The Era of Choice

The Era of Choice

The Ability to Choose and Its Transformation of Contemporary Life

Edward C. Rosenthal

A Bradford Book
The MIT Press
Cambridge, Massachusetts
London, England

First MIT Press paperback edition, 2006
© 2005 Massachusetts Institute of Technology

MIT Press books may be purchased at special quantity discounts for business or sales promotional use. For information, please email special_sales@mitpress.mit.edu or write to Special Sales Department, The MIT Press, 55 Hayward St., Cambridge, MA 02142.

This book was set in Sabon by Graphic Composition, Inc., and was printed and bound in the United States of America.

Library of Congress Cataloging-in-Publication Data

Rosenthal, Edward C., 1959– .
The era of choice : the ability to choose and its transformation of contemporary life / Edward C. Rosenthal.
    p.   cm.
"A Bradford book."
Includes bibliographical references and index.
ISBN-13: 978-0-262-18248-5 (hc : alk. paper)—978-0-262-68165-0 (pb : alk. paper)
ISBN-10: 0-262-18248-3 (hc : alk. paper)—0-262-68165-X (pb : alk. paper)
1. Philosophy and civilization. 2. Culture—Philosophy. 3. Decision making. I. Title.

BF611.R67 2005
153.8′3—dc22

                                            2004062536

10 9 8 7 6 5 4 3 2

To my parents, Florence and Harold, who nurtured me
To Bryony, who has given so much, and
To our lovely children, Jordan and Chloe

Contents

Preface

The essential thesis of this book is this: for the majority of us, having *choice*—and having to make *choices*—has become and will continue to be the most important factor that influences both our personal lives and our prevailing culture.

Years ago, I was struck suddenly by the notion that being "modern" means being *able to choose*. Most of us in the developed world, particularly in the United States, have vastly more choice both on a daily basis and with respect to our life paths than did our predecessors just one hundred years ago.

Often, people say that the United States of America is an *idea*. Central to this idea is, of course, freedom. Freedom to *choose*. People first came to America to exercise the right to choose their religion, and others followed hoping to shape a new and more prosperous life. For one reason or another, throngs have chosen to come here for nearly four centuries. Choice is practically in our blood.

But other parts of the globe—especially Europe and much of the Pacific Rim—have now caught up to the U.S. and Canada in terms of material bounty and democratic freedoms. What we will discuss in this book applies to those prosperous nations as well. They too embrace a world of choice that was only a dream a century ago.

Being able to choose means being *free* to choose. But freedom need not entail choice. Indeed, for most of human history, the realization of pure freedom had usually been met by the cold reality of a *lack* of reasonable choices. People were therefore not truly empowered to shape their destinies. In fact, as I shall argue, the dearth of choice that has characterized the great majority of human lives has rendered true freedom a mere hypothetical concept. Until now. Only in relatively recent times has our standard of living been high enough, for enough of us, to feature *the ability to choose* as the preeminent influencing importance of cross-fertilization (Jung would have preferred "synchronicity") of ideas in art and science (and chess), a theme more vital than ever in today's age of hyperspecialization. Perhaps it was this early exposure to the application of imported ideas that led to my interest in the oppositions between breadth and depth and between specialists and generalists.

I have been fortunate to experience countless hours of stimulating conversation with Martin Czigler, Bryony Kay, Fred Murphy, Krishna Prasad, Arvind Rajan, and Eric Theise on any number of issues. I want to thank Yasmina Mobarek for introducing me to Gallic intellectual thought. Martin, Fred, K. P., Arvind, and my mother, Florence Rosenthal, each carefully read an earlier draft and supplied me with numerous valuable comments. I have learned a great deal from Barry Schwartz. T. L. Hill took the time to educate me about the publishing industry. Mark Liberman, Lisa Meritz, John A. Paulos, and Miriam Solomon have been very helpful as well. Others who read my work and offered comments and encouragement were Don Hopkins, Cindie McLemore, Desmond Nazareth, Howard Weiss, and Bryony Kay. Most of all, I want to gratefully acknowledge Bryony's ideas and support.

Everyone at The MIT Press who worked on this book put a lot of care and expertise into it; many thanks are due to Anne Bunn, David Cecere, Susan Clark, Judy Feldmann, Erin Hasley, Gita Manaktala, Katy Papagiannis, Cristina Sanmartín, Ann Twiselton, and David Weininger. Thanks also to Todd Nudelman. Finally, I want to thank Tom Stone at The MIT Press, who had the vision to pursue this project and turn it into something real.

1 | Choice: More Than Wanting to Have Your Cake and Eat It Too

Choice is everywhere. It profoundly affects our lives. Compared to our ancestors—even those of just a century ago—we have more things to choose and manage. Therefore it is no surprise to declare that the presence of choice and its resulting complexities of decision making constitute a central part of our lives.

But this book is about far more than that. My claim is that the relatively newfound presence of choice in the developed world is a force that has penetrated not only our lives, but also our lifestyles and our culture. In short, choice has transformed not only how we live but also *how we think* and who we are. It is the influence of choice that has recently—since about 1970, if we had to pick a single year—separated us from who we used to be.

The startling revelation about choice is that its presence in our lives manifests itself in a fantastic variety of intellectual and cultural contributions. But rather than simply muse in wonderment about all of the marvelous things out there and the joys and anguishes we experience in having to pick and choose among them, we will sample an abundant cross section of modern creative expression and demonstrate the impact that the era of choice—which began roughly a century ago—has had. Choice has influenced specific scientific and philosophical theories and in addition has helped bring about movements, the most notable of these being postmodernism, which for many thinkers has become our defining cultural mode. In addition to surveying the altered cultural landscape, we will also examine choice at the individual level with both its personal and sociological implications. Finally, we will consider examples of how thinking through the oppositions that choices present to us can guide policy decisions in business and government.

What is "choice"? In ordinary speech we talk about having choices, alternatives, or options. We also speak of actions: having to make a choice (which seems to imply a burden), and making a decision (with its air of finality). There is certainly a difference between the potential states and the decisive state. As we are often painfully reminded, it is one thing to be gratuitously awash with choices, and quite another to pick one. Since each of these decision-making aspects influences themes that we will consider, I want to define "choice" as referring both to environments in which choices abound, and to the ramifications of having to act decisively. Obviously, the gravity (or lack of it) of any situation is related to the stresses we create. But even in the happiest of circumstances, when impelled, and not compelled, to choose, we generate some anxiety in building up to the moment of action, the instant in which the decision is executed. A linguistic aside: here, "executed" is consistent with psychiatrist Irvin Yalom's observation that to *de-cide* means to kill; that is, in making a decision, we understand that the excluded candidates are no longer "alive" for us. In fact, the Random House dictionary gives "to cut off" as the etymology for "decide"; semantically, this corresponds with one's finally acting, cutting off the process itself as well as the unchosen alternatives.

As we will discuss, the overplentiful commodification cultivated since the maturation of the Industrial Revolution has been an integral theme, an inescapable core of our lives, for more than a generation now. This cornucopia is wonderful, yet dreadful. We are literally spoiled for choice, but even those cheerful situations in which we are like a kid in a candy shop can turn momentous. In our delight at picking the prize, we confront the regret of lost opportunities. Of course, the degree of regret depends on the situation's importance and on our assessment of its risks. But as our wants become needs, we magnify even trivial decisions and heap ostensibly unwarranted attention and analysis on them.

The fact is, every situation is unique and can never be revisited. Consider a dining experience. You are at the restaurant (one of many you could have visited). It is a unique event (whether a regular Wednesday night out with friends or a first date or an anniversary); you are contemplating the wine list (which may never again be the same). You can either invest yourself in the decision process, or you can divest—opt out, if you will—in a number of ways, including the nondecision of leaving it up to someone else. To put it differently, you can be active or passive, involve yourself or not, live life or let someone (or something) else manage it for you. This leads right to the heart of what existentialist thought is about, and we will trace that path later on.

But back to the wine list. If you thoroughly engage yourself in the decision process, you must consider many variables: price, taste preferences, familiarity, reputation, complementarity with various foods, and—more superficial but nevertheless key—concerns like nationality, region, vineyard, and vogue. Your information is incomplete, the wine list, in its limitations, may weigh on you with omissions, and you can't think about this all night. Finally, you are not alone—you are responsible for others' enjoyment as well.

This all sounds tense, analytical, and obsessive. Just pick a wine—but that is opting out, disengaging. So you take the plunge and think it over.

To put this into perspective, the wine will come, it will probably be suitable, because most wine would be, and since you are still reading this, your diligence and taste are no doubt of a high standard. You'll never quite know how the other wines would have worked out, but, stepping back a bit more, we're only talking about some wine with dinner.

But so many—most?—decisions are complex ones. If you aren't fazed by the wine example, try an experiment. Invite several friends over to watch a movie. Tell them that you'll all decide on a choice once everyone has arrived. What will probably occur is a fumbling, hesitant blend of conflict and cooperation. Most of those present will attempt to be reasonable and at least mildly accommodating, thereby curbing their enthusiasm for certain picks and softening their veto positions for other ones. Anyone with strong preferences and a personality to match would be taking a chance in attempting to force the issue—there is more at stake than merely choosing a film. We try to maintain the appearance, at least, of cooperation, reasonability, and kindness. We also wish to minimize the wrath and criticism engendered by being responsible for a disliked choice or for vetoing something favorable to others.

The inevitable fact, however, is that we have dissimilar preferences and this creates conflict. The movie situation provides only tame drama (it is hardly *World War III: The Sequel*). But it *is* significant that after some initial statements and a bit of jousting, one or two of your friends will withdraw ("anything except horror movies," or "just no musicals") because the discomfort of the *process* outweighs any mild disappointment from a lesser-preferred pick. This discomfort has been well expressed by the philosopher Søren Kierkegaard: "When I behold my possibilities I experience that dread which is the 'dizziness of freedom' and my choice is made in fear and trembling." Perhaps Kierkegaard had no friends come around to socialize, but the fact remains that many of us admit being terrible at decisions.

It is clear that any choice we make involves contemplating the inclusion of certain things and the exclusion of others. Once a decision has taken place and between disciplines that excessive analysis and specialization has created. The same trend is developing in our private lives, as we find ways to have our cake and eat it too.

To put it differently, choice demands that we form oppositions. Having to make a decision sharpens and reifies the opportunity costs of the excluded items. (As we will see later, these potential losses often seem to outweigh the possible gains.) In our attitudes toward marriage and divorce, in our debates over multiculturalism, in our theories of particle physics and in our evolving literary criticism, the newfound prevalence of choice has spawned a keen interest in oppositions, dualisms, dilemmas, contradictions, and paradoxes. This world of the complementary creates anguish (you can't have your cake and eat it too!). To alleviate this anguish, we have developed mechanisms to hedge, to compromise, to sample, to avoid, to delay, to get another chance, to *synthesize,* in order to soften the blows of exclusion and irreversibility that choice carries.

You may question what is new here. I claim that the presence of choice and its derivative themes of opposition and synthesis are responsible for much of the mentality of the twentieth century and beyond. But what about postmodernism? Isn't the subject of this book just a restatement of, or another angle on, postmodernism?

My rejoinder is no, this is not another fresh, but ultimately tiring, tome on postmodernism. Postmodernism is a notorious term, largely on account of being multifaceted and indeterminate—we shall revisit it later. Certainly theorists of postmodernism have dealt with the subject of oppositions. In one broad interpretation, postmodernism is itself antimodernism; but there exist many other subthemes that we will explore. And certainly, both postmodernism and choice are largely due to the mass production and delivery triumphs of industrial society, which are evidenced by today's consumerism.

But let me make a crucial distinction. Postmodernism—and there *is* such a thing, and it is not mere pastiche, pluralism, and everything-goes—seeks to explain a relatively new cultural norm, one that seems to transcend the established modernist norm of progress. But postmodern theorists, although they might discuss implications of natural-scientific ideas (the Heisenberg uncertainty principle being a favorite one) or social-scientific ones (in, for example, Marxist critiques of the market economy), or report on various popular trends in music, fashion, or film, are not able to trace these elements to a common theme. Instead, they have supplied a hodgepodge of origins: antimodernity, late capitalism, the rise of popular culture, multiple coding, pluralism, and other sources that we will later review. Although these analyses are valid in part, they lack unification, and ultimately, postmodernism becomes hard to define and its development is difficult to explicate. Further, postmodernism, in concentrating on the products, cultural and otherwise, of our society, does not provide insight into our psychology and decision making. Postmodernism seems to have pervaded countless aspects of contemporary life and has been celebrated since the 1970s, and therefore one is tempted to believe, simply, that everything today is postmodern. And given the enormous changes over the last thirty years (among them being shorter memories), life indeed seems different from what it used to be. Hence, we are postmodern whereas the ancient 1950s and 1960s were modern. This argument, of course, begs the question of why this transformation was bound to happen.

With my focus on choice, I am simply highlighting a stark and fundamental element of our existence that provides a theme, a first principle to explain how and why our lives have in fact changed. Our atmosphere of choice and its attendant dilemmas, anxieties, and evasions, has attained such scope (penetrating every aspect of our lives) and scale (affecting the great majority of us in developed countries) as to transform how we think about everything, thereby shifting humanity into a new phase of civilization.

Although such transitions are gradual, we will be able to trace a buildup of this new mentality (let's skip that word "paradigm") from the late 1800s onward. By the 1950s American society was well on its way (but not quite there yet); by the 1970s, we had achieved a critical mass, as it were, reaching a point of no return. This, of course, marks the 1960s, that decade of societal upheavals, as the watershed period. We will look back at that era later.

I must be careful to avoid claiming that choice has directly *caused* particular attitudes, ideas, and behaviors to surface. I cannot exactly assert, for example, that physicist Niels Bohr's theory that light is *both* particle and wave (depending on the context) is literally a result of his having been swamped by an abundance of choices. Nor may I claim that Robert Frost's poem "The Road Not Taken"—although it directly expresses the anguish of choice that we all confront—could not have been written in an earlier era. So just how does choice—more specifically, the enhanced choice first widely seen in the twentieth century—affect our minds and our culture?

To answer this, I have to fall back on the notion of *correlation,* one of the cornerstones of both natural and social science. Any discussion about behavior, decision making, lifestyles, and ideas must entail consideration of social and intellectual phenomena. If we have learned anything about such things, it is that they are complex—beholden to no one simple schema. We can't say that poverty causes violent crime, or that television viewing causes obesity. We can, however, suggest that, under certain, perhaps not fully understood, conditions, there is an association, a *relationship,* between poverty and violent crime, or between TV watching and weight gain.

When these notions are *quantified,* that is, when poverty is measured by income or assets, and obesity is measured in pounds, we can design experiments and gather data that, when analyzed, may be shown to support our hypotheses. Correlation, a statistical tool of social and physical scientists, provides a numerical measure of how strongly the phenomena in question are related. Scientists can pinpoint what percentage of the variation in the behavior they are studying, like obesity, is explained by the factor(s) they have singled out to explain it, like TV viewing. We say, loosely, that things are correlated when an increase, say, in one factor, is consistent with an increase (or a decrease) in another.

But caution again: nobody said anything about cause and effect. If you found out that stock market behavior was in sync with the phases of the moon, you could invest accordingly and make a fortune—even with absolutely *no* causal relationship whatever between the two. (Let me concede up front that, regrettably, I have no financial advice for you in the pages ahead.)

So, I am not planning to demonstrate that people in the twentieth century have had x percent more choices to make than did their forbears in the nineteenth century and that their such-and-such output measures were up by y. (Note, however, that researchers are beginning to do this: recently Christian Broda and David Weinstein estimated that the fourfold increase in the variety of imported products available in the United States over the past thirty years accounts for a rise in our collective welfare of approximately 3 percent.) What will become clear in the pages ahead is that over the past century or so there has been an explosion of choice in our personal lives and a simultaneous introduction of intellectual ideas and social behaviors that I link directly to choice or its derived oppositions. These instances are countless, diverse, and surprising—surprising in the breadth of connections that can be made. Some of these connections are straightforward, like relating choices on life's path to the Robert Frost poem, or to Hugh Everett III's many-worlds theory in quantum physics, or to nondeterminism in computer science. (Straightforward but still fascinating.) Other connections are not so obvious, like relating Einstein's relativity, Saussure's linguistics, Gödel's logic, and Disney's trailers.

At this point, it is fair to ask, in our increasingly bottom-line-driven society, of what *use* is this theory? It is all well and good to identify choice as the crucial element in our lives, but how can we employ this awareness in order to live better? In other words, how can we profit from it? Choice is a great challenge—agreed. Having to live with excessive choice is what delineates more modern from less modern society—fine. What can we do about it?

Although I will save predictions and prescriptions for the last chapter, I can touch on the essential theme here. Our exposure to choice has brought us not only the repeated anguish of decision making, but also the realization that sometimes we *can* have our cake and eat it too (or at least come close). We have discovered that oppositions can tear us apart; but, as we are frequently able to reconcile them successfully, we feel, increasingly, that we *need not give something up*. We no longer accept that something *has* to go. As with so many other aspects of our consumer society, when we sacrifice less, our wants become needs.

To put it differently, over the last couple of generations we have conditioned ourselves not to give up on contradictions. Thus we have developed profound needs, not just passing urges, to trace divergent paths. To this end, we have formed various strategies: we change cars and houses; we change jobs; we change careers, even spouses. Yet there is little compromise in all of this, except regarding lasting commitment. Nothing endures; time becomes the next variable that we attempt to control, in our determination to reverse the irreversible, to go back and find out what we missed.

This necessity to travel down all of life's branches is *real* for us. It wasn't for our predecessors. It is here to stay. And the lesson in this is that in so many natural dualisms—security versus risk, conformity versus rebellion, familiar versus new (to name a few)—we cannot completely neglect one in favor of the other. I am not recommending a simple balance, or compromise, or a hedging of bets. But I am saying that to maximize the potential of an individual, or a relationship, or a society, we must attend to complementary needs. How this takes place depends on many factors. Couples that marry permanently may need to find fresh activities; risk takers, some stability. The point is, trade-offs are not always the exclusionary dilemmas that they seem.

How the Era of Choice Came About

Is it possible to back up the claim that our lives differ, choicewise, from those of our ancestors? A focus on the twentieth century would entail a comparison with the nineteenth century, at the very least. We will examine this historical context in the next chapter. But there are two catalysts of choice we should consider right now: First, the "usual suspect" of industrial society, namely, the growing prosperity brought on by burgeoning production and distribution systems, and second, the loss of the absolute, originating in the nineteenth century. These two factors are complementary. That is, our newfound prosperity alone would certainly have complicated our lives, and expanded our day-to-day choices. Without the loss of the absolute, however, our sense of importance as free and empowered individuals would have remained stifled, and choice as a concept would never have attained its current importance. Only at the turn of the last century did both of these factors emerge.

The loss of the absolute, as we shall see, involved a collection of events that reduced humankind's confidence in underlying objective truths about the world. This loss was felt both spiritually and scientifically, and had various sociopolitical and psychological implications. Waning objectivity was accompanied by rising subjectivity, which meant two things. The lack of a definitive moral or scientific foundation left, literally, an existential void in which people had to develop an identity and accept more responsibility for their actions. Then as now, it was easier to discover an identity in products and possessions than it was to build one emotionally and spiritually. At the same time, the lack of particular objective norms freed up the attitude to accept alternative viewpoints—the "relativity" that has seeped into so many areas of discourse with such controversy.

As for the plethora of new products available to ordinary people, the trend, which has snowballed over the past century, began in America and spread to Europe and beyond. A brief glimpse at some facts and figures will prove most instructive in understanding to what extent choice truly pervades contemporary living and how little, comparatively, it influenced mainstream life prior to 1900.

We all have some idea about just how much our standard of living has increased over the past century. But what *is* "standard of living"? Is it the availability of (virtually) unlimited fresh water, proper sanitation, and central heating, as well as plentiful and enjoyable food and opportunity? Or is it more than that? We usually resort to various quantifications: how much discretionary income, how much free time; how many labor-saving appliances; how much stuff. This topic invariably ignites the old debate: does a higher standard of living—as commonly measured by *acquisition*—indicate a better life?

This is dangerous ground to tread on. There exists, of course, a long-standing tradition of criticism of the consumer economy. Economist Stanley Lebergott, cites, among others, the vituperations of Thorstein Veblen and Stuart Chase from the 1920s, Henry George from an earlier era, and Vance Packard, Joan Robinson, John Kenneth Galbraith, and Tibor Scitovsky from a later one. Rather than begin a diatribe against our vanishing values, let me attempt to gain some perspective with selected data (all of which, unless otherwise specified, is from Lebergott). A century ago, life expectancy itself was much shorter; however, as that figure is an average, and is therefore fraught with all the peculiarities of averages, perhaps a different measure will give you pause. Consider the following diseases that are rarely fatal today: measles, diphtheria, typhoid, polio, whooping cough, mumps, rubella, influenza, pneumonia, tuberculosis, and gastritis. In 1900, people were *one hundred* times as likely to die in the United States from one of these diseases than from AIDS today. This alone would lead you to suspect that life is a lot more secure today. With more time to live, we have more choices to make, both for the short- and long-term.

More convincing are measures of relative wealth, free time, and purchasing power. One thing we take for granted is the ability to work and play around the clock. It is a very natural course of events that so many things are becoming 24/7. But a mere century ago, only 3 percent of U.S. households even had electric lighting. We easily forget how the simple extension of the day provides numerous opportunities that our forebears could only dream about. And "dream" is the right word; they worked harder than we do and surely needed their rest. A century ago the great majority of people worked on farms or toiled in factories. Farmers worked from before sunup until after sundown. The typical week for nonfarm workers in 1900 consisted of six ten-hour days; the "normal" forty-hour work week became regulation only in 1938. The sixty-hour work week of 1900 shrank to thirty-nine hours by 1975.

"Just thirty-nine hours? Who? No one I know," you might be thinking. Indeed, as the economist Robert Frank points out, numerous measurements indicate that since the mid-1970s, our work weeks have increased, on average, by a few hours. This phenomenon is not due to any loss of purchasing power for our wages. It is a probably a consequence of what Frank calls "luxury fever," an updated version of "keeping up with the Joneses" that we will discuss later on. Despite this upturn, however, we still work far less than our ancestors of 1900 did.

How about work inside the home? Meals, laundry, and cleaning consumed a household average of over fifty-five hours per week in the early 1900s and had dropped, by 1975, to less than twenty hours per week. (For many households, the surplus thirty-five hours were often negated when the housewife joined the work force. Unfortunately for these women, they usually kept the privilege of being responsible for the other twenty hours too.) By *any* measure, though, discretionary time is relatively abundant nowadays.

What was, and is, done with this time? Pursuit of weekend recreation? Vacations? Back then, the "weekend" was Sunday alone; clearly, recreation could not have been a major societal priority. To validate this, note that annual per-capita spending on recreation (in constant 1987 dollars) was all of $83 in 1900, but was $1,026 in 1990 and is considerably higher now. If they didn't spend money on leisure a century ago, what *did* they do with it? Well, not nearly as much as we can. Every hour of work (in constant 1982 dollars) could buy only *one-sixth* the (dollar) value a century ago as compared to today; in other words, one hour's work buys six times as much now as it did in 1900. Moreover, there was less discretionary money back then. According to journalists W. Michael Cox and Richard Alm, the basic needs of food, clothing, and shelter consumed 76 percent of the average household budget in 1901 as opposed to just 37 percent nowadays. If you prefer to believe the Federal Consumer Expenditure Survey, the latter figure is about 50 percent; either way, there's a lot more money floating around now.

It is instructive, also, to compare the United States to other industrialized nations. At one extreme, we have been conditioned to believe that planned (communist) economies create bland uniformity in all of their products. Choice, therefore, would be a prerogative solely of the West. Alas, Lebergott surprises us by indicating that the USSR *planned* the production of 600 varieties of wine and 2,500 varieties of confectionery items a generation ago; in 1958–1961, China began to grow 1,500 varieties of tea. So although choice has certainly predominated in the West, it has not been absent in other economies and other cultures. A different surprise is in store when considering Europe's lag in conveniences. In 1960, 96 percent of U.S. households had refrigeration. Compare this to only 52 percent in (West) Germany, 41 percent in France, and 30 percent in Great Britain and Italy. What about hot running water, present in 93 percent of U.S. households in 1960? Britain checked in at 77 percent, but France recorded only 41 percent, West Germany, 34 percent, and Italy an astonishing 24 percent. One could go on and on with such figures. The point is, we forget how good we have it, and how recently so many did not (or still do not). In three generations in the West, we have progressed from a typical life being one of working hard in and out of the house just to survive, to one where we all waltz daily into attractive supermarkets that have 30,000 items on display.

Choice is certainly something new in the world, manifesting itself on a scale never before seen. For those who see merely the return of well-known cycles, such as the peaks of commercialism found in ancient Greece or Rome or in the Renaissance, I will have a rejoinder in chapter 18. Principally, however, what I hope to examine in the rest of this work is how choice as a newfound phenomenon has manifested itself. Before we review its important nineteenth-century foundations in the next chapter, let's summarize what we've seen so far.

To recap: over the last century we have seen an astronomical improvement in our material well-being. The associated explosion of goods and services has led to a wealth of choices in our daily lives and life paths that had never before existed. This transformation, unique in history, makes us realize that being able to choose defines what it means to be "modern." Thus I claim that our newfound presence of choice better defines our contemporary culture than do the usual theories of modernism and postmodernism. At the very least, we need to explore the implications of choice as well as investigate modernism and postmodernism.

But we realize that even the stratospheric rise of material wealth is insufficient to explain an ethos, a cultural transformation. Something else, something spiritual, must have come about, and this is what I call "the loss of the absolute" that began in the mid-1800s. This is the rudderless feeling that we can't depend on anything—not religion, not science, not capitalism, not communism, and, finally, not liberalism, that is, our attempt to create a tolerant society that provides a foundation for individual freedoms and public functions.

Our current mindset, then, arose from a cornucopia of choice, injected with a strong dose of individual freedom but beset with attendant insecurity and responsibility. We are constantly, wonderfully awash with choices but in making these choices we feel the weight of deciding among alternatives, of considering inclusion and exclusion, opportunity and regret. We realize how keenly we consider these decisions, and how the overwhelming availability of choice *is* overwhelming—a blessing and a curse—and it strikes us that people didn't always have such a persistent abundance of choice as we do now.

In trying to discern just what impact choice has had on our world, in the pages that follow we will explore the ways in which choice has directly influenced our personal lives. But to see the larger picture we also need to explore the changes in our cultural output—in science, philosophy, social science, art and architecture, and more. We will examine this in the context of how our society's increased focus on the resolution (and often dissolution) of oppositions and dualisms has come to affect how we view the world. We will find that choice and the consequent emphasis we place on oppositions have altered our views about reality itself. Let's begin our journey.

Any study that looks back faces a natural problem: how far back to go. Movements in the twentieth century depend in part on events of the nineteenth; these, in turn, depend on the eighteenth, and pretty soon, you are talking about Copernicus, Thomas Aquinas, and Plato. But here, I feel confident that to understand the impact of choice requires us to retreat only to about 1850.

Invention and progress are often what come to mind when we recall the nineteenth century. Indeed, the 1800s supplied such unprecedented advances in science and technology that the philosopher Alfred North Whitehead would comment that the *idea* of invention was itself the greatest invention of the age. I don't think we need to enumerate the diverse world-changing innovations that emerged in the nineteenth century, from the perfection of the steam engine to the railroad to the telephone to the harnessing of electricity. Nor is it necessary to spend too much time detailing the well-known rise of industrialization in the West.

However, it is useful to observe some measures of growth of the leading industrial powers. Great Britain, the United States, and Germany, in that order, were the most industrialized nations in 1900, combining for over 55 percent of the world's manufacturing output at the time. The historian Paul Kennedy (drawing from Paul Bairoch) tells us that as the per-capita level of industrialization in Britain had risen fourfold from 1830 to 1900, the United States had seen nearly a fivefold increase, and Germany (achieving its initial unification during this era), an even steeper rise. Clearly, these soaring levels of industrialization swelled the output levels of all manner of goods, which began to penetrate the world's markets. Not incidentally, the extent of penetration even as far back as the mid-1800s was tremendous, as evidenced by the observation that the economies of China and India became *less* industrialized during this era, their fabric industries shattered by the influx of cheaper and better textiles from Britain. GNP growth in the West easily outstripped that of the population, and although by today's levels the people of 1900 endured a poor standard of living, their real wages had increased 80 percent since 1850.

The industrial revolution had significantly transformed society well before 1900. The substitution of machines for human work, generating skyrocketing productivity, was widespread. Improved technology was driving people off the farms, and factories in teeming urban centers absorbed much of the rural population by drawing it to the only ready source of jobs (albeit menial ones, created by endlessly subdividing work into small repetitive tasks). What's more, the economy had organized itself into a complex *system;* industry begat industry, and different sectors had become increasingly interdependent. Much of the impetus for expansion carried downward from production to distribution, and created a vast interconnected ship and rail network. Another demand was self-referential; the explosion of machine tools precipitated the development of a machine tool industry—"machines to make machines," to quote critic Neil Postman. (Today, our analogue is the entertainment industry, spawning self-referential entertainment products.) By the early 1900s scientific management, as the work of people such as Frederick Taylor was called, had documented a host of organizing principles that led to further gains in efficiency as well as better working conditions. Soon to come was the single decisive step in this evolution, Henry Ford's auto assembly line, which he introduced in 1913. Ford's ideas were quickly and widely adopted, just in time for the mass production madness of World War I, which, as my colleague Fred Murphy points out, came about through a perceived lack of choice.

The Rise of Secularism and the Loss of the Absolute

Certainly, economic growth led to a staggering increase in the availability of myriad goods as well as the means to procure them. To understand the implantation of choice into our society, however, we also need to comprehend a set of crucial *attitudinal* changes that developed over the latter half of the 1800s. These I generalized in the first chapter as the "loss of the absolute."

Perhaps the most important component of this loss and the subsequent ways in which people would compensate for it was the diminished belief in what organized religion provided. I have worded this carefully, because it is not the same thing as a diminished belief in God—one should not leap to conclusions on the basis of, say, declining churchgoing statistics. One can *believe,* independent of an authority or affiliation, and conversely, one can participate in a religious organization without accepting every article of the faith. In any event, the fact that religion has made a recovery, worldwide, over the past two decades would seem to discredit the simple theory that people a century ago, in losing religion, gained a belief in the subjective and the relative, and put their faith in acquisition. Although it is difficult to determine precisely what the relationship is between the nineteenth century fade-out of religion and the subsequent fade-in of other values, we certainly need to examine what went on between, say, 1850 and 1900.

Historian Owen Chadwick provides great insight for us in his study of the secularization of the nineteenth century European mind. He delimits the critical era as starting in 1859—when Charles Darwin published *The Origin of Species* and John Stuart Mill *On Liberty*—and finishing at 1900. Perhaps Darwin, more than anyone else, rocked the foundations of people's belief in the absolute as embodied, so to speak, in the Almighty. It was religion, after all, that early giants of sociology like Émile Durkheim and Max Weber took to be the foundation of social and moral life.

By the end of the nineteenth century Durkheim was furthering the understanding of the depths of religion's roots. The older school took religion to have sprung from people's fears of acts of nature. This point of view would assert that as our knowledge about the world increases, our need for religion decreases. But the newer approach claimed that religion serves a social, ritualistic *function* in society that rationality is not going to oust. Religion, in fact, is intimately connected to an essential, irrational dimension of human nature, and is not merely a societal phenomenon that knowledge will eliminate. Weber, in the early twentieth century, advanced his famous theory of the Protestant work ethic. This theory purported, in part, that the notion of predestination fostered increased industriousness among Protestants (the assumption being that their hard work would result in worldly success, a harbinger of a good afterlife), which became the engine of capitalism.

Naturally, Weber's theory has been repeatedly critiqued. For our purposes, though, the important point is that he showed how ordinary, day-to-day, secular activities were still ultimately directed toward heaven. The prior emphasis was on *being* (good); the newer emphasis was on *doing*.

To look back further for a moment, there are reasons why secularization is a topic of the nineteenth century and not of the eighteenth-century Enlightenment. One reason is that the Enlightenment's emphasis on rationality was, by itself, not sufficient to develop a more secular society. But more to the point, after 1859 liberal thought, expressed for example by the principle of tolera- tion as well as the concept of evolution, gave secularization roots from which to grow. And this growth and spread of secularization would contrast against that of the Enlightenment, which was enlightenment of the few—of the upper classes who had access to education and to ideas (typically portrayed to us as proliferating via the salons). As mentioned above, however, the newer school of sociology linked religious thought to deeper individual and societal struc- tures, and therefore secularization, if it took place at all, would extend across class boundaries. Associated with this trend in sociology was a trend to study history at the level of ordinary people instead of the titled few. Secularization, then, would seem to be of the many.

But what exactly is secularization? Simply turning from the godly to the worldly? This slippery point is nicely finessed by Chadwick: secular belief is that *"miracles do not happen"* (his italics). Another, perhaps more functional take on secularism is that it is not derived from a religion of the divine.

Liberalism

How Darwin and evolution might have contributed to secularization is clear enough. But what about Mill's *On Liberty?* That is, what impact would the notions of liberalism and toleration have in ultimately decreasing Western use for religion's message? To begin with, toleration forms the basis for the twen- tieth century ethos of subjectivity and cultural relativism, although, of course, the concept is ancient. Its link to religion would go back at least to the Refor- mation—this cleft in Christianity created a minority, and if one minority would be tolerated, why not others? It was an integral concept in America's forma- tion. What toleration did was to undermine conformity. And if conformity could be destroyed, then an individual's idea could be worthy.

Mill had to decide how far "liberalism" could be taken. For many, then as today, the term represented *too much freedom,* for example, *libertinism* as in the wickedness of the Marquis de Sade. Although, ultimately, people like Thomas Jefferson, in writing the Declaration of Independence, had looked to "natural rights" for guidance, freedom had to be reined in to some degree in an organized society. Mill articulated the notion that members of a civilized community can exercise power over other members against their will only in order to prevent harm.

Toleration, as established through religious difference, was not the only driver of nineteenth-century liberalism. Another was the rise of the state, which occurred in fits and starts across Europe throughout the century. Centralized power was frightening to many citizens who, in losing "local" rights, looked to natural, universal rights as compensation. Another impetus for ordinary people to renounce centralized leadership may have grown from what historian Daniel Boorstin has called the "graphic revolution." Technology new to the mid-nineteenth century enabled the easy reproduction of pictures. The resulting proliferation of images of political and religious leaders perhaps cheapened them in the public's eye.

But more important still were the social upheavals of the Industrial Revolution, in which vast numbers of people took active roles in moving away from their villages to seek employment. In this way a person could break from the traditions that bound his or her forebears; in so choosing a life path, one would be able to appreciate change, and observe that customs and laws are merely artificial.

According to Mill, liberty developed from an instrument to yield justice (or improved government or society) to a quality of life, a good in itself; that is, it became an end rather than a means. Further, liberty as an individual right ought to be a quality that society not only tolerates but fosters. Chadwick calls Mill's essay the "first modern exposition of a theory of the secular state." Opposition was certainly present in Mill's Victorian era. Whereas Mill's liberalism is founded on the assumption of every individual's ability to reason, the conservative backlash denied this supposedly universal characteristic.

In addition to conservative opposition, Mill's liberalism eventually ran into a backlash that ceded some moral authority back to the Church; one result was that liberal theory in general withdrew from Mill's impractical ideals. To begin with, the doctrine of noninterference (as it was often perceived) seemed to extend too far. Accelerating industrial growth created a disturbing chasm between the rich and poor. In addition, liberal politicians were eventually perceived to desire to suppress their opposition with charges of fascism or intolerance (much like the political hypercorrectness of today). And further, as organizations (whether corporations or unions) grew, churches took back some of their role as "houses of conscience," not beholden to companies or other interest groups. To balance this, it seems that the press was mildly critical of the Church, but they went only so far. Seeing that most of the European population of the time was Christian, if not exactly churchgoing, papers remained in business by not venturing any radical opinions.

Marx

You may have been wondering when I would mention the influence of Karl Marx. This juncture is a good spot to do it. Marx's initial objective was to critique religion. Later on, Marx sought to reduce religion's role, but he realized that the way to do this was not through secularizing the state. The United States, Marx noticed, was a secular but religious nation. Therefore he needed to go deeper—to tackle religion, he had to address earthly needs. We create and cling to religion because of alienation in society. This alienation develops because we become commodities much like the very items that we (workers) produce. The illusion of religion is that it will repay the injustices suffered in this life with a future of eternal redemption, thus reinforcing our alienation by detaching us from reality (the "opiate of the people"). The remedy is not, then, simply to establish a secular society—it is to correct the materially rooted alienation by creating a classless society, where communal ownership and its implied forfeiture of individual ownership and possessiveness and all its associated evils will dissolve the alienation in society and, in so doing, strip us of our need for religion. It is interesting how Mill and Marx advance secularization from two different platforms.

One cannot blame Marx too much for his probable naiveté regarding human nature. After all, in many parts of China, and even in a Western locale like Cambridge (England), bicycles, for example, have been communal commodities, unowned and interchangeable (provided, of course, that there are enough to go around). And even today, there are tribes in, say, Tanzania, where the very notion of jealousy is so foreign that it is not signified by any word in the (tribal) language. Nevertheless, it seems promising that if we turn Marx around, we will be on the right track. The Bible told us that money is the root of all evil. It took two thousand years for a riposte from George Bernard Shaw: "Lack of money is the root of all evil." We chuckle at this, and deep down, we may suspect, in our new-millennium minds, that he is right.

So we answer Marx with Shaw and believe that the surer road to eradicating inequality and envy across classes is to provide surfeit and excess to all. Perhaps had Marx lived a few generations later, he would have been most impressed with the ability of advanced capitalism to produce and distribute a vast array of goods to a market where all but a small minority possessed (or had the ability to borrow) a sizeable amount of disposable wealth with which to exercise choice of consumption. But whether even unlimited wealth combined with virtual immortality would ease our existential angst or convert a present-day Marxist is a different issue. In any event, Marx's theory, of course, was developed in a world devoid of our contemporary massive production capabilities, where so many are significantly able to shape their lives.

Marx aside, Chadwick is inconclusive in general as to whether it was religiousness or irreligiousness that was more dominant among the eighteenth-century European working classes. There do exist some statistics on declines in churchgoing in the 1880s and there is a correlation between town size and decreased attendance, but confounding factors appear. Many poor country folk who migrated to cities lived in ghettos, had no "Sunday clothes," and did not feel respectable enough to attend. They also perceived the Church as an authority that had joined forces with the State, or at least with the established powers. The upper classes did, visibly enough, attend church more often, fueling distrust and antagonism. The summarizing point is that the working classes, although not religious, were not anti-God. Atheism was abhorrent to most and did not catch on. Even the far-left-wing German Social Democratic party heeded the doctrine, "religion is a man's private concern." (Today, this might be known as "don't ask, don't tell.")

Although Marx's influence obviously mushroomed, Marxist sociopolitical transformation did not take place until well into the twentieth century. Before that, other secularizing influences were taking their toll. For example, whatever liberalism exactly was, it was threatening enough for Pope Pius IX to condemn it in his 1864 Syllabus of Errors. Unfortunately, by then, liberalism, as inherent in such concepts as tolerance, equality, and liberty, had enough of a positive ethical spin to it that, to many, the Pope appeared morally wrong. This reiterates the above point that secularization, in general, involved *anticlericalism* if not the renunciation of God. The fact that the nation-states of Germany and Italy were beginning to develop touched patriotic nerves and further contributed to the relative decline of the Vatican.

We have already noted the Industrial Revolution, which had deeply impacted society at all levels by the mid-1800s. Clearly there were social and economic effects from adoption of the new technologies, but there were intellectual consequences too. Although technological advances and inventions were always eye-catching, over the years it was also becoming clear that science was steadily uncovering nature's secrets. Interestingly, it took a long time for the Enlightenment and its overarching principle, *progress*, to become influential, intellectually, in Great Britain. Chadwick points out that John Morley, a positivist and a critic of religion, "put the French Enlightenment on the British intellectual map" in 1865. (Prior to that, the German term *Aufklärung* was used to refer to the [contemptible] eighteenth century in French thought.) For Morley, progress required the elimination of the supernatural from our consciousness. As we will see, he was just one contributor to the mushrooming debate and, as some see it, power struggle, between science and religion.

The Scientific–Religious Gap

Although many people, even today, believe that one aim of science is to disprove religion, it does not have such an agenda. Those who believe—whether in 1870, 1917, or 2005—that science refutes or otherwise vitiates religion, especially in the general population, are quite naive. Voltaire's remark of 1769, "If God did not exist, it would be necessary to invent him," still rings true. However, the influence of science in the latter half of the nineteenth century was consistent with the secularization and anticlericalism that we have described.

Another writer who incited antagonism between religion and science was John William Draper, a minor scientific figure known primarily as a popularizer of Darwin. In his 1874 book, Draper, in the name of science, skewered the Church (at least, the Catholic Church). He is obscure now, but at the time was important enough to be translated into eight languages. Other, more important, scientific materialists sprang up after the 1850s. Karl Vogt was an influential Darwin popularizer who maintained, in speeches and textbooks, that science directly contradicted religion, spirit, and God. Various theories of the time seriously discredited any spiritual basis of our being. Jakob Moleschott, a physiology lecturer, coined a curious remark: "no thought without phosphorous," which inspired the well-known expression (due to Feuerbach), "man is what he eats." However this is interpreted, it emphasizes our material essence. As Darwin's theory caught on—that is, fueled intellectual foment, even among the middle classes, on science versus religion—in the early-to-mid-1860s, the proponents of the religion-is-ignorance school had something deep and lasting that appeared to back them up.

Other minor scientists typified the popular expression of the new materialist, antispiritual, antireligious views. One was Ludwig Büchner, whose *Force and Matter* (1855) was a huge bestseller that sold hundreds of thousands of copies, reached its twenty-first edition by 1904, and was translated into fifteen languages. Another, Ernst Haeckel, added to the scientific materialist movement with *Riddle of the Universe* (1899), which also sold hundreds of thousands of copies. How influential were these or any books? Perhaps not overly so, but nevertheless they provide a convincing snapshot of the zeitgeist. Chadwick claims, "These books . . . tell us, not what people thought, but what they wanted to read about, and what they wanted to say they had read about." Moreover, evolutionary science was not just for bookish bourgeois; it also trickled down to oppressed workers. Socialist agendas, like that of the Social Democratic journal *Volkstaat,* co-opted evolution as an argument for socialism. Indeed, it was the merging of intellectual and social forces—considerable scientific advancement coupled with a common-man, proletarian element— that differentiated nineteenth-century secularism from the fashionable atheism of the Enlightenment. But probably the outstanding emblem of secularization was the figure of Darwin.

Darwin published *The Descent of Man* in 1871 and it is fair to say that within a decade the recognition that humans had evolved (or, if you prefer, *descended*) from earlier primates had spread well beyond the scientific community. The degree to which popular society had assimilated the new ideas is exemplified by the search for, and references to, the "missing link" (which became the subject of various circuslike exhibitions). By the 1880s, though, there were other scientific and philosophical developments that were consistent with the conservative backlash against Mill's liberalism.

One element of conflict was that, despite the amusement of those missing-link exhibitions, many people deep down could not quite bring themselves to believe scientific materialism in its pure form because this would seem to imply determinism and lack of free will. Of course, this ancient debate is still troublesome, and will be discussed later. We need to keep in perspective that scientific materialism, riding on the coattails of evolutionary theory, did not enjoy an easy and steady rise in popularity but faced, and still faces, waves of opposition. Even today a very significant minority of Americans favors the teaching of "creationism" (and not evolution) in our schools.

Another barometer of the dynamic climate of the second half of the nineteenth century is its historical writing. Generally speaking, as I have noted, the overall trend is that the presentation of history itself became more secular. This was expressed not only in the rejection of religion and its appeal to miracles, but also in a *striving* to be more secular, more positivist, and more reliant on scientific method. A subsidiary theme, however, is that history grew more social and more personal; it became less the study of great people and ideas moving the world, and more of the view that change emanates from the socioeconomic conditions of the masses. The *many* were becoming important, not just the few; this, in turn, was related to a historical determinism that originated mid-century. This determinism, partly a product of statistical studies of particular acts such as murders and suicides, presumed to involve deeper biological laws or social conditions.

One important example of the secularizing influence in historical work was Ernest Renan's book *The Life of Jesus,* published in 1863. This was the first biography of Jesus that excluded the supernatural. Renan sought to bring us Jesus as a *historical* character, where history is portrayed scientifically, that is, secularly—without miracles. His work seemed to fit the times, with readers drawn to a figure they could embrace as a sublime human being, yet stripped of a mythology that was by then difficult to accept.

The reaction to Renan's book illustrates the breadth and depth of acceptance of the scientific materialism of the day. But twenty years later, even with declining populations of churchgoers, the backlash against scientific thought gained momentum through the notion that science, although perhaps not wrong, was *insufficient.* Science could not solve all of our problems, in particular, not our moral problems. Ferdinand Brunetière, a leading French intellectual of the 1890s who was a literary critic, a materialist, and a Darwinian, personified this eventual dissatisfaction with science. In the mid-1890s, Brunetière abandoned his lengthy program of attempting to found a social morality by distilling "religion" from organized religion. His newfound *rapprochement* with Catholicism was partly due to his impatience with science, seeing as it had not, by that late date, erased the problems of humanity, nor had it replaced religion. (And partly, it was fueled by a private audience that Brunetière had with the Pope in 1894.) Brunetière was interpreted, wrongly, as having claimed that science had failed. Interestingly, in the face of proscience, prorepublic youth rallies against him, Brunetière subsequently abandoned Darwinism and drifted toward the right and the Church. Religion had indeed gained some ground against science.

Passionate Writers

Brunetière's friend, the Vicomte Eugene-Melchior de Vogüé, introduced Russian authors, particularly Dostoevsky and Tolstoy, to France in 1886 with the publication of his book, *Le Roman Russe.* Ironically, this popularizing of Russian authors led a movement *away* from materialism. The new wave of weighty novels ran counter to the Victorian principles of liberalism, order, and "doing good." They did not foster belief in positivism and progress. Rather, they exuded the subjective and darker side of humanity through their inner torment, doubt, disorder, and mystery. They stressed the opposition between the intellect and the heart, the objective and the subjective, and in doing so, created a serious problem for the materialist program.

The Russians did not have a monopoly in undermining the clinical, passionless, and ostensibly objective liberalism that had gained so much ground. Friedrich Nietzsche equally brought attention to the individual. Nietzsche's iconoclasm and his sometimes insulting remarks won enemies as well as followers; his aphoristic and powerful writing style was easy to misconstrue and take out of context.

Much of Nietzsche's writing involves the foundation of moral thought—which is crucial to our outline of the power struggle between the Church and the secular movement for moral predominance. Nietzsche was very clear on this: he saw, over the next two centuries, *"the advent of nihilism"* (his emphasis) grounded in "one particular interpretation, the Christian moral one." Christian humility reduces us to mediocre beings, mired in a "slave morality" based on resentment and ultimate recompense. Worse, Christianity is based on a fiction, with God having emerged from our insecurity. Since, indeed, "God is dead," it is solely up to us to create higher-value beings.

Thus emancipated from our misguided faith, Nietzsche compels us to exercise our free will, keeping in mind that "the extraordinary privilege of *responsibility,*" that is, conscience, rests entirely on our shoulders. In his words, "we discover that the ripest fruit is the *sovereign individual,* like only to himself, liberated again from morality of custom, autonomous and supramoral . . . the man who has his own independent, protracted will and the *right to make promises*—and in him . . . a consciousness of his own power and freedom, a sensation of mankind come to completion" (his emphasis).

Nietzsche's main outpouring of work came in the 1880s (he broke down in 1889, went insane, and never recovered), which is significant to us as a period in which European liberalism, after large gains, had ebbed. Evidently, the double barrel of liberalism and scientific materialism that appeared in 1859 established a foothold for secularism, but despite weakening the Church, did not wipe it out. People found no spirituality in the new intellectuality. What role were their emotions to play? Nietzsche, Dostoevsky, and Tolstoy were able to provide a sense that one's moral compass could come from *within*. Within each of us lies a unique cradle of consciousness in which our belief system grows through life experiences. This point of view necessarily puts significant weight on the subjective—a component that the scientific materialists (and their twentieth-century successors, the rat-running behaviorists) ignored. Further, on a number of levels, one could embrace Darwinism, be moved by Dostoevsky and persuaded by Nietzsche, keep one's belief in free will, and waffle on the issue of God.

This sounds very much like the ordinary person of today, who is likely to accept evolution and various other scientific theories as absolute truths about the world (but leave room for a bit of the supernatural), embrace liberalism in its democratic tradition (but abhor taxes), and honor relativism as a supreme right to one's opinion (yet hold others to be mistaken). Most of us are devout believers in our right to freedom, tacitly based on our unshakable belief in free will. And despite our puritanical streak, we (Americans) accept, even encourage, free spirits in our midst (as long as they're not our kids). Nietzsche wrote for "free spirits"; we tolerate them more nowadays, in part because of him. Nietzsche's polemics helped break down the absolute; with greater emphasis on the individual, the world of ideas could better balance the objective and the subjective as well as the individual and the group. We will explore these oppositions further, but for the moment we need to mention yet another foundation of the absolute that crumbled in the 1880s.

The Pillars of Science Begin to Shake

Possibly the greatest scientific triumph of the nineteenth century was the unraveling of the mysteries of electricity and magnetism. This success proceeded in stages culminating in the brilliant theory of James Clerk Maxwell, who summarized electromagnetic phenomena in four expressions, now called Maxwell's equations, in the 1860s. (These equations are occasionally seen on T-shirts worn by physics students.) Maxwell's theory not only unified electricity and magnetism, but light and other electromagnetic waves (like infrared and ultraviolet) as well.

The scientists of the day assumed that these waves needed some medium in order to propagate. After all, sound waves vibrated air (and other media) and water waves rippled water. How could waves travel through a vacuum? It was proposed that there existed a medium, undetectable though it seemed, called the *ether,* to conduct light waves. It was supposed that the ether permeated all of space uniformly and that the earth and other bodies drifted through it. Now, one mathematical consequence of Maxwell's theory was that light emanating from a source travels at the same speed in *all* directions, even when the source itself is *moving*. This was hard to explain. After all, if you were in a moving car and turned on a light bulb, wouldn't the light, augmented by the speed of the car, move faster forward than backward? Resolutely, physicists rose to the challenge and developed experiments to measure relative velocities. However, twenty years after Maxwell, into the 1880s, not only couldn't physicists detect the ether, but when they tried to measure the velocity of the earth relative to the motion of light, they failed; the experiments yielded no velocity at all.

In the 1880s, Albert A. Michelson, another physicist, launched a long career of studying the nature of light. He built an apparatus for this purpose, called an interferometer, which used mirrors and half-silvered mirrors to reflect and combine light waves in order to measure wave interference and changes in propagation times. Michelson and his colleague E. W. Morley devised an ingenious experiment to measure the speed of the earth as it travels through the ether. They measured this speed in different directions, and lo and behold, found none. That is, the earth did not move relative to this uniform ether, despite our orbital velocity of about eighteen miles per second. Something was wrong, and every explanation for this—like the presence of an ether wind—was inadequate.

One of the explanations, offered by H. A. Lorentz, was that objects contract in the direction of their motion. This alone did not suffice to explain wave propagation through the ether; too many other experiments revealed difficulties with the ether hypothesis. But the mathematical transformation that Lorentz applied to Maxwell's equations was seized on in 1905 by Albert Einstein, who employed it in his theory of special relativity.

Our superficial notion of relativity, for example when we declare that "everything is relative," has virtually no relation to what Einstein was talking about. However, Einstein's new theory rocked popular as well as scientific thought because the maxim of relativity is comforting to the average person.

Let's pause and review the major themes of this chapter. Throughout the nineteenth century, scientific progress vastly increased our knowledge about, and more significantly, our *control of,* the world. At the same time, a new liberalism emerged with its emphasis on freedom and tolerance; alongside this, powerful voices in literature and philosophy emphasized individual forces and values. Meanwhile, a dual ideology, one that was communal and socialist, had caught on. The synergy of the scientific and technological advances together with the new social movements helped establish a new secularism that, unlike that of the Enlightenment, was broad based and not restricted to the salons. This new secularism diminished the role and power of the Church.

However, despite the heady progress felt so universally, people realized that utopia was not just around the corner. Social problems still remained; some got worse. Disease was still prevalent, and daily life, though changing, was still hard. And deep down, secularization did not chase our fears of or hopes for a God—it just left people uneasy. Science could be trusted only so much. Unfortunately, after Michelson–Morley, even the scientists were shaky, as Newtonian mechanics, which explained so much about the world, was at odds with Maxwell's electromagnetic theory.

Another perspective on the new and growing uneasiness of the era is this: a century before, when Ben Franklin was fooling around with kites, science was *incomplete* to such a large degree that inconsistency among competing theories was not the primary issue. But by the 1880s, with mechanics and electromagnetism fairly well understood (the wonderful inventions of the time providing validation), the inconsistency discovered between these theories was seriously disturbing. Such inconsistency was additionally felt on moral and social planes, through various oppositions. Liberalism and socialism crossed swords and both of these assailed the Church. Even Christ had a dual nature now, both as a deity and as a purely historical human being. Prior to the late 1800s, people knew what they were *supposed* to believe, even if deep down, they were skeptical or just unsure. But, nearing 1900, conflict multiplied—along with places in which to invest one's trust and faith. The link between the Church and God was threatened, if not severed altogether. And science?—science not only was incomplete but was now self-contradictory. What was one supposed to believe?

In summary, there were two profound nineteenth-century developments that led to choice becoming a major, unprecedented force in our civilization. One was the acceleration of industrial growth, which rapidly raised the standard of living in the West. This acceleration would continue into the twentieth century and create a widespread consumer culture as early as the 1920s. Concurrent with this—and not unrelated to it—was the loss of the absolute. Two general symptoms of this societal disposition were rising secularization and its associated subjectivity. There were several contributing factors to this. One was the advent of Darwinism, which, more than anything else, undermined our belief in the influence of an Almighty in our earthly affairs. Another was the spread of liberal philosophy, whose principal virtue, toleration, eroded conformity. In liberalism the Church, already weakened by natural science, was challenged in its moral authority. As we will discuss, Kierkegaard (religious though he was) focused on the individual as a responsible decision maker, and Nietzsche, Tolstoy, and Dostoevsky showed us that our morality could be generated from within. By the 1890s, however, when the initial confidence in science and liberalism waned, the Church regained some of its influence. Indeed, for a century since then, the same pattern has repeated itself as we continue to vacillate between the forces of technology and spirituality. Although by 1900 much progress had been made, our doubts about the world were, paradoxically, stronger than ever.

These reinstated doubts of the late 1800s were confirmed, or at least reinforced, in 1912 by the hype and sinking of the *Titanic*. The next big setback—a much bigger one, of course—was the (First) World War just two years later, nullifying any claims to our having mastered any moral control. As if that weren't enough, science, although it would take even larger steps forward, would continue to fall apart at its foundations. The deepening loss of the absolute would diminish objectivity and emphasize subjectivity. Nature and society would lose their power over us, and relativity and pluralism would become central to twentieth century thought. These are events we will discuss throughout the rest of this book.

I think it is clear that the period from 1850 to 1900 saw a great deal of social, cultural, and scientific and technological change. The world had modernized considerably, and the era of choice was ready to emerge.

Nearly a century has passed since the horrors of World War I, and most of us are immersed in a sea of consumerism. What's more, we are flooded with information and frantic with communication. It wasn't always like this. If you are a Generation X-er or a baby boomer or older, then you can probably remember the days prior to, say, 1985, when life was a little bit simpler. Sure, there were computers and investments (though not as pervasive), and electronics, and most of the comforts and gadgets that we have today. But consider what there *wasn't:* no Internet or e-mail, no voice mail or even answering machines, no fax machines, no laptops, no wireless phones, no pagers, no PDAs, no satellite uplinks, and only a smattering of cable TV, personal computers, and word processing. Give yourself pause, and contemplate how much life has changed in twenty years.

There is nothing profound in this observation. Everything I listed above involves information, communication, and convenience, and for most of us, despite bug-ridden software, inadequate support, and the occasional mechanical breakdown, the above features have enriched our lives.

Of course, when things go wrong, and they invariably do at the worst times (not because of Murphy's Law, but because *any* time is a bad time once you're completely enslaved to these gadgets)—we may wax nostalgic and long for those days when there wasn't any of this stuff to screw us up. Those who are a bit more cynical and sensitive than the rest wonder at such moments whether we indeed *are* better off than before, just as we wonder whether offices are more productive now (not by certain measures) or whether less paper has been generated by the electronic revolution (definitely not). Moreover, investments in information technology are often ephemeral, and what we need to master doesn't just increase, it multiplies.

We've grown into an information-rich society over these twenty years, much as a college student grows into a responsible adult. College students with full course loads and relationships and maybe a job and a car think they're over-loaded—and they are—but in fifteen years, when they'll have families and mortgages, job stress, not enough sleep and too little time off, they'll realize that school had its advantages. As adults they will take on a treadmill of re-sponsibilities and worries that won't wind down in a couple of months. It's the *management,* the planning and juggling, that seems to suck up time and effort, not the actual events (which we're too tired or rushed to completely take in). We operate, in part, at a *metalevel,* a step removed; it's at this stage that we transfer so much of our commitment and engagement to our children, or, des-perate to make a difference, to some other cause.

The crux of the issue is that, indeed, the more you have, the more you have to manage what you have. This *vicious spiral* grows. You begin to metamanage, that is, to manage your management. The perfect example of this is our love affair with the computer, or more precisely, with information technology. We spend so much of our time mastering the tools that we neglect the substance. When was the last time you took a pen and wrote a heartfelt letter to a friend? Now that everyone has e-mail, we can easily reach more people more frequently, but our e-mails are careless and rushed, and sent and received with all the clinical feeling of a "virtual" letter.

Computing provides a good example of how we transfer our emphasis from subject to medium (Marshall McLuhan), or from object level to metalevel, or from actual to virtual. But it is only an example of what pervades so much of our lives. We manage our commodities similarly. The more we consume, the more we attend to consumption. The more money we make, the more we manage how our money makes money. (Indeed, finance has replaced pornography as the most popular Internet application.) We divert our engagement from the *products* to the *process* of consumption. Consider our current societal foci: malls, together with the rising wave of e-commerce. Shopping has become an end rather than a means. This self-referential hierarchy is again the vicious spiral. It is what we are ceaselessly ascending, both as individuals and as a society. As individuals, we spend most of our free time and discretionary income in this consumer trap, while we lose sight of what the sought-after products will do for our lives. On the societal level, education and health care, two of our most important institutions, are getting ruined by top-heavy bureaucracies and spiraling administrative expenses, which can outweigh the basic costs of providing the intended services. The result is that administrators control our medical treatments, and many of our schools can't even provide books for the students.

For many, the vicious spiral is an inescapable vortex that eventually may collapse under its own weight. We realize that we need help, so we hire nannies for our children and accountants for our taxes; we employ stockbrokers, lawyers, doctors (and specialists), therapists, travel agents, and contractors. But that's just the beginning. The nanny has to be able to contact you, so you get a pager. Obviously, you need (yes, need) a wireless phone. At home you have a cordless phone too, for convenience, and maybe an extra line for the computer or fax machine or one for the kids. This pretty well satisfies your communications requirements, but what about information? You need the Internet, so you have to learn your way around it, but then you have to keep track of all of those passwords and log-in IDs. But, for Christ's sake, you have all those other phone numbers, PINs for bank cards, alarm systems, ATM cards, calling cards, phone-in services and voice mail—a worse nightmare than the six remotes all over your living room. (Many of us ease this problem by using the same PIN for everything, and God help us if someone finds it out.)

Of course, such a situation can be pleasant. Later on we will discuss Maslow's hierarchy of needs, from physical necessities to the desire for self-actualization. If the vicious spiral I have just described indeed depicts your life in part, you are probably beyond having to worry about the basic struggles for food, clothing, and shelter. You are more concerned with the process of choice than you are about the choices themselves. Perhaps you enjoy the new communication- and information-intensive lifestyle in which you are enmeshed. Simply put, we have access to a vast proliferation of things, most of which are not immediately at hand, and we need tools to spare us time and difficulty in reaching them. In addition, one could say, we delight in toys. We relish technology's mastery over the triple hurdles of nature, time, and space. Perhaps our infotech existence is a harmless manifestation of Daniel Bell's postindustrial society, in which information (and not energy) is the primary resource, processing (and not fabrication) is the chief output mode, and where knowledge (and not capital) is the underpinning of technology.

Metamanaging Our Lives

But these explanations do not address the impact the vicious spiral has on our lives. To say we like tech toys is to miss the point. To identify a symptom of a new era is important, but does not grapple with the central issue. This issue is one of *meta*management, not just information management. In this environment there are several constraints that bind us. The obvious ones are money (rather, the lack of it) and time. Another one, though, is our dwindling understanding of our increasingly technical world.

As technology advances, we become generally more clueless about how things work. Very few of us even pretend to understand DVDs (let alone older technologies like TV or radio). For that matter, most of us don't understand the workings of a water faucet. This distancing from the nuts-and-bolts is surprisingly pervasive. Take a typical stockbroker, for example. If you ask him or her about "beta," a market measure of volatility, the chances are that you can get an explanation of what it means, but the broker will not know how it is calculated.

In spite of this growing breach, to some extent we can succeed in managing our affairs. We decide which gadgets and services to ignore, use, master, or seek help with. If we want to record programs from our TV, we learn how. If our taxes are complicated, we invest in software or get an accountant. For the difficult tasks, we have specialists' specialists, a logical consequence of society's division of labor. Nevertheless, most of us are frequently driven to helplessness, which does not foster independence. This helplessness clashes with the increased sense of self that our era of choice has given us. And *driven* by choice, that is, driven by the desire to provide more and better choices (i.e., "features"), the systems that are supposed to ease our lives are becoming more complex and harder to use. With each new purchase, consideration, and decision, we are increasingly burdened to either deal with it ourselves or to rely on others (much like the "make or buy" decisions that plague so many companies). Manufacturers, looking to "add value," prey on our thirst for features—the more, the better. However, we must also weigh the time and effort involved in mastering their use.

Is there a silver bullet? Sometimes, something comes along like the universal remote that reduces your living room aggravation. Sometimes a help menu is developed that really helps, and sometimes "user-friendly" is not oxymoronic. Our incompetence is tempered by gadgets that we can program, tax software that holds our hands, and shiploads of books for beginners and dummies. Since knowledge is so enormously specialized, most of us are dummies at most things, and are ironically proud of it. Ignorance has become a strange sort of common denominator for all of us and we don't need to hide the for-dummies books in a brown paper wrapper. In general, though, we sometimes have to get our hands really dirty, and we have neither the time nor the desire to do so. Unable to plunge into the trenches, we instead manage our lives on a metalevel, ceding control over our lives to experts and gadgets. Ascending the vicious spiral involves more than making choices about our affairs; it involves making choices about choices. As we become better able to pack more and more into our lives, the ascent will continue—and the more difficult it will be to come down.

We so frequently feel empowered by technology that we seldom realize how imprisoned we are in the vicious spiral. We are so busy returning e-mails and playing with our financial portfolio that we fail to realize how much autonomy we have lost. This issue of dwindling control calls into question the opposition between free will and determinism. This dualism is one that we will continue to visit because choice itself seems so dependent on a foundation of freedom.

Freedom, Responsibility, and "The Grand Inquisitor"

We have already discussed the importance of nineteenth-century secularization and its assault on the absolute. No literary passage better conveys the core issues of freedom and responsibility on the societal as well as on the personal level in this context than Fyodor Dostoevsky's masterful "The Grand Inquisitor" chapter from *The Brothers Karamazov.* The scene is set by Ivan, one of the brothers, in sixteenth-century Seville, in an era when heretics were burned in the autos-da-fé of the Inquisition. Christ appears silently among the people. They recognize him and he is beseeched to perform a miracle or two, which he carries out. On seeing this demonstration, the Grand Inquisitor has Christ taken away by guards and shut in a dark cell.

The Inquisitor cautions Christ, "You have no right to add anything to what You had said of old," and then informs him that he will be burned as a heretic the following day. The reader may ask, why this time, and the answer soon follows: the Inquisitor does not want Christ to undo fifteen centuries' worth of work. That is, Christ desired man's faith—faith as a product of *freedom.* But the Church believed the vast majority of humankind to be weak, unable to handle true freedom. Thus, over those fifteen centuries the Church worked to relieve the masses of the burdens of true freedom by substituting the lesser, but tangible, rewards of a false freedom.

The Inquisitor asks, "Did You forget that man prefers peace, and even death, to freedom of choice in the knowledge of good and evil?" And, although "Nothing is more seductive for man than his freedom of conscience," we are told that because "nothing is a greater torture," the freedom that Christ wanted for us is too oppressive, and "utterly beyond the strength of men."

Are any of us up to Christ's expectations? The Inquisitor allows that "for the sake of the bread of Heaven, thousands and tens of thousands shall follow You," but points out that "millions and tens of thousands of millions . . . will not have the strength to forego the earthly bread for the sake of the heavenly."

Heavenly rewards are vague and mysterious, and await us only in a far-off, incomprehensible future. Christ overestimated our ability to hold out for eternal good, and underestimated our craving for the bread that satiates our hunger. Moreover, the Inquisitor continued, "They will be convinced, too, that they can never be free, for they are weak, sinful, worthless and rebellious." And they know it. But there is a deeper insight: the Inquisitor declares that bread and freedom are incompatible *among* people; they "will never be able to share among themselves." People are not only weak; they are unable to govern themselves. Therefore, the Inquisitor concludes, "In the end they will lay their freedom at our feet, and say to us, 'Make us your slaves, but feed us.'" At this point, what can the Church do but "feed them in Your name, and declare falsely that it is in Your name."

Dostoevsky's Ivan has more to say through this Inquisitor. The Church, it is claimed, by "feeding" the people is actually providing more succor for the great majority of humanity than Christ himself. There are two initial reasons for this. One is that Christ, in predicating faith and eternal happiness on individual freedom, "scattered the flock and sent it astray on unknown paths." The Church will bring that flock together and provide the secure community that lone individuals need. The other reason is that, unlike Christ, the Church "shall give them the quiet, humble happiness of weak creatures such as they are by nature." But beyond this, the Inquisitor reveals, the Church will, in its supreme authority, render the masses first awestruck (and grateful for it) and then entirely at their master's mercy. Finally, in complete control, the Church will be able to create happiness for its followers in promoting simple joys and even through allowing sin, all the while sparing folk of the anxieties of confronting the big questions. (The thing is, the Inquisitor, heavy with the weight of the belief that the other kingdom does not exist, would prefer the flock not to know that they simply "expire peacefully in Your name," where "beyond the grave they will find nothing but death.")

To reiterate, not only are we too weak to accept personal freedom and individual self-determination, we are also too weak to accomplish self-determinism as a people. The Church will not only look after our individual needs, relieving us of worrisome freedom, but will serve to unite us as a community. Our security in this pact is further guaranteed when people "remember the horrors of slavery and confusion to which Your freedom brought them," a slavery in which to face alone the "insoluble mysteries" that will prove unbearable and destructive. Finally, the small comforts that the Church will provide its flock in this life certainly outweigh those of an afterlife whose nonexistence is kept secret from the masses.

Other teasers from "The Grand Inquisitor" are tangential for us, like the relative integrity of Orthodoxy versus that of Catholicism. But Dostoevsky's central opposition, dramatically staged, is a fundamental human condition: we desire freedom, but its responsibility can weigh so heavily on us that we need to be released from it. This antifreedom soothes us; it lifts a weight off of our chests. Christ insists that we have freedom; the Inquisitor, slavery. Who is closer to the truth? Practically speaking, since only the Nietzschean superman can follow the former path, the real question is, what mix of the two ways will provide the greatest good?

"The Grand Inquisitor" initially focuses on the question of human individuals and their inability to freely choose their course, but ultimately provides a template for social control. One such model was in place long before the Inquisition—the Roman example of providing bread and circuses. We should note that "bread" need not be taken metaphorically; witness the dénouement of Marie Antoinette centuries later. Other models might dispense with the (hopefully benevolent) autocrat and, within a democratic system, attempt to maintain stability among the populace through the distribution of a wide choice of commodities.

Bread would evolve into salad bars and diversified ethnic gastronomy; circuses would become cable TV, multiplex cinemas, and cruise holidays, all of it more or less organized by a ruling consortium. This consortium is none other than the usual suspects—sociologist Theodor Adorno's "culture industry" to some, the media, to others; in short, giant conglomerates whose power dwarfs that of the Church.

Of course, the steady succession of disasters that crop up—like the spread of AIDS—as well as lower profile, but endemic practices such as drug abuse and racial discrimination—provide fuel for the recurrent cries of "conspiracy," in which "the government" is suspected of manipulating the system to weaken certain interest groups. But in prosperous periods dissent is minimal and the consortium of power brokers, as it were, is able to keep the masses well away from the gates. Call this system what you will; one of the more provocative terms I have heard for it is the "monkey cage" theory. This expression serves to hyperbolize the Frankfurt School thesis that the culture industry pacifies the populace, thereby repressing social change.

Who runs the show? After all, even the Inquisitor reckoned that maybe tens of thousands (out of billions) would be strong enough to follow Christ. This small percentage of us are the chosen, as considered through whatever lens (courage, intelligence, etc.) that is relevant.

In any monkey cage, or us-versus-them theory, we're in charge because we deserve to be. To convey this notion, Herbert Spencer, a contemporary of Dostoevsky, coined the phrase "survival of the fittest" in his attempt to tailor Darwinian theory to sociology. We *should be* in charge; we've proven ourselves fitter. As critical theorist Thomas McEvilley points out, Spencer's social Darwinism was well suited to the modernist ethos of progress that permeated his era. With technological progress in full swing, it only made sense that the cream would rise to the top. This concept also justified the colonialism through which Western powers grabbed their shares of the lesser-developed world.

As an aside, I personally do not subscribe to social Darwinism or to conspiracy- or monkey-cage-style theories. Our reasonably fluid market seems to provide ample opportunities for most, and besides, the world's increasing complexity is probably not centrally controllable. The key issue, perhaps, is whether enough people are learning skills that can secure them valued pursuits. Whether people are getting smarter or not (college-entrance exam scores say no, IQ scores say yes), I can testify that the proficiencies our twenty-two-year-olds possess when they venture out of school and into responsible lives are terribly uneven. Despite my rejection of social Darwinism, it can't be denied that some individuals' profiles are better adapted to the prevailing conditions, and that these people enjoy success, at least as measured by our usual criteria. Regardless of our abilities, though, we all have dismaying career choices that must be faced in adolescence and early adulthood. These choices rock us to the core since they form our identities. We find, though, that our decisions are not irreversible. Stockbrokers become chefs, chefs go back to school, and anyone with a niche can venture into the world of start-up.

The economic dimension of the social control issue might persuade one to reject the Inquisitor's argument. But it remains unclear, on the whole, how best to manage our society. Obviously, we're still learning. It seems fair to say that some regimes go too far, and not just the blatantly totalitarian or fundamentalist ones. (In Singapore, for example, chewing gum is prohibited except for certain medicinal purposes.) But, for certain specific issues, it's crazy not to side with the Inquisitor. Consider guns. Guns serve *one* purpose—to kill—and whatever benefit gun owners believe they derive from their possession, it doesn't outweigh the cost of murder. For most of us, this became clearer than ever in 1998, when school shootings by young teens became commonplace. Other concerns, like abortion, are more problematic, and policy paths are not easy to derive. The question of noninterference versus intervention, Christ or the Inquisitor, is perhaps best handled issue by issue.

Choice seems to involve two different freedom–determinism axes. Along one dimension, there is the degree to which a person may take charge. One's actions can range from total passivity to complete responsibility. But, even when we never relinquish control, our actions intersect with exogenous ones. These outside factors may constrain us completely or not at all. How frequently do we talk about luck, or fate, or being in the right place at the right time?

When we consider our life-defining situations, most of us think about our partners and spouses (past and present), our children, our careers in general and jobs in particular, our homes and surroundings, our possessions, and our hobbies—as well as our tastes, our ideas, and our values. For so many of these attributes (*this* job, *this* spouse, *this* book [I hope], *that* house—I'm just reflecting our collective materialism), we can, at least in theory, trace our lives back to some defining point when we embarked on that path. At some point in time we had to make a choice about a particular feature. Frequently we opt out, and of the "choices" that we do make, we often don't decide in the usual way. Therefore we believe that certain things just happen to us.

But regardless of the extent to which we make conscious decisions, something results. We take one job and not another. We break up with people, or let them break up with us—or we just drift apart, or let ourselves drift apart. We take one house over another; was it sunny when we visited? Did it rain when we saw the other one? And because our friend was heavily into one band, are we also? Much of how we choose ourselves is well thought-out, and when we look back on these paths we feel that we made the correct decisions. But how much of our lives has *not* been the product of a conscious procedure?

We all do look back, and muse, "what if." I doubt, though, that we spend too much time on circumstances beyond our control. We all realize, eventually, that "if my grandmother had balls she'd be my grandfather." What really gets to us are the decisions that we *can* (and *did*) control. These constitute the domain of "what-if" retrospection. With choice such a central part of our lives, is it mere coincidence that "what if" has become such a significant phrase for our society, or that the ability to perform "what-if" analysis has become an integral part of finance and engineering? Doesn't the complexity of this dense network of paths taken, ignored, rejected, disdained, accepted, feared, desired, and dreamed vastly enrich our lives, now postindustrially shorn of the narrow, necessary drudgery of previous eras?

Don't we yearn—in weak moments, or sentimental moments, or merely philosophical moments—for those lost opportunities to have at least tried out a different path? And for those tough choices we presently make and will continue to make, can't we tinker and explore, rather than face the all-or-nothing? (Can't we have our cake and eat it too?)

The Inversion of Choice

Thus far, I have argued that human beings have faced far more choices than ever before, and that this abundance of choice has significantly altered our lives. I need to point out, however, that the presence of choice, especially when it is overwhelming, can have the effect of negating itself. In this *inversion of choice,* too much choice can equal none at all. Suppose you need, for example, a phone of some sort, and walk into an electronics store with ten minutes left on your lunch hour. There you are with maybe seventy phones in front of you. Such a situation can be bewildering, intimidating, and even paralyzing. Not knowing where to start, and not having all day either, you could well walk out speechless and empty-handed. We often take the vast selection available in stores for granted, but if you were to transport most people from outside the West and plunk them down in the shampoo aisle of the local megadrug store, their wide-eyed, open-mouthed bewilderment would shock you.

The inversion of choice is shaping both consumer behavior as well as business's responses to it. As e-business authors Ravi Kalakota and Marcia Robinson point out, consumers burdened by the plethora of retailers and electronic distribution channels are increasingly seeking integrated, "one-stop shopping" solutions to simplify their shopping decisions.

Inversion of choice haunts the cable television industry too. Some years ago, as cable TV was making inroads into our homes, there was much anticipation of expansion to five hundred channels. After all, the increase from a handful to a hundred was hugely popular and, together with the remote control device, it revolutionized the viewing process, turning it into a peregrination from station to station (and channel flipping, in turn, had a great impact on other media). But soon thereafter—concurrent with the advent of the World Wide Web—the excitement over five hundred TV channels was dampened. Now fifteen hundred channels are available, but the marginal gains are minimal. How do you find out what's on? It takes forever to search the menus, and until a good search device is developed, hundreds of channels might be worse than the seventy phones.

There exist other, more subtle, inversion of choice effects in our society. Wander through the lingerie or the men's underwear sections in a department store, and you will find brassieres and underwear in countless sizes, all of which feature the same (female or male) model. One might have thought that for a particular size, the person photographed on that package would embody (literally) the particular merchandise (so a size 32 will look like a 32 and a size 40, a 40). But no, whether a 32 or a 40, you have to settle for the same photo to aspire to, which is to say, by buying this garment, you *would be* that model.

If that seems like a frivolous example, then let's examine a related, more serious, inversion of choice. Over the past decade, providers of goods and services have tried harder than ever to cater to the customer. Customer satisfaction drives business, from product design to customer service. Some of the last bastions against change in this regard have been universities. Recently, though, a new educational mentality has emerged where the students have been transformed from a population attempting to gain education from taking courses with experts, to customers and clients (even "shareholders") of institutions of higher learning. Accordingly, a lot of emphasis has been brought to bear on the notion of discovering what these consumers demand from a course or a degree program. This inversion turns the decision process upside down. The experts, who used to believe they knew what was important about their subjects, now scramble to develop multiple degree programs and curricula to satisfy a broad spectrum of customers—those who, ironically, as potential students, do not know the subjects or their applications. This inversion, which begs the question of what ought to be taught, is not entirely without merit, because in the very competitive world of education, the students' being treated as customers is predicated on the very real situation of their having a choice in the matter. No wonder there are so many programs, and consequently so much administration, at universities nowadays. But then we're left with a pool of customers who are hardly better off picking the right program than they are choosing among the seventy phones.

The More Choice, the Worse?

I'm sure that you can recall situations in your life in which a multitude of options made the decision more difficult. Perhaps, vaguely aware of this, you had consciously wished that some of those options didn't exist. It turns out that research has shown that sometimes, a wider set of choices actually does lead people to be less happy than they would have been with fewer alternatives. This and many other empirical results have been described by psychologist Barry Schwartz in his book, *The Paradox of Choice: Why More Is Less*. Indeed, the main point of Schwartz's work is to show that, contrary to what most of us seem to believe, having lots of choices in life can in fact make us worse off; as the number of choices we have grows, at some point "choice no longer liberates, but debilitates. It might even be said to tyrannize." Why is it, though, that "many Americans are feeling less and less satisfied even as their freedom of choice expands"? Experiments conducted by Sheena Iyengar and Mark Lepper show that groups that were offered smaller numbers (e.g., six) of jams or chocolates to sample were more satisfied than were groups offered larger numbers (e.g., twenty-four) of the items. In addition, Jatin Atre and Elihu Katz have found a similar result with broadcast media, namely, that increasing the number of news and entertainment channels induces viewers to become more likely to successively pick the same type of program. These studies provide some indication that having more choices can actually be damaging; Schwartz provides several additional angles on how our cornucopia of choice has its hidden costs.

If we consider the phenomenal range of choices that we experience in our lives, we realize that it has led to a wealth of experiences for many of us. But the downside is that we adapt to these experiences and thereby raise our expectations. Luxuries of a generation ago, like air conditioning, have become the bare necessities of today, and as our list of necessities has lengthened, there is more to complain about should something not measure up. Given how quickly we adapt to new comforts like air conditioning or leather seating or gourmet dining, to continue to get the same kick out of things we end up embracing runaway consumerism. But then the problem is that our ever-increasing consumption is counteracted by "hedonic adaptation," in which we need ever-higher quantities to obtain the same *boost* in satisfaction. This sounds like addiction, and for many of us, it probably is.

Another downside of choice is regret. As Schwartz explains, regret comes in many forms—the usual "postdecision regret," when you wish you could take it back, "anticipated regret," when you wonder, "what if a better deal comes along," and other variations. Clearly, the more choices we're offered, the more we must deal with this demon.

Yet another difficulty with our world of choice involves a growing desire to make decisions reversible—to change our minds, postpone finality, and avoid commitment. Although we might think such behavior is valuable, Schwartz cites empirical evidence indicating that people who are able to change their minds end up *less* satisfied with their picks than those who have to stick with their original choices!

Our list of ills is not complete. We compete for status, and many of us lose. Then there's the sad fact that the grass is always greener anyway. We constantly worry about missed opportunities. And too many of us obsess about getting the maximum out of any situation instead of accepting what will be surely good enough.

Indeed, choice is a multiedged sword. An abundance of it presents opportunities as well as stress, while a surfeit of it can leave us with virtually no choice at all. And the issue of choice itself is confounded by two additional points: the philosophical question of whether we truly *have* free will, and, if we do, the extent to which fate and luck influence the outcomes. Indeed, so many of our decisions are complex and their outcomes unclear. Isn't there a systematic, scientific *method* through which we can improve our decision making?

The answer to this is yes—sometimes. Decision science in its many forms and appellations has been a major analytical development in our era of choice. We will discuss it later on. For the moment, though, let's explore a tangent. Earlier I had mentioned the evolution of our defining attributes as represented by a network of paths. Although decision science can assist us at a particular juncture, and help us plan for the future (much as a chess player who anticipates an opponent's moves), it cannot, of course, unravel our lives and retrieve a spurned job opportunity, or have us marry person B instead of person A. The network of paths that maps one's life is a maze like any other maze, and it turns out that such structures have provided us with some fascinating intellectual contributions.

Mazes—usually in the form of caves—have intrigued us for thousands of years. Caves naturally offer themselves for exploration, but since they often branch out to form labyrinths, the dangers of getting lost forever have led people to devise methods that allow entry, exploration, and escape. The challenge of how to best search caves has left its legacy in unlikely places such as countless kiddie games and diner place mat puzzles.

The late nineteenth century saw the publication of serious research on foolproof maze traversal procedures. These early efforts have been only slightly modified by contemporary computer scientists, who call their basic methods "depth-first" and "breadth-first" search. The ideas behind these procedures are straightforward. The maze is broken down into distinct segments, delimited by junctions called *nodes,* where they meet (or branch off into) other segments. During a search, the segments and nodes are marked in such a way that an explorer can determine if he or she has been there before, and if so, from which (other) segment the discovery was made. In this way one can make an exhaustive search, while able to backtrack all the way to the starting point.

Contemporary researchers (often motivated by the problem of obtaining tenure at a university) have made numerous advances in searching mazes and other structures. In addition to trying to most efficiently find a pot of gold (or an ancient wall painting) and get out alive, these investigators also concentrate on problems of trying to catch elusive prey. They tackle progressively more difficult problems—the structures get more complicated, the researchers need to determine how many agents are necessary to catch a certain number of fugitives, and so on—doubtless all with some military application.

To get the feel of these problems and to see what they have to do with us, let's consider a simple branching sort of maze in which each segment, as we proceed away from the single entrance, forks into two. Our objective is to find a pot of gold buried at one of the nodes. At the opening fork, we have to choose right or left, after which we arrive at what I'll call level one. We then proceed to the *next* level inward. Suppose that *each* of the two level-one nodes has another fork to confront us. This yields a total of four level-two nodes to explore. What if the maze continued like this? Level three would have two more possibilities from each of the preceding four, for a total of eight; level four would have sixteen nodes, and so on. With only a few more levels, the search could become seemingly endless. Consider the time needed to traverse each segment (an hour? a day?). If the maze had enough levels, you'd start to doubt whether you'd ever find the treasure. You'd wish you *knew*, at each fork, *which way to go*. If you did, with a ten-level maze, you'd find your prize in no more than ten steps; otherwise, you might have to search all 1,024 nodes at level ten (and all 512 nodes at level nine, and so on). You would certainly pay for some "inside information."

Being endowed with such information is basically what computer scientists, who began studying related "complexity" problems in the 1970s, call *nondeterminism*. The idea is that, at each fork, you'd simply ask a Delphic oracle, "do I go right or left?" and a mysterious voice would reveal the correct way. Imagine the time and trouble the oracle would save you. Without it, each additional level *doubles* the number of nodes of the previous level, and this exponential increase will soon run you out of time or money or both, rendering the pot of gold literally not worth your while.

Of course, we mortals are unable to tap into such powers, although we fervently try. We—and for other applications, the computers we program—can only slog through the maze and hope we find the gold (or for the computer, the answer) sooner rather than later. The procedures we employ are *deterministic*, not nondeterministic.

Any theory involving "oracle-powered" nondeterminism may seem senseless, since by its very nature, a nondeterministic algorithm would require a heretofore most elusive divine providence. But, remarkably, this fairy-tale device enables computer scientists and operations researchers to classify thousands of practical problems. Generally speaking, these real-world problems such as logistical vehicle routing and scheduling problems are so difficult that optimal solutions are known to be found only through an "oracle computation" as above. The classifications that researchers have developed help them know what they're up against, and even suggest strategies for the best plan of attack for complex situations. With some problems, even if the *optimal* solution is unobtainable, certain methods are guaranteed to come close (say, within a certain small percentage). Ultimately, the concept of nondeterminism, in which our choices are made with divine aid, has far-reaching effects, which include putting the logic in logistics and advancing the field of computational biology—nothing less than helping to unravel the genetic code!

What about "inside information" and growing our own little pot of gold? Nondeterminism won't make us rich, but thinking about it can provide a perspective on investments and market predictions. We all look to the forecasters who seem to "guess right"; we believe, of course, that there is more to their magic than mere guesswork. (For some, perhaps there is.)

Consider four different stocks (or four mutual funds) in which you may invest. Suppose that, over the next year, each of the four will go up or down considerably and, to keep things simple, the ups and downs are each fifty–fifty in likelihood. Suppose, too, that there is no interaction effect—so no one stock's price movement will affect that of any other stock. (A mathematician would say the stock prices are *independent*.) Whatever you invest will be committed at the outset for the full year.

Let's assume you feel lucky and invest, despite the fifty–fifty nature of things. If only you had some inside information—you'd avoid the stocks destined to drop and buy those slated to rise. But you *don't* have any good information, so, more or less blindly, you buy some but not others. A year later, when you assess the situation, you will probably find that your actions were not optimal; that is, you didn't pick the winners (and avoid the losers) with complete accuracy.

At one extreme, some poor sap could have guessed incorrectly on every single stock; at the other end of the spectrum is an investor who can't go wrong. If you could relive this situation over and over (without the benefit of knowing the outcomes), sooner or later, merely by chance, you will stumble on that magic luck. What's really going on is this: on any one stock, your chance of success is the same as with a coin flip. Given a lot of investors, roughly half of them will guess correctly on that stock. Half of the correct investors will guess right on the second stock also; then, half again will guess right on the third stock, and so on. With four stocks, roughly one out of sixteen investors will have guessed correctly. When it comes time to compare performance next year, the lucky few will appear to have been remarkably prescient.

Visually, the structure that best represents both the branching maze and the investment scenario is a *tree:* from the trunk come two main branches; from each of these grow two more branches, and so on. This tree is just the typical family or organizational tree in a different context. Unlike real trees, however, I must mention that in mazes, the branches can sometimes *join*. So, at times, the same position can be reached two different ways, like when two different chess games reach the same configuration through transposition of moves.

In any event, a search of the tree would require a systematic tracing, unless you can invoke an oracle or provide for *parallel processing* (in which multiple paths can be traced). What if we could invoke parallel processing on our life tree? Of course, we know we can't; such an idea is surely science fiction; indeed, it is the standard science fiction theme of parallel universes. But is it just science fiction? Let's consider what physics has to offer.

Pick Your Universe

You don't have to be an expert in physics to have had some exposure, through various popularizations, to the building blocks of matter: subatomic particles. Most of us have some more-or-less dim awareness that there is more to this subject than protons and electrons. Its study is expensive and politically charged. For example, way back in 1993 the United States Congress denied funds for a costly "supercollider," with which ultra-high-energy experiments might have turned up yet more exotic particles in the increasingly complex quest for nature's ultimate truths.

We're also vaguely aware that the subatomic world is strange (a pun!), that its energy comes in tiny quantum units (which ironically give rise to the hefty "quantum leaps" that people colloquially refer to), and that its behavior is uncertain. One aspect of this uncertainty is described by the celebrated Heisenberg uncertainty principle, which we interpret as saying that the subatomic world is hard to pin down. Another aspect is that each subatomic particle can only be described at any given moment as possessing a *probability distribution* among certain possible states.

So we know that the quantum world is weird and uncertain. But what most of us may *not* be aware of is that the quantum world is so weird and uncertain that not only are the best theories vaguely understood by us, they're controversial for physicists too. The consequences of these theories are so bizarre and counterintuitive and the different theories so contradictory, that the whole business is simply unclear to everybody.

Some of the contradictions and bizarre conclusions are not only amazing, but also are indicative of the depth to which the presence of choice, in shaping a new era, has permeated our very ways of explaining how the world works.

A quandary central to quantum physics is this: consider a particle that is to be measured by some device. Before measurement, the particle is described only fuzzily—by some set of possibilities and their associated probabilities. Quantum theory holds that the fuzzy description is, strictly speaking, the actual *reality* of the particle. Note: this is not like a flipped coin that someone is hiding from you, where the probabilities of heads and tails are fifty–fifty but you know that the coin is in one state *for sure*. The particle is in a particular state for sure only after we observe it. "For sure" indicates *irreversibility*, where the squishy probabilities have been firmed up and no longer apply. This reduction from probability to certainty is what physicists call the "collapse of the wave function." Exactly when did the measurement yield information transcending the prior uncertainty and how does the measuring device bring about this collapse from squishy probability to concrete reality? The usual answer seems to be that the particle is in the squishy state until an observation is made. But this view implies that *objectivity* itself—in this case the state of the particle—requires an *observer* to be part of the system, and this necessity seems unreasonable. ("If a tree falls in the forest, and nobody hears it, does it make a noise?" would be, as a semantic riddle, roughly along the same lines.)

The collapse of the wave function is an irritating topic for physicists. Of interest to us, though, is a theory, one of various theories that address this problem, that is simply far out. It was published in 1957 by physicist Hugh Everett III, and for all any lay person could tell, it might as well be science fiction. Everett's theory claims the following: consider any particle and all of its possible states. When a measurement is carried out, the particle plus the measuring device together do not end up in exactly *one* configuration. They will split into as many configurations as there are possibilities. In other words, the initial universe consisting of the indeterminate particle and the measuring-device-with-observer has multiplied, after observation, into many parallel universes. This branching gets around the collapse-of-the-wave-function conundrum. Everything that had some chance of happening, *happens*—but in *different* universes. In one universe, the particle has been measured as being in one state, in another universe, a different state, and so on. And all of these universes are constantly multiplying (talk about a vicious spiral). All of them *exist*—but the catch is, you can't go from one universe into a parallel one. You can move along the tree but not hop from branch to branch.

With a modicum of imagination, we can bend this theory in all sorts of science-fictiony ways. We can imagine the development of increasingly unlikely worlds, ones in which we won the lottery, and poets and sanitation workers were revered. And we can be consoled, or infuriated, to know that these unlikely worlds exist, just as ours does, that there is a clone of ourselves out there leading a similar (or not) or happier (or not) life. No, not really a clone—that's *us* out there, or used to be.

As could be expected, Everett's theory has been controversial. Indeed, perhaps the most bizarre aspect of the theory is that many leading physicists, including Murray Gell-Mann, have championed the basic approach. These scientists believe in it, because, as a mathematical explanation of how the world works, it is very compatible with what we think we know. But even though he has tried to tone down the parallel-universes interpretation, Gell-Mann nevertheless concedes that this science-fiction scenario is possible, that is, that there may be a large set of "inequivalent . . . domains, of which the familiar one is just a single example."

Everett's theory is not nondeterminism. We can't travel from one universe to another, but traversing an entire maze, or database, *is* (at least in theory) possible. The latter just takes time (perhaps too much). But both theories are intimately related to the joy, anguish, loss, or general wonder that we feel in our personal lives when we ponder those "what ifs" regarding past and present choices.

Considering what Everett's many-worlds theory together with nondeterminism imply about our personal lives is irresistible. Interpreting Everett's theory leaves us to imagine numerous parallel universes, in which all of our choices have been played out separately. Parallel to your very own and unique life path is a huge array of "you": there you are in Los Angeles with a different job; there you are in Manchester with a different husband and more children; there you are in Boston, at a different school; there you are on that remote island you've always dreamed of. Of course, Everett does not allow us to step into any of these realities.

Nondeterminism opens the door a bit. Invoking an oracle to tell us the correct path is merely a computational device. If we only had more time, it seems, we could explore some of those other paths, at least modestly (remembering, though, that our *actual* decisions are still irrevocable). I believe that, subconsciously, this attitude has shaped how we run our lives. We want to explore that maze in its depth and, particularly, breadth. We have second and third careers; we have second and third spouses; we have shortened many dimensions of our life cycles in order to fit multiple sets of them into the one life we do have.

Quantum theory in general provides plenty more counterintuition and controversy, some of which we will discuss later on. Issues like nonobjectivity or Everett's many-worlds theory are by no means the only twentieth-century scientific assaults on the security that belief in some sort of an absolute brings. We have already mentioned Einstein's special relativity theory of 1905 and alluded to its distance from the "everything is relative" manifesto that drives cultural relativism. The latter is the attractive notion that different points of view can all be valued and are thus valid. One reading of this pluralism is *inclusiveness*—that many alternative beliefs can all be right. A different interpretation is that there is no single "right" opinion; this viewpoint opens up the discourse to pure subjectivity. In any event, it is tempting to think that pluralism has increased in legitimacy by riding on Einstein's coattails.

Even Physicists Can't Pin Things Down

Of course, the general theme of cultural relativism is in no way what Einstein had in mind. Simply put, Einsteinian (special) relativity posits that physical laws are the same for Joe, a fixed observer, and for Moe, who is moving uniformly relative to Joe (I paraphrase and follow physicist Richard Feynman here). A consequence of this is that, for Moe, zooming along in a spaceship while Joe is standing still, when he shines one light ahead of him and one behind, the light beams are moving at the same speed from *either* of their points of view. That is, the speed of Moe's spaceship is neither added to nor subtracted from the light's speed. But there are startling consequences of this principle. It turns out that Moe's clock will run more slowly than Joe's clock. Roughly speaking, one second will take *longer* to happen for Moe than for Joe because Moe's clock mechanism will be (slightly) slowed down due to its having to cover extra distance created by the craft's motion, although Moe won't perceive it. Not only is Moe's clock slowed down, but everything else about Moe runs slower as well. Now suppose Moe has two clocks, one at each end of his ship, and he synchronizes them by means of a time signal sent from a source halfway in between the clocks. These two clocks will *not* be synchronized from Joe's point of view, because to *him*, the light takes slightly longer to reach the clock in the front of the moving ship than to reach the one in the rear (the light needs to catch up to the front clock, which is moving away from it, while the back clock catches up to the light). Thus we speak of the destruction of the notion of *simultaneity*—what it means for two events to happen "at the same time." To maintain a consistent and ultimately experimentally accurate physical theory (including telling what periods of time have elapsed in the Joe and Moe coordinate systems) Einstein made use, as we have said, of mathematical transformations first hit upon by Lorentz. At speeds approaching that of light, these equations imply significant contractions of space and time (the latter of which we have touched on), a notion that is revolutionary and hard to accept.

The different coordinate systems that Joe and Moe might use were popularized as "frames of reference," a concept that has a legitimate application in the social sciences, for example, in prospect theory (which we will look at later on). Cultural relativism is centered on reducing the emphasis on traditional frames of reference (Eurocentric, male, etc.) and increasing the attention paid to nontraditional frames of reference (global, female, etc.) But the next step taken in relativity's popularization was, "it doesn't matter what your point of view is," implying that *any* point of view is acceptable. The invariance of the physical laws somehow got lost. Ironically, Einstein's rigorous theory, which deepened our understanding of objective truths about the world, seemed to provide ammunition, indeed justification, for any amount of subjective interpretation of an event.

The conflict between the objective and the subjective was clearly central to the continuing decline of the absolute, but was not the only relevant friction generated at the turn of the last century. Part of the attraction of cultural relativism is that inclusion provides a positive comfort while avoiding the negative aspects of exclusion—the theme of choice softening that we have already discussed. The inclusion–exclusion opposition is worth a brief digression. It is central to quantum theory in at least two arenas that both date from the 1920s: one is the aforementioned Heisenberg uncertainty principle; the other is the Copenhagen interpretation of the dual nature of light, due to Neils Bohr. Heisenberg's principle considers certain pairs of properties (position and momentum, or energy and time) of a particle and asserts that you cannot specify both attributes with certainty; that is, the determination of one property to a certain degree of exactitude will necessarily blur your measurement of the other property. Thus inclusion of the one property requires the exclusion of the other.

Equally interesting is Bohr's thesis on the nature of light. Facing an apparent dilemma, he invoked the bold, novel principle of *complementarity* that, in spirit, is unique to twentieth-century intellectual thought. We have already mentioned light in relation to the Michelson–Morley experiment, which rang the death knell for the existence of ether. But what *is* light? Modern responses to this question can be said to begin with Isaac Newton (light is a particle stream) and Christiaan Huygens (light is a wave) in the late seventeenth century.

These contrasting notions were unresolved in the early twentieth century. Both the particle theory and the wave theory were well developed and each had an experimental basis. The nagging problem was that existence as a wave seemed to rule out the particle theory, and conversely, light-as-particles would deny the wave theory.

Bohr took this proverbial bull by the horns and went in between. His Copenhagen interpretation of this dilemma maintained that light was *both* particle *and* wave! The way out was to involve the observer (again): if you wear your particle hat and look for particle behavior, light behaves exactly as you would expect; but if you choose to observe wave behavior, you will find exactly that too. One viewpoint neglects—in fact excludes—the other, but they are meant to be taken together. As to whether Bohr's theory satisfactorily answers the question, "what is light," the fact is that the complementary pair of theories provide, together, a reliable physical framework. Pragmatism had carried the day, and now, more than seventy years later, we have nothing better to say about the nature of light. Altogether, complementarity provides a beautiful example, as testimony to our era, of physicists defying logic, having their cake and eating it too, and softening, even in their "hardest" of sciences, one of nature's most essential dualisms. As with the collapse of the wave function, or with Heisenberg, the physical objectivity that a theory is meant to describe involves an observer. Once more, objective "truth" and nature herself are hard to pin down, and seem to depend on the subjective hands and imperfect tools of people.

We thus have returned to the subjective–objective rift. Backpedaling momentarily into the nineteenth century, it turns out that physics was not the only science in crisis. Mathematics itself, an even more "objective" edifice, was cracking at the foundations.

Choose Your Math

As I have already argued, it is not surprising that humanity's considerable ability by the late nineteenth century to produce, transport, and communicate, the ability to overcome, or at least escape, some of the forces of nature, gave us heady confidence even in the power of mere individuals. This actualizing of our power was, naturally enough, accompanied by a paradigm shift—in the West, at least—to the acceptability of a more subjective, more individually tailored viewpoint at the expense of pure objectivity. Reality as God-created nature was no longer immutable. The whole of it was assailable, malleable. Even mathematics.

Despite the fact that there had been controversies in mathematics for ages, it was only in the nineteenth century that mathematicians began to give up on their search for a single, absolute, objective truth and instead accept alternative systems. Let me emphasize that despite the way we learn elementary mathematics in school—"there is always a right answer"—mathematics does *not* equal absolute truth. It is based on a set of *assumptions,* and different assumptions give us different results. The maxim "garbage in, garbage out" that we hear for computers applies to mathematics as well. The most celebrated alternative system in mathematics was the development of non-Euclidean geometry. Euclid compiled the standard exposition of geometry that we learn in school to this day. To obtain his theorems, he had to begin with some definitions—of slippery notions such as point and line—and then set out a few more-or-less self-evident truths to work from. The most controversial such axiom, one somewhat unsatisfying to Euclid himself, essentially stated that parallel lines will never meet (and that lines that are not parallel will meet eventually).

Even by the late nineteenth century, long after alternative geometries had appeared (most notably due to Bolyai and Lobachevsky, who both rejected the parallel axiom—think about lines of longitude on the globe), certain eminent mathematicians still accepted the Euclidean version as the true structure of reality, simply because the alternatives seemed less plausible. Einstein, in his general theory of relativity, refuted this conventional view by demonstrating that the geometry of the space-time continuum was curved, that is, non-Euclidean.

Another case in which our security and faith in mathematical objectivity began to crumble dealt with the nature of the infinite. Generally, the infinite had always been considered in the usual ways that appeal to us naturally—as an indefinite extension of the finite. But in the 1870s and 1880s, mathematician Georg Cantor began to explore the nature of the infinite, and came out with strange reports.

To understand the issue, let's consider what Feynman once said at dinner to a five-year-old (a colleague's son): that there are twice as many numbers as numbers. When the kid protested, Feynman said, pick a number. If the kid said three, Feynman said six. If the kid said ten, Feynman went twenty, and so on.

This little riddle goes back to at least Galileo; had the kid read Cantor, he could have set Feynman straight (not that Feynman didn't know this) by demonstrating that the one-to-one correspondence between the counting numbers and even numbers implied that both sets had the same "size." Cantor's result, of course, is counterintuitive because there seem to be twice as many counting numbers as even numbers.

Cantor went on to prove, however, that infinities do come in different sizes. For instance, consider numbers like the square root of two—irrational numbers. Cantor showed that there are *more of these* than there are, say, counting numbers. If you are not quite ready to accept this, neither were some mathematicians of the day.

More trouble was on the way. As 1900 approached, mathematicians were growing increasingly critical and rigorous, and were more apt to scrutinize subtleties inherent in their underlying assumptions. One such subtlety that was being employed at the time was the innocent-sounding device of *choosing* elements from various (finite or infinite) sets in the construction of a new set.

Some of the best mathematicians of the day—Borel, Zermelo, Lebesgue, Baire, Hadamard, Brouwer, and Poincaré, to name several who are legendary to people with advanced degrees in mathematics and to virtually no one else—became embroiled in a controversy, around 1904 1905, as to whether you could *arbitrarily* make such choices in a mathematical proof or whether you needed a well-defined *rule* by which the choices were made, with elements methodically selected to make up the set you were attempting to construct. The "axiom of choice," as the arbitrary selection device came to be known, turned out to be quite a useful trick for mathematicians. It was also shown to be logically equivalent to some other assertions that were more easily swallowed, and over the years, objections to it gradually disappeared. Indeed, as contemporary mathematics, logic, and science and their attendant technology have in general become so extraordinary, so far removed from experience and intuition, and so often devoid of objective truth, it is hard to see now what those brilliant and angry young men of 1904 objected to. From our point of view, why do we have to precisely define which elements we wish to select? Why can't we just allow for the method to be flexible instead of rigid, and arbitrary instead of specific?

In retrospect, it is evident how desperate some leading mathematicians felt about having to solidify their field. In an international congress in 1900, the mathematician David Hilbert set out a list of twenty-three problems that he thought important for the progress of mathematics. His second problem appealed for a proof that arithmetic itself be *consistent,* that is, not self-contradictory. And in addition to that, Hilbert wanted to demonstrate that every mathematical proposition had a definitive answer. In 1931 the logician Kurt Gödel smashed Hilbert's hopes for any kind of consistent and complete mathematical system, as we will discuss later. But in the meantime, other theorists were working hard to found mathematics on an indisputable basis; the most famous such effort was the immense *Principia Mathematica,* by Bertrand Russell and Alfred North Whitehead, which first appeared in 1910. All in all, one can characterize such efforts as doomed attempts to attain something (objective truth) that they felt was slipping away.

Artists Strut the Subjective

As we are reviewing the decline of the absolute and the rise of the relative, you may be wondering where else this shift has been manifested besides science, mathematics, and philosophy. Consider art, at the other end of the spectrum. It is well known that Impressionism, which began in the mid-nineteenth century, encompassed a set of techniques that revolutionized how an artist might achieve *representation.* Briefly, Western painters, starting in the 1400s, had developed a set of techniques in an attempt to portray the visual field. Chief among these was the device of monocular linear perspective, utilizing a "vanishing point" to achieve the appearance of depth within a flat composition. In addition, Western artists and their commentators had also cultivated various conventions regarding the subject matter and layout of a painting. It is interesting that the conventional set of techniques and conventions was often taken for granted as the correct, objective system (fiercely defended by the salon judges), instead of being recognized as one of many ways to depict a subject.

The Impressionists challenged the usual perspective, subject, and layout criteria in several ways. Their departures from classical painting included shifting the point of view through the use of strange angles, exaggerated perspective, and asymmetry; allowing some interpenetration of objects and environment; freeing color as a subject in itself; rejecting the conventional, balanced composition by focusing on a small, arbitrarily cut-out piece of nature; minimizing perspective and depth, thus reducing the canvas back to two dimensions; and by creating disturbing color associations. Impressionism brought a novel subjectivity into art and paved the way for further exploration.

Impressionism matured by the 1880s with certain artists on its cutting edge moving further away from the movement's mainstream to forge even more revolutionary styles. In this context we think of Vincent Van Gogh, Georges Seurat, Paul Gauguin, Paul Cézanne, and the other post- and neo-Impressionists. In different ways they each accelerated the transformation of painting from representation to abstraction. Three of them—Van Gogh, Gauguin, and Cézanne—inspired the two most important artistic movements of the early twentieth century, Cubism and Fauvism.

Much has been made of how Cubism, which was brought on the Parisian scene by Pablo Picasso and Georges Braque in 1907–1908, visually expresses the theme of relativity. Critics who believe in such a connection focus on the idea that a cubist picture illustrates *simultaneity* in its fracturing of the subject into many juxtaposed planar views. The idea is that these planes cover an object in a three-dimensional, sculptural ensemble to be seen all at once (instead of having to walk around it), thereby compressing time, the fourth dimension. Absent, however, is any *intention* by these artists to create a style that conveys scientific theory. Art critic Douglas Cooper states that such an intention never existed: "Such an interpretation is certainly false, for neither Picasso nor Braque imagined either himself or a spectator walking around or among the objects they were representing." A few years later, Robert Delaunay and then the Italian futurists evolved a technique to impart a dynamic element to a composition, called "simultaneity" by the futurists. According to Cooper, for the futurists "'dynamism' and 'simultaneity' lay in the forcefulness and movement inherent in the subject itself, in its extension in time and space, and in the expressive means by which the spectator was made to feel himself situated in the middle of it all."

Concurrently, Picasso and Braque began to augment their "analytical" cubist works with other media, for example, by mixing sand into the paint to give it texture, or by attaching pieces of cloth or strips of newspaper to the canvases. Thus started a more abstract, synthetic Cubism in which the artwork gained some independence from mere representation. Before long, Picasso withdrew somewhat from the synthetic, nonfigurative abstraction by combining it with naturalistically drawn objects. Although this was perhaps an attempt to portray reality simultaneously cubistically *and* traditionally, and although it is important as an attempt to balance the abstract and the concrete and reconcile two different approaches to representation, there is no evidence of any scientific thought.

Finally, despite statements such as painter Umberto Boccioni's in 1913 that futurism intends to show "an object experienced in the dynamism of its becoming, that is to say the synthesis of the transformations that the object undergoes in its two fluctuations, relative and absolute," in which one might imagine a kernel of scientific thought, we can safely say that neither Cubism nor futurism (nor any other idiom of the day) was inspired by relativity theory or made any serious attempt to express relativity on canvas.

But nevertheless we can see parallels, at least broadly speaking. One is the revolution in both relativity and Cubism in the way they have conceptualized and transformed space itself; that is, Cubism and relativity are each based on the principle of examining something simultaneously from multiple points of view. Another parallel is that of the introduction of a significant amount of abstraction in Cubism and a considerable element of transintuitive thought in relativity. And both relativity and Cubism rocked their respective establishments. Relativity overrode time-honored, intuitively satisfying physical theories, while Cubism rejected an equally traditional adherence to depth-giving perspective. Cubism and relativity both consider the interdependence between different components of a system. In this context art critic Robert Hughes quotes Alfred North Whitehead, "'There is no such [independent] mode of existence. Every entity is only to be understood in terms of the way in which it is interwoven with the rest of the universe.'" Perhaps the most important parallel, though, is the diminished objectivity and increased subjectivity brought about, intentionally or not, by both. The result is that no single point of view may necessarily dominate.

Cubism was not the only avant-garde art movement of the early 1900s. We have already mentioned Fauvism. *Les fauves,* "the wild beasts," was a critic's name for a group of artists who exhibited at the Paris *Salon d'automne* in 1905. These artists, principally Henri Matisse, Maurice de Vlaminck, and André Derain, startled viewers by employing spots, splashes, and patches of bold, loud colors in somewhat crude, primitive compositions. An observation of Kees van Dongen, a peripheral figure who maintained that Fauvism had no underlying philosophy, leads us to question the depth of the movement. In his view the protagonists, less rebellious than the Cubists, simply intended to deliver bright, cheerful, sensual canvases.

But there is compelling evidence to refute this. The Fauves revolted against both the Impressionist and neoclassicist programs of trying to capture nature. As art historian Sarah Whitfield writes, the "anarchic measures introduced by

Derain and Vlaminck to disturb and disrupt the picture surface were a demonstration against what they regarded as the refinement of the Impressionist sensibility." To this end, for example, Derain intentionally employed annoying elements in order to repudiate established conventions. And although most Fauve works were landscapes rather than abstract compositions, Whitfield indicates that Matisse and Derain nevertheless strove "to free the picture from any imitative or conventional contact" with nature, aiming to find a middle ground between the natural and the artificial. The Fauves also expressed emotion in their canvases through the use of color. Matisse claimed that he and Derain "were at that time like children in the face of nature" in expressing their temperaments. In fact, music served as an inspiration for them to infuse painting with an expressive spirit, and new dance forms that appeared in Paris in the early 1900s were quite influential on the Fauves as well.

Overall, perhaps the Fauves' most important contribution was to extend the liberation of color as an independent medium that was begun by Van Gogh and Gauguin, and sought even earlier by the poet Charles Baudelaire who in the mid-1800s wrote, "I should like red-colored fields and blue-painted trees. Nature has no imagination." Artists would now create, instead of copy, landscapes.

Starting with Impressionism, and continuing with Cubism and Fauvism, the objectivity at which neoclassicism had labored for four hundred years was suddenly disappearing from art. Obviously, I haven't described all of the influencing factors. From about 1850 onward, photography increasingly affected how artists (and the rest of us) view the world. This medium, in outward appearance, provided a new objectivity and invariant permanence. Photography seemed definitive and factual. Paradoxically, though, it increased one's choice about what to depict, inspiring the Impressionists to compose spontaneous, unbalanced, chopped-off scenes. Aerial photos by Nadar gave artists a fresh way to see things, projecting three-dimensional landscapes onto two-dimensional prints. The accessibility of the works of Japanese artists (after Admiral Perry's "black warships" forced open Japan's ports in 1854) with their lack of a convergent vanishing point augmented the trend to experiment with multiple perspectives.

The subject matter in landmark works like Édouard Manet's *Le déjeuner sur l'herbe* and Picasso's *Les desmoiselles d'Avignon* made it clear to the viewer that he (and here I mean "he") was implicated in the scene—and therefore part of the work. Various techniques reinforced such subjectivity, like catching the subject off guard or painting from creative angles. Perhaps more significantly, Paul Cézanne, around 1900, began to break down form itself. In his Mont Ste.-Victoire canvases, among others, he attempted to extract an underlying reality of the landscapes by exposing the geological foundations, as it were, and letting them float, without depth, like the layers of a tiled collage.

Cézanne's landscaping was picked up and amplified by Braque, and brought to the domain of the personal by Picasso. Not incidentally, this block tiling of the plane also serves to remove perspective, primarily by disorganizing and eliminating spatial distinctions, and secondarily by disfiguring time through disabling our somewhat predictable visual trip across the scene from foreground to background, from light to dark, from large to small. Thus our ordinary mode of viewing is challenged as well. When a man with a pipe is dissected on canvas and becomes a disembodied, dissonant, hard-to-recognize vibrating ensemble of images, we are personally challenged to make what we can of it, knowing that someone else will see something else.

But overall, the salient feature of twentieth-century art, what differentiates it from its precursors, is its emphasis on *abstraction*. In brief, abstraction is a powerful generalizing technique. It is the use of a model to represent (represent) a set of specific objects or ideas, all of which share a common essence, or set of properties, which are hopefully captured by the model. Abstraction itself is certainly not new to modern times; indeed, Euclid's geometry was a system that expressed relationships among forms. Further back, and also refocusing on art, we have the Lascaux cave paintings, which, in their elegant simplicity, can be viewed as abstractions of hunting, rather than as depictions of particular episodes.

It doesn't matter whether you accept my endowing of the cave drawings with relative sophistication or prefer to see them as efforts of utter naiveté; the fact is, in the West, we have devoted tremendous effort over the centuries to depict forms realistically, that is, to develop representational likenesses, to visually capture and reproduce in two dimensions (three if you include sculpture) *objective truths* about the visual properties of forms.

Abstraction departs from concrete realities, but the real issue is, does abstraction necessarily sacrifice reality itself? In mathematics, despite the difficulties that I have described, abstraction certainly expands what we know about the world. Algebra, for example, allows us to state facts about surfaces that cannot ever be visualized or even physically exist. And yet this abstraction, in turn, enables management scientists to discover optimal output levels for very real resource allocation problems. In less rigorous fields, abstraction organizes a handful of specific cases into a general theory, which can then be applied to new instances (provided the latter share the abstracted properties). For example, in psychoanalysis, there are competing theoretical perspectives that give rise to different theories regarding our emotions and behaviors. These perspectives have different assumptions and therefore may result in different diagnoses (like the different "truths" of different geometries). The objective truth of the situation seems to be obscured. This is not a result of abstraction per se—it is a result of needing to choose among conflicting theories in an uncertain situation.

We began this chapter discussing mazes, nondeterminism, and many worlds, and have ended it by discussing ebbing objectivity and rising subjectivity in art and science. What ties these strands together is the failure of the nineteenth century to capture reality, and the recognition, by the early twentieth century, that reality is multifaceted. When we lose faith in the absolute, when we are freed to create our own reality—or at least a vision of it—we become free to *choose*. I now want to explore how reality became blurred as the twentieth century moved along.

New technology is being introduced so quickly these days that it is hard to keep up with what is fact and what is fiction. For example, years ago, desperately hungry, I ordered a pizza from a large chain. At the end of the phone conversation, I realized that they did not have my address, something obviously necessary for a delivery. When I said, wait a minute, you don't have my address, Big Brother Pizza said, "oh yeah, we know where you live." Thinking fast (a rarity for me), I realized that they must have some sort of *reverse* phone directory; continuing to think fast (equally rare), I realized that I had moved just a month ago, and that their newfangled reverse directory would not be likely to have my new address. So I said, "no you don't know where I live," thus saving myself from cold pizza. Of course, reverse directories are commonplace now, but probably you have been humbled enough by information technology to sympathize, having already modified your *a priori* views on what is possible.

By "the blurring of reality," though, I mean much more than this. The twentieth century, with its arsenal of powerful media, forever changed how we relate to fact and fiction, reality and fantasy, genuine and counterfeit. In fact there is now a third player, the "hyperreal" of theorists Umberto Eco and Jean Baudrillard, *more real than real*. As we shall see, our loss of the absolute is profound enough for reality itself to be called into question. The blurring of reality—the confusion among the real, the imaginary, and the hyperreal—is now eternally part of our lives.

More Real Than Real

While I'm in the mood for storytelling, here's another personal incident from a while back. My wife and I were in northern Italy, crossing Lake Garda from Limone to Malcesine on a motor launch and enjoying the fresh breeze, warm sun, and soaring mountains, when we noticed a fellow passenger videotaping practically the entire boat ride. We must have expressed some knee-jerk contempt at the time, simply because there is something bothersome about people who video everything in sight. But let's think about this. The idea of the video, of course, is to go home and use the segment to literally recreate the experience. But the paradox is that the cameraman is substituting that ersatz reality for the real thing, because what he (and it's usually men doing this) is actually experiencing on the boat is his preoccupation with the process of videotaping. He won't enjoy the wind and sun on his face; his sensuality as well as his cognition will be intertwined with and contaminated by the camcorder. He gives up on the real experience and sells his soul, as it were, to a digital devil in order to eternally facilitate his memory. But all he will recreate in his home is his experience of videotaping, not the sensual ride.

There is something about photography and tapes that possesses us. Literary theorist Roland Barthes in *Camera Lucida* writes that, "Photography . . . *authenticates* the existence of a certain being [his emphasis]," it freezes and "certifies" life-as-it-was. I want to generalize this powerful notion. Photography is an example of *facticity,* which is "the condition or quality of being a fact" (*Random House Dictionary,* second edition). Another example: a woman's pregnancy is the facticity of her having had sexual intercourse (which is why the Virgin Mother was such a shocking notion).

But times change. Photographs, especially in digital form, can be easily doctored. Women can be impregnated without intercourse, and video and audio tapes—what do they prove anymore? (Indeed, in late 2001, when a tape appeared showing that Osama Bin Laden supported the September 11 terrorist attacks, many in the Muslim world believed the recording was fabricated and inauthentic.) Yet seeing (and hearing) images through various media has a religious quality for us, in fact, a hyperreality. What if you were to see, for example, Madonna (surely *not* a virgin mother) in your local mall? This event would combine a media "reality" with a common reality. What we find exciting is the rare penetration of the larger-than-life hyperreality into our more personal, quite ordinary circumstances. In this infiltration of show business into our lives, show business has become real, and real life has become show business—a phenomenon exploited in recent years by reality TV, in which ordinary people are propelled into stardom. Although we say the stars are larger than life, it is often the characters they portray that are hyperreal, in fact, more so than the stars themselves. At a gut level the public understands this, for example, when TV actors quit a series or have their contracts discontinued. Usually these terminations are announced well in advance of the viewed episodes and the public is led to speculate how and when an actor will be written out of a series. Thus the departure, both in real life and in the TV series, becomes a media event in its own right.

Another inversion of the importance we put on media stars has cropped up recently in various self-conscious, tongue-in-cheek radio and TV advertisements pointing out that the persons they feature are *not* actors. Presumably the audience knows that "satisfied customers" ordinarily are actors, so the non-actor commercials carry more veracity. More to the point, these ads reject the typical testimonial style. That is, the "real" customers hardly provide testimony for the product; their presence testifies more to their reality as a regular human being and not as an actor. It is curious how the emphasis in such ads is shifted from the product to the facticity of customer as customer. Overall, though, the key notion to reiterate is the noticeable incursion that TV and movies have made into our lives, as seen in comments such as psychoanalyst Edgar Levenson's that "people are increasingly having difficulty distinguishing between reality and virtual reality—people are no longer making distinctions between movies and reality."

As an aside, it is interesting to note that "digital" has become a sexy, magic word. Today a great deal of our information and communication technology is digital, which simply means that images (or text or sounds) are encoded in a binary alphabet (of zeros and ones), stored or transmitted, and then reconverted faithfully at the receiving end. But many of us forget (and others never knew) the extent to which digital technology has superseded that of analog. Generally speaking, going digital has been a good thing, so why bring it up?

Stepping back, the digital–analog distinction is an example of a dualism well known to mathematicians: the discrete versus the continuous. Certain things, like weight or velocity, can take on any possible value (perhaps within some bounds) and are therefore treated as continuous variables; other things, such as a coin flip or dice roll, can only take on a (usually small) set of outcomes, and are thus considered differently.

The reason mathematicians make a distinction here is for the purpose of expediency. Sometimes continuous variables are more easily manipulable, and other times discrete quantities are. In applied work, usually one approach or the other is the clearer, more "natural" way to model the given phenomena, although sometimes the clear and natural way proves insoluble. Note how these considerations stray from the reality of the underlying physical or economic situation. Often mathematics is a game of approximation. A good example is the Taylor series, where, to get close to a certain unknown value, one sets up an infinite sequence of terms, keeps only the first couple of them, and shows that the infinity of the discarded ones is negligible.

What, then, about the blurring of reality? Well, digital data is merely a mathematical approximation of its subject. But as a data stream such information is extremely corruptible—not that the alteration of photos never happened before. A good example is the celebrated D-Day photo by Robert Capa. Its perfect simulated-action image was created, ironically, from an unblemished still photo altered by a lab assistant's mistake. But we have reached the stage where a small child can scan photos, add and delete images, and reprint them; people and places are frozen as facticity no longer. Thus, we are torn between, on the one hand, a predisposition to exalt a media image and endow it with transcendent properties, and on the other hand, to assume that everything we see is adulterated, airbrushed, and touched up (yes, even those before-and-after shots). Our skepticism is fueled by more than a distrust of media images. Another source of the paradox of facticity can be found in the misuse of statistics. Statistics, as compiled by experts and presented in the media, take on a holy status. But as we get increasingly inundated with information, we are likewise swamped with facts and figures. Many of these, of course, are presented with the intention to mislead, and we have become increasingly aware of this. Therefore statistics, computed *numbers* that might ordinarily appear incontrovertible, have lost, through overkill and deception, their power to persuade.

Another example of the public's fascination with media facticity emerged when the television program *ER* staged a live broadcast. There was considerable hype preceding the airing, including self-conscious references to the injection of "reality" into the upcoming program. Viewers would be aware that the actors were not acting in the usual fashion; they were performing in real time, and were therefore transcendent, that is, more believable. The stakes were higher and the program had a hitherto absent edge. The downside, however, was the implicit weakening of ordinary TV drama.

To make matters worse, although our sacred media has been losing its credibility, we have become accustomed to its hyperreal presentation, brought to a new level by the recent generation of disaster movies like *Independence Day*. Filtered, focused, and concentrated high-fidelity stimuli on large screens have an intensity that renders ordinary day-to-day reality bland by comparison.

Back in 1993 television viewers were exposed to an extraordinary segment in which a shocking domestic murder interrupted an otherwise ordinary interview. Briefly, what happened was this: a woman was being interviewed on a sunny suburban Florida sidewalk by a minor local station. In an instant, the interviewee was violently shoved to the lawn by a man lunging into the picture. He immediately produced a handgun and banged several bullets into her prone body, killing her.

Oddly enough (or maybe not), the obvious horror of the incident was largely absent. Any regular television viewer has seen countless such violent incidents. What's more, on TV shows and in films the staged violence is rehearsed, choreographed, and amplified, with hyperreal close-ups of blood and guts, often replayed and sometimes in slow motion (intended, of course, to soak the viewer, almost literally, in the blood). But this actual incident was over in five seconds, and had no gore or close-up.

The only feature, in fact, that this clip *had,* as a violent episode of interest, was its *authenticity.* It was also very personal and did not feature a national media figure. Because the hyperreality of television reduces even magnified violence to banality, the five-second, unadorned bang-bang of the real thing was relatively mild and undisturbing. Television stations realized this and promptly aired it with little fuss—not because it was a murder, or of national interest, but as a curiosity, a brief snuff film from your station affiliate. It was made into entertainment, and, unintentionally, became an art segment.

Unfortunately, this murder was an actual event. But what if it were merely staged? Surely, such "art," long since absorbed by the viewing public and diminished by the hyperreal, is well past its power to shock. It is the hyperreal, after all, where art and reality become indistinguishable. For Baudrillard, when the distinction between representations and their referents breaks down, we are in the world of the *simulacrum.* For example, suppose one person makes a copy of an object, and another person copies the copy, and so on; the simulacrum is one of the copies that lives on as the real thing and this blurs the relationship between original and reproduction.

Facticity and Ordinary Stuff

The blurring between real and fake is definitely big business. Obviously being real has serious cachet; real products have a natural appeal. Witness Coca-Cola (the real thing), Budweiser (genuine, true), and so forth. New York City has its own little skirmishes between pizza (and, separately, bagel) establishments suing one another over which is the original eatery. Related to this is the distinction between name brands and designer labels, and regular merchandise. One banal feature of our society is, as everybody knows, there is street credibility through the possession of a designer article as opposed to some nameless item. It's the hood ornament on your car or the little leather tag chained to your bag that you really purchase, and they certify a dual facticity: one, of the article's authenticity; and two, of the owner's being able to afford the item. On account of this street credibility, a feedback loop forms where the inflated prices boost the distinction.

Once name brands held a vogue accessible to the population at large, it wasn't long for imitations to spring up. But fairly recently, two subthemes have developed here. One is that ordinary brands—for example, department stores' own labels—began marketing themselves like name brands. In the new mix, some customers don't even know which ones are "real," and thus, ordinary merchandise is taking on some of the élan (and market share) of the designers. Second, many imitations have become high quality. When they began to spring up such imitations were poor and easily identifiable. But nowadays, some imitation merchandise is the real thing, made off the books with the same materials and by the same craftspeople who make the limited-edition originals (and they're satisfyingly one-third of the price). The tremendous international scale of the problem was reported in 1997, and prior to that, author Richard Appignanesi claimed that "the postmodern premise that reality and its simulacrum are indistinguishable has espoused [in Southeast Asia] a thriving culture and economy based on fakes . . . An astonishing 20% of the region's economy is generated by this simulacrum industry."

What about "buying American?" People are often dismayed to find out that their "American" product has been assembled abroad using largely foreign components; conversely, many Japanese cars, we are reminded, are made in the United States.

Imitation designer goods aren't the only simulacra on the market. The more well-established practice of imitation involves the use of vinyl as a substitute for leather, or aspartame for sugar, and so on. In these examples, either your funds or your caloric intake are scarce, hence you are marketed a presumably inferior raw material with little intention to deceive behind it. But even this arena has become blurred. For example, you can buy leatherlike athletic shoes, whose artificial uppers are advertised as superior to leather. Fascinating: you're holding, weighing, a leather sneaker but the tag tells you, boasts, in fact, that the fake stuff is better than the real thing. You're left to wonder if it's true, or if they're just marketing a reverse snobbism. Blurring real and fake goods is traumatic enough, especially if you're in retail, but the effects of the blurring of reality go much further; they penetrate our speech and the way we think.

There's an old song by Robert Palmer with the refrain, "I didn't mean to turn you on." This lyric is wrapped in a rhythmically rising, falling, gasping, in–out sexuality. Fine; it's a nice tease. But also consider the ubiquitous "I don't mean no disrespect." Nowadays we believe that after a spell of flagrant disrespect with every intention to do so, this disclaimer properly neutralizes the offense. One denies the truth of the situation, sidestepping retribution instead of properly apologizing. And it works most of the time. Such denials, incidentally, neatly fit in with contemporary "political correctness"; that is, politically incorrect behavior can be blurred out of focus by a standard disclaimer (of course, one has to be careful that the disclaimers do not mock their very denials).

This notion of not meaning any disrespect—just because you say it—has even been exploited at the presidential level. In 1993, after Bill Clinton met with the controversial author, Salman Rushdie, Clinton was branded by the head of Iran's judiciary "the most hated man before all the Muslims of the world" (outside of, presumably, Rushdie himself). Realizing that he could not so easily get away with meeting Rushdie, Clinton decided on a hedging strategy, instead of either apologizing or affirming and justifying his actions. He claimed that he did not mean Muslims any "disrespect," and that he met Rushdie for only a "couple of minutes" anyway.

Often action replaces speech to produce polite insincerity. For example, you sit down in the subway train next to a big guy who is taking up considerably more than half of the pair of joined seats. You "politely" mutter a gruff "excuse me" as you sit down. In response to this he shifts himself around slightly to both acknowledge your presence and ostensibly give you more space, but he doesn't actually move over at all. His gesture is courteous, but in reality he does not perform the signified courteous act—which could, of course, be achieved only by moving his butt over. Such incidents happen an untold number of times every day, mostly in cities where time and space are squeezed, and those millions who carry out such falsehoods are practicing what the philosopher Jean-Paul Sartre calls *mauvaise foi* (literally, bad faith, or better yet, self-deception) in blurring the distinction between make-believe and true courtesy.

These gestures, often enough, may well be conscious parodies, used as effective foils against the enemy. But we're starting to believe in them ourselves.

Some of the actions, some of the choices people make, perhaps unintentionally involve an escape into fantasy. If someone's entire life is acted out in a fantasy world (i.e., they experience a reality that intersects "objective reality" as minimally as possible), we are apt to diagnose them as schizophrenic and have them institutionalized. But indeed many of us adopt at times this fantasy mode, especially for what we perceive to be storybook situations.

This occurs particularly in romance: we make ourselves act in artificial ways, "like in a book" (*roman* means "novel"); those who don't read choose to act self-consciously, as if they were being watched on film, or in a TV soap. Pornography influences how we make love; people imitate the actors' remarks (here, consider the wry inversion, as reported by Baudrillard, "what are you doing after the orgy?").

Sex fantasies themselves require some plausibility to be effective, but *too much* plausibility, and they're absurd. You realize that you cannot simply have Britney or Brad knock on your door, as that would never happen, so you try to imagine another situation in which you might come across your flame—perhaps on a flight to Los Angeles. But then you have absolutely no reason to fly to Los Angeles except to visit your in-laws, probably the last people you want to conjure up in this setting. So, before you lose the mood altogether, you make it a flight to Miami, or maybe not a flight at all; how about the bar at the Four Seasons? The Four Seasons is closer to home and less trouble to develop, so you go with that. Is it late afternoon or night? Perhaps nighttime is sexier. But you never go out at night. Do you include a call to your spouse (honey, I've got a lot of work at the office)?

If you develop the fantasy like hypertext, you will find yourself "clicking" through an endless sojourn of detail checking, in order to realistically and seamlessly incorporate the fantasy into your life. Doing this would not only take forever, but also might include a shower afterward and a script of conversations regarding what you worked on at the office that night, as well as the prohibition of certain actions regarding the deed itself (as if you were cheating in real life).

Basically, what I am describing is the same mentality that notices that if you win a million dollars in the lottery, fifty percent is taken away as tax, so you'd only get half a million . . . and half a million doesn't buy what it used to, so you'd better win two million, or maybe four. This is too detail oriented, erasing the creative whimsy.

But in other aspects you need this attention to detail to ripen and intensify the fantasy. You want, after all, to feel the suppleness of Britney's skin, or to loosen the buttons on Brad's shirt. You want to live through the encounter in real time—and surely, this would include some opening conversation, some intrigue, some buildup (OK, not too much). Without it you will have reduced Britney or Brad to the anonymous two dimensions of a pornographic magazine.

We are left to conclude that fantasy design is a tricky business. At one extreme, you are compelled to resolve an ever-expanding world of minutiae in order to render the episode realistically. This clearly is not satisfying. At the other extreme, you avoid serious questions, you forget about your father-in-law meeting you when you disembark at Los Angeles International, but in sidestepping life's contingencies, your fantasy world is little more than a cheap centerfold. At both of these extremes, the book-keeping dullness of the one and the impersonal superficiality of the other, you lose the palpable aroma, texture, yes-this-is-really-happening excitement of an engrossing tale. The trick, then, seems to be to keep the fantasy elements without forsaking a grounding in reality. A tightrope to walk on.

Virginity and "Born Agains"

Sex is rampant enough to figure into even this book. As with any trend, there is always a backlash. Fairly recently a number of interest groups, most of them with religious or "pro-life" affiliations, have launched a revival campaign for virginity. If you ride public transportation, you've perhaps noticed their ads, for instance, one with teens hanging out in a spacious (suburban) living room. The caption provides authentic, anxious voices aimed at the opposing sexes: "she expects me to," or "he'll find someone else," and so on. But the teenaged reader is reassured that virginity is cool.

A presumed subtext of these messages is that virginity preservation sows measurable societal rewards: fewer babies born to poor, unmarried teens; more girls completing school; and a lower incidence of sexually transmitted diseases (not to mention the moral improvement). But the message is generally ineffective. Kids are curious. Kids throb with hormones. Kids have long absorbed the omnipresence of sex. They're going to try it. In the face of this, what message has a chance? *Secondary* virginity. The reasoning goes, OK, you've lost it. But you can get it back. Why not? Reinvent it! Restore your dignity: revirginize! Nurture, preserve, this newfound virtue; make it the real thing.

As with "born agains" in our present society, which so easily mixes the natural and synthetic, truth and fiction, and even subordinates reality to hyperreality, it does seem possible to elevate secondary virginity to, and even beyond, the real thing. But this will be a vain attempt. Although secondary virginity is the last bastion, since we won't accept tertiary virginity or anything beyond, it's doomed. Interpretations aside, people are no more likely to be able to stick to it than they are to diets. One can always go on another diet, or try, for the sixth time, to give up smoking.

Replacing virginity by secondary virginity is, at bottom, an attempt to trump the real with the hyperreal. One might conjure up a likely teen exchange: "Like, if you're a virgin, it's no big deal to keep it, cuz all you have to do is stay the way you are." "But, like, someone who's a secondary virgin, they gave in, they didn't have any willpower the first time, and now they try to act superior." "No, like, OK, now that you know what it's about, it's harder to stay a virgin the second time, you've got a real choice to make, there's like much more sacrifice."

I guess I'm not convinced. It seems to me that any such hierarchy has to collapse. Virginity—a purely personal virtue anyway—is virginity, and once it's gone it's gone, and no amount of subsequent abstinence is going to change it.

Having mentioned "born agains," there's definitely a connection here. Not that this notion is exactly new; after all the original born-again individual was Saint Augustine of Hippo, fourth century, Christian Era. Not so long ago, however, there was a bit of a trend to it, and I think it's worthwhile to reflect on the concept.

What is inspirational seems simple enough: redemption, a second chance. The born agains confess: I drank, I stole, I gambled, I whored, I sinned (isn't it true, in your mind's eye, that to say "I sinned" is, in its generality, greater than the sum of all of its parts, and therefore the ultimate?). And they continue: But now, in my chastity, in my sobriety, in my simple honest life, and my love of the Lord [or Jesus], I am consciously rejecting those pleasures of the flesh, pleasures that, I must say, are acutely tempting, especially as I have already tasted them. And in my self-aware, deliberate leap of faith, I am making a sacrifice that is all the keener because I know, and therefore truly understand, those vices.

Thus the born agains seem to get a leg up on the merely faithful. By transgressing and then returning to the flock, their faith is not merely renewed; it is stronger than that of others. They derive more authenticity in their new positions than they would have had by not sinning at all. (The Amish pursue a similar line of reasoning: they allow their youth a period of time to live the other life in evil places like Philadelphia; some are lost to the decadent outsiders but they were likely unfit anyway. [Of course, they can't live a double life because they risk excommunication in which they are shunned by their family.] The ones who return to the fold, and these seem to be the great majority, have rejected the outside world with its temptation and technology, and are apt to become stronger adherents to the Amish beliefs. It's like giving the young a vaccine. Not all Amish are completely virtuous. Witness [no, not the movie] two Amish youths who were busted in mid-1998 for long-term drug dealing in collaboration with a motorcycle gang.)

The born agains may seem to be more authentic, *more real in their faith,* precisely because they know what they're giving up and what they're returning to. Let us not overlook, however, the simple facts of the situation. The born again argument, like secondary virginity, attempts to elevate a hyperreal condition over a simpler faith. This argument, if accepted, would replace on the high ground the untainted morals of those who have not sinned with the tainted morals of those who have. In the eyes of a lawgiver who exhorts us not to sin— period—this inversion cannot be correct.

"Get Real" at School and at Work

I would like to close out this chapter with the blurring of reality in the workplace and in the university. Let's consider our society's new veneer—the glorified titles that so many people have. An old one is "superintendent" for janitor. But over the past decade or so we've spawned a whole new taxonomy. "Sales associates" are salespeople or sometimes just checkout clerks. "Sanitation engineers" are garbage collectors. "Travel consultants" are travel agents, "salon coordinators" operate the reception desk, and so on. "Consultant" is perhaps the leading such designation. In so many instances, particularly as we have moved into a service-dominated economy, low-paying, unskilled jobs have been elevated, in name anyway, to positions of false identity. Perhaps some of this has been forged by the good intentions of political correctness, to avoid denigration in general. However well intended, this process blurs together the real consultants, superintendents, and so on, with the pretenders; but worse, the workers themselves and those they interact with, through this device, are ultimately removed from who they are and what they do.

One related and particularly insidious form of this feel-good philosophy appears in the awarding of college degrees in the United States. It is not too radical to insist that a good majority of undergraduate degrees awarded in this country are to people who have learned very little in general and are largely incompetent in their so-called major subject as well (not to mention in everything else academic).

Standards have fallen to where, at a typical college or university, passing grades are often obtainable through hardly more than decent attendance, and even grades of B are handed out indiscriminately. Now, in itself, grade inflation need not be a tremendous evil, except when one wants to select the truly exceptional. The real danger lies in the fact that it becomes difficult to distinguish among almost anyone graduating these days.

One million or so undergraduate degrees are conferred each year in the United States, and outside of the relative handful from worthy institutions, we are loading ourselves up with several hundred thousand folks entering the workforce each year, in whom have been invested countless billions of dollars merely to inflate their egos and infuse them with misdirected expectations (and to keep lots of faculty members gainfully employed).

Many of our graduates, when hired, are mistaken for individuals with a mastery of well-defined skills that are appropriate for the tasks at hand. Needless to say, in-house training becomes a universal necessity. Its presence, as in a self-fulfilling prophesy, makes future students even more apathetic in the classroom (why should I learn this?—they're gonna train me anyway). Perhaps most unfortunate of all, since an undergraduate degree means so little now (and even if it did, everyone has one), ambitious people have to go up the ladder and seek a master's degree simply to differentiate themselves. Thus, now a master's degree serves roughly the same function that a bachelor's degree did a couple of generations ago. Sadly, much of the undergraduate inertia carries over, so as long as the tuition is paid, *voilà*, a master's degree.

The blurring of reality that we have reviewed has mushroomed over the past quarter of a century and is an important part of contemporary life and thought. This is a good juncture to examine what some commentators have identified as a root cause of so many new trends: postindustrial society.

There have been two major sets of thought on how the twentieth century has broken with its predecessors, or, more boldly envisioned, on how society has been transformed in a significant and irreversible way over the past century. The broader, more recent and more popular discourse is postmodernism, aspects of which I want to discuss mainly in chapters 14 and 15. The precursor discusses postindustrial society (after sociologist Daniel Bell), focusing on our transformation from the industrial society of 1900 to a new set of conditions. I want to introduce some of Bell's and others' ideas because they represent an important explanation of how our world has changed over the past century and retained some validity. This validity, however, is limited. Classifying various phenomena as being postindustrial (or postmodern) is not adequate to describe how and why they surfaced.

Let me reemphasize that by focusing on *choice* and the oppositions that our ability to choose has brought about provides a unifying concept that spans various social and intellectual trends. Looking back at what we have covered— the vicious spiral of choice, nondeterminism, the many-worlds theory, the loss of the absolute in physics, art, and mathematics, and the blurring of reality— we have hit on paradigm-shifting, tectonic-plate-rupturing concepts that have changed how we live and think. The same is true of ideas we will meet in later chapters—decision science, structuralism, existentialism, the individual versus the group, and more. These key developments of the last century have forever altered our world views. To say they are postindustrial or postmodern does not strike at their core. Choice does.

Controlled by a Dominating Society

Criticism of postindustrial society has been important, though, and a good way to introduce some relevant themes is to consider sociologist Herbert Marcuse's

1964 book *One-Dimensional Man*. Marcuse was heavily influenced by Marx and Freud as well as by his Frankfurt School contemporaries Theodor Adorno and Max Horkheimer. He wrote during the depths of the cold war, and we will see that his formulations of the prevailing zeitgeist are significant but somewhat outdated.

The basis of *One-Dimensional Man* is that society—"advanced industrial society"—dominates individuals more than ever before. This society's growth is maintained by repression, and "its peace maintained by the constant threat of war." Advanced industrial society differs from its predecessor (plain vanilla industrial society) in several ways. Technology and scientific management have conspired to change the modes of production. As a result, physical labor is reduced and our energies are transferred into a mental arena. Workers contrast less conspicuously (than, say, in Marx's day) with what they produce; that is, they don't live in poverty and filth anymore. And this means that the working class is no longer the antithesis of the establishment. Simultaneously, high culture is being eradicated, and what results is a reduction in the conflict between high culture and the facts of social reality. High culture is brought down to earth by transforming its alien, misunderstood components.

In other words, the prevailing production and distribution systems "indoctrinate and manipulate" all the individuals they reach by providing pleasant products that improve everyone's lives. So, by swallowing up the populace, the production-distribution system will either reject transcendent notions and objectives, or else reduce them to the terms under which the system itself operates. The latter takes place through wholesale incorporation into the established order by means of reproduction and display on a massive scale. Hence one-dimensional man, who is transformed by this industrial psychology to a mimetic personality defined by and identified with the larger technological system. Each member of society is in fact brainwashed, with his or her individuality becoming "swallowed up by its alienated existence." For Marcuse, this one-dimensionality would virtually preclude the potential for social change.

Marcuse gives a number of examples of the consequences of one-dimensional society. One is his illustration of how our language "imposes in truly striking constructions the authoritarian identification of person and function," citing *Time* magazine's use of phrases like "U.S. Steel's Blough" and "Egypt's Nasser." He also comments on the blurring of various oppositions, as in a 1960 newspaper ad, "Luxury Fall-out Shelter." But in many respects, the world he observed has changed, and the theoretical underpinning of his commentary is, to some degree, misplaced.

A good example of the sort of ultimately flawed analysis that Marcuse and other critical theorists embarked on is Marcuse's lengthy discussion of the Freudian notion of *sublimation,* which is the civilizing repression of biological (usually sexual) drives by way of diverting these impulses and energies into more acceptable outlets. Marcuse argues that advanced industrial society has reversed this by encouraging what he calls "institutional desublimation" in which the realization of sexual urges is to some extent sanctioned by the controlling system. This is well enough, but then, relying on Freud in assuming that the energy available for distribution between the two primary drives, Eros and Thanatos, is constant, he concludes that the increased expression of the libido in society would imply the diminution of aggressiveness. However, I think it is clear without referring to crime statistics that any reasonable index of aggressiveness in the West has risen since his writing. In this instance the Freudian energy-is-constant approach is an artifice based on the concept of conservation of energy in physical systems. It need not apply to psychological phenomena (of which the Freudian theory is an abstraction) and to extend it in a literal sense to sociological phenomena is mistaken.

By the way, many such notions of classical physics like energy conservation and equilibrium were applied to the social sciences over the last century. For example, neoclassical economics, which was reaching its theoretical peak in Marcuse's day, relied heavily on notions of equilibrium, conservation, and decreasing returns. Game theory, which grew out of economics, in its infancy began by focusing on "zero-sum" games in which one agent necessarily loses what the other gains. Zero-sumness was a natural concept for Marx, who held that the interests of the owners of the means of production were at odds with those of the workers. It was natural too for traditional manufacturing management, where cost and quality traded off against one another. Our obsession with sports and its metaphors reinforces this notion and insinuates various connotations of "winner" and "loser" into our language. Admittedly, many situations *are* zero-sum; when there is only so much to go around, winners indeed gain what others lose.

But we are emerging, slowly, from this restricted conception. Objectives of management can be consistent with those of workers. Higher quality can often cost less. In the past two decades, economist Brian Arthur has shown us many important applications of *increasing* returns; various scientists have profitably studied systems *far* from equilibrium, where new agents self-organize; game theorists have understood that the interesting cases are not zero-sum. In short, the classical constant-sum paradigms are giving way to a broader world view. Hindsight shows us that even the penetrating analyses of the critical theorists of the mid-twentieth century were too steeped in Marx's and Freud's constrained universes. In the newer landscape, someone asks, do you want chocolate or vanilla, and you answer, "both!"

Even when stripped of its zero-sum, Eros–Thanatos connection, Marcuse's idea that advanced industrial society has enabled a degree of desublimation retains some relevance. One manifestation of our enhanced ability to choose among goods, consistent with Marcuse's view, is the commodification and increased availability of sex. And conversely the denial and relative *lack of* choice that the less fortunate sector of our society experiences certainly correlates with the increased aggressiveness (expressed as violent crime) recorded since the 1950s.

However, Marcuse's theory is off base in other respects. Another example where he lacks true applicability is found in *Eros and Civilization*. Marcuse describes the Freudian transformation from the *pleasure principle* to the *reality principle* as a key element of advanced industrial society. This transformation, as he outlines it, takes human beings from immediate satisfaction to delayed satisfaction, from pleasure to restraint of pleasure, from joy to toil, from receptiveness to productiveness, and from the absence of repression to security. For Freud, this transformation corresponds to the development of civilization. Marcuse critiques Freud here by noting that our transformation to the reality principle stands on the "fundamental fact" of scarcity. In advanced industrial society, however, this scarcity is artificial; it is imposed on us, "the consequence of a specific *organization* of scarcity . . ." (his emphasis). Marcuse is largely correct in this. However, he believed that the only way out from under the domination of the production-distribution system was a revolution that would topple the reality principle and restore the primacy of Eros. Although logically speaking, the one-dimensionality Marcuse exposes appears incontrovertible— since this process eliminates or absorbs any alternative—I believe that he underestimated the potential for value change coming from within the system.

Marcuse does not seem to consider the possibility that the system's underlying values are dynamic and that new values can self-organize. Today, the very modes of production and distribution have radically changed since the 1950s and 1960s. In those days the Frankfurt School's primary target in its accusations of cultural indoctrination was television. Indeed, the television of that era was controlled by a small number of like-minded corporate interests, so it is not surprising that critics felt sensitive to its narrow range of expression. However, our new communication and information media, very much examples of chaotic, self-organizing systems, cover a wider creative and political spectrum and are less alienating than the examples of twentieth-century advanced industrialism that Marcuse describes. Furthermore, in their essence, contemporary media are too uncontrollable to be part of an organized economic exploitation. What's more, technology has become—despite the obvious correlations that persist between technology ownership and income, class, education, race, and so on—remarkably egalitarian. And technology users are no longer passive receivers of indoctrination. Indoctrination abounds, but dialogue and interaction are becoming universal. To a large degree control has shifted from above to below.

In summary, I find the one-dimensional argument to be a case of what I have called *inversion*, in which ostensibly too much choice really boils down to none at all. There is an analogy here to Baruch Spinoza's determinism, where we think we have all manner of choices but in fact have to adhere to the parameters of the system in which we are inextricably bound. The argument stating that this inversion serves to repress transcendent expression, although reasonable forty years ago, has lost much of its appeal today.

The Wane of Delayed Gratification

But before moving on to discuss Daniel Bell, I would like to revisit the transformation to the reality principle. Back to Freud for a moment. The idea was that the transformation from the pleasure principle to the reality principle goes hand in hand with the development of civilization. Is the inverse of this transformation underway? Is the reality principle unraveling? Perhaps one key to this is that so many taboos have been liquidated. So many people have broken so many codes that the codes are no longer codes. Reflecting on this leads to one facet, looking ahead, of postmodernism, in its eclecticism and pastiche and "anything goes" practice.

More to the point, though, in our eagerness to explore as many of life's branches as we can, we have developed a "now" mentality. Frugality is out; debt is in. Our young have come to expect things pronto. For example, college students are no longer willing to wait several years to reap the financial rewards of adulthood. Facing the dual pressures of needing to pay for school and desiring to accelerate their completion ("I can't wait till I graduate"), many students work long hours and attend school full-time (and perform poorly enough so the professors end up having to alter their standards, contributing to the grade inflation that we have discussed). On top of this they travel widely and own cars in addition to piles of electronic goods.

But we can't lay all or even much of the blame at the feet of students. Over the last several years numerous retailers have offered deals that are "buy now, no money down, pay nothing" for six months or a year. With ordinary credit, which is tempting enough, people know that they will (someday) pay a penalty to borrow. The no-money-down modification expands our already swollen living-on-credit mentality by providing a free, long-term loan.

Simply speaking, the public has become completely absorbed in an instant gratification mode. No longer do we save up for something. Routinely we hear of people who, in deep debt, buy a new vehicle to replace their aging but functional car. So what if you're fifty thousand dollars in debt. What's another ten grand? (Indeed, this is somewhat compelling on the face of it; what *is* the difference between fifty and sixty thousand?) Same thing, of course, for the college students, who are some of the biggest spenders around. Not so long ago, when the total cost of a year in college—when textbooks were thirteen dollars—was no more than several thousand dollars, students scrimped and saved and swatted cockroaches. Now that costs, in real dollar terms (no accounting for inflation can equalize it) are astronomical—the texts are over one hundred dollars—students live in luxury apartments and do spring break in Cancun. If they're going to end up fifty thousand dollars in debt even if they're thrifty, why not enjoy being a real person and put the trip, along with all the books, on plastic? Fifty thousand, sixty thousand, what's the difference? Why wait when you can have it now? This attitude can, of course, be measured. Consumer debt in the United States totals more than two trillion dollars. However you want to divide this sum—by individual, by family, or by household—it amounts to several thousand dollars per person!

Capitalism Dances with Modernism

In the 1970s Daniel Bell published *The Coming of Post-Industrial Society* and *The Cultural Contradictions of Capitalism*. The former work demonstrates how technology, in a general sense, has reshaped social and economic order. The latter volume, which I will concentrate on, is concerned with the reshaping of culture—specifically, how the values of capitalism and modernism have brought about unsettling friction and contradiction in our society's beliefs.

The collision of the worlds of capitalism and modernism is still going, and has even reached a new stage—the emergence of the bourgeois bohemians—described by commentator David Brooks in his book, *Bobos in Paradise: The New Upper Class and How They Got There.*

For Bell, the culture of capitalism is the freedom from family and other traditional restrictions, freedom that enables the ability to realize oneself, to succeed. Modernism, which we will revisit later, for Bell is the conscious striving to be in the vanguard, to keep ahead of the curve. He dates it from about 1830 onward, and attributes it to our newfound physical and social diversity and mobility. This dynamism brought about a *culture of the new.*

Bell claims that capitalism and modernist culture shared (at the beginning) a common source: liberty and liberation, embodied in "rugged individualism" economically and the "unrestrained self" culturally. But these two drivers became adversarial, diverging in multiple ways. One sense of this is Freudian, the clash of the work and pleasure principles. But, more significantly, while modernist culture emphasized self-expression, capitalist culture, driven by efficiency, dissolved individuals into their organizational functions. The key point here is that, initially, bourgeois culture embraced an ascetic capitalism as well as modernism's renunciation of the past. But not only would capitalism and modernism conflict, but the values of each would become corrupted, undermining society's backbone and bringing on instability.

Before religion receded, work and the accumulation of wealth had a "transcendental justification" in the form of the Protestant work ethic. But as religion's role shrank, work and its byproducts lost their former justification. Capitalism, therefore, began to be driven more by *acquisitveness* than by the Protestant, efficiency-based asceticism that initially inspired it. And in tune with this, gradually *"the legitimations of social behavior passed from religion to modernist culture"* (Bell's emphasis). With this came a shift from divinely inspired moral codes to an emphasis on one's personality and self-enhancement. The latter qualities were quintessentially expressed by artists who, in their modernist role, rebelled against the bourgeois establishment. Eventually, this modernist model won out, paradoxically becoming the normal mode of cultural change. For Bell, runaway greed—as seen in capitalism's growing acquisitiveness and modernism's increasing emphasis on the self—would be an ominous portent, threatening our economic, social, and political soundness.

We have already seen the building blocks of Bell's formulation: Mill's liberalism, the Weberian grounding of capitalism in Protestantism, the advancing secularization of the latter half of the nineteenth century, the rise of modernity and the dislocation brought on by the Industrial Revolution, as well as one more ingredient. This ingredient is the surge of mass consumption, consisting in the acquisition of once-luxury goods by the middle and lower classes. Mass consumption arose in the 1920s, brought about by technological advancement as well as the spread of assembly-line production, sophisticated distribution (marketing), and installment plans for payments. Regarding the installment plans, Bell points out that linguistically and spiritually, *debt* was not a widely acceptable concept, and therefore the notion of *credit* (although amounting to the same thing) was attempted, and it caught on. Gradually, our mass consumption brought on "institutionalized expectations of economic growth and a rising standard of living . . . converted . . . into a sense of *entitlements*" (Bell's emphasis). Unfortunately, capitalism's trajectory is endless. Bell cites sociologist Werner Sombart (who coined "capitalism") writing in the early 1900s, "'There are no absolute limits to acquisition, and the system exercises a psychological compulsion to boundless extension. . . . Acquisition therefore becomes unconditional, absolute. Not only does it seize upon all phenomena within the economic realm, but it reaches over into other cultural fields and develops a tendency to proclaim the supremacy of business interests over all other values.'" But focusing also on insufficient resources, Bell noted that "we realize the incompatibility of various wants and, more important, of diverse values. . . . The problems of choice are inescapable." Although acknowledging choice as an issue, Bell did not recognize it as a fundamental aspect of our society that is itself a primary force in forging new cultural and intellectual directions. Most important for him are the problems that stem from uncontrolled consumerism and decayed modernism.

Bell's focus on modernism begins with what we have called the loss of the absolute. Religion's retreat leaves a lacuna; he held that modernism grew out of our preoccupation with literature and art, which substituted for prior interests in religion. But this modernism is unremitting; "our culture has an unprecedented mission: it is an official, ceaseless search for a new sensibility," also known as art critic Harold Rosenberg's "tradition of the new."

There are several dimensions to Bell's conception of the loss of the absolute. To begin with, he notes that we have over time lost our moorings in a world awash in choices. Tradition and familiar bases are gone. We eschew our inherited roles. Old standards and the authorities and critics that uphold them are gone by the wayside. And, for the first time in social history, we are perpetually awash in choice—with respect to careers, lifestyles, political representation, and more. He believes that we cannot find a style, "a single principle" of modernity, for four reasons. One, mass society creates and seeks diversity and the enlargement of experience. This would tend to militate against a common theme or thread. Two, "the lack of a center." There is no more Paris in the '20s. Three, we have an increasing emphasis on visual culture; and four, the "breakup of the rational cosmos," meaning several things. Modern painting rejects the rational, traditional methods of proportion and perspective, foreground and background, figure and ground, that gave a mimetic window onto reality. Instead we get impressions and sensations, not depictions, of objects. We get two dimensions, not three. We get multiple simultaneous viewpoints, and transformations, feelings, and impact. The viewer is involved in the work and not at a (contemplative) *distance*.

In literature, we find multiple meanings, streams of consciousness, and a cutting back and forth in the narrative to effect a simultaneity of sensation. In music, emphasis shifts from melody and harmony to sound itself. Bell's overarching point is that in all of these modernist works, *expression* enters in, and erases the "psychic distance," the reflection and (cold) objectivity that the spectator once had. With this immersion in the work, the natural flow of time is often displaced or lost. Bell also notes the loss of *social distance* in which "distinctions of speech, taste, and style become erased" and privacy is lost. Finally, he laments the loss of ordering principles, boundaries, objective time and space, and a religious anchor. The result can be alienating. Durkheim's dualism between the sacred and profane leads us to ineluctably conclude that, as the sacred seems to recede, we increasingly face the profane.

For Marcuse, and to some degree, for Bell, advancing consumerism began to engulf modernism, converting it into a mere commodity. At that point in time, dissolving modernism on the one hand and untrammeled capitalism on the other engendered the upheavals of the 1960s from which Bell perceived it would be difficult to extricate ourselves. In 1996 Bell scanned the social and cultural landscape and concluded that things had gotten even worse. Capitalism had further accelerated—or deteriorated—into Wall Street greed and designer extravagance. Modernity, having reached the end of the line, had degenerated into a mostly vulgar "PoMo," that is, popularly expressed postmodernism, that through its commercialism, its retreat from reality and disregard of history, is extinguishing culture. And finally, in the wake of the turmoil of the 1960s, America today is "confused, angry, uneasy, and insecure," wallowing in moral decay at every level.

Whether Bell's pessimism has validity is moot. For each such concerned commentator, there is an exuberant counterpart who delights in the limitless possibilities that are rapidly unfolding. The correctness of Bell's thesis is not our primary concern, although, for the record, I do not share his pessimism regarding our social, political, and economic future. In addition, I believe there is a richness to postmodernist culture that he has failed to appreciate.

When *The Cultural Contradictions of Capitalism* first appeared, Bell was labeled, perhaps unfairly, as a neoconservative. The fact is, anyone who either decries recent trends or backs the *conservation* of particular practices (which may be two sides of the same coin) will be categorized as a conservative. But every society has to face the question—because we have the choice to—of how to resolve the opposition between tradition and trend. Bell makes it clear that he feels it is necessary for a culture to keep its past. We need to know how our forebears dealt with the same big questions; this, he says, is essentially what culture is about.

The issue of how to balance between trend and tradition probably has no right answer. It may be a matter of taste. One point to be made, however, in our trendy times, is that tradition cannot ever completely vanish, because there would be an eventual trend to restore it.

Overall, Bell has advanced a cogent framework to explain our socioeconomic shifts as resulting from the relentless nature of the free market. But, although he focuses mostly on the dual branches of capitalism and modernism, Bell's aim is ultimately to stem our alienation, to save our moral foundation that he claims is being eaten away. My thesis, to demonstrate that the new centrality of choice has been a fundamental force in shaping not only the twentieth century but also future generations, is strengthened by what Bell has had to say.

To Belong or Not to Belong?

One theme that we will revisit in different contexts is *alienation*, which we had already mentioned vis-à-vis Marx. So much has been made of this term over the past one hundred fifty years. Surely for Marx, alienation had some foundation in the growing division of labor brought on by the Industrial Revolution. But what about now? Alienation never quite disappears. It seems to come in waves, for example, that of the 1960s. Somewhat rhetorically, I want to ask what exactly *is* alienation. Roughly speaking, it is estrangement or disaffection with a touch of indifference or hostility. But that's not enough. Alienation conjures up a separation, possibly irreconcilable, as well as a sense of incomprehension and perhaps wistfulness, for what once was. Since this term has come to represent a cyclical, general disconnection in our society, it is important to spend some time discussing it. Alienation, I believe, is a feeling we get when a basic human need is not satisfied: the need to belong.

Marx claimed we leaned on religion on account of our alienation. But religion was a false cure. Marx sought to treat our alienation by creating a classless society with communal, and not individual, ownership. This structure would de-alienate us, and eliminate the crutch of religion.

Alienation did not, of course, begin with Marx. But its mysterious, debilitating, and melancholic force has repeatedly surfaced in numerous voices of difference, dissent, and rebellion, from Dostoevsky's Underground Man to Camus's Stranger. Alienation seizes—or is seized by—every disenfranchised interest group and every unhappy youth, suicidal or not. Indeed, it seizes us all at some time or another.

To be an alien is to be foreign, excluded. An alien does not belong; it (it, not he or she) is unlike one's own. This rejection, as it were, quells a basic need, and leads to isolation and hostility. But there's more to it, in the form of the following opposition: we all strike a balance between the heartfelt, warming desire to belong, and the angry, rebellious urge not to. This dualism between the desire to recognize our unique self and the desire (brought about by alienation) to belong was recognized by the psychologist Alfred Adler.

But Adler aside, given a particular set of cultural norms and styles, there are those of us who more or less adhere to them and play the game—and those of us who do not (I suspect a genetic basis for this). The latter individuals—*individuals*—need to signify their estrangement in some understood ways. They isolate themselves; they differentiate themselves from the greater set of conformists and are isolated in return.

But is society in fact a set of conformists together with a collection of uniquely differentiated individuals? What we observe instead are alternative groups that define themselves through commonly held rebellious tendencies. Such groups are identifiable, for example, by various modes of dress or behavior; in short, the individuals do not, *qua* individuals, break off from the mainstream—they join other dissidents. They belong to the set of those who do not belong.

Such relationships are dynamic and unstable; too much belonging, and many balk. But the interesting thing is, once we partition society into those who belong, and those who belong to the set of those who do *not* belong—then we have a logical contradiction. (If you belong to the set of those who don't belong, then you belong but you don't.) It is called Russell's paradox, after Bertrand Russell, who at the turn of the last century, as we have discussed, was trying to protect mathematics and logic from such conundrums.

As we all know, so-called alternative people, those on the cutting edge, sooner or later begin to attract some company. They eventually feel that they've been caught up in too much belonging and then set themselves loose and chart a new course. Alienation: now it sounds like fashion. But sensing that the mainstream has caught up with you is just Russell's paradox breathing down your neck. First comes alienation; soon, membership in a club you don't want to belong to. You have gone from Karl Marx to Groucho Marx!

Inclusion and Exclusion

The subject of belonging and the alternative is a manifestation of one of the principal oppositions that choice brings about, namely inclusion–exclusion. There are other examples where this opposition looms large. As Fred Murphy notes, libertarians will never be successful politicians because they don't wish to belong—but politics is fundamentally a process of belonging. To close out this chapter on postindustrial society I will consider the inclusion–exclusion opposition in the context of postindustrial society's gathering place—a place where everyone belongs: the mall.

One universal, and indeed, universalizing, feature of malls is that they are, by their very nature, inviting. Their very popularity rests on their being amiable public spaces. Everyone knows this. Malls are *inclusive*.

Contrast this with another fact that everyone knows: that boutiques are very private spaces. They are not for the general public. They are *exclusive*—their privacy and intimacy are derived from the exclusion of the lesser-valued majority of the populace. By featuring a select, and by definition, limited array of merchandise, boutiques develop a personality and create the atmosphere of a club. Their well-defined, well-refined style is carried out to the extent of being exclusive of most tastes. The club atmosphere then is extremely intimate, warm, and personal, but only to the self-selected members who bask in the self-reflective glow of being accepted in such a cultivated and exclusive venue. Of course, the indicator of that refinement is usually found in the prices of the goods on sale. The elevated prices—to be interpreted as club membership—exclude the general public. Coupled with the personal nature of boutiques, which forces potential buyer-members to interact, the exaggerated prices serve to discourage the unfit.

Malls and many department stores, on the other hand, encourage all comers in their wide-open, unthreatening, anonymous egalitarianism. The inherent downside, virtually necessary in such an enterprise, is to carry merchandise that in design, style, material, and price appeals to the lowest common denominator.

The trade-off between *haute couture* exclusivity and generic common denomination is a key to the marketing success of both merchandise lines and retail establishments. In facing the horns of this dilemma, however, we have seen the emergence, over the years, of boutiques within malls and boutiquing within department stores. This is a brilliant strategy that allows the feature of exclusivity (for those who can afford it) within the all-inclusive egalitarian structure, providing an initially democratic mechanism to satisfy the masses and yet eventually stratifies them anyway. We are reminded of Alexis de Toqueville's observation that in a democracy, people *start,* but do not necessarily *finish,* equal.

Delving deeper into this subject of membership, one can find countless things to say about the formation of groups, the identification of individuals within a collective, and so forth—such study is a cornerstone of anthropology and sociology. But certain observations can be easily made. To begin with, many of us seem to enjoy identification, in various segmented arenas, with certain establishments, places, and brand names, that after due course, provide us with a familiar and reassuring context. (Repeat customers form the backbone of any business that intends to endure.) Our propensity to identify has amazing manifestations. Countless persons adhere to a unique brand of, say, Scotch whisky, yet they are in fact completely unable to distinguish between makes by taste. Others subscribe to particular types of detergents or gasolines when the competitors are virtually identical. It is remarkable how many mediocre restaurants are repeatedly visited (and how many mediocre dishes consumed) just for reassurance.

The point is that out of the many such loyalties a person may exhibit, almost none of them is by itself that meaningful in the person's overall self-profile. I don't suggest that saying you're a Coke (and not a Pepsi) drinker is going to reveal your true nature. But many of us do identify ourselves, to a large extent, with the activities in which we engage. (Just check the personal ads.) And the whole interacting set of identifications seems to provide, for many, a frighteningly hefty bulk of their actual *identities.*

In considering the advantage evidently obtained by identifying with a certain item or movement, we face the inevitable problems of choice: which brands are worthwhile adopting, which establishments do we pick as our haunts, and which activities do we engage in (and at what levels)? When we exercise a selection, our inclusion therein carries the dialectic of exclusivity, which we presumably think adds value to our lives. But as we continue with certain goods or activities, their messages often change, as we periodically check if there exists the fit that there used to be. Sometimes we feel insecure, not knowing if we truly belong. We begin to feel alienated, perhaps finding it difficult to distinguish our true identity from what appears. Undesirable qualities—that are perhaps first seen in others—begin to get reflected back on ourselves, as revealed in part by the Groucho Marxism, "I wouldn't want to join any club that would have me as a member." Finally, too much of an identification with one entity, in the face of various constraints on time and money, can ruin other possibilities. Politicians, of course, know this all too well, and therefore withdraw from extremist positions.

Postindustrial society has seen the transformation from a plentitude of goods to a plethora of information. Yet we still retain the bugaboos of scarce time and limited resources; worse, the vicious spiral ensures that these problems will multiply. How can we possibly manage complex decisions that are subject to numerous constraints? Over the past fifty years, this subject has finally started to receive scientific treatment. Let's turn to a discussion of decision science in the next chapter.

In chapter 2 we discussed the origins of various ideas that emerged in the twentieth century as the need to analyze complex decisions reached a certain criticality. The applications of division of labor and economies of scale were widespread by 1900. Steamship and rail had widened the distribution of commodities. Moreover, by that time the paradigm of increasing efficiency had become natural and was given greater urgency by the newfound global competition that developed principally among Great Britain, the United States, and Germany. Therefore it is not surprising that "scientific management" arose, paving the way for the development of industrial engineering, production and operations management, and management science. These fields continue to undergo extensive development; two of their more recent contributions have been total quality management and business process reengineering. We will discuss some of what management science has to offer in this chapter and return to it in the context of risk and uncertainty in chapter 10.

The disciplines listed above—a hodgepodge of ideas, theories, and techniques—have been extensively pursued in universities but have only somewhat recently filtered into the consciousness of engineers and MBAs, if not the general public. One reason that these concepts are not better known is that they are found in the unions and intersections of different fields. These are, bewilderingly, decision theory, decision science (what's the difference?), management science, operations research, risk management, game theory, quantitative methods in business, industrial engineering, engineering management, and God knows what else. Most research universities, and even some teaching colleges, have one or more departments from that list. Moreover, some of the subject matter, which can be highly technical, is taught in more traditional areas, like mathematics, statistics, and economics, or in more specialized areas like computer science, civil engineering, or even marketing and finance—talk about interdisciplinary!

Management Decisions: Optimal Use of Limited Resources

To try to clarify this picture, let me identify what some of the major developments have been. The single most important methodology, both in its own right and as an influence on other work, is the mathematical modeling and solution procedure known as *linear programming*, or LP, introduced by George Dantzig in 1947. Dantzig's technique put the science of *optimization* on the map. The formulation of a linear program requires a decision maker to focus on a goal and to enumerate available activities or alternatives in a certain situation. These activities are typically constrained, either naturally, through resource limitations or other conditions, or artificially, through factors like staffing requirements or demand restrictions. The decision maker wishes to obtain the "program" specifying those activities and their levels that will provide a maximum (say, profit) or minimum (say, cost) subject to the constraints present.

Obviously, not every problem or even every management problem can be solved by LP. To use the technique, your objectives, tangible or not, have to be boiled down to a single item, like money. Then, you have to know the net profit (or cost) from a unit of each possible activity. You also have to know precisely what your limitations are and how they affect your activities; for example, you would need to know how various outputs use up resources.

To illustrate this, suppose you craft tables and chairs from lengths of pine that you purchase every week. Let's say that you have an unlimited supply of screws and glue and other such things, so that the only limited resources necessary for producing the tables and chairs each week are the lengths of pine and the hours that you work. Let's further assume that you can sell, at certain fixed prices, as many chairs and tables as you can make. How much profit would each table or chair generate? The two types of furniture use up the lengths of pine and the labor time at different rates; for example, tables use up more wood than chairs do, but chairs require more time. Taking this into account, you can determine how much profit you obtain from each table and each chair by subtracting the cost of each item's production from its selling price. If you decide to manage your furniture production like a business, your aim will be to maximize the total profit of your enterprise, subject to the limited wood and time at your disposal. A properly formulated linear program, when solved, will indicate the profit-maximizing mix of table and chairs.

In this instance there is an inherent linearity—which expresses, for example, that two tables use double the resources but yield double the profit of one table and that the total profit is simply the table profits plus the chair profits. But often this characteristic is not present in the situation being studied. For example, if you were planning, for a certain geographical region, the optimal number of drugstores to open up (and in my neck of the woods these stores have multiplied faster than rabbits), LP would be suspect as a tool, because it is hard to determine just how much business one drugstore will cannibalize from another one.

However, LP (as well as its cousins, integer and nonlinear programming) has had enormous application and impact in a variety of areas, ranging from portfolio selection to production planning to staffing to logistics. Airlines completely depend on it. Indeed, optimization, the handmaid of efficiency itself, would hardly exist without it.

If you probe into the mathematics of LP and its associated techniques, you will find precursors going back three hundred years. Calculus deals in part with the minima and maxima of functions. Beginning students learn about *uncon*-strained optimization, such as finding where the highest point on a curve will lie. More advanced students study constrained optimization; a typical textbook problem will challenge the student to find the dimensions of, say, a milk carton that holds a certain volume with the minimum possible amount of cardboard (i.e., surface area) used. Incidentally, the standard U.S. milk cartons do not achieve this objective—they use extra cardboard to look bigger, but in Britain, for example, with a stronger tradition of facing scarce resources, the cartons are less impressive but waste less cardboard (and fit more easily into the smaller fridges).

The other mathematical component, linear algebra, that is used to solve systems of equations, evolved later than calculus but still much earlier than LP. What is it that makes LP more advanced, and why didn't it appear earlier than it did? The typical (but nevertheless reasonable) answer is the argument of necessity. World War II brought a variety of unprecedented large-scale tactical and logistical problems involving the deployment of scarce resources. As an example, the RAF had a significant number of expatriate (mainly French and Polish) pilots with different skills and language fluencies and a very short supply of planes. Experienced pilots were more successful than novices, but lengthy training would reduce the pilot supply in the short run. Assembling competent flight crews that could communicate among themselves was one challenge. Beyond that, different theaters of operation all competed for the limited stock of men and material. These theaters changed, both geographically (from the defense of London to antisubmarine operations in the Bay of Biscay to long-range bombing over Germany) and in criticality. With all this and more going on, how could the RAF best meet its demands?

An important factor is that, unlike World War I, scientists and mathematicians were sought after to solve such complex problems. Also, the conditions of World War I were largely the static grind of trench warfare, led by generals who were not trained in an age of scientific management, whereas World War II's circumstances were more dynamic. Finally, although computers, as we know them, had not quite evolved by the 1940s, the new quantitative emphasis created a demand for calculation that only computing machinery could adequately meet. (The premier professional society of computer scientists, the ACM, founded in 1947, is still called the "Association for Computing Machinery.")

This warfare-based argument of necessity may be adequate, but we have left out the *mathematical* component regarding optimization's development. What was well-known for ages was how to solve "simultaneous equations." You learned this in school (or, at least, they taught it to you). But the textbook renditions (which seem pointless to most students) generally treat forced situations, situations where the variables end up having to take on particular values, for example, the exact coordinates where two straight lines intersect. There is no leeway, no *choice*. (You may recall that normally when you would solve two equations in two unknowns, you'd obtain a unique solution.) There is a good reason for this: classical physics and economics were formulated mechanistically. Physicists were modeling the natural world; economists emulated the physicists, hoping that markets were essentially no different from moving bodies. In either case, one came up with "the answer"—the correct velocity, distance, price, or quantity.

But with the new problems—resource allocation, transport, scheduling— came a new challenge: how to choose. What had motivated physicists and economists was description: how did the world work? But in the military and more generally in other organizations, the models were prescriptive: *what* to do. In these situations, assessing the multitude of choices and possible solutions posed a formidable problem in itself. On top of that, the decision maker had to somehow evaluate the alternatives with respect to a cost or benefit to be optimized, as we have mentioned. Not surprisingly, Dantzig's method to solve such problems, and other associated methods, grew into a science—a decision science. It burgeoned with the advent of stored-program computing in the early 1950s. Some gave it the wartime name *operations research;* others, *management science.* As we have mentioned, its interdisciplinary nature housed it in many places in academia and industry, but, to this day, it has rarely found a true home. Unlike more standard disciplines with a defined scope of affairs, like biology or anthropology or accounting, management science has no single, concrete core to it. It deals with *systems* and strives to find applications. Management science evolves as the world does, and management scientists are always on the lookout for new applications of their techniques and new outlets of influence. Recently, for example, as a result of the sustained bull market of the 1990s, some management scientists have ventured into finance, peddling "financial engineering" in degree programs. The methods they have imported into finance have been used on various problems, for example, the pricing of options. ("Options"—the perfect name for a financial instrument in the era of choice. Incidentally, it is absolutely staggering how the financial services industry has evolved the galaxy of options, including "options," that are currently available to investors.) In any event, the main strength of management science—its being an interdisciplinary tool—has also been its biggest weakness.

The Best Plans for Unknown Amounts of Business

At home or not, understood or not, there have been some major successes besides Dantzig's linear programming. A broad area of management science deals with stochastic systems, where uncertainty and probability lurk everywhere. With LP, the possible choices are confounding, but the models depend on known (i.e., assumed) profit margins, known consumption rates, and known resource levels. In stochastic systems, the inherent uncertainties restrict us to the fog of statistical analysis and probability estimation. Here's an example: suppose you have to set up a call center for customer support. How many customer service representatives will you want to employ? This would obviously depend on your expected volume and pattern of calls concerning your products, as well as on the speed with which calls could be handled. But calls arrive irregularly and conversations vary in length. Moreover, even for a particular pattern of calls, it isn't clear what to do. Hiring swarms of reps provides great service—callers will not be on hold too long—but it's expensive. And attempting to skimp on the reps saves a few bucks in the short run, but creates long waits. The unhappy callers may then abandon your products, which would hurt you in the long run.

It turns out that *queueing theory,* which originated in the 1950s, gives remarkable analyses of various waiting line situations. From decent estimates of call arrival patterns and conversation lengths, one can determine how long an average on-hold wait will be, what the likelihood of a line of a certain length will be, and more. This theory allows phone companies to plan capacity expansions; it enables a supermarket manager to staff checkout lanes.

Some problems, though, are too complex for queueing models and formulas. For example, in the customer service setting, queueing models can't handle additional twists like callers hanging up out of frustration. If you are involved in planning a large, complex capital project, you don't want to discover, after it's too late, that you were way off the mark. Such problems are perfect for computer simulation. Simulation, not possible fifty years ago, is now a feature of any number of computer games as well as serious software. By allowing users to test different parameter values, to play with different configurations, to ask "what if" to their hearts' content—all this while performing thousands of runs in the blink of an eye—simulation serves as a keystone in building a science of decision. It also provides an apt metaphor for today's world of choice: rather than commit yourself, toy with all the possibilities first.

Management scientists have been able to tackle a variety of industrial-strength problems with their tools. Where do you locate a new facility? How much inventory do you need to carry? What delivery routes and schedules are the most efficient? In the old days, we located the steel mills near the coal mines. Today, we need to weigh new factors, from labor-force education levels to global currency exchange rates. Before, we carried extra inventory to cover our problems. Now, we shed inventory to lower our costs and, while doing this, we make ourselves more flexible in adapting to the market and offering choices. In the past, we'd ship and truck things without much science to it. Now, we have *logistics,* and we meticulously plan our vehicle routes.

Optimization as we have discussed it above is very much a discipline that arose out of the need to choose among alternatives in complex situations. It is usually conceived, however, as a theory in which a decision maker controls human activities restricted by nature or in general by exogenously generated, static constraints. Neither nature nor the artificial constraints are particularly out to subvert the decision maker. They simply represent the environment and its limitations.

Game Theory and Political Choice

At about the same time Dantzig was developing linear programming, another important branch of decision science was being introduced, called *game theory*. Despite the name, game theory is a serious attempt to analyze how multiple decision makers, who have different interests, should act in the presence of conflict and uncertainty. The actions of the decision makers (called *players*) change the outcomes that are obtained. Therefore, not only is the static nature of the optimization models gone, but all of the decision makers act in self-interest. That is, the other players are *willful* agents and pursue objectives that may be contrary to yours. We've already discussed zero-sum games in chapter 6, where (for two players) one player's gain must come at the other's expense. Such situations are purely competitive. Many other situations, though, despite being rooted in conflict, are non-zero-sum and less competitive, and can turn out happily (or badly) for all involved. Incidentally, game theory represents one of Bell's criteria for the postindustrial age—that one is playing a strategic "game between persons" and not a "game against fabricated nature" (for example, deciding what to do given a particular weather forecast). Aside from decision making under conflict, the other aspect of game theory, uncertainty, is a hallmark of the newer era, as opposed to the deterministic, mechanistic Newtonian paradigm that dominated the previous two centuries.

The person most responsible for the launching of game theory was the mathematician John von Neumann, who published the first book on the subject—applying it to economics—with economist Oskar Morgenstern in 1944. Initially, von Neumann's interest was, at one level, playful. He was interested in modeling the game of poker, specifically, how best to employ bluffing. Bluff too much, and the other players will get wise to you; bluff too little, and you won't win many hands. But the others may be bluffing as well. How do you develop a successful strategy?

In such decisions, the crux of the issue, as we will see with existentialism, is that you have to act, picking one of your alternatives. But worse than the usual existential dilemma is that now there are opponents. In poker, if the best strategy overall is to *sometimes* bluff, how do we carry it out? The answer is to *randomize,* for example, by rolling dice, having decided to bluff if you obtain a seven. Most people find it strange to let a chance event like a dice roll (or a coin flip) determine their action. But, if you remember choosing, as a kid, who went first, you played a game where each of two kids throws out one or two fingers; one kid wins when the sum of the fingers is even, the other kid, odd. Even young children, through playing the game repeatedly, come to realize that they have to mix up their choices randomly or else the other kids will catch on and defeat them. Intriguingly, as biologist John Maynard Smith and others have shown, even fish and birds carry out such "mixed strategies" in their struggles for mates, territory, and food, although they obviously don't know, in a calculating sense, what they are doing.

Researchers in many areas have applied game theory either to explain behavior or, more aptly, to provide rational direction. To illustrate more of the subject's scope, let me discuss three examples from political science. It must have occurred to you when you voted in a (U.S.) presidential election, that your single vote is hardly likely to matter. Yet, clearly there is some chance that your vote could be the decisive one. Can this likelihood be measured? There are two components to the problem: first, your vote has to "swing" your state; second, your state has to swing the electoral college, the way Florida did in the 2000 U.S. presidential election. Although the probabilities involved are very small, they *can* be calculated—and, for voters in different states, they *vary.* Game theorist Guillermo Owen has used a technique called the Shapley value (due to Lloyd Shapley) to show that under our electoral college system, voters in the larger states can have more than three times the power of voters in some of the smaller states. And law professor John Banzhaf preceded Owen's work with a similar analysis and conclusion. These results not only contradict the founding principle of "one adult, one vote" (I had to reword it) but also have tremendous policy implications for resource allocation in political campaigns. By the way, many people, including sophisticated analysts, believe that the electoral college system confers disproportionate power on the *smaller* states, so I'd better justify the opposite claim.

Let's compare a large state, say, Florida, with about sixteen million people (2000 census) and twenty-seven electoral votes, with a small state like South Dakota, with its 750,000 people and three electoral votes. First let's understand the naïve viewpoint. This holds that Florida, with twenty-one times South Dakota's population, ought to have twenty-one times South Dakota's number of electoral votes for Floridians to have the same per-capita voting influence as South Dakotans. But Florida only has nine times South Dakota's number of electoral votes, and therefore we might conclude that the Coyote State gets the better deal. Such a disparity can be observed for all such large-small pairings; indeed the Founding Fathers believed they overcompensated the small states when they added two electoral votes to every state's apportionment, regardless of size. How does game theory refute this belief?

Game theory analysis begins by observing that the electoral college ultimately divides the states into two groups: winners—those in the victor's camp of at least 270 electoral votes (out of the total of 538)—and losers (those carried by the losing candidate). Think about the ballot counting on election night and the sequence in which the states are (correctly, we assume) declared to have gone for one candidate or the other. There is always a single state that actually puts the winner over the top. In 2000 it was Florida. But in another election the decisive state could equally be any of the other forty-nine states (or Washington, D.C.), on account of time-zone differences, varying ballot formats and precinct reporting, or other factors. In how many scenarios could a small state like South Dakota actually make the difference? The only ways South Dakota can be decisive are when it joins a group of other states that total exactly 267, 268, or 269 electoral votes. (With fewer than 267, South Dakota's three additional votes would not put a candidate over the top, and with more than 269, the outcome would already have been decided.) There are relatively very few ways that these scenarios in which South Dakota swings the election could come about.

Florida's twenty-seven votes, on the other hand, will put a candidate over the top whenever that candidate has already accumulated anywhere from 243 to 269 electoral votes. Mathematical analysis shows that this category of Florida's swing scenarios is far more numerous than South Dakota's set. Now, it is true that a voter in South Dakota has a much higher chance of being the decisive vote there than a Floridian has in Florida, because South Dakota is far less populous. But since Florida's chances to swing the national election vastly outnumber South Dakota's, in the final analysis an individual voter in Florida has roughly three times the influence of one in South Dakota.

This theory leads us to conclude that the large states ought to receive far more of the candidates' money and attention than their proportional share of the electorate, while, unfortunately, some small states like South Dakota may well be largely ignored. Surely the Founding Fathers did not anticipate such consequences of their design. In recent campaigns there has been increasing awareness of this inequity, and media pundits tell us that states like California are virtually must-win battlegrounds. (This, incidentally, makes George W. Bush's

2000 victory all the more remarkable, given that he lost six of the eight largest states, including California.) All in all, perhaps it is time to revisit whether the electoral college should be abandoned in deciding the chief executive.

The discovery of power inequities among states is just one application of game theory to politics. Another game-theoretic analysis begins by asking the provocative question, "why vote for just one candidate?" Why not vote for all candidates that you approve of (given, of course, that the one with the most votes still wins)? This notion, called *approval voting,* is attributed to researchers Steven Brams, Peter Fishburn, and Robert Weber. The idea is that, with more than two candidates, each voter is less pressured to manipulate his or her vote. That is, if you favor candidate A who is a distant third, wouldn't mind B, and dislike C, you need not worry about throwing your vote away in choosing A (or else voting for B simply to defeat C): you could vote for *both* A and B. Thus, approval voting would reduce misrepresentation of our preferences. It would also encourage third- (and even fourth-) party candidates to join the fray. The extra diversity would more closely express our national profile and eradicate the current, bland, two-party system, in which each party needs to maximize appeal by maintaining a fairly centrist position.

Perhaps the most important work in applying a mathematical decision theory to the problem of designing a voting system that represents voters' preferences is the economist Kenneth Arrow's *Social Choice and Individual Values,* first published in 1951. It had been well-known that voting systems, for example, that simply asked voters to rank the candidates and then used either majority rule or a weighted numbering system to determine a winner, were inherently flawed. Realizing then, that designing an incontrovertible "social choice," or voting, system that guaranteed certain hard-to-define desiderata like "fairness" or "justice" was a tall order, Arrow instead began by setting down some reasonable conditions that any decision procedure ought to meet. At the individual level, Arrow assumed that all pairs of alternatives were comparable for every voter. That is, for each voter, every pair of candidates A and B he or she could consider was such that either A was preferred to B, B preferred to A, or that the voter was indifferent between them. In addition, Arrow assumed transitivity, meaning that if a voter preferred A to B and B to C, then the voter must prefer A to C. He added a couple of more technical conditions too (which we will disregard). So far, so good.

Next, Arrow considered the range of possible decision procedures themselves and pondered conditions that appeared innocuous and universally acceptable. One was *nondictatorship,* that no single voter's preference can solely determine the outcomes. Similar to dictatorship is when an outcome is *imposed* on the electorate, for example, when A is ranked higher than B even though no one preferred A to B. Reasonably, Arrow sought a decision procedure that would rule out both dictatorship as well as the imposition of choice. Furthermore, Arrow believed a social choice procedure should obey *independence of irrelevant alternatives.* The idea is as follows. Suppose an election takes place, the individuals' preferences are polled, and then, before the votes are examined, a certain candidate dies. Surely the choice to be made from among the surviving candidates should not depend on the preferences for the dead candidate. One more intuitively appealing condition that Arrow included was *positive association of social and individual values,* which, roughly speaking, said that if candidate A rose in every voter's ranking, then A's overall ranking should rise.

Given these conditions (which had to be revised a bit in order to provide the correct result), Arrow proved his celebrated *impossibility theorem,* which is that the ostensibly innocuous and desirable conditions above are *inconsistent.* That is, there does not exist a voting procedure that satisfies all of the conditions simultaneously.

In our context, one reading of Arrow's theorem is an increasing loss of the absolute. For centuries, most politically savvy people must have suspected that no democratic political system was perfect, but now there was a formal analytical result that supported this view. On the other hand, it must be noted that Arrow's framework, as evidenced in his assumptions, is not the only feasible one. Plato would have rejected the premise that the formulation of a just society (in which a political decision procedure would play a part) should depend on the preferences of all of that society's individuals. To supplement this line of thought, we have already seen how the Grand Inquisitor claimed that the masses are incapable of making decisions. As political scientist Robert Abrams indicates, the "fear of the tyranny of the majority, in de Toqueville's terms, has also been a recurring theme in political philosophy"—and this fear is recognized, for example, in the U.S. Bill of Rights. Indeed, the philosopher "José Ortega y Gasset . . . argued that the political problems of the twentieth century, and especially the rise of fascism, resulted from 'the revolt of the masses,' in which people of no particular ability (not simply the rich) have taken power." Such criticisms challenge Arrow's predicating political decision on a system of collective choice.

Another approach is to accept most, but not all, of Arrow's assumptions. The hope is that by modestly changing (or, if necessary, eliminating) some of his conditions, the impossibility result would vanish without significantly compromising justness. A good deal of work has appeared in this vein, but none of it has decisively established an acceptable collective-choice procedure.

Another issue of concern is that voters may misrepresent their true preferences in order to manipulate the outcome, as we had discussed with approval voting. One hopes that we could develop a "strategyproof" collective-choice method that would duly represent individuals' preferences and yet thwart strategic misrepresentation. In the 1970s, however, researchers Alan Gibbard and Mark Satterthwaite proved yet another impossibility result, namely that no such strategyproof method could exist.

Incentives to Play Fair

Misrepresentation of our preferences, bluffing, and lying are behaviors that social and biological scientists and management researchers have begun to study over the last quarter of a century. We've discussed politics. But what if you're selling telecommunication spectrum rights, or oil drilling rights, and you want to discourage bidders from underbidding? How do you design a process that will keep bids honest? How can a community, with a limited budget but various ways to spend the money, elicit honest revelations from its citizens as to how much money to spend on what projects? When the community plans to raise money for the provision of a public good, how can the problem of free riding—using the good without chipping in for it—be avoided? (How many times have you watched public television without contributing, or walked away as soon as a street performer started to pass around the hat?)

What happens in organizations? If they're very small, the owner can keep tabs on the employees. But successful organizations grow, and at a certain point no one person can manage everything. Delegation is necessary, responsibilities are allocated, and structural subdivisions emerge. Now these divisions, although hopefully part of a team, in fact engage in competition. Advertising budgets, workforce, sales force, and other resources are limited, if not fixed; how should the organization allocate them among the divisions? Should the top performing division be rewarded with more resources or should the less efficient units get a boost so they can improve? The real issue is, how can top management provide incentives that elicit nonmanipulative behavior by the division heads? The latter may attempt to push an agenda that champions certain activities at the overall expense of the organization. (This is an example of something called a *social trap* we will investigate later on.) The details of the divisional operations are unobservable to top management; no one can micromanage all the branches.

The problem we outline is really one of *information*. To solve it, information economists have developed various "principal–agent" models with modest success. The idea is that a "principal"—an abstraction for top management—has to provide incentive for the "agent" to optimize the principal's profits. The sticky part, of course, is that the agent, whose actions are hidden to the principal, naturally acts in self-interest. So the principal has to ensure that the agent's self-interest is consistent with that of the principal's, which usually is not as easy as it sounds. Keeping many agents honest and unified in a team sense, though difficult, is imperative and is a top priority in both private and public enterprises.

It is interesting to note that the information-management problem inherent in an organization's growth is another instance of the vicious spiral. We could ask why organizations grow, and discover that the answers range from the obvious greed (related in part to economies of scale) to the less obvious insecurity. Growth, diversifying an organization's products and services horizontally, vertically, or geographically, can serve to spread, and thereby reduce, risk. In seeking this risk reduction as well as additional profits, organizations face an agonizing set of decisions regarding products, markets, locations, financing choices, and so on. Because of these complexities, larger enterprises cannot be managed in the same way smaller ones can, and therefore the "agency" problems that challenge economists and management theorists will not vanish. Not as long as micromanagement remains infeasible or undesirable, and different members of the illusory "team" continue to have different objectives and vie for scarce resources. Of course, as technology critic Gene Rochlin indicates, the degree to which computerization enables "penetration across and through the lines of authority" may soon erase the informational asymmetry and resulting privacy that underlings currently enjoy. Managers may before long have the ability to thoroughly monitor the work of anyone serving under them.

Constraints and Progress: The Four Stages

The salient point here is that, even in our world of plenty, limited resources have played and will continue to play a central role in the way individuals and organizations make decisions. No wonder that a hallmark of our era is *constrained optimization*. We have clearly moved a long way from the fledgling industrial era of the nineteenth century, when most lives were still tightly determined and discretionary time and income were almost nonexistent. Now most of us have tremendous latitude in making both large and small decisions. What does the future hold for us?

As our technological sophistication continues to increase, it is safe to say that our productivity will likewise continue to rise, as will our standard of living. Our jobs will continue to become more service- and information-oriented, less physically demanding, more specialized, but more flexible. One hour of work will buy a greater value of goods than ever before, and more of these goods will be discretionary and presumably entertainment oriented. We may not be happier, but the constraints on our lives will be eased. When the great majority of us are focused on self-actualization as opposed to basic survival needs, we will have moved into a world where mortality is the primary constraint on our activities. We only live once. The world of tomorrow will be one of *almost unconstrained optimization.*

Presently, we are forging a world where at the turn of the twenty-first century, fiction is starting to become possibility. *If* we are able to solve our terrible problems of warfare, ecosystem instability, disease, and social friction, it is not too soon to look ahead to a remarkable world where we will be able to prolong our lives. Mortality—obviously a formidable opponent—will be a final barrier to *un*constrained optimization. What do I mean by this challenge? It is hard to predict the path of science; however, biologists are already not only unraveling our genetic code, but also beginning to discover the mechanisms through which we age. Cloning is now a reality. Neuroscientists are starting to discover the physiological bases of brain functions. It is not too far-fetched to wonder whether some day we will be able to genetically alter ourselves, halt the aging process, map our brain states (including all of our memories) onto an external storage device, and repair body parts and organs from cloned individuals. At this hypothetical *omega point* (no relation to the teleology of Teilhard de Chardin here), we will be virtually immortal, and virtually able to experience anything and everything.

To summarize what I have outlined above, I have broken down human development into four stages, two of which have yet to appear, if ever they do. The first stage is that of essentially *no choice,* which characterized the overwhelming majority of the world's inhabitants through, roughly speaking, the end of the nineteenth century. The second stage is our current one of *constrained optimization* that is typical of most people in developed countries today. Our lives are complex and we are regularly inundated with a multitude of products and services to choose among. These goods and services are the product of a globally interconnected economy that is made ever more efficient through advances in technology as well as in organizational management, the latter brought about through the widespread application of management science principles. However, our cornucopia is attenuated by the limitations on our money and, especially, our time.

The third stage, which may be in the relatively near future, is one of *almost unconstrained optimization.* It is the foreseeable continuation of the past century's advances. This stage is, however, qualitatively different from our current situation, in that all of our requirements will be comfortably met and the only real constraint on our activities will be our mortality.

The fourth stage, the *omega point,* is at the present time distant and merely hypothetical. In this logical extension of the other stages, to actualize all of our possibilities we must prolong our lives—ideally, to establish immortality. In such a world, so many of the choices that are so central to our current lives and so many of the oppositions that are derived from these choices will have been softened or dissolved altogether.

After such speculation, it is time to come back to reality. Our lives are very much captive to the complex choices that we have to make within our current limitations. As we have discussed, choices bifurcate our possible paths. Oppositions we must consider not only cause us anguish but also literally change the way we think. Let's return to this theme and examine how binary oppositions have made an impact on linguistics, anthropology, literary criticism, and more.

In a series of lectures from 1906 to 1911 at the University of Geneva, Ferdinand de Saussure revolutionized the way we think about language and communication. Unfortunately, when he died in 1913 he had not yet published his ideas. Two of Saussure's colleagues put together lecture notes from some of his students and published them in 1916 as *Cours de linguistique générale*. Saussure not only redirected the study of linguistics, but also founded semiology (semiotics in the Anglo-American world) which is the more general study of signs. Saussure was the direct inspiration for structuralism, one of the important intellectual waves of the twentieth century, which saw broad application in anthropology, literary criticism, philosophy, and beyond.

Until Saussure, linguistics, the science of language, was largely historical and comparative. Scholars had attempted to find relationships among different languages and track how languages had developed. By the late 1800s, these studies had become strongly evolution driven, in keeping with the times. Saussure, however, was convinced that this approach would never address the key questions about what language was. His highly original theory, founded on a powerful set of oppositional pairs, provided important insight into language and communication.

Oppositions and Language

The essential component of Saussure's thought was that the fundamental unit of any language is the *sign*. The sign itself consisted of two components: the *signifier*, which is the spoken utterance, and the *signified*, which is the concept referred to. It is important to note that the signified is a mental notion, not a physical object. Signifiers and signifieds always come in pairs. In other words, one does not exist without the other, and every sign is a relation between them.

The binary feature of the sign is important because it means that language and, to some extent, thought itself has a dual nature. This principle, when extended to other realms of analysis, becomes quite powerful. Of course, many signs that we come across are not verbal ones, and therefore it is not surprising that an analysis of signs extends fruitfully to beyond linguistics itself. To use author John Sturrock's example, a wreath of flowers, in our culture, is a signifier "whose signified is, let us say, 'condolence.'" But messages sent, for example, by flowers are culture sensitive and as such are interpreted within a certain *code*. Thus we have entered the realm of anthropology.

To return to Saussure, a central attribute of signs is that they are *arbitrary*. This means more than the simple fact that the signifier "red" in French is "rouge," or, even within the same language, that Brits say "lift" while Yanks say "elevator." Signs are arbitrary because they are merely socially agreed-on relationships between spoken utterances and mental concepts. And, contrary to what we might at first believe, they are *not* based on connections to natural objects. In the *Cours,* Saussure noted that even fashion is determined in part by the "requirements dictated by the human body." But, the *Cours* continues, "A language, on the contrary, is in no way limited in its choice of means. For there is nothing at all to prevent the association of any idea whatsoever with any sequence of sounds whatsoever." Indeed, this arbitrariness differentiates language from other (social) institutions.

At this point, I presume that you still want to believe that the physical things many signs correspond to are definitely *not* arbitrary. Animals are animals and furniture is furniture. But even on this point, anthropologists have found a surprising extension of the arbitrariness of language; different cultures carve up the physical world differently. One culture sees in a totem pole animals carved onto a column of wood; another sees a complex set of associations. What you see as a phone cord someone else sees as a laundry line.

Another linguistic dualism for Saussure is the difference between *langue* (language) and *parole* (speech). Language is the formal system of syntax and semantics that enables communication; speech is the ordinary practice of this system that individuals carry out. Saussure moved the emphasis in linguistic study toward language and away from speech. His work in attempting to uncover "deep structure" foreshadowed that of Noam Chomsky, who in the 1950s showed that our linguistic performance was predicated on the existence of a universal, innate grammatical structure.

Another important oppositional pair for Saussure was that linguistic elements fall into two distinct categories, corresponding to two complementary mental functions that are each necessary to process language. The first category arises out of our inability to simultaneously utter two words. Our speech, therefore, must necessarily be strung out in some sequential fashion. The resulting linear arrangement of words or phrases will then generate various combinations of relationships among them. These words or phrases then obtain their value in direct opposition to what was uttered before or after (or both). So if you say, "I climbed the steps," two such relationships, for example, are between "I" and "climbed," or between "I climbed" and "the steps." Saussure called such sequential relationships between linguistic elements *syntagmatic*.

The second group of relationships is complementary—in opposition to the syntagmatic category. Here, Saussure focused on associations between words that we make in our brains. These relations—now known as *paradigmatic*—are substitutional in nature. For example, instead of saying, "I climbed the steps," you might have said "I climbed the stairs" or "I descended the stairs" or "I climbed the Matterhorn."

One interesting consequence of this Saussurean dualism is that certain figures of speech that used to get lumped together are now seen to work in opposition to one another. Perhaps the most common figure of speech is the metaphor, which operates via the recognition of some aspect of similarity. "Her smile was sunshine itself." Metaphors, through the act of substitution, form paradigmatic relationships. There are two less well-known but nevertheless common figures of speech that, despite a superficial resemblance, act as polar opposites to the metaphor. These are *metonymy* and *synecdoche*. In metonymy, an attribute of an object or concept is named for another. For example, you might say, "I smoked some cancer sticks" instead of "I smoked some cigarettes." A synecdoche uses a part for the whole or the whole for a part. For example, "I've got wheels" means "I've got a car." Metonymy and synecdoche, because of the context generated by our perceptions of contiguity or juxtaposition, are syntagmatic, not paradigmatic, relationships. Below, I will describe an application of this theory to an actual physiological condition.

With respect to oppositions in general, after Saussure we have come to realize that language, in both its phonetic and semantic components, is a system of *differences*. Without differences, no phonetic or semantic segmentation can exist, and without that segmentation, we would not be able to represent either the variegated stimuli that the outside world presents to us or the multitude of conscious and unconscious thoughts that we generate from within. What we now call *structuralism* is a set of approaches to linguistics, anthropology, literary criticism, and sociology in which analyses of the signs that comprise human discourse are based on Saussure's methods of defining terms oppositionally.

Perhaps the most influential of the Saussurean dualisms was the breakdown of linguistic analysis into the *diachronic* and the *synchronic*. Diachronic analysis is the evolutionary, historical focus that scholars had always followed. Synchronic analysis unravels the structural properties of a given language at a certain point in time, entirely disregarding the historical influences.

The diachronic and synchronic axes of analysis are complementary. Each method provides a framework for examination that excludes the other. One field where this exclusion is particularly powerful is literary criticism. For example, using the diachronic approach, you take a literary work and immerse it in rich historicity. You consider the childhood circumstances of the author. You identify the orthodox and avant-garde artistic influences present at the time of publication. You point out political events, or psychological considerations. In short, you are searching for causal factors involved with the author's end product.

Although Saussure was more concerned with unearthing a structural model for a particular language at a particular time than undertaking a historical analysis, he recognized that the latter was still necessary. Still, pure structuralism would drop the diachronic component, and this approach became popular in literary criticism, beginning in France in the 1950s and 1960s. This general application of synchronic analysis rejects causal factors and isolates a creative work even from its creator. Analysis shifts from the quasi-objective to the purely subjective, where we would disregard even the author's own annotations!

At this extreme, the text itself is completely divested of historical context and even of authorship. It lives and breathes its own multiplicities of meaning. Each meaning is valid to the beholder, but like the skin of an onion, more layers can be uncovered if one peels them back. This is Roland Barthes's famous "death of the author," proclaimed in 1967. Theorist Jacques Derrida, labeled a "poststructuralist" or "deconstructionist," carried this view farther. Derrida attacked our very notions of meaning and reason. Meaning can reside only in relationships between signs, not in any inherent characteristics of signs or an underlying "reality." Reason itself is never certain. And oppositions are dissolved. As author Barbara Johnson (as quoted by Bell) has pointed out, deconstruction in general "'attempts to elaborate a discourse that says *neither* "either/or," *nor* "both/and" nor even "neither/nor," while at the same time not totally abandoning these logics either.'" We had already seen with Nietzsche that God (the creator) is dead. Structuralism's aftermath—deconstruction—first kills off the author-creator, and beyond this, reason itself. Clearly, such textual analysis is closely allied with cultural relativism, and radically extends the loss of the absolute.

Structuralism: Some *Real* Applications

Let's return to structuralism and discuss two different applications. The first is the validation of the syntagmatic–paradigmatic opposition by linguist Roman Jakobson in the 1950s. Studying aphasia, a speech disability due to brain disease or injury, Jakobson found that certain aphasic disorders could be divided into two categories, similarity disorders and contiguity disorders. Aphasics with the similarity disorder were restricted to the syntagmatic axis of expression. These patients had lost the ability to use, or understand, substitutive terms. For example, Jakobson wrote, "The sentence 'it rains' cannot be produced unless the utterer sees that it is actually raining." When such a patient "failed to recall the name for 'black' he described it as 'what you do for the dead.'" This deficiency binds one to literal descriptions.

For aphasics who suffered from the contiguity disorder, "the patient is confined to the substitution set . . . and his approximate identifications are of a metaphorical nature, contrary to the metonymic ones familiar to the opposite type of aphasics." These sufferers, stripped of the context that syntagmatic relationships yield, are limited to the paradigmatic axis. According to Jakobson, this contiguity disorder tends to give rise to rudimentary single-word utterances. It is fascinating that structural theory was found to have this physiological manifestation.

Structuralism also served to revolutionize anthropology, largely as a result of the work of Claude Lévi-Strauss, whose first of many books was published in 1948. One cornerstone of our activity as human beings is that we *classify*. Classification is necessary for carrying out decisions among choices, as we need a mechanism to generate distinctions as well as similarities among competing alternatives (objects, concepts, stimuli, and so on). And that we all classify is central to Lévi-Strauss's work.

Lévi-Strauss wrote in an era in which empiricism had grown to dominate the social as well as the natural sciences. Observation and experiment determined the boundaries of theory. In psychology, behaviorism dictated what we knew about the mind, and in Lévi-Strauss's own field of anthropology, it seemed as though in our social customs, exceptions to the rules became the rules. The vast storehouse of ethnographic data, in its variety and complexity, compelled one to accept cultural relativism. Therefore, universal absolutes regarding human customs and beliefs came to be regarded as indefensible. In this light, it was reactionary to some degree for Lévi-Strauss to develop an anthropological theory based on the invariance of innate, shared structures.

Lévi-Strauss draws his inspiration from Saussure in his emphasis on analyzing our customs and beliefs as abstract, but universal, relational systems (I use the present tense to underscore the synchronic and not the diachronic approach). He studies anthropological phenomena—kinship, totemism, myth—as linguistic systems. In his studies of *la pensée sauvage* (which critic Dan Sperber translates as "untamed thinking"), Lévi-Strauss advances the thesis, somewhat discredited at the time, that "primitive" peoples are capable of abstract thought and that, in fact, what we see in the oral folklore of such peoples is a type of synecdoche, the substitution of concrete forms for abstract notions. It may surprise us that so-called primitives transcend mere pragmatic interest in the objects of their environment, but the argument is that "untamed thinking" is much deeper than the merely practical. Lévi-Strauss establishes that universally, humans take an extraordinary interest in the variety present in their environment, and that this variety is classified in ways that are locally different but that globally are similarly structured.

In other words, not only do we all naturally and universally differentiate and classify our environment, but we also utilize an ability to conceptualize the resulting notions and their relationships on a higher level. That this fact was obscured for so long was a result of different cultures viewing the world through different cultural lenses. An interesting corollary here is the extension of this theory to our decision making: choice itself is laden with higher-level baggage. That is, the concrete choices and consequences we ponder also represent wider, more abstract categories; simple and uncomplicated dilemmas, then, may entail deeper conflicts.

It has been noted that Lévi-Strauss's thought took shape at the same time as the study of cybernetics and, more generally, information theory and computer science. These disciplines, of course, were based on the binary (0, 1) alphabet that most starkly exposes how communication is built on a system of oppositions. Sperber has described how some of Lévi-Strauss's early work was meant to contribute to the nascent "development of a unified science of communication based on semiotics, cybernetics, and information theory." Fifty years have now passed and very little progress has been made toward this goal.

Nevertheless, it would be well to examine an application of this binarism to anthropology. A nice example, mentioned above, is Lévi-Strauss's insight into the phenomenon of totemism. An enormous amount of effort had been expended by anthropologists to explain totemism, with incomplete and sometimes contradictory results. The main questions, in Lévi-Strauss's own words, are first, "why it is that mammals, birds, reptiles, and trees should be symbols of the relationships between spiritual power and the lineages," and second, "how may it be explained that social groups, or segments of society, should be distinguished from each other by the association of each with a particular natural species?" Most anthropologists had pieced together partial explanations based either on the idea that totemism was a prereligious practice, or that a group's totem was thought to be helpful to the group, or that there was an association between the totem and the group's ancestors, which led to taboos such as the prohibition of killing of that animal or plant.

Lévi-Strauss rejected such explanations. For him, the correct approach was to uncover *structure* as he did with the interpretation of myths, in which we represent the animal world in terms of social relations that mirror our own. This approach involved classifying the natural species "in pairs of opposites . . . on condition that the species chosen have in common at least one characteristic which permits them to be compared." He provides an example illustrating why (for a particular tribe) certain birds were selected to represent twins. The reasoning is thus: because of their special characteristic, twins are a manifestation of spiritual power. So they are "children of God." Since the sky is the "divine abode," twins may be considered to be "persons of the above." In this sense they are *opposed* to ordinary humans, who are "persons of below." Since birds are themselves (literally) "of the above," twins are therefore logically associated with birds. However, twins, despite their special nature, are still ordinary people, and therefore "of the below." The problem of which birds to associate with twins is solved when considering birds' diversity. In particular, some birds fly higher than others do. The appropriate birds, then, to use are "terrestrial" ones like guinea fowl.

Lévi-Strauss claimed that "this kind of inference is applicable not only to the particular relationships . . . but to every relationship postulated between human groups and animal species." So, we conceptualize the animal world through our social constructs in many subdivisions according to function, location, habitat, and so forth. Interestingly, Lévi-Strauss credited an earlier anthropologist, A. R. Radcliffe-Brown, with implicitly having hit upon the structuralist oppositional-pair mappings, at least in specific cases. But Radcliffe-Brown refused to believe in general that "it is the logic of oppositions and correlations, exclusions and inclusions, compatibilities and incompatibilities, which explains the laws of associations. . . ." By relying on the structural logic of relationships alone, Lévi-Strauss was able to dispense with the usual explanations by which the animals in totemism are "solely or principally creatures which are feared, admired, or envied. . . ."

Totemism and aphasia might strike you as obscure applications of linguistic and, more generally, structuralist theory. What about something closer to home? In fact, linguistic theory, and more generally, semiotics, enter our lives daily—most prominently through advertising. For example (speaking of cancer sticks), author David Lodge points out the Marlboro Man as an advertising metonym. The idea is that by purchasing the Marlboro cigarette, you take on the Marlboro Man's persona or lifestyle. Innumerable such images confront us constantly. Subtle or not, these ads communicate powerfully. In this vein, Umberto Eco writes that the clothes we wear provide us with an attitude. Of course, this goes equally well for haircuts, eyeglasses, and accessories, although things get confusing when people wear those "authentic" sports jerseys. In our commodified world such attitudes are easily obtained through frequent purchases. Having so many attitudes to choose from, we seem increasingly to be adopting a pluralistic style that embraces many attitudes at once. Incidentally, this pastiche threatens to become yet another inversion of choice, as the multiplicity of attitudes and styles merge into stylelessness.

There is a connection here with the blurring of reality. For example, British punks of the 1970s were tough, rebellious, working class youths, whereas American punks of the 1980s were more often than not suburban middle-class kids dressing up as punks, as if for Halloween. But, "punk" or not, they were taken to be punks, and—more to the point—they believed in it themselves.

Consider the Opposite: Turn Facts on Their Heads

We have seen the importance of polar oppositions in the development of structuralism and its relatives. Of course, my claim is that oppositions gained salience as choice evolved, and thus structuralism emerged. As we have seen, structuralism is not the only arena where oppositions, sometimes logical ones, have played a primary role. Let's look at a few other instances where oppositions change, and sometimes blur, our sense of reality.

One sophistication that our society is developing, as critical thinking in general becomes more emphasized and more public, is listening to what is not said, or, to put it differently, examining the *complement* of the information presented to us. Sometimes, turning communication on its head introduces problematic ambiguity; sometimes it provides fresh clarity.

A couple of travel recollections illustrate the ambiguity I refer to. In various places at home and around the world, security concerns prompt the appearance of armed policemen and sometimes soldiers. Generally, in most of the West, security personnel are deployed discreetly, and are not visible beyond a certain minimal level. But if you travel to some other countries, *wham*—there are armed soldiers swarming all over the place, with submachine guns at the ready. A simple dilemma is unavoidable: do you feel safer, on account of the copious omnipresence of armed protectors, or do you feel more threatened for exactly the same reason?

Similar ambiguity is found in other settings. Several years ago my wife and I visited the town of U. in a semideveloped country. On arriving at about 8 A.M. on a soon-to-be-blazing morning, we noticed an insecticide cloud (what else could it be?) billowing through the streets. Shortly, a noisy truck swung into view, continuing on its spray circuit. Immediately we both had the same sinking thought—that there must be an acute bug problem in this place. The enthusiastic man at the information office, although admitting that the thick cloud was indeed fly-control spray, gave (of course) the opposite spin: U. was an extremely clean town. As you could guess, Bryony and I remained skeptical. Over the course of the next few days, however, we came to accept the dual truths: that U. was a very tidy town, but, nevertheless, had a serious fly problem.

If you wait for more information, sometimes the ambiguity is lifted. During spring finals week of my sophomore year in college, my roommate Mark took in a stray, untrained puppy. Having already had enough stress from the exams, I didn't need any more from the introduction of "Jessica" into my life. Since I felt sure this dog would befoul my belongings, I made Mark keep her in the foyer. One afternoon Mark brought Jessica in from outdoors; she bounded onto my bed, and I immediately chased her off. Mark assured me that Jessica would not soil my bed—"she's already gone eight times today." As you could guess, I figured that the odds were pretty good that she wasn't done yet. Well, after I chased her away she bounded into the next room, where the door was ajar. A moment later, Jessica had bestowed her latest gift on Jim's comforter.

Sometimes you have to seek out the other information, instead of waiting for it. You remind yourself to read the fine print. Sometimes there is none.

Maybe you're out to purchase a car, rent a vacation home, or buy a certain electronic gadget. Some features that you would find desirable simply may not be present. And the salesperson is not going to point out, "there's no air conditioning." For this you need some savvy, perhaps some experience. Other situations are quantifiable, but statistics blur the real facts. A university may boast of 16,000 applications for 2,000 seats in its freshman class. This sounds like a one-in-eight chance to get in—very selective—but the real story could be that 10,000 (more than half) of the applicants are accepted, and only one in five of those accepted choose to attend. Or perhaps you're worried about errors, but you're told about quality. One product is 99 percent reliable; a different product, 99.5 percent reliable. Not much difference? One product is twice as likely as the other one to go wrong! Same thing with fat-free percentages. Looking at what you're not told can certainly be revealing.

Is There *One* Quality?

Quality is certainly a term for our times. Its manifestations, and our perceptions, have created various shifts in the global economy over the past twenty-five years. Quality is now a cornerstone of most successful manufacturing and service companies. But "quality" is sometimes hard to pin down, and its transcendence has been discussed in two books by Robert M. Pirsig: *Zen and the Art of Motorcycle Maintenance* and *Lila*.

What *Zen* primarily addresses are various dualisms in Western thought, many of which date back to the ancient Greeks. These dualisms, which include mind versus matter, subjective versus objective, substantive versus methodological, empirical versus rational, and substance versus form, for Pirsig provided unsatisfactory ways of partitioning the world in order to explain it or establish an approach to explain it. His solution was effectively to establish an undefinable, monistic reality called Quality. Mind and matter derive from Quality. Indeed, Quality is not just part of reality, "it was the whole thing." It inhered in everything, but remained mysterious. Conceptualized in the right way, quality branched out into certain categories that formed a "true" basis of reality. Quality consisted of the union of "romantic quality," also referred to as "pre-intellectual reality," and "classic quality," also known as "intellectual reality." The latter, in turn, breaks down into the more familiar "subjective reality" (or mind) and "objective reality" (or matter). Thinking about Quality the right way unifies religion, art, and science. Ultimately, Quality is essentially the tao of Lao Tzu, the dharma of the Hindus, the virtue of the Greeks—in short, the omnipresence that unites Eastern and Western thought.

After some years, Pirsig, bothered by the undefined nature of Quality, attempted in *Lila* to elucidate it. A character criticizes the undefined Quality from *Zen,* pointing out that a quality present in all of us is no quality at all. Such a lowest common denominator became an excuse for lowlifes to be above the law, and have their behavior absolved. This is the inversion that we have discussed, where an absolute, through its infinite manifestations, is watered down to virtually nothing. A monism becomes an anythingism.

Lest Quality be appropriated by criminals (and to answer the criticism more generally), Pirsig tries to establish that Quality is, at bottom, morality. He develops a "Metaphysics of Quality" (MOQ) that interprets our world better than "subject–object metaphysics" because it is more inclusive. Through MOQ, the values of morality, religion, and art are empirically verifiable. When the challenge of trying to locate such values is cited, Pirsig notes that our usual procedure of describing them in terms of substances fails, but that with MOQ, we see that concrete substances emanate from value and not the other way around.

At this point, there is a need for specificity. The main tool for Pirsig is an improvement on his prior division of Quality into romantic and classic; he now has hit upon static quality versus Dynamic Quality. (We note that despite Pirsig's attempt to rid us of our nasty dualisms, he needs to invent others in their place.) Like mathematical models whose simplifying assumptions only approximate the workings of the world they are meant to explain, philosophical models suffer the same fate. Without a substructure, Quality has (somewhat literally) no legs to stand on if we want to take it seriously as a correct version of reality. So, the key substructure is the polarization of Quality into static and Dynamic. The capitalization indicates an asymmetry of value.

Dynamic Quality "is the pre-intellectual cutting edge of reality, the source of all things, completely simple and always new." This is what you recognize the first few times you hear a great song; thereafter, the tune lapses into static quality, when the song thrills you no longer but you could still recommend it to a friend. In addition, "Dynamic Quality is not structured and yet it is not chaotic." Now Pirsig must demonstrate that his dual axes will stand up to various philosophical riddles. One example is our recurrent theme of free will versus determinism. For Pirsig there is a simple solution: one component of our behavior is deterministic, which corresponds to static quality; the other component is free, corresponding to Dynamic Quality. A scientific example is evolution. Evolution is an upward-spiraling process that continually tests the adaptability of new forms. It is a process loose enough to transcend rigidity but not loose enough to be chaotic. Therefore it falls squarely under the umbrella of Dynamic Quality.

At this point Pirsig lacks an adequate structure to model various phenomena, including those of cultural history, so he introduces a hierarchy itself based on the principle of evolution. Intellectual quality dominates social quality, which in turn dominates biological quality, which lastly, dominates the inorganic. For Pirsig, our societal order was for the first time essentially intellectual only after the end of World War I. Only in the 1920s did Victorian social mores cease to be dominant. Pirsig sees twentieth-century social turmoil as an example of conflicts between different layers and dimensions of Quality. The "hippie revolution" he sees as a moral movement directed "against both society *and* intellectuality." This revolution was difficult to understand, he claims, because its dynamism lay outside of "'understanding' itself," that is, static intellect. In attempting to transcend both society and intellect, though, the hippies who rejected social and intellectual norms had two options: to head toward biological quality or to Dynamic Quality. And, when "biological quality and Dynamic Quality are confused the result . . . [is] an extremely destructive form of degeneracy of the sort seen in the Manson murders, the Jonestown madness, and the increase of crime and drug addiction throughout the country."

We need to address Pirsig's Metaphysics of Quality because it is a serious attempt to model, macroscopically, the course of social history—more, in fact, reality itself—not only in the twentieth century but also before and after it. However, there are numerous flaws. Everything that seems to be explained by the theory undergoes some amount of simplification. For example, free will versus determinism is *not* solved. Embedding the problem in terms of the static versus dynamic axes only provides a linguistic overlay. Or consider the Dynamic Quality that comes through in the first few encounters with a great song. This Quality soon lapses into static quality. But what about ten or twenty years later? We hear the same tune (on an oldies radio station) and—nostalgia or not—it is great again, though perhaps not quite as fresh as that first time. What has happened? Did we rediscover Dynamic Quality statically? This would seem to violate the theory. Did the static quality itself simply dwindle away? Very doubtful. We still know the words, the melody, the drumbeats.

Turn to the 1920s. Pirsig puts a great deal of emphasis on the way 1920s intellectuals embraced sex as a vehicle to reject Victorian domination of society. Some of the impetus toward freer sex came from cultural relativism, for example the anthropological studies by Ruth Benedict and Margaret Mead. But Western society had gone through such a stage before: the discovery of the "noble savage" in the 1700s, which had far deeper social, political, and economic consequences. And, compared to the tidal wave of counterculture in the 1960s, the 1920s was a mere hors d'oeuvre.

Most of all, though, my objection is that Quality itself, still undefinable despite the structures and hierarchies invoked to model our social development, is a deus ex machina, a red herring. Quality is posited to have an underlying absolute value, but there is no convincing case for this. It is as remote as ever. Quality's only explicatory usefulness comes through when it is mapped onto a structure and a hierarchy that by themselves cannot cover all of the complexities of our sociocultural ascent. Ultimately Quality gives us neither value nor substance. What *is* powerful—as a guide, a heuristic—is Pirsig's opposition of static and dynamic, and the hierarchy, replete with its own conflicts, from inorganic to intellectual.

Schrödinger's Cat and Its Ordinary Psychology

I would like to close out this chapter on oppositions by studying another celebrated paradox of physics, "Schrödinger's Cat." This cat is interesting not only in its bizarre physical theory—which has been discussed extensively—but also in a psychological application.

"Schrödinger's Cat" is another apparent paradox in quantum theory that nicely expresses a discomfort contingent on choice. Like everyone else, physicists like to have their cake and eat it too, and the particle–wave nature of light (indeed of all matter–energy) and the collapse of the wave function are not the only controversial dichotomies with which they entertain themselves. "Schrödinger's Cat" is a thought experiment ("not tested on real animals") devised by the physicist who came up with the idea of the wave function in 1926. We can briefly summarize it as follows. There is a box with an ordinary, live, and healthy cat in it. In this box is some sort of quick-acting death agent, say, a poisonous gas, which is to be released if and only if a certain switch inside the box is activated. But this switch is activated by (and only by) a particular quantum event: the radioactive decay of a single unstable particle.

Now let's say the box is soundproof, and that you can't see into it or shake it or do anything else to determine the cat's condition. What about the radioactive decay? These particles pop off at random unpredictable moments. Statistically, though, their behavior is well-known. Physicists know the *likelihood* that a particle will decay during a certain interval of time. Suppose you stick this poor cat in the box at lunchtime, and later, at around two o'clock, you are informed by the resident physicist (Schrödinger's Ghost, if you like) that the odds are now exactly fifty–fifty that the particle has decayed. In other words, because of the poison gas, the odds are fifty–fifty that the cat has died.

The paradox is that the usual interpretations of quantum theory tell us, incredibly, that the cat itself must be half alive and half dead. The reason is that quantum theory states there is a "wave" representing the decayed particle and a "wave" for the undecayed one. The decay has a 50 percent probability, and the "wave function" for the particle is given by the superposition of the two alternatives, both equally likely. Max Born's universally accepted interpretation of the wave function—in the absence of an observation—is in this case probabilistic: the event half happened and half didn't. And this literally means that the state of the particle is: decayed with probability 1/2, and not decayed with probability 1/2. (This does *not* mean it's half gone.) Since the cat is alive if and only if the particle has not decayed, it seems that we have to conclude that the cat is both alive *and* dead. So this thought-experiment cat, which everyone knows is *either* alive *or* dead (but not both), is predicted by quantum theory, in some sort of literal way, as *both*.

Schrödinger, of course, did not want to accept this consequence and he avoided it by excluding macroscopic objects from the domain of quantum theory. Thus he hoped to save his wave equation from silly misinterpretation. But what about an extended domino effect from particle to atom to molecule and so on?

This cat bothers physicists even more than it bothers us; after all, it's not *our* theory. Physicist Stephen Hawking has said, "when I hear of Schrödinger's Cat, I reach for my gun." Hawking's parody (or not) aside, it is frustrating that quantum theory, which has served humankind for seventy-five years now, providing a wonderfully accurate model of our world, seems to indicate that reality need not choose between one state and another. Reality is some of both, even when, as for the cat, it *cannot* be. When physicists speak of nonobjectivity for subatomic particles it is disturbing, but is something we can overlook; not so for a furry pet.

Of course, some commentators have tried to wriggle out of the paradox. Heinz Pagels analyzed the cat-in-the-box-plus-observer as an *information system,* and concluded that we need not accept "quantum weirdness" for the cat the way we would for subatomic particles. But his argument hinges on the irreversibility of the cat's death; if we substituted "asleep" for "dead," his argument fails. Eugene Wigner tried to modify the Schrödinger equation in its application to sentient beings, but this seems too artificial. Everett's many-worlds theory of chapter 4 would have one world with a dead cat and another with a live one (both replete with all the necessary consequences, such as the observer's reaction). Gell-Mann sidesteps the whole issue by denying even the (physical) possibility of the thought experiment. He notes that in either scenario, the box would *have* to react in some way with the outside world, thereby eliminating any mutual interference that would yield the wave superposition and the resulting paradox. That is, Gell-Mann claims that because the live- and dead-cat scenarios "decohere" (meaning they are mutually exclusive), there is no difference between Schrödinger's Cat and a cat that has been in a box on a long plane trip, perhaps alive and perhaps not. In other words, for the cat—a "real quasi-classical object"—we can't use the "smeared-out" quantum probabilities to say that it is both dead and alive, or anything similarly weird. Although Gell-Mann's point is well-taken, it is still interesting that physicists are so divided when they themselves popularized the weird interpretation. (In addition, we must remember that Gell-Mann bases his model on Everett's, which postulates its own weirdness.) Finally, mathematical physicist Roger Penrose suggests that applying quantum theory to macroscopic entities like cats and cricket balls is simply *wrong*—and therefore quantum theory in its correspondence to the real (macroscopic) world is *incomplete.*

As described thus far, Schrödinger's Cat is a technical paradox that annoys physicists but does not seem to otherwise impact our lives. This view is surprisingly off the mark. To be more precise, the *ideas* behind the cat paradox, at the confluence of how we think about logic and probability, often seep into our daily lives.

For example, suppose a heinous act (e.g., murder or rape) has been committed by someone with whom you work. The perpetrator's identity is unknown, but suppose you are aware that it is either person A or person B (and not both). You see both of these individuals frequently, passing and greeting them in the hallways. Now, one of them is entirely innocent and the other is entirely guilty, but which one? As you pass them in the hall, you cannot help associating the dreadful act with *both* of them. Not that both are partly responsible—but with *each* person, you cannot stop wondering, you cannot resist assigning a *positive probability* (maybe not 50 percent, but certainly not zero) of guilt. Although you remind yourself that each person should be considered innocent until proven guilty, you nevertheless feel some revulsion for both. You cannot deal normally with either of them. You still greet each one in the hall, but you are uneasy. You look at each of them differently than you used to. You are surely biased, and realize its unfairness. Perhaps you look away when either one approaches and feel guilty about your awkwardness. You try to evaluate which person did it; you try to analyze them, you try to decide for yourself who is guilty, but the fact that either one could be capable of such a crime is incomprehensible to you.

This cat is not so easy to shake off.

Schrödinger's Cat provides a wonderful example of blurred oppositions, both physical and psychological. The blurred, or "smeared-out," quantum probabilities are transferred onto the macroscopic cat. It makes no sense but we don't know where our error is. In the psychological scenario, however, the crime's uncertainty *does* apply to both suspects, and the fifty–fifty quantum indeterminacy is not a silly model at all for our puzzlement and uneasiness. What the scenarios do share is the question of absolute truth and the blurring of objectivity in the attempt to decide the cat's state or the culprit's identity. In the next chapter I would like to address that question of deciding for oneself in a blurred world where absolutes have receded, freeing decision makers to choose their paths.

One recurrent theme for us has been the debate between free will and determinism. One aspect of this debate is purely philosophical, but there are practical dimensions to consider as well. For example, our ability to produce, transmit, and store information is advancing at a phenomenal rate, but at the same time we are becoming ever more beholden to its technology. This clash between empowerment by technology and imprisonment in its vicious spiral is a variant of the opposition of free will and determinism. As this dualism will continue to appear, and since choice itself seems to be dependent on a foundation of freedom, it is worthwhile to discuss the origins of freedom as a Western concept. Here I will draw heavily from sociologist Orlando Patterson's *Freedom*.

Are There Different Freedoms?

For Patterson, freedom is the loftiest of our values. And surprisingly, he tells us, "most human languages did not even possess a word for the concept before contact with the West." Most of us think of the American and French Revolutions, and the aforementioned liberal notions that date back to the philosopher John Locke when we think of freedom's origins. But contrary to this popular belief, the concept of freedom has long been important in the West. It dates back to the fifth and sixth centuries B.C.E.—and it derives from the experience of slavery. Ultimately, although freedom's roots took hold in Greece, it grew with Rome. Rome, in dominating the Western world, redeveloped large-scale slavery and refashioned Christianity into a religion (the only religion) "that placed freedom—spiritual freedom, redemption—at the very center of its theology."

Patterson breaks freedom down into three components. First, consistent with Mill, is "personal freedom," which allows you to do what you like without being constrained by others and yet not impinging on others' abilities to act similarly. Second, is a dictator's freedom. "Sovereignal freedom" is unconstrained, where you can do what you like regardless of others' desires. Third, is "civic freedom," which recalls Athenian democracy; it is the ability of responsible individuals to participate in community life and governance.

In general, individual freedom as a concept was untenable and, therefore, moot. No one in ancient times was free in the sense of the ability to live independently. But from the seventh to the fourth centuries B.C.E. in Athens, important transformations occurred. One was economic, in which new industries developed, largely supported by slave labor. The others were intellectual: the advent of democracy; the flowering of rational philosophical thought; and, Patterson says, the "social construction of freedom as a central value."

Prior to this, in Homeric Greece, men generally were not enslaved. Women, however, were (in war, for example, the defeated men were killed but the women enslaved), rendering freedom a concept initially more relevant for them. But, gradually, the male slave population grew. The Persian wars (c. 480 B.C.E.) spread newfound fears of possible enslavement throughout the male population. They also contributed to Greek unity and a sense of desire for liberation and freedom, including the freedom that was a Greek but not a Persian value. The Greeks were fighting for freedom, both positively as a concept to maintain, and negatively to avoid being enslaved.

As the slave population grew, so did the institution of democracy—which excluded both women and slaves. Eventually, roughly one-third of the total population were slaves, and one-sixth metics (an intermediate class between slaves and citizens), so democracy was certainly restricted to a minority of the population. But democracy notwithstanding, even middle- and upper-class Athenian women were *more* confined to the household than they formerly were. Furthermore, according to Patterson, "women had almost no freedom of choice in selecting their husbands, and while they could, in theory, initiate divorce proceedings, this was rare." And, incredibly, "men who violently raped women were punished less severely than those who seduced them, since the latter case entailed the corruption of the woman into a person who dared to exercise her freedom of choice." It is interesting to add that this period was the golden age of Greek tragedy, and in these tragedies (written by men, for men), women were strong, central characters.

This fledgling democracy left much to be desired, but it did reflect a growing sense of civic freedom, which lasted until Rome's conquest of Greece. When the Greeks' civic freedom disappeared, however, they maintained not only their personal freedom, but also a spiritual freedom that came from within. For Patterson, this inner freedom is exemplified by Prometheus in Aeschylus' play *Prometheus Bound*. When comparing his chained doom to Hermes' "lackey" situation (Hermes being Zeus's loyal, trusted messenger), Prometheus exclaims, "'Be sure of this, when I set my misfortune against your slavery, I would not change.'"

Other discussions by Greek philosophers on personal and political ramifications of freedom remain fresh today. Plato's *Gorgias* provided a platform for endless debate. In it, Callicles, a student of Gorgias, sees democracy as quashing the natural order. We find echoes of this character not only in various Sophists but also in Nietzsche and the writer Ayn Rand. These ideas, repeated by conservative intellectuals today, are close to the notion of sovereignal freedom, which has its roots in associating freedom with power and superiority. This notion is brought to perfection by Tom Wolfe's phrase "Master of the Universe" (to describe a rich Wall Street trader). Many people who are wealthy or otherwise powerful (through managing subordinates and sizable budgets) come to believe they deserve to be rich or powerful. Similar to the principle of social Darwinism, life is just for Masters of the Universe because they think they truly *are* superior. For Plato water finds its own level in that rulers rule, soldiers fight, and so on. Although Plato rejected democratic rule, finding Athens to have a "reckless excess of liberty," he repudiated extremely monarchical states as well, because they excessively curtailed liberty.

Other thinkers set down additional ideas for us to revisit. Diogenes gave an early version of the vicious spiral in showing us that a master, by taking a slave, institutes his own enslavement by becoming dependent on the slave. Epicurus preceded Jeremy Bentham's nineteenth-century utilitarianism by noting that some pleasures are not worthwhile, and, moreover, it may be advantageous to endure short-term suffering for long-term benefits, as found through a sort of cost-benefit analysis. Epicurus's pleasure-seeking philosophy (as we commonly understand it) was based on freedom; he rejected determinism through various arguments.

Eventually came Roman rule, with Roman emperors. Without democracy (which failed for other reasons) it is easy to imagine how a Roman emperor could embody sovereignal freedom. And some tried to, like Nero. Interestingly, Patterson relates that Seneca, in a letter to his former pupil, wrote that the emperor who exhibits the highest form of freedom is the one who enables the freedom of the masses. This sovereignal freedom would therefore entail moral responsibility through social design. Perhaps Nero may have taken Seneca's words to heart and deliberately aimed to find a greater freedom than that championed by his old tutor. But in this Nero was at the mercy of his base impulses, and therefore not wholly free.

A later emperor, Marcus Aurelius (d. 180 C.E.), fell prey to an ironic inversion in which his empire and its people constituted a bondage from which he could never escape. Marcus was thoughtful enough to be considered as a philosopher. Constantly torn between his duties and his personal freedom, he postponed his own redemption, as he saw himself the protector of his subjects. Yet Marcus yearned for true freedom, that sought later by the existentialists. He strove to "'perform every action as if it was the last of your life'" but was completely unable to do so. Marcus's stoicism and rationality *prevented* him from breaking through to freedom. What he needed was *faith*— which would help bring about *spiritual* freedom. This, of course, was what Christianity provided.

Christianity was well developed by Marcus's reign. To obtain the ultimate good—salvation (as important then as now)—Jesus gave the message to give ourselves completely to God, who in turn commands us to *love*. No freedom there. So how did Christianity acquire freedom as a central dogma? The Gnostic view was that Jesus liberated us from our state of ignorance. He enlightened us, showing us that the undiscovered self was one with God. But this conviction lost out to the Pauline one, which, according to Patterson, best "related the religious expression of freedom . . . to the actual experience of freedom as the release from slavery." Here, Christianity brings us out of spiritual slavery; what it provides is spiritual freedom. This freedom "is the essence of being in Christ."

As stated, the spread of such a Christianity is problematic, but Patterson argues that powerful forces enabled its wide dissemination. One was the likening of Christ to an emperor. Another was that Paul's theology utilized secular notions. And in Romans, Paul transitioned from the personal freedom that he had previously emphasized to a sovereignal freedom that we entrust to God. Later on, with the crumbling of the Roman Empire and loss of an earthly model of sovereignal freedom, Augustine, like the disillusioned freedman, could move around and make choices, but found freedom to be something we cannot grasp on our own. We need the city of God.

For Patterson, freedom has been singularly important: it is the force that is responsible both for the remarkable creativity of Western culture as well as its ascendancy over other cultures. This somewhat "end of history" view is certainly arguable, as is his assertion that nearly all peoples cherish the ideal of personal freedom, regardless of their political structures. To be fair, he notes that the concept of personal freedom has been repeatedly criticized, and, further, that freedom's pursuit has at times been disastrous, resulting in selfish and dehumanizing behavior.

A final gem is the discussion of the symbol "Y" that denoted *choice* among the Pythagoreans—the fork in the road—as observed by Werner Jaeger. Remarkably, Patterson writes, "Less obviously . . . we see the permanent horror of constraint; in the image of the wooden cross—the vertical crossroad, the Pythagorean 'Y'—we see the ultimate veneration of choice. Whether we chose to believe this or not, it is this strange, terrifying vision, at once mortal and divine, that has fashioned the culture and genius of the West." Whether the cross symbolizes an emphasis on choice is debatable, and in any event I have already argued that choice as an everyday phenomenon is fairly recent. Nevertheless, this is an apt way for us to conclude a work meant to explain freedom's rise from origins in slavery.

We saw that Nero may have attempted to transcend the evidently limited freedom that Seneca recommended to him. Marcus Aurelius had the opposite problem; loyalty to his subjects presented a constraint that he could not elude. Christianity asks us to subordinate our earthly freedoms to the sovereignal freedom of God and thereby, paradoxically, gain a greater freedom than we would otherwise have. Clearly, the notion of freedom encapsulates that of constraint; that is, freedom has to transcend itself by the inclusion of its negation. There are two aspects to this. One is to be able to avoid the false freedom of uncontrollably giving in to impulses (think of addiction). The other is this: although we desire freedom to choose—this is empowerment—we also want to be divested of the burden of choice. This conflict certainly adds to our angst, which is why so many of us just collapse and let inertia take over. Perhaps we let others choose for us; in general, we *opt out*. So freedom is freedom *to* choose and freedom *from* choice. When we do surrender our freedom to others, Erich Fromm has shown that this relinquishing of choice can have deleterious effects in the political as well as the personal sphere—leading, for example, to the rise of totalitarianism.

As for those who grasp for, or who at least accept, free choice and its burden and responsibility, only the Nietzschean superman can always, relentlessly, truly take the reins. Others among us pretend to take charge. We act, but simply by going through the motions. We deceive ourselves, we choose without our hearts or minds; we are not engaged in the process. Our action is a limp hand-shake; it lacks passion and commitment, and deep down we know that we are not comfortable with our choice. We have selected for the sake of selection, primarily to convince ourselves and others that we have not opted out, and secondarily to get the process over with.

Just What Is Existentialism?

In chapter 7 we examined a science of decision that has developed over the past fifty years. On the humanistic side, if there has been a philosophy or mode of thought that has focused on decisions, it has been existentialism.

Existentialism, once a fashionable signifier, has been largely ill-defined and therefore misunderstood. A great many philosophers and writers with little in common have been placed together in the existentialist camp. Worse, "existentialist" has for many conjured up "nihilist," "atheist," and "Marxist," among others. To be an existentialist you have to be a revolutionary beret-sporting café habitué, cigarette dangling from your lips, with neither ties nor morals.

Philosophically speaking, the term "existentialism" stands in opposition to "essentialism." One's essence would be an immutable core, the something that makes a thing what it is. Existence, though, is contingent on variable material properties. Existence is allied to matter whereas essence is related to form, and traditionally Western philosophy from Plato onward has concerned itself first with essence. For example, René Descartes's *"cogito, ergo sum"* ("I think, therefore I am") shows that only through the acknowledgment of our essence, mental activity, can we infer some sort of existence. Existentialism, though, rejects the primacy of immutable forms and focuses on our situation in the world and the necessity to take action—the necessity to make a decision. Additionally, existentialism can be seen to promote the subjective at the expense of the objective.

The first author who is identified as an existentialist is Søren Kierkegaard who in the 1840s turned our attention to man as a decision maker, one who must choose. He presents to us the human condition—perhaps the prototypical human condition—in Abraham's predicament of deciding whether to sacrifice his son Isaac for God. Kierkegaard confirms Abraham, who acted in faith, as the first existentialist. In this view, Kierkegaard meant to overthrow pure philosophy as a foundation for our actions: "Philosophy cannot and should not give faith." Kierkegaard focused on the individual acting alone, making a decision, and thereby forging into the unknown void. This decision was transrational; as he put it, "The instant of decision is madness."

Unfortunately, Kierkegaard's rejection of reason and his shift to the subjective invoked unbearable responsibility. The "dizziness of feelings" he experienced facing the world led him to despair, which turned on him with dilemma's horns, "in Despair at Not Willing to be Oneself; in Despair at Willing to be Oneself" (this from the aptly named *The Sickness unto Death*). The only way to cope, it seemed, was to turn to faith, "the paradox of life and reason," faith in the absurd, faith in Abraham's God.

Forty years later Nietzsche threw off the shackles of the (or "an") Almighty. It was a very different world from Kierkegaard's. The Industrial Revolution had accelerated, empowering people technologically and providing them with increasing control over the elements. The physicist James Clerk Maxwell had largely demystified the workings of electricity and magnetism. Many thousands of miles of rail and cable had been laid; trains shrank the world and cable (and soon, widespread telephone service) gave us virtual *telepathy*, or so it must have seemed. Karl Marx had claimed that religion was a mere construct we devised to combat alienation. So perhaps it was easier, or at least more natural, for Nietzsche to proclaim "God is dead," which of course left it up to us to invent, and to choose, our own values.

In stripping God from us, Nietzsche required that we morally be able to pull ourselves up from our bootstraps. This meant that, as individuals, we would have to shed the "slave morality" that is so pervasive in our society, underpinning, for example, Christianity. Such a morality is false and hypocritical. As for faith: "'faith' means not *wanting* to know what is true." Diminishing the slave morality would require developing a "master morality" based on self-affirmation, the Dionysian ethic that "says Yes to life," as commentator Walter Kaufmann puts it, "with love and laughter." And gaining this would require possibly a superhuman effort. Indeed, Nietzsche has wrongfully been given a bad name by both his "will to power" and "superman" having been associated with the Nazis and other evils. But unlike Kierkegaard, his focus remained on the macroscopic issues of morality, and away from the microscopic—where the conscious individual confronts the dread of decision.

Exploring the microscopic would involve a preoccupation with consciousness and psychology. In the 1890s a revolution would take place in psychology, led by Sigmund Freud. But more thematic for us is the elevation, within philosophy, of psychological processes such as consciousness and intent to the highest priority. The program of phenomenology as championed by Edmund Husserl in the early twentieth century gave these subjective phenomena an essence. If mere thought, and objects of thought, were considered to have this primacy, the next step would be an inquiry into the relationship between consciousness and being itself. This next step was the existential philosophy of Martin Heidegger. Heidegger never got around to resolving just what the ultimate nature of being is, but he did set down an analysis of the Being we can grasp most easily: human existence. This existence is very special: "Man alone exists. Rocks are, but they do not exist." What sense can be made of this? Our existence is, for Heidegger, the *Dasein* ("being there"). On this point, it is worth recalling the bewildered, literally engaged-in-the-world Peter Sellers in the film *Being There*. The Sellers character—a mentally handicapped man— charms us with fresh "insights," like noticing that an elevator is a very small room. His comments on tending gardens are taken by Washington sophisticates as brilliant metaphors for our complex world. We are amused by his direct naiveté because it reminds us how to look at the world in a very simple way. In fact, most of us need to be reminded of our primitiveness. We do seem to take it on naturally in new situations, for example, when we travel. The near-caricaturish postures of tourists are well-known and universal. When we remove ourselves to unfamiliar surroundings, we delight in *engaging*. We open our eyes (and our mouths) widely, we crane our necks, we grow young. We invite bewilderment (although only up to a point; exhausted by the effort, we too often give in to eating at a McDonald's or staying at a sterile chain hotel).

But it is not only travel that gets us in touch with our world and the mystery of why we are *here now*. All of us on occasion are given over to wonderment over our arbitrary, I-didn't-ask-to-be-born, what-do-I-do-now placement in the world.

Thus far, Heidegger does not give us a usable philosophical framework. Let's go further. We are not merely *placed* in the world. Our existence is finite. We are free. Free to make *choices*, although we realize that our boundedness spurs us to make these choices count. To do this, we have to consider our personal and unique relationship and discourse with the larger world. In carrying out our lives, we can trivialize this relationship by either going through the motions or conforming socially. That is, we can live *inauthentically*. Or, we can take care as to how we confront our choices in relating to the world. We can strive for understanding and create our own opinions and solutions; that is, we can live *authentically*. (There is a definite echo here of the Nietzschean superman.) To live authentically is to make oneself vulnerable, to accept the *angst* that permeates us. In our acceptance of inevitable death, in the suffusion of our being with nothingness, our actions, which allow us to take our fate into our own hands as individuals, are what enable us to transcend the void and create a life worth living. Few, if any, of us possess this Nietzschean spirit that surpasses the ordinary, hypocritical morality of the masses.

Whether this sounds good is up to you. To professional philosophers, who pick apart every word and dissect every argument, Heidegger's logic is usually upside-down and backward. They ask, "why is freedom a given?" "How does this *Dasein* relate to other things exactly?" and so forth. On these points Heidegger and others renounce logic. If his writings defy logic, then "so much the worse for logic." Heidegger suffers from two other problems. One stems from pro-Nazi remarks that he gave upon becoming the Rektor of the University of Freiburg in 1933. The main problem, though, plain and simple, is that he's generally incomprehensible.

Abstruse though he may be, Heidegger was one of a growing camp of authors who called out in protest against the rational methodology of traditional philosophy. Enough of proceeding by splitting hairs, arguing over abstract categories. This has not answered any of the "big questions"—which indeed have to do with human beings grappling with a complex world. Let's turn our attention to the human condition. If we forsake logic—at times—we are at least on the right track.

Accepting this plea involves something of a paradigm shift, and perhaps the best mottoes for this revolution come from the philosopher Miguel de Unamuno, who claimed that "the primary reality is not that I think, but that I live," and further stood Descartes on his head by declaring, *"sum, ergo cogito"* ("I am, therefore I think"). In this he accepts our pure existence as the fundamental truth. Unamuno shifts his emphasis away from rational thought to *feeling*, and acknowledges that for many of us, "the real, the really real, is irrational, that reason builds upon irrationalities."

Sartre Shows Us Hell, Then Goes on a Date

When writers seize on faith and passion, and dispense with logic and rationality, they cease to be philosophers (well, "real" philosophers). And if existentialism had ended here, it would have languished in obscurity and perhaps never quite become a movement, let alone have any impact. Some of the ideas we've sketched needed more development. And rigor. And a *lifestyle* that people could admire, even emulate. At just the right time, someone came along with the necessary goods: Jean-Paul Sartre.

Sartre was almost unique in being able to combine an oeuvre of serious philosophical work with an ensemble of other, more popular, writings, all the while maintaining a romantic and rebellious lifestyle. His work in the Resistance, his ties to Marxism, his café writing, and his many affairs (despite his relationship with feminist author Simone de Beauvoir) personified, for many, the excitement of the Left Bank.

Like Heidegger, Sartre began with exploring the concept of *Being*. This he bifurcates into separate components: one is Being-in-itself, the ordinary nonconscious existence of tables and chairs; the other is Being-for-itself, that is, *our* being, our consciousness. Again we are seen to be unlimited in our freedom in how we navigate ourselves through life.

But Sartre offers us more. He concentrates on our placement in a series of *situations,* in which we need to choose, to act. For example, the character Garcin in *No Exit* arrives in Hell expecting the worst of tortures, but finds instead that he is one of three people in an ordinary room. It's not long before all three get on each others' nerves, and they soon realize that each acts as a torturer for the other two. Garcin, unable to bear the situation any longer, leaps up to beat on the door. He'll endure "anything . . . red-hot tongs, molten lead and racks," in place of the room. Suddenly the locked door opens, offering Garcin a ticket into the void. But he stays, refusing to take the chance he so desired.

For Sartre, our reality is to choose our actions in such situations. But at a higher level, through these choices we *choose ourselves;* in fact, "for human reality, to be is to *choose oneself.*" Choosing on a small scale is hard enough, but now Sartre requires us to see these choices as part of a more orchestrated, cosmic picture. Like Nietzsche and Heidegger, Sartre realized that most of us, like Garcin, are not up to this task. We back away from the responsibilities entailed in making choices. This recoil is what we have referred to previously as *mauvaise foi,* literally "bad faith" but more accurately, according to Kaufmann, "self-deception." Translator Hazel Barnes writes, "Through bad faith a person seeks to escape the responsible freedom of Being-for-itself." To illustrate our denial of responsibility, in *Being and Nothingness* Sartre chooses a situation that is commonplace but nevertheless charged with sexual potential.

"Take the example of a woman who has consented to go out with a particular man for the first time. She knows very well the intentions which the man who is speaking to her cherishes regarding her. She also knows that it will be necessary sooner or later for her to make a decision."

How does she abnegate her responsibility, that is, decide to put off deciding? How does she respond to her date?

"If he says to her, 'I find you so attractive!' she disarms this phrase of its sexual background; she attaches to the conversation and to the behavior of the speaker, the immediate meanings, which she imagines as objective qualities." So in her mind she transforms her date, his compliments and his desires, into objects, because she is not sure what she wants. At the same time, she is aware that her process of objectifying him is not wholly satisfactory, that is, as Sartre says, "she would find no charm in a respect which would only be respect."

The date might thus continue, uneasy but without damage or regret—but then the man makes a move: he takes hold of her hand. This action changes the status quo and requires an immediate response. Sartre then describes the woman's decision: "To leave the hand there is to consent in herself to flirt, to engage herself. To withdraw it is to break the troubled and unstable harmony which gives the hour its charm. The aim is to postpone the moment of decision as long as possible. We know what happens next; [she] leaves her hand there, but she *does not notice* that she is leaving it . . . during this time the divorce of the body from the soul is accomplished; the hand rests inert between the warm hands of her companion—neither consenting nor resisting—a thing."

This behavior (bad faith) that all of us engage in under a variety of circumstances is by itself enough to be disturbing. But Sartre probes the psychological self-deception further: "while sensing profoundly the presence of her own body—to the point of being aroused, perhaps—she realizes herself as *not being* her own body, and she contemplates it as though from above as a passive object. . . ." This he calls *transcendence*.

A number of thoughts come to mind regarding the woman's behavior. Perhaps she should be excused; she wants to spend more time with him before she decides what to do; she is a bit of a victim of his too hasty advance. Or perhaps you believe her decision is a foregone conclusion—given the lens Sartre provides for us, you feel that her intentions, conscious or otherwise, were to welcome, or at least not rebuff, the man's advances until a more critical moment approached, when she could have extricated herself quietly and at little cost. Maybe you believe that she enjoys the attention, the company, the free (?) dinner. Or maybe she simply had planned to wait and see, and then make a conscious deliberation.

Sartre's description of the woman passively allowing her date to take her hand may have been appropriate for the era. More relevant perhaps, for today's audience, would be a version in which a person may rely on artificial means (drugs or alcohol) to vascillate between facticity and transcendence, that is, to carry out an act but evade responsibility for it.

Imagine, say, a college student who gets drunk and ends up sleeping with someone that he or she doesn't really like. In answering a friend's question, "why did you sleep with this person?" the response is, "I was out of it." This absolves oneself of the responsibility for the action (it wasn't really me) while nevertheless retaining any pleasure derived from the experience.

When people rely frequently on chemical highs, for example daily, this is addiction—at least as viewed by others (only when the persons involved can recognize this behavior and put an end to it is, ironically, when they call themselves addicts or alcoholics). So we can interpret a major component of addiction—the usual escapist motivation—as the Sartrean *mauvaise foi* carried out to pathological extremes.

Let's return to Sartre's woman. Maybe she is a more deliberate planner than she is made out to be. Elsewhere in his tome Sartre has something to say about willful consideration. He believes that the choices we make are not brought about consciously, that "voluntary deliberation is always a deception." Further, he holds that "when I deliberate, the chips are down [*les jeux sont faits*]." In his view, then, the freedom—and, in this, the free will—that we possess is actualized by means other than deliberate conscious pondering. We use deliberation simply as "a procedure which will make known to me what I project and consequently what I am." It is essentially the cart following the horse.

To found a philosophy on freedom and then to announce that one's choices are not the products of rational deliberation is to walk a fine but ultimately disappointing line. If all of our voluntary decision processes are mere rationalizations of foregone conclusions, how were these conclusions reached? Although Sartre suggests that we employ other modes such as passion, or decision simply through action, which is what demonstrates our true feelings (which our language in turn narrates for us), his conceptions smack of the *uncontrollable* elements of our thought that seem so unsatisfactorily wed to the possession of freedom. Language, which structures our voluntary deliberation, is not only *not necessary* for our decisions and actions, but is wholly removed from the process.

Some readers may find the notion of "non-verbality of thought," as Penrose puts it, to be disconcerting (if not the crux of the issue). But Penrose documents an impressive list of scientific luminaries, which includes the mathematicians Poincaré and Hadamard, the social scientist Galton, Penrose himself, and Einstein who emphasize this dimension of thought. To top it off, Penrose and Hadamard quote Mozart as noting that melodies "crowd into my mind as easily as you could wish. Whence and how do they come? I do not know and I have nothing to do with it." Contrary to this, mathematician and game theorist Ken Binmore claims to "have to calculate" in order to properly express a *preference*. However, this would seem to beg the question of how he would initially come up with the quantitative assessments of the "utility" of the various elements of the alternatives he faced.

The tension between free will and nondeliberate, perhaps unconscious, thought is by no means the only paradoxical aspect of existentialism. In fact, existentialism has been misunderstood precisely because of such apparent inconsistencies. Another example is that although the majority of writers associated with existentialism are atheists in the Nietzschean tradition, quite a few are believers, following Kierkegaard. Although religion tends to split the category, one unifying issue is the phenomenological emphasis on our psychological processes and the human condition as the primary concern for philosophy. But, philosophically, any focus on the Self and its functions will necessarily flirt with solipsism, which formally claims that only the self can be proven to exist, and informally promotes self-centered egoism. So, unfortunately for Nietzsche, Heidegger, and Sartre, although they espouse a higher morality, strength of character, and sense of responsibility, through various interpretations (or misinterpretations) of their works and others', there has been a pervasive association of existentialism with nihilism, anarchy, and egocentricity.

After all, Sartre's very title *Being and Nothingness* indicates that negation itself is a fundamental characteristic of our existence. For Sartre, nothingness continually punctuates our past, present, and future. Psychologically, as nothingness assails us it burdens us with ceaselessly having to choose (to choose oneself, to make oneself, to create oneself). This apprehension of our freedom and its enormous responsibility is what leads to angst, the notion of dread and anguish that also is a common denominator of existentialist writers. But lacking this critical insight, many casual consumers of existential works focus more on nihilism and less on responsibility as the message.

Probably Sartre fueled much of the nihilist and anarchic connections by his own actions. To maintain his independence of thought, he dissociated himself from various institutions—he resigned his professorship at the Lycée Condorçet while quite young, and later on he refused entry into the Legion d'Honneur and declined the Nobel Prize for literature. In addition, Sartre supported Algerian independence and protested against U.S. involvement early on, when it was seen as subversive to do so. Therefore his behavior, however self-consistent and admirable, surely won a constituency that was more willing to tear down rather than build up moral structure. Finally, Sartre's sympathy for Marxism and the Communist party in France augmented his set of supporters with extreme leftists who focused on the alienation brought about by, among other things, capitalist society in general and the Western military-industrial complex in particular.

To close out this look at existentialism, I want to consider some of the writings of Albert Camus, a fellow Resistance member. Like Sartre—Camus's close friend until their positions on communism drove them apart—Camus developed his ideas in both literary and philosophical works. His best-known book, *The Stranger (L' étranger),* presents an alienated hero-antihero, perhaps a victim of his society and contingencies beyond his control, but nevertheless one whose thoughts and actions might well be misunderstood as a nihilist manifesto. Note that *étranger* also connotes foreigner or outsider. (I'll never forget an occasion in a small town in Aquitaine when a couple drove up alongside me to ask directions. After I responded that I did not know, they started to drive away and the man dismissed me, with that superior and scornful way the French have mastered, as an *étranger.*)

Although Camus claimed not to be an existentialist, he too is concerned with the themes of alienation, absurdity, death, and angst, and, as the other writers, he comes down squarely on the side of constructive responsibility, not destructive amorality. Philosophically, for Camus, *the* fundamental question is whether life is worth living. To wit, "There is but one truly serious philosophical problem, and that is suicide." Camus finds our human condition to be absurd. However, he exhorts that triumph lies in one's self-created mastery over this absurd fate—mastery being not simply creation, but also control and responsibility. Instead of fruitless resignation, the absurd man "says yes and his effort will henceforth be unceasing." Implicit in this saying yes to life and its problematic choices is the responsibility of making decisions.

Although Camus's intentions may have been misunderstood by disaffected youths who believe they see a case for the "pointlessness of it all," he found, even in the depths of war in 1940, that "within the limits of nihilism it is possible to find the means to proceed beyond nihilism." While Kierkegaard saw Abraham as the first existentialist, carrying out an absurd act on account of his faith, Camus instead offers us Sisyphus, eternally condemned to rolling a boulder up to the top of a mountain only to have it fall back down, as the absurd man. But even in this situation, without Kierkegaard's God to believe in, Camus tells us, Zenlike, "Each atom of that stone, each mineral flake of that night-filled mountain, in itself forms a world. The struggle itself toward the heights is enough to fill a man's heart. One must imagine Sisyphus happy."

Accepting Responsibility . . . or Not

At this point you may be skeptical about existentialism. In particular, if you are a pragmatic person, you may be wondering about existentialism's usefulness. Can anything we have discussed—self-deception, living authentically, accepting responsibility—really be applied advantageously to our lives? One difficulty that existentialism faces, paradoxically, is an increasingly permissive society. As we find that we (as well as others) can get away with more and more, our lesson is that we need not accept responsibility for our actions. There are numerous examples of this in our society. The saddest one, perhaps, is the alarming number of (single) teenaged girls having children. Many of these girls are not mature enough to understand the awesome responsibility a child entails, and the results are too often that such children are not brought up in a nurturing environment. Our growing liberty and widening subjectivity and tolerance frequently serves to dilute the notion that each of our actions has a consequence, and that some consequences are superior to others. Assumption of responsibility, then, becomes blurred.

Nevertheless, one useful application of existential thought has been to psychotherapy, and it will be interesting to see the planting of some of the ideas we have reviewed in this particular milieu. My source here is Irvin Yalom's text, *Existential Psychotherapy*. Of the many problems that might trouble a patient, Yalom characterizes the existential domain as conflicts that arise *"from the individual's confrontation with the givens of existence* [his emphasis]." These conflicts, in turn, are grouped into four major categories: death, freedom, isolation, and meaninglessness.

Perhaps death is the most daunting of these conditions to face. Yalom observes that Kierkegaard was the first to delineate between *fear* (of *something*) and *dread*, which is of *no thing*, that is, *nothingness*. A common mechanism we develop to minimize dread is displacement. We fight anxiety by *"displacing it from nothing to something* [his emphasis] . . . . It is what Rollo May means by 'anxiety seeks to become fear.'" A psychotherapist discovering that various fears are such displacements would hopefully be able to help a patient overcome them.

Interestingly, in Yalom's section on death he comments a great deal on free will versus determinism. The reason for this is that Freud, and Freudian-influenced theorists, failed to recognize death as a major source of anxiety. This is surprising. How could someone as astute as Freud dismiss the fear of death as either an extension of the fear of castration, or as a concept that was ungraspable and therefore essentially meaningless? The underlying reason for this neglect was that Freud was a determinist. Fear of death, a future event, would necessitate the involved mental activity of planning for and projecting into the future. But for Freud, the unconscious forces that determine our behavior "are primitive and instinctual." Therefore any complex thought concerning death does not influence our behavior. We have already seen that Sartre is a determinist on the same order, and Yalom notes that Freud too is similar to Nietzsche, who believed that our behavior is unconsciously, mechanistically determined and that conscious thought follows involuntarily.

Regarding therapeutic treatment, Yalom moves from the fairly nonspecific and mundane to the more specific and pressing. In the former category, he notes an important dream of a middle-aged "empty nest" patient, and her eventual improved attitude. The dream made her truly realize that her time was finite, and this realization inspired her to appreciate time, and life's events, in a more fulfilling manner. This shift brought her closer to Heidegger's notion of the *authentic;* as Yalom put it, "she wondered not at the *way* that things are but *that* things are." On a more critical front, Yalom reports on terminally ill patients. It appears that we desensitize ourselves to death to some extent. Aware of this, a therapist may help a patient by repeatedly exposing the fear "in attenuated doses." "Over and over a patient approaches his or her dread until gradually it diminishes through sheer familiarity."

The next important category is freedom. Consistent with what I have claimed regarding people's increased choice in recent times (as opposed to, say, Freud's era c. 1900), Yalom contends that, "Today's patient has to cope more with freedom than with suppressed drives." In other words, we are not as compelled or impelled to act as our forebears were. People today have to face, Yalom says, "the problem of choice—with what he or she *wants* to do" (his emphasis). The correct question is then Yalom's "why are decisions difficult?" and in reply he quotes a John Gardner character: "Things fade; alternatives exclude." Decisions are indeed difficult, and Yalom catalogues some techniques we use to assuage their pain. One is "trading down," where we arrange our alternatives so that there is less to give up (for example, by finding some compromise). Others are "devaluation of the unchosen alternative" and "delegating the decision to someone."

Regarding Heidegger's *Dasein* and Sartre's *Being* (both in-itself and for-itself), Yalom notes that we all have the dualistic nature of being an object in the world as well as a "transcendental" ego, a bridge to the world and a source of responsibility. Therefore our very existence is bound up with the freedom that ultimately derives from responsibility. And—as we have already noted—he points out that we are responsible for our *failures to act* as well as our actions. In addressing our anxiety vis-à-vis freedom, Yalom focuses on the clinical details of responsibility avoidance, which he equates to inauthentic behavior, that is, bad faith. He also considers therapeutic techniques available to bring about responsibility assumption. Numerous therapeutic movements have focused on responsibility assumption, the most successful of them being EST, which goes back to the 1970s.

The long reach of responsibility avoidance in our society is illustrated in the following common (and perhaps vulgar) example. Consider an average heterosexual man who sees a couple pass by. The woman is fabulous looking, and obviously enjoying herself while draped around an ordinary guy. This scene is not infrequent, and is therefore—precisely on account of its banality and prevalence—important. What are the thoughts of our observer, Mr. Average? Most likely, at first, "what is *she* doing with *him?*" Next comes a comparison, not unfavorable, of himself with the lucky guy. There is brief confusion, on account of the anomaly, and a search (visually) for a reason why the two are together. Perhaps Mr. Average realizes that he might not *like* this particular woman. But he has seen it before and, bitter and scornful, he will invariably trot out the two usual conclusions: either the guy is rich or has a large member.

These two possibilities—pathetic though they may be—are not arrived at arbitrarily. In some sense, they represent the two extremes that cover the concept of "luck." Money, though it is often a product of one's ability and hard work, is nevertheless easy for us to isolate as an independent factor. It has nothing to do with "us." Similarly, a large sexual apparatus is a physical characteristic over which one has no control. Why do so many (men) think this way? Rarely will they seriously consider the plausibility of the two typical reasons; rarely will they give women more credit, either. A few thoughtful men might consider alternative explanations, but for most guys, these will be summarily rejected.

To begin with, most people share a long-standing belief that lovers and companions are more or less similar in their degree of attractiveness (depending on what we call attractive). We all empirically verify this every day, and moreover, such a principle makes sense biologically and in terms of market economics. But historically there have always been exceptions. Powerful men have traditionally had easy access to obtaining "possession" of attractive females ("women" is less to the point here). Such as this was—and still is—the assumption of wealth is quite understandable.

More germane, however, is the fact that in bygone times (and in many cultures today) there was much less choice about whom to marry. Lack of physical mobility limited one's freedom to roam and correspondingly reduced one's supply of candidates. Class systems were much more dominant than they are today. In addition, I need hardly mention how singles bars, parties, personal ads, dating services, and chat rooms have replaced (however well or poorly) the old-fashioned family network.

So, without belaboring the issue, there certainly seems to be much more choice of a companion these days than there ever was. How this weighs on our excluded Mr. Average is simple. He acutely feels cheated—and it's nobody's fault but his own. Deep down, he does not believe that money or size matter, and therefore, deprived of excuses of luck, he realizes that he had the same opportunities as the ostensibly successful man. He had the same choice and chance to meet and win over an outstanding woman and failed. Since such *personal* inadequacy is hard to face, Mr. Average has to transfer his failure to an exogenous source.

This transfer is nothing more than responsibility avoidance. And not only will Mr. Average exonerate himself for his past lack of success, he will tacitly do so for the future as well. Such a path is much easier to follow indefinitely than the admission of not doing the best one can. And, come to think of it, Mr. Average would have to confront this painful issue in various situations, and not only when he sees Mr. Ordinary with Ms. Outstanding. No wonder he has gotten so quick at blaming it all on luck.

Returning to a theoretical base, one could ask, how is failure to accept responsibility internalized? One manifestation of anxiety over freedom is *guilt* which, as Yalom indicates, Heidegger associated with responsibility. More important, though, is Yalom's quote from theologian Paul Tillich, who reformulates the notion as follows: "'he is required to answer, if he is asked, *what he has made of himself*. He who asks him is his judge, namely, he himself.'" Psychologist Rollo May adds that existential guilt is "a perception of the difference between what a thing is and what it ought to be." This notion—reaching one's potential—Yalom traces back to at least Aristotle. In psychology, it is called "self-actualization" (probably first used by sociologist Abraham Maslow) and "self-realization," among other things. How do we find our potential, or know we haven't reached it? Through guilt. Thus we can gauge the extent to which we have not lived up to the assumption of responsibility. Yalom finds that when a therapist attempts to flush out the patient's perception of responsibility, the specter of guilt will quickly materialize.

Awareness of one's guilt and lack of responsibility assumption does not in itself modify behavior. The patient has to have the will to bring about change. But here, it is interesting to note the same problem as before: if our mental activity is deterministic, what is will, and how can it be utilized to change our behavior? Leslie Farber (who in turn quotes W. H. Auden) claims that will can only be inferred after a particular behavior; otherwise it is not consciously experienced. Otto Rank, however, rejected this Freudian determinism and centered his therapy on the clash of the two involved wills. The patient's will would surely resist the therapist's, but the therapist can then work around this conflict by attempting to transform the patient's "counter will" into "creative will," which would be used to further the patient's progress. Rollo May believes that will needs "wish" as an antecedent. A wish is a specific desire, and will is the subsequent drive to bring that desire about. In his words, "If you have only 'will' and no 'wish,' you have the dried-up, Victorian, neopuritan man. If you have only 'wish' but no 'will,' you have the driven unfree, infantile person who, as adult-remaining-as-an-infant, may become the robot man."

It is clear now that freedom entails a lot of baggage: responsibility, guilt, and will. This baggage can even be retrospective. One such example of the difficulty that we have in assuming responsibility is offered in the case of a woman whose continued smoking directly ruined her health and then her marriage. When confronted with a demand to "choose smoking or marriage," she kept smoking. Why? She realized that "if she stopped smoking now, then that would mean *she could have stopped smoking before*" (Yalom's emphasis). Yalom's point is that quitting smoking now would create existential guilt, because quitting would involve the smoker's admission of the damage that she had been doing to herself for years. In therapy, she had to be shown that she needed to "accept the crushing responsibility for her actions in the past by grasping her responsibility for the future. . . . One can atone for the past only by altering the future."

Yalom addresses *meaninglessness* as the last of the basic existential concerns. He finds Camus's "absurd"—the predicament of trying to find meaning in a meaningless world—to be an accurate portrayal of the basic human condition. Given our absurd situation, Yalom poses the questions, "What then are we to do? Are there no guidelines? No values? Nothing right or wrong? Good or evil?" Of course, if we have indeed lost these absolutes, then "everything is a matter of indifference."

As I have argued regarding other issues of choice, "today's" meaninglessness was not abundant in preindustrial, agrarian times. For Yalom, meaninglessness cannot be disassociated from leisure and the detachment of alienation. How does meaninglessness come about? For starters, Yalom observes that "'free' time is problematic because it thrusts freedom upon us." This can lead to boredom, apathy, cynicism, and lack of direction, which for Victor Frankl characterize the "existential vacuum." Frankl claimed that these feelings are on the rise and spreading worldwide, shown in 30–80 percent of young people (most studies, of course, were of college students). In more extreme cases, people develop "existential neurosis," categorized by *crusadism* (also "adventurousness"), for example, found in demonstrators and activists who latch on to one cause after another; *nihilism,* found in those who seek to cut down the meaningful efforts of others; *vegetativeness,* where "one sinks into a severe state of aimlessness and apathy;" and, finally, *compulsive activity.*

What is the therapist to do in the face of meaninglessness? Yalom notes Frankl's remark, "happiness cannot be pursued, it can only ensue." A strategy consistent with this observation is "dereflection," which basically urges the patient to stop concentrating on himself or herself and to try to find meaning externally. But perhaps a more fruitful therapy for meaninglessness is what Yalom calls "engagement," which is initiated by relating personally, not superficially, with the patient. This creates a role model with whom the patient can identify.

Yalom goes back to Camus and Sartre in search of positive qualities. He interprets Camus's *Myth of Sisyphus* as saying that the only path we have available to reach inner fulfillment is to rebel against the absurd by living with dignity. And, although to Yalom, Sartre does not provide such guidelines *philosophically,* in his fiction (e.g., *The Flies*) he endows characters with a "leap into 'engagement.'" In this they are able to restore a sense of justice, freedom, dignity, self-realization, and a search for meaning (which we create and commit to). In summary, Yalom lists certain activities that "provide human beings with a sense of life purpose": altruism, dedication to a cause, creativity, hedonism, and self-actualization. He also notes, after Erik Erikson, that as we pass through our life cycles, we evolve new meanings, often ones concerned with future generations or with the human species as a whole.

What Are Our Needs?

Existentially rooted problems will surely continue to make up a significant portion of our anxieties. But, moving away from psychotherapy, how do existential problems fit in the more general matrix of human existence? Abraham Maslow, who developed the hierarchy of needs that I mentioned in chapter 3, explored this question. Maslow claimed that we need to fulfill our basic physical needs before we go on to fulfill other needs. The entire set of human needs he depicts as building up a pyramid. At the bottom are the fundamental needs such as hunger, thirst, and sex. At the next level up are concerns of safety and security. In the middle of the pyramid are psychological needs. Of these, the lower level ones are belongingness-related: love, affiliation, and acceptance. At a higher level is the need for esteem; the need to achieve, be competent, gain approval and recognition.

Finally, at the apex of the hierarchy are self-actualization needs; as psychologist James Vander Zanden puts it, "The need to fulfill one's unique potential." What is interesting here is that it almost appears as if Maslow has worked backward, having identified admirable people such as Abraham Lincoln, Eleanor Roosevelt, and Albert Einstein, and then developed a laundry list of attributes that aspire to the Nietzschean superman and Heideggerean authenticity ethic. These attributes (taken mostly from Vander Zanden) include having a firm perception of reality; accepting themselves, others, and the world for what they are; exhibiting considerable spontaneity in thought and behavior; being problem- rather than self-centered; having an air of detachment and a need for privacy; being autonomous and independent; resisting mechanical and stereotyped social behaviors (but not assuming deliberate, flamboyant unconventionality); being sympathetic and seeking to promote the common welfare; establishing deep and meaningful relationships with a few persons rather than superficial bonds with many; having a democratic world perspective; being able to transcend, rather than merely cope with, the environment; and finally, being creative and susceptible to "peak experiences" marked by rapture, excitement, insight, and happiness.

Of course, Maslow could well have set out his own social and political agenda, and then found individuals who seemed to meet these conditions. If the long list above appears indulgent, it is perhaps true that the emphasis that Maslow and other humanistic psychologists place on the self flirts with solipsism. Overdeveloping self-centeredness can lead to an underdeveloped sense-for-others, that is, deficient community spirit. Thus we stray toward a familiar debate that we will revisit, namely the Ayn Randists and libertarians at one extreme and the socialists at the other.

One notion that we have not touched on but that goes along with responsibility is that of *risk*. Many decisions are motivated by *risk avoidance,* not just responsibility avoidance. Risk avoidance is not, categorically speaking, unreasonable, but then there is the old cliché, "nothing ventured, nothing gained" (which modern finance has dressed up as stating that the largest potential gains come precisely from the riskiest investments). We have discussed the quintet of freedom, choice, responsibility, guilt, and will. But, generally speaking, actions that we are free to choose may have downsides; these pitfalls vary not only in magnitude but also in perhaps unknown degrees of likelihood. This is the domain of risk. What is its role? How do we account for it? How should we? Let's give some thought to these questions in the next chapter.

Risk expresses two distinct notions: one is the magnitude of loss in a certain situation, and the other is the chance, or probability, of this loss occurring. Of course, such evaluation is based on the possibility of exposure to loss to begin with. As we are faced with more and more choice in our lives, we are faced with more and more risk. And our attitudes toward risk are present even in scenarios in which we face only positive options. In these happiest of situations, we compare relative merits and develop a sense of *regret* (if we select the raspberry cheesecake, we may be sorry we didn't pick the chocolate mousse).

Thoughts on risk weren't always amalgamated in this fashion. Some writers have treated risk as just the probability of loss; others, the magnitude of loss. Still others have differentiated risk from uncertainty, pointing out that there is a difference between being informed (say, knowing or believing in a probability distribution) and uninformed regarding the likelihood of various possibilities. In considering the overall picture it seems to me more clearheaded to dissolve these partly semantic differences and simply accept that weighing a risk requires evaluating both the likelihood as well as the amount of loss.

Author Peter L. Bernstein advances the view that what separates the moderns from the ancients is an ability to quantify, assess, and control risk. The watershed was, more or less, the Renaissance, and the reasons are as follows. Risk management relies heavily on probability theory and statistics, both of which are calculation intensive. The Greeks, Romans, and other ancients had clumsy number systems that were satisfactory for display but ill adapted to calculation (which is why everyone used abacuses). It wasn't until the thirteenth century that the Hindu-Arabic numerals we use today were widely employed. Moreover, the sciences of probability and statistics greatly rely on the notions of sampling and experimentation. The Greeks, being more concerned with absolute truths, were not interested in empiricism. Closer to the Renaissance, one may wonder why Arab mathematicians, who were relatively quite advanced, did not develop a theory of probability. The answer, perhaps, lay simply in their fatalistic culture: God wills.

With the flowering of the Renaissance, burgeoning trade meant that long-range planning, including forecasting and contemplation of risk factors, was a problem faced by an increasingly large class of merchants. This sounds like a sufficient condition for the development of risk sciences like insurance, but, as Bernstein does indicate, probability theory was not developed until the 1650s—by mathematicians Blaise Pascal and Pierre de Fermat (of the "wager" and the "last theorem," respectively) in response to a nobleman's questions about gambling. Finally, after the Reformation began in the early 1500s, people (well, Protestants, anyway) had to adopt more of a *culture of responsibility* for their deeds—and therefore had to develop more of a framework for contemplating alternative actions and their consequences. Adding to this, we note that Max Weber's interpretation of the Protestant work ethic illustrates how predeterminism does *not* imply fatalism. In looking for signs of our future state, we realize that our present condition serves to prognosticate our future. We also understand that a good deal of our present condition is brought about by our own actions.

Mortality Tables: Live Longer, More Choices

Another turning point for Bernstein in the development of modern risk analysis was the pioneering of actuarial tables by John Graunt and later, Edmund Halley. In 1662 Graunt, a "haberdasher of small-wares" (as stated at the time, according to James R. Newman's *The World of Mathematics*), published a "Pamphlet" of observations, "not two hours reading," based on birth and death tables from London during the period 1604 to 1661. The tables themselves are interesting enough; for example, in the year 1632, sixty-three different causes of death were listed, ranging from "Executed, and prest to death" to "Rising of the Lights" to "Teeth" to "Aged." Incidentally, about one in every fifteen deaths (excluding infants) were attributed to "Teeth," which certainly makes you realize how potentially serious a gum infection is. But much more important are the inferences that Graunt made, accurate or not, from the tables. For starters, he was able to estimate London's population (an unknown) from the tallies of births. Graunt also discovered that there were more males born than females (139,782 to 130,866 from 1628 to 1662, a ratio of 1.068 males to 1 female, remarkably close to that of 1.06 to 1 today, worldwide), but that males have a higher death rate. Most important of all was a table of survival rates for certain ages. For example, Graunt estimated that 36 percent of all those born died before age 6, that only 25 percent survived until age 26, and that only 6 percent survived until age 56. No wonder the philosopher Thomas Hobbes wrote of our lives being "poor, nasty, brutish, and short." As we mentioned in chapter 1, our longer horizons certainly contribute to providing a series of both short- and long-term choices far beyond what our ancestors could have expected. Graunt developed an estimate of what we would call life expectancy at birth to be 16 years. William Petty, a friend of Graunt's, used data from a parish in Dublin to estimate the same thing; his figure was 18 years.

In 1693 Halley, the astronomer (who lived until age 86), took Graunt's work further. To calculate what we now term mortality tables, Halley used data from the town of Breslau, which, he noted, had several advantages over London and Dublin. For one thing, the Breslau records furnished age at death; for another, Breslau's population was more stable. Halley calculated the odds that a person of a certain age would survive a certain number of years. For example (following Bernstein), having found 567 individuals in Breslau aged 25, and 560 the following year aged 26, Halley concluded that the odds were 560 to 7, or 80 to 1, that a 25-year-old would survive to age 26. Similarly, noticing 531 persons aged 30 and that 265.5 (half of 531) would fall between the population sizes at ages 57 and 58, Halley figured on a fifty–fifty likelihood of a 30-year-old living another 27 or 28 years. Median lifetime, according to Halley, was 17 years, leading him to conclude that one's years beyond 17 are a "Blessing." A note on life expectancy is in order here. Naively, one might assume a life expectancy of, say, 40 means that most people die at around 40. A more sophisticated, but still incorrect, view is that 40, being an average, would be obtained from numerous septuagenarians and octogenarians canceling out a high infant mortality rate, with relatively few dying at intermediate ages. Examination of Halley's data proves this wrong (at least for the Breslau population). Halley himself was astute enough to use the median lifetime to avoid misinterpretation. Finally, Halley had the ingenuity to calculate "the *Price* of *Insurance* upon *Lives*" based on his tables, thus founding, in effect, the modern life insurance industry. (Insurance itself is ancient; it goes back, Bernstein mentions, at least to the Code of Hammurabi in 1800 B.C.E.)

Today—and only in the past few generations out of the whole history of *Homo sapiens*—we can expect to live far longer than twenty years. We have already discussed the relative material wealth that we have only recently started to enjoy, but the most important gift of the twentieth century was the gift of longevity. Medical advances—most significantly, antibiotics as well as access to clean water—have given most of us an excellent chance to live a full and long life. Our life expectancy, dramatically higher than ever before, is radically altering the way we conceptualize our life paths. No longer is it unlikely that one lives to old age. The future, then, is more probable, brighter, and more important than it ever was—and is something to plan for.

Ironically, though, just as mass production was introduced, just as the West began to turn out modern conveniences, the First World War erupted; not simply a world war but a partly mechanized war introducing tanks, airplanes, and chemicals as destructive agents. The casualty lists, doubled by disease, flew in the face of life expectancy. Just twenty years later, another ghastly counterpoint to progress ensued. The Second World War was ended, with fitting horror, by an atomic device floated down from the heavens—technological energy (and not mere scientific abstraction) that annihilated one hundred thousand people with the push of a lever. The century that taught us how to save millions also taught us how to take millions. The atomic firestorm gave way to a cold war that has bestowed, as its legacy, an awareness—I admit it's slight for most of us, at least presently—of living on the brink of destruction. How ironic that our technological prowess—the result of studying the very large and the very small—has made our lives more important by lengthening them, but has made existence itself hostage to a gnawing, inextinguishable fear of a nuclear trigger. This trigger, furthermore, will likely always be a possibility, due to terrorists, rogue states, or simply accidents, in spite of any recent cutbacks and declarations the Americans, former Soviets, Chinese, French, North Koreans, Pakistanis, or Indians may have made. And despite our advances in understanding risk, how can we possibly estimate this ultimate risk of self-annihilation?

Turning back to risk and choice on the personal level, I wonder whether contemporary people, with our hard-fought accumulation of consumer products and our well-planned lengthy futures, are more risk-averse decision-makers than our forebears were. I am tempted to make such an assertion, or, at least, conjecture; this would be a good topic of inquiry for social historians. It does seem that people grow more conservative as they grow older—and sensibly so, at least in part because so much more has been invested, while the aging process deprives us of our youth-derived immortality. (There's a good reason why eighteen-year-olds are prime Army recruits.) In what ways do we change when we really believe we'll live past eighty? How was the typical outlook different in, say, seventeenth-century London, when at *any* age, there was a significant chance of not making it past another few years? More to the point, what do we really know about how people assess risk, and how risk attitudes affect our decision making?

Some Quirky Aspects of Decision Making

Decision making under conditions of risk and uncertainty is only partly understood. To begin with, most of the quantitative studies that have been carried out treat our risk attitudes regarding money. Although money does provide a divisible and universal medium of exchange, the understanding of our risk attitudes with respect to money alone can hardly provide a comprehensive theory. For another thing, we don't know why people differ considerably in their attitudes. One individual prefers a sure win of $300 to a fifty–fifty gamble (or lottery) at either $1,000 or $0; another person would require a sure payment of $375 not to gamble; someone else, $450. The difference between the expected value of the lottery (which is in this instance $500) and the "sure win" amount that a person would value equally with the lottery is called a "certainty premium." It is the amount of "expected" gain from the lottery that one will forego to obtain the security of the sure payment. For a given situation, certainty premiums will vary widely. How can we explain this?

The best that theory has to offer treats how an individual's preferences change as alternatives vary, or predicts how most people would behave, but does not explain differences *among* decision makers. Psychologists have performed loads of tests of these sorts of preference profiles, and partly on the basis of these findings economists have developed theories centered on the idea that decision makers have utility (or satisfaction) for money or for bundles of commodities that exhibits decreasing returns to scale.

For example, the gift of a million dollars to you would impart a certain amount of utility, but a gift of two million would most likely not quite double that amount of satisfaction. Similarly, a third million would probably give even less additional (i.e., marginal) utility than the second million, and so on. Such decreasing returns also express that we are risk-averse, meaning that nearly all of us would prefer a sure amount less than $500 to the fifty–fifty gamble between $1,000 and $0. The two state-of-the-art theories, which are "expected utility theory," originated by von Neumann and Morgenstern in the 1940s and advanced by mathematician L. J. Savage in the 1950's, and "prospect theory," introduced by psychologists Daniel Kahneman and Amos Tversky in 1979, overlap as well as compete. They explain much about our behavior but are far from comprehensive in explaining what we desire and what we avoid. Prospect theory can be viewed as an updated and improved extension of expected utility theory, despite some objections from quite a few eminent mathematical economists and game theorists. In any event, by putting together different findings, expected utility theory and prospect theory hope to explain, at least in part, real-life behavior, such as people taking out insurance policies or pursuing ordinary gambling. But such a synthesis is a huge job.

How can we characterize our undependable behavior with a coherent theory when there's so much that's unknown, and when so much seems inconsistent? For example, which of the following situations would you prefer: lottery one, in which you win $200 1/4 of the time, $100 1/2 of the time, and $0 1/4 of the time, or lottery two, in which you have two fifty–fifty chances at either $100 or $0, executed consecutively? Think about this for a moment; and now observe that lottery one, a compound lottery, is in fact identical to the repeated gamble in lottery two. You can imagine that an attempt to evaluate risks and associated returns from different portfolios in a truly integrated way—a way that accurately measures our preferences—would be extremely daunting. Perhaps not surprisingly, many apparent paradoxes abound in this literature. The most understandable one is the Ellsberg paradox: jar A has fifty red marbles, fifty black; jar B has one hundred red and black marbles also, but in unknown proportions. You will select a single marble at random (blindfolded) from the jar of your choice. You win $100 if it's red, and nothing if it's black. Would you prefer jar A or jar B? Now change things: you win when the marble is black. Which jar do you prefer now?

Most people prefer jar A in *both* cases; the fifty–fifty chance seems more reliable than the unknown mix. But think about this: if you prefer jar A for red, you seem to be claiming that the probability of obtaining a red marble from jar A (which is 50%) exceeds the probability of obtaining a red marble from jar B. But by this reasoning, the probability of obtaining a *black* marble from jar B would have to be *greater than* 50 percent—and then you should prefer jar B for the black marble. But you didn't. Now, is this a real paradox, or is there something going on in the way that it's expressed that you can't quite put your finger on? And if it is a paradox—by which I mean that we simply cannot deduce that the preference of one gamble over another implies that we think our probability of winning (the same prize) is higher, and that people are therefore risk averse even when it seems illogical—can we explain such inconsistent preference behavior (which researcher Daniel Ellsberg called "ambiguity aversion") in a consistent theory?

Kahneman and Tversky pioneered a voluminous theory on such quirky lotteries and made a number of interesting discoveries. For example, "losses loom larger than gains." To see what this means, would you take a fifty–fifty gamble to either win or lose $1,000? Most people would not. More curiously, Kahneman and Tversky found that we are risk averse when considering *gains,* which is consistent with the von Neumann–Morgenstern theory, but that we *take risks* when faced with *losses.* Consider the following comparison: you could either win a sure $3,000, or gamble on a lottery in which you would win $4,000 80 percent of the time but win nothing the other 20 percent of the time. Most people (80 percent, in Kahneman and Tversky's sample) prefer the sure $3,000 to the lottery. However, when the tables are turned, something strange happens. Suppose you face either a sure *loss* of $3,000, or a gamble in which you lose $4,000 80 percent of the time but lose nothing 20 percent of the time. Now, with identical numbers but in the realm of losses rather than gains, most people (92 percent for Kahneman and Tversky) will go for the gamble, in what Kahneman and Tversky call the "reflection effect."

In chapter 4 I mentioned that relativity's treatment of different coordinate systems gave rise to the notion of "frames of reference," which had application in, among other things, prospect theory. To illustrate the concept, let's use another of Kahneman and Tversky's examples. A local epidemic surfaces and 600 people are expected to die. There are two alternatives in dealing with it. Plan A will save 200 people. Plan B provides a one-third chance to save everyone but then two-thirds of the time no one will be saved. (Notice that plans A and B yield the same expected number of survivors.) Kahneman and Tversky found that 72 percent of their respondents chose plan A.

Now frame the alternatives differently. Under plan C, 400 people will die, while under plan D, there is a one-third chance that no one will die and a two-thirds chance that all 600 people will die. Plan C is identical to plan A but it specifies that 400 will die instead of saying that 200 will be saved; plan D is identical to plan B, except that it, too, describes victims instead of survivors. In this framing of the dilemma, 78 percent of the respondents sought the gamble (which, in the original description, was preferred by only 28 percent).

Here's a less grisly illustration: suppose you have just won $1,000 on a game show. The show host proposes an additional game: to either accept an extra (sure) payment of $250, *or* to try a lottery where you win another $1,000 25 percent of the time, and nothing 75 percent of the time. In this situation, most people would decline the gamble in favor of the sure $250. Now suppose that you have won $2,000 on the game show. The show host asks you to either pay back $750 of your purse, *or* to try a lottery where you lose $1,000 75 percent of the time and lose nothing 25 percent of the time. In *this* situation, most people would accept the gamble, although again, the odds and returns are identical.

More generally, prospect theory tells us that much of what motivates our behavior is *loss aversion*—simply, that we hate to lose. In both of the above demonstrations of framing, loss aversion is what motivates the gambling behavior. In the realm of gains, risk aversion takes over and most people prefer security to gambling. But the key point is that the way the situations are framed induces us to conceptualize the scenarios as those of gain or loss. In one case, we considered either survivors or victims, and acted accordingly; in the other case, the different starting points (from which we either increased or decreased our wealth) influenced our actions.

There are other peculiar behaviors that have been observed; for example, people seem to overestimate small probabilities but underestimate large probabilities. Worse, we seem to compartmentalize our funds in a process called "mental accounting." To update Kahneman and Tversky's example, suppose you spent $60 on a ticket to a show. You arrive at the theater and find that you have lost the ticket. Would you spend another $60 to replace it? And what about in this scenario: you haven't bought the ticket yet, but when you arrive at the theater you discover that you have lost $60 of your money. Would you now spend $60 for the ticket?

Clearly, in each case the outcomes are identical. You either just go home $60 poorer or else see the show for a total cost of $120. But people conceptualize the situations differently. In the first case (where the ticket is lost), most people will give up and go home, whereas in the other instance (when the money is lost), most people will spend the additional money for another ticket. Mental accounting would seem to dictate that in the first situation, our theater fund was too depleted to support another purchase. But in the second case, we had lost $60 from a more flexible general-funds account that could withstand another withdrawal.

Another irrationality—this time in a market setting—that Bernstein reports is what finance professor Richard Thaler has called the "endowment effect":

that we would value a certain item much more as an owner than as a buyer. For example, in one experiment, students were given Cornell University mugs and then asked the lowest price they would be willing to sell the mugs for. Other students were asked the highest price they would be willing to pay to purchase a mug. The seller's prices averaged $5.25, while the buyers' highest offers were centered around $2.50. Was one mug in the hand worth two on the shelf? No. The endowment effect is a different psychological phenomenon, and Bernstein points out that it has important consequences for investors. He writes, "Once something is owned, its owner does not part with it lightly, regardless of what an objective valuation might reveal," and goes on to use the endowment effect to explain the relative lack of cross-national investment worldwide. Such effects, which are studied in the field of behavioral finance, threaten the conventional view that markets behave rationally.

There are other important instances of how different frames of reference alter our behavior. Robert Frank observes how our attitudes toward consumption are contingent on what others consume. In particular, conspicuous consumption by those wealthier than we are changes our frame of reference so powerfully that we feel compelled to follow suit. That is, our utility for keeping up (competing) outweighs that derived from other activities, no matter how much we try to minimize our envy. In addition to this component of our framing, which is driven by loss aversion and rivalry in addition to jealousy, our perceptions of value will change as well. Although we would ordinarily be satisfied with a $150 watch, enough exposure to $1,000 timepieces makes even a $500 watch seem inexpensive, and renders the $150 one cheap and ultimately inadequate.

Finally, whether we feel that we have *control* over a situation seems to change our decision making within it. For example, we generally have more fear of commercial flying than we do of driving a car, even though statistically, commercial flying is much safer than driving. And in the so-called Lake Wobegon effect, we overestimate our relative skills. As Frank points out, the great majority of us believe that we are better-than-average drivers. Such overconfidence tends to distort our perceptions of various likelihoods and thereby warps our decision-making processes.

Unfortunately, though, as we saw, most of this risk analysis involves fairly simple, well-defined situations with money as the sole medium of exchange. What about preferences over apples and oranges? What about when probabilities are unknown? Note that in most of the laboratory experiments (which, like most psychology experiments in general, are performed on college students; we only hope that students reflect the behaviors of the rest of the population) from which we gain our knowledge of and confusion about this field, the probabilities are given. Prospect theory may explain gambling and insurance but it does not address the pleasure we obtain from the gambling act itself or the utility inherent in the secure feeling that insurance provides. And what of other risks? In the example of automobile versus airplane travel, what elements exist other than control? How can we separate and account for emotional as well as intellectual factors? And in general, in what ways do our findings from certain situations (like the airplane-versus-auto case) apply to other situations?

Other Decision-Making Methods for Risky Propositions

The wider field of decision theory encompasses many branches of inquiry, all of which have been developed, if not entirely originated, in the era of choice. Another slant on risk and decision making under uncertainty is offered by introductory management science texts. They typically cover a limited set of analytical methods that are meant to evaluate managerial decision problems involving uncertain events. An example is decision trees, which depict sequential branching processes over time. At certain junctures, a decision maker has a number of available alternatives, of which one must be chosen. These are represented by "decision nodes" in an evolving tree diagram. At other points there are multiple actions that are beyond the decision maker's control, and are uncertain to boot—for example, market behavior. In the tree diagram, these possibilities are shown as branches that emanate from "chance" nodes. As possibilities, they are assessed (numerical) probabilities. The decision maker is supposed to model the real-life situation (which might be to find the ideal output of a newly introduced product) by forming the tree diagram and then using it to find the best decisions at each decision node. This may be done by computing expected values (average costs or benefits) at chance nodes and picking the best alternatives available (minimum cost or maximum profit) at each decision node. Two clever techniques often employed in tandem with the decision trees are "minimax" analysis and Bayes's theorem, which focus on the uncertainty present.

Minimax minimizes the maximum possible losses. The idea is to assume, out of the possibilities that exist beyond your control, that the *worst* one will happen. Then, when you can exercise a choice, you pick the best (hence, minimax) from these worst-case scenarios. This provides a guarantee that nothing worse than the minimax outcome can happen to you. There are subtexts: one, minimax does not treat 99 percent probable or 1 percent probable events differently under its law. In fact, this is the whole point—that the low-probability events are accorded equal weight or respect as the likely ones. Two, there is a certain skepticism present; maybe you *believe* an event only has a 2 percent chance of occurring, but how do you really know what its likelihood is?

Bayes's theorem is an attempt to use *information* to sharpen those probability estimates. You *think* the new product will sell, but you aren't sure: do some market research and you'll have a better idea. You *think* you're pregnant, but, of course, you may not be: take a test and be more assured. Or you believe someone's guilty, but the evidence is circumstantial: a DNA test result might convince you.

In the above paragraph, the degrees of certainty increased from the first example to the second to the third. But, as nice as Bayes's idea is—we'll skip the details of how the estimates get revised—we are never left with absolute certainty. There are two aspects to this. Suppose our market research yields a probability of 50 percent that your new product will be successful (perhaps ten out of twenty similar products had succeeded in the past). The uncertainty inherent in this situation can only be estimated from an incomplete population, or a population that does not perfectly match the case in hand. In other situations, fairly precise laboratory tests are performed for a particular sample. DNA tests are much more reliable than market research data. But all laboratory results are to some degree unreliable, since false positives and false negatives result from test inaccuracies, mishandling (sometimes deliberate), and faulty data entry. And this implies that any figures at all that we derive from experiments are themselves suspect.

All of this quantification, incidentally, and the very concept of decision analysis, reminds me of John Stuart Mill's having had an important decision to make, writing down all the reasons in favor and all those against, and then selecting the heavily outnumbered choice. Decision theory is fine when everything about your problem is clear-cut and quantifiable. But the next time you're agonizing over where to go for a vacation—will it be the Jersey shore or Florida again, or will you venture to a new destination, like North Carolina, or maybe something more exotic like Jamaica or Brazil?—it's one thing to compare costs and quite another to compare the intangibles, like Jamaica's beauty versus the Shore's familiarity. The unknown, of course, always presents elements of risk that the familiar does not. Quantifying those risks, especially the intangible ones, is hard to do and, in a sense, is the prime objective of the mathematization of the social sciences that is itself very young. A hundred years ago, none of this mattered to the vast majority of people. As we have seen, there was little free time or discretionary income, and the contemporary avalanche of commercialism was all but absent. Today, almost anyone, at home or work, can track down on the Internet any number of details about New Jersey or Jamaica or anywhere else.

The trade-off of security versus risk is a thread that runs through several choice-introduced dualisms and ties them together. The secure choices correlate with the familiar ones, with the static status quo, with keeping an equilibrium, and with promoting depth of experience. Weighing in against these are the unexplored, the dynamic, disequilibrium, and breadth of experience. We have already seen Garcin's risk aversion in *No Exit,* so typical of human nature. All of us have suffered numerous lost opportunities, and the worst thing about it is, we rarely get to know what things would've been like had we taken the plunge. Once again, we have Kierkegaard's fearful and trembling choice and its accompanying dread, our very existence contingent on uncertainty and decision. Garcin, who merely typifies our pervasive inertia and timidity, is necessarily an antihero (heroes, of course, overcome their fears and strike out boldly into the unknown). But in the face of an unknown hell, and in the face of the possible *irreversibility* of a decision, who could act otherwise?

So many of our choices pit the dynamism and temptation of the new with the comfort and predictability of the old. Of course, some individuals lean toward the risk-seeking, let's-try-something-new end of the spectrum; others tend to pick the usual tried-and-true; still others mix it up. As long as there have been choices (and of course, there always have been, just not in the concentration we experience nowadays) there have been people in each category. One question we will return to is: to what degree are we undergoing a societal shift in favor of the new and trendy, while eschewing the old and traditional? But before we deal with that issue, we need to emphasize that our focus in the past two chapters has been on individual decision making. The era of choice, as we have already observed, has greatly expanded the power and scope of what we can control personally—but at a price. We seem to be diminishing our emphasis on the groups to which we belong. Let's explore this theme next.

11 The Individual versus the Group

Thus far we have been primarily concerned with choice as a major influence for changing the way *individuals* have viewed and interacted with the world. The by-products of this new environment of choice that we have examined range from the concrete to the abstract, from the philosophic to the scientific, and from the practical to the theoretical. Common to all facets, though, is a *personal* quality. Existentialism concentrates—perhaps too much so—on an individual who must decide and then carry out his or her intentions responsibly. Decision science and risk analysis evolved to provide a quantitative framework for managing choices. Although the management science context subsumes the personal domain under the organizational, the point of view is still egoistic. It's "us" (instead of "me") against "them." The vicious spiral of choice spins its individual webs around us. The science we have discussed—the foundations of modern physics and mathematics—can be seen as an ongoing attempt to discover nature's secrets; again, a dyadic struggle, us versus the elements. Structuralism, a key idea in the development of recent social science and the humanities, also has, at its core, the individual attempting to make sense of the world. And freedom, at the heart of being able to choose, although necessarily involving the consideration of others in one's environment, is primarily an individual virtue.

Only in our discussion of postindustrial society have we thus far addressed concerns that reach beyond individual ones to the larger community. Let's return to this issue of choice in society. Doing so will expand our domain from the narrow, almost purely individual province that we have explored to one that considers each of us in the broader societal sphere. Here, oppositions—the progeny of choice—will continue to form the foundation of ideas and the catalyst for social change. The first and most natural dualism to consider is the friction between the individual and the group.

Good for One, but Not for All

"Social traps," as termed by mathematician and social scientist Anatol Rapoport, are situations in which the self-concerned actions of individuals result in consequences that are detrimental to the collective good. More precisely, in these situations *individually optimal* behavior is *group suboptimal*. The prototypical example cited in contemporary print is an old parable, described by ecologist Garrett Hardin in 1968 as "The Tragedy of the Commons," in which all members of a bovine-owning community allow their cows to graze unhindered on a common field. Eventually the uncontrolled grazing compromises the field, and the cows are unable to feed adequately. This is to everyone's disadvantage. In such situations, the collective good endures as long as certain levels of things are maintained, but these levels are not sustainable against the pressure of individually "rational" behavior—that is, greed.

There are a variety of situations that fit this general scheme: overfishing is one, pollution is another, and volunteering is a third. Clearly, greed on everyone's part can lead to disaster. Hardin had two suggestions, on different sides of the political spectrum, to prevent tragedy. One is to distribute the collective resource to the individuals, who may then utilize it as they wish (this amounts to privatization). Another is to apply regulatory constraints on the individual consumption of the resource. Each solution has disadvantages but avoids the social trap.

Studying the relationship between individual behavior and group outcomes is a critical area of exploration in both the social and biological sciences. Individual greed can lead to group disaster, but what about individual generosity? It is well-known that people often display altruistic behavior, most dramatically in cases of people sacrificing their lives to save others. Various theories are trotted out to explain such phenomena, for example, kin selection, or superior, though initially paradoxical, "selfish gene" theories. Under such theories, altruism still is behavior in one's best interest, where "best interest" refers to the objective of the gene (or genes) that "programmed" the people to sacrifice themselves in order to preserve additional copies of the same gene in others. In this way, selection theories manage not to contradict a higher-order axiom of behavior, which is that people act as utility maximizers in some, perhaps not obvious, sense. This principle, of course, itself gives rise to controversy over whether we truly are utility maximizers, or whether we maximize our *perceived* utilities (or at least try to), all the while acknowledging exceptions to this rule, like those actions that arise out of sheer stupidity. In any event, the other side to social traps is that occasionally, individually suboptimal behavior can be group optimal.

Altruism fascinates us, so it must be true that greed is more common. It has certainly been much celebrated and maligned. And two things seem clear: no one has to search hard to find examples of it and no one needs to theorize about it. Or do we?

In fact, for almost half a century social scientists of many callings have studied greed, often in the context of a well-known game called the prisoner's dilemma. The prototypical story goes like this: a serious crime has been committed. Two suspects have been arrested and are then separated. At this point there is not enough evidence to convict either of them for the crime. The district attorney (D.A.) attempts to squeeze a confession out of each of them separately. The background here is that if neither confesses, all the D.A. can get them on is a minor charge, like drug or weapons possession (amounting to, for example, six months in jail). However, if one suspect confesses but not the other, the confessor gets immunity while the other takes the full rap for the crime (say, a fifteen-year prison sentence). If both confess, then of course the D.A. will get them both for the crime (say, ten years each). Now if the suspects could both keep mum, they'd be fairly well off, but immunity is more attractive. After some reflection, both prisoners discover the fundamental temptation: that no matter what the other suspect does, confession is the better course of action. And the next very deflating realization for each is that the other prisoner will realize this too! Therefore, through both fear of the other's confession, and the temptation in one's own, the prisoners will likely each confess, resulting in the mutual ten-year sentences that they could have avoided by keeping silent.

Many of our interactions are in fact prisoner's dilemmas. The general schema is that there are two actions (or families of actions): to cooperate or to defect, for each of the parties involved. The best outcome for you is when you defect while the other cooperates; the worst outcome is the opposite scenario. Mutual cooperation works out well, but not as well as the "temptation" scenario. The situations range from the trivial—like whether you'll help clean up the mess two of you made—to the significant, like whether two automobile giants involved in a joint venture will honor the agreement. In pitting cooperation versus defection, the prisoner's dilemma weighs sacrifice and greed. It's a nasty game, and it has a political interpretation too: author William Poundstone goes so far as to equate liberals with cooperators and conservatives with defectors. Fair or not, his remark is provocative, and shows the extent to which the game can get under one's skin.

Is there a cure for the prisoner's dilemma? The only sure antidote seems to be not to play, but, of course, evasion is not always a viable strategy. Some authors look toward the possibility of repeated scenarios as a way out of the dilemma. This we will examine shortly. But perhaps the best medicine is to follow the general advice of game theorists Adam Brandenburger and Barry Nalebuff: when the game is bad, change it. That is, try to modify the conditions of the situation to nullify the prisoner's dilemma aspects. For example, in a joint venture, reduce the temptation the other organization may have to defect by establishing legal consequences for not cooperating. At the same time, sweeten the deal—sign a contract committing to a long-term partnership, with a considerable reward for cooperation.

Returning to the wider array of social traps, do situations exist other than pollution and overfishing that require cooperation or altruism for the greatest good for all? It turns out that such situations are becoming the rule, and not the exception, in all of our lives. In these predicaments a certain action when carried out unilaterally ends up improving one's standing. But when many others act similarly, everyone becomes worse off, as in the prisoner's dilemma. Robert Frank characterizes such situations as "smart for one, dumb for all." As *hors d'oeuvres* Frank reminds us how people need to stand up at concerts (because the people in front of them are standing) or talk more loudly at a cocktail party (because everybody else is talking loudly). More seriously, we engage in advertising wars and arms races. In each case the instigator gains an advantage that is neutralized when everyone else follows suit. At the end of the day, no one's relative position has changed but everyone has suffered higher costs. City dwellers who "must" send their children to private school fall into this trap, as do suburbanites who "need" three cars and end up in Sunday traffic jams en route to the mall. In fact Frank claims that all of our conspicuous consumption, itself a product of luxury fever, is landing us in the exact same smart-for-one-dumb-for-all situation. This component of the vicious spiral is simply a social trap.

Greed and the "Invisible Hand"

But to assert the prevalence of social traps is to deny the universal success of greed. Greed itself is easy enough to renounce, but if we rename it by the kinder, gentler term "self-interest," we are suddenly conceding that self-interest often does not win. And to make this last assertion is to contradict the prevailing socioeconomic principle in the West over the past two hundred years: the "invisible hand" of Adam Smith.

Although Adam Smith did not extol greed—in fact he based his moral philosophy on sympathy—his famous "invisible hand" theory purported to show that the welfare of a community *generally* derives from each member pursuing his or her own self-interest. The natural order through which this mysteriously would come about can perhaps be attributed to God.

It's a nice idea but it doesn't always hold. More to the point, Smith's sentiments provide the cornerstone for a belief—almost literally a holy belief—in free markets and an absence of protectionism and regulation. As with so many principles, the holy belief that I allude to goes beyond what the originator had to say. In this case, Smith's only mention of the famous phrase is the following: "by directing that industry in such a manner as its produce may be of the greatest value, he intends only his own gain, and he is in this, as in many other cases, led by an invisible hand to promote an end which was no part of his intention. Nor is it always the worse for the society that it was no part of it. By pursuing his own interest he frequently promotes that of the society more effectually than when he really intends to promote it." Smith gave no explication of this credo, but did state, more boldly, that "the study of [one's] own advantage naturally, or rather necessarily leads [one] to prefer that employment which is the most advantageous to the society." It is curious that in one passage, Smith was circumspect in his language, clearly not setting down a natural law, while in the other passage, he proclaimed that self-interest "necessarily" leads individuals to their (and everyone else's) greatest welfare. Interestingly, economic historian Jerry Z. Muller points out that Smith did not believe we always acted *correctly;* indeed, he felt that often, on account of our basic lack of rationality and our subsequent mistakes, we lose and the community wins. Lest we take Smith too literally, Muller comments that the "image of the 'invisible hand' . . . is a metaphor for the socially positive unintended consequences of the market, which through the profit motive and the price mechanism channels self-interest into collective benefits." Metaphor or not, too many modern commentators and analysts seem to believe that self-interest is somehow guaranteed harmless to others.

Smith was surer of himself in his rejection of government regulation, the complement to the invisible hand. (*Let me do my thing;* it will work out to everyone's advantage.) He wrote, "every individual, it is evident, can, in his local situation, judge much better than any statesman or lawgiver can do for him. The statesman who should attempt to direct private people in what manner they ought to employ their capitals, would not only load himself with a most unnecessary attention, but assume an authority which could safely be trusted, not only to no single person, but to no council or senate whatever, and which would nowhere be so dangerous as in the hands of a man who had folly and presumption enough to fancy himself fit to exercise it." To this day, the orthodox mantras invoke free markets, on the one hand, with the emphasis on "free" and all its associated heartfelt themes, and decry government intervention ("laissez-faire" being the phrase once in vogue; "small government," which encompasses more, is newer) on the other. But we note that just as self-interest cannot always lead everyone to the promised land, neither will the absence of government intervention.

Adam Smith is by no means the only eminent partisan of self-interest. The primary emphasis of liberal philosophy—in its development from John Locke, in his stipulation that life, liberty, and property are natural rights; to Jean-Jacques Rousseau, who somehow believed that despite entering into a social contract in which we relinquish our natural rights to the community, we will nevertheless retain our freedom, because the common good will provide for the individual good; to Thomas Jefferson's provision for inalienable rights in the Declaration of Independence (and the successful American and French Revolutions); to Jeremy Bentham, for whom the community was a "fiction," no more than a collection of individuals striving to maximize (his neologism, Daniel Bell tells us) their situations; to John Stuart Mill's view of liberty as the advancement of freedom and individuality; even in the Marquis de Sade, whose libertine philosophy argued that each person's pleasure from his (or her) own initiatives will outweigh any pain he (or she) might receive at the hands of others—is that the individual is valued over the community. I have to point out that, as we will see in chapter 17, there are really two philosophies at odds that have been lumped together in what I have called "liberal philosophy": egoism and utilitarianism. Adam Smith, it has been claimed, belongs to both.

With the above thinkers, not only is the individual preeminent, but *all* individuals can be preeminent; that is, we are always reassured, impossible as it may seem, that no one, acting in self-interest, will ever step on anyone else's toes. It is somewhat incredible to me that each in this succession of great minds goes out of his way to encourage self-interest and yet claim it is consistent with the common good. What we have is an interesting Möbius strip of a political spectrum, in which, by following liberal philosophical principles far enough, one ends up coinciding with views held by the right—the reduction of taxes and subsidies (especially social programs), small government, and so on, the logical extension of which seems to be libertarianism, an odd mix of ultraliberal philosophy with ultraconservative political economics. (Incidentally, if we follow this Möbius strip around the other way, we get the curious, Stalinesque confluence of communism and fascism.)

Let's Play Nicely and Share

The invisible hand plus a hands-off government engenders free markets. Free markets are fine for a wide range of endeavors. The competition that free markets stimulate is vital for providing incentives to innovate and to create new products, services, and efficiencies that maintain healthy economic growth. But certain things are public goods, things we share but do not trade, for example, armies and police forces, the Centers for Disease Control, libraries, roads, water and gas . . . well, maybe it's not so clear after all. Maybe you believe that you should only have to pay for what you use. Let's carry that to its logical conclusion. You walk or drive down street A and not B; your tax, which is now a toll, is charged for A and not B. But perhaps street C is a cheaper alternative to A, so you start using street C. Now apply this toll-road mentality to every aspect of your life. How much of your tax money currently goes to the police department? How many times have you "used" a police officer? But what about a nuclear warhead? Space station? Never? Then you need not have paid. But if no one paid, we wouldn't have these institutions. And conversely, if we could adopt "pay-per-view" for literally everything, wouldn't that alter how you did what you did? Of course—and this illustrates what the insurance industry calls "moral hazard." In the insurance setting, the idea is that you'll be a lot less careful with your car if it is insured for $50,000 instead of $15,000. The point is, traditional economic, free-market notions don't, can't, and shouldn't apply to all goods and services. Starting with the family, if we consider any community of any size (ultimately the global community), there is a natural dichotomy of goods and services into those that we own and those that we share, that is, those that are private and those that are public. And this fact renders the price-mechanistic, free-market, laissez-faire, egoistic system unsuitable as an approach to solve all of our socioeconomic problems.

I am not employing this argument as a paean to, say, communism. But we do live within a larger community. Politically, we need to govern ourselves, and economically (especially in our current stage of technological development and our reliance on limited resources), we need to share among ourselves. Even if you can dispense with armies, the Centers for Disease Control, the space shuttle, and a thousand additional major capital-intensive works, I bet that you cannot dispense with many others—such as insurance, which is by necessity a pooled monetary resource. Clearly, the rampant pursuit of individual happiness on everyone's part is not sustainable. We have conflicting preferences and goals, and in the face of scarce resources, some of our interactions are indeed zero-sum. Such situations create, sadly, a loser for every winner. In addition, analyses of the prisoner's dilemma and the wider category of social traps demonstrate that universal egoism can lead to universal misery.

Put differently, a community of individuals *can all lose*. Fortunately, however, the news is not entirely negative: our messengers here, the game theorists, have also brought us "win-win" scenarios. Even in the hopeless-looking prisoner's dilemma, we have evidence that the meek actually can inherit the earth, largely through the experiments of political scientist Robert Axelrod in the early 1980s.

Axelrod conducted tournaments in which various strategies (submitted as computer programs by international experts) competed against one another in prisoner's dilemma games repeated many times. In each play, two programs would square off by each choosing to either cooperate or defect. The best payoff (the "temptation") was five points for defecting while the other player cooperated; mutual cooperation netted three points, mutual defection scored one point, and the "sucker's payoff" from cooperating when the other defected, was zero. Each program played all of the other ones two hundred times apiece, and in the end, they were ranked by their point totals. The programs ran the gamut from "nice" ones that would tend to cooperate (despite defection being the better strategy in any one play of the game), to "mean" ones that would sometimes cooperate but then throw in a random defection, to calculating ones that would modify their play according to how they sized up their opponents. There were two remarkable results of Axelrod's tournament. All of the nice programs ended up substantially outperforming all of the mean ones. And, perhaps more surprisingly, the simplest and most transparent program of all emerged victorious. This program, "Tit for Tat" (TFT), submitted by Anatol Rapoport, started out by cooperating and from then on simply duplicated its opponent's previous action. If its opponent cooperated last time, TFT would continue the harmony. But if the opponent defected last round, TFT would punish it with a defection this time.

The main lesson gleaned by Axelrod—provided we have a future to consider—is that through acting cooperatively, curbing our fear and greed, we can provide superior long-run outcomes for ourselves and others. "Acting cooperatively" does not entail servile submissiveness. One must be tough also, Axelrod instructs, and quickly punish greedy "defection" in order to discourage actions that seek to prey on a generous partner. Sensible as these lessons are, they have largely been excluded from American culture, except in a few books for managers that appeared in the 1990s, urging them to compete through cooperation. (No doubt most managers viewed this oxymoron cynically.) Although this genre inspired a modest following, to bottom-line oriented business people it sounds as gimmicky as the latest self-help or New Age trend. We cannot help but be suspicious of such pop prescriptions as "compete by cooperating," because we are so steeped in the Vince-Lombardi-style winning-is-everything doctrine. (One of the worst things you can be called in the United States is a loser.)

Our reluctance to abandon our greedy ways is additionally fueled by our culture of individualism. Further, although social scientists such as Axelrod and Rapoport strove to demonstrate the extent of the conflict between the individual and the group, a huge socioeconomic transformation erupted on the world scene: the breakup of the Soviet bloc and of the USSR itself, and their subsequent "renormalization" (still happening) to a free-market economy. The Polish struggles for democracy, the demolished Berlin Wall, and the Soviet collapse were high drama. For many in the West, particularly in the United States, these events not only chalked up a victory in the forty-four-year-long cold war, but validated, even sanctified, the free market and capitalism itself, as the right path. The late 1980s were the death knell for Marxism and for communism in general (China, it was well known, had been steadily growing a market economy, if not the associated politics; North Korea and Cuba were visibly suffering).

Remarkably, hardly anyone pointed out that the Soviet collapse and the loss of its satellites need not imply that communism itself was faulty—imagine if all of chemistry, for example, were shelved on account of a few bad experiments. As the 1990s progressed, the tribulations of ordinary folk in Eastern Europe who had had the rug pulled out from underneath them were overshadowed in the U.S. press by stories of triumphant home-grown entrepreneurs as well as savvy Americans who capitalized on various new opportunities. In addition, we were occasionally fed stories about troubles in some partly socialized

Euro-nation. But when the Asian monetary crisis hit in late 1997, we were told that these up-and-coming capitalist tigers just didn't do it by the (our) book.

The point is, communism as it was experienced in the twentieth century was rotten, but this doesn't imply that all socialist incarnations are doomed. If we—the global *we,* which finally solidified in the 1990s—pursue untrammeled free-market exchange as the foundation of our economy, we will surely continue to create losers along with winners. The attendant problems of a sufficiently large underclass will eventually lead to a mandate to redistribute wealth: to subsidize, to socialize. Perhaps this mandate will be triggered by a fear of the underclass; perhaps it will be motivated by spiraling costs themselves as we all keep up with the Joneses. It is simply part of a natural cycle. The Clintons' initiative some years ago to establish universal health coverage was halted, but it will, in some form, return. Other public services and goods—like education—will likewise be scrutinized. The conclusions will be that capitalism went too far, and should not apply to certain universal needs.

Of course, communism couldn't possibly be the answer either, simply because of its absence of focus on the individual. Viability of a socioeconomic-political system requires *dual* foci. The individual must be valued through the provision of the freedom necessary to create, produce, and possess, as well as something larger: the freedom to *choose.* Simultaneously with the preservation of individual freedom, we must together uphold our community—not just to maintain law and order and provide for shared goods and services, but also to fulfill our need to *belong.*

Individualism liberates, but it separates and thereby excludes and alienates. A balance must be struck, both at the individual and societal levels, between emphasis on the self and emphasis on the group. Human needs for both poles are profound. Our need to express our individualism will always simmer, as will our need to belong to a larger group. Voltaire's observation about God is equally true in this sphere: if our communities are degraded, they will necessarily self-organize out of the resulting chaos of teeming souls; and if these souls are suppressed by the emergent group, they will eventually break their chains, too.

Fiscally, striking a balance between individuals and the group requires emphasis on community-based taxes, as well as a healthy dose of what I'll call "pay-per-use" activity. A cautionary note here is that, as our information-gathering and -processing ability continues to improve and seduce, we need to resist the urge to transfer the bulk of our public spending to the private, pay-per-use mode. Not that pay-per-use must have Orwellian consequences, but it would first erode our public goods and services and next erode our *civitas,* our sense of belonging. Public goods are not only necessary; they are the economic manifestation of our belonging to the larger group.

Let's expand on the public–private good dichotomy as a crucial dimension of individual-versus-group friction. If you live in the United States, it cannot escape your notice that a politician who increases taxes (or one who the people perceive as a tax hiker) faces almost certain doom at election time. The larger philosophical debate of individual versus group values, for us, has come down to the issue of raising taxes and allocating subsidies. As to recipients, not even the military is free from scrutiny anymore. Americans are particularly averse to community structures like taxes. Although they are not ungenerous, they do detest the loss of control over how their money is spent once they relinquish it.

This theme is worth a bit of exploration and conjecture. Why are Americans ostensibly less community minded than, say, Europeans? How else is this manifested? In what circumstances is it the other way around, for example, when American "can do" spirit prompts the organization of groups to carry out tasks?

Two culprits in the American retreat from community are automobiles and geography, both of which have helped to create sprawling, amorphous suburbs where those with the means have made their homes their castles, in opposition to the compact, snugly knit villages of Europe. Perhaps we can also blame our geography for our farther-flung families. But the real point is this: Americans have largely gravitated to a pattern, almost a style, that emphasizes exclusion as opposed to inclusion. I do not refer to the connotations of these terms with respect to class or race or gender. I simply mean the principle of not believing in subsidies. This spurning may derive from a particular concept of equity that is based on the monetary exchange of getting what you pay for, which also means paying the same price for the same provisions. And this "fairness" principle is the logical extension of self-reliance, itself derived from national traditions of independence as well as—to go back well over a century—our frontier mentality and our isolation.

But we have to remember that to subsidize is basically to share. Sharing is an essential human characteristic that occurs most naturally among, but is not limited to, family and friends. Why is it that as society "progresses" we are phasing out this trait? It's not just Margaret Thatcher and Ronald Reagan.

Now, many years after their tenure, the 1980s reforms continue to be extended to new arenas, often under the heading of "cost centers." This approach dictates that anything unprofitable must be dropped. Universities are less willing to tolerate esoteric seminars for four students that were formerly subsidized by running introductory sections of four hundred. Each class now has to generate a profit, so those with enrollments below a certain "break-even" point are canceled. Public transportation is more than ever a business, not a service, and bus and train routes must generate profits or face the axe. And the same bottom-line mentality pervades private concerns. We have to wonder when this principle will be applied to human life itself.

To recapitulate the above, I am speculating that a good deal of our national raison d'être involves the historical development of an independent people; that our isolation in the nineteenth century fostered this independent spirit; and that this spirit underlies our traditional sense of fairness. In addition to this, our attempts to tolerate multiple religions and classes (if not always races) diminished their importance and produced a singular emphasis on money as the only worthwhile carrier of value. Therefore money has served not only as a medium of exchange but also as a vehicle for expressing self-reliance as the foundation of equity. The consequence is that we don't like to pay taxes to support projects for others. No wonder that when an invention like the automobile comes along, the first thing our society does with it is to create suburban housing through which we can exclude those others (as signified by the white picket fences that so many seem to value).

Choice: The Right to Abortion and Its Linguistic Nuances

There are certainly other areas in which the struggle between the individual and the group is carried out. One, for example, that we will leave for chapters 14 and 17, is the blurring and intermingling of the public and private. Another one, with which we close this chapter, is whether society at large can dictate what a woman can do with her fetus.

The question of abortion divides our society like few others. And despite the fact that the U.S. Supreme Court decision *Roe v. Wade*, in which states were denied the right to prevent or restrict abortions in the first trimester of pregnancy, has stood unreversed since 1973, abortion remains an active concern in the United States (and some other Western countries). It is almost constantly in the media: there are occasional murders and acts of terrorism that, sadly and ironically, are committed in order to prevent abortions; the issue of whether public funds should be used to provide abortions is frequently revisited; and on abortion more than any other issue, politicians are required to commit unequivocally (as either "pro-choice" or "pro-life"). When politicians are forced to take a stance—and of course they are risk averse to do so, since any meaningful stance will lose as well as win votes—we know that the matter is a passionately fought one. Abortion presents perhaps the ultimate expression of the tug-of-war between the individual and the group. It also provides a good example of how linguistic nuances, which center on choice, emerge through widespread debate over a charged issue.

There are three reasons that those who support abortion term themselves "pro-choice." The primary reason is the straightforward one: proponents, some of whom would not personally opt to have an abortion, believe in the *right* to an abortion. There is a secondary reason, though: using "pro-choice" to signify pro-abortion links the right to an abortion to the higher right to *choice* that is so deeply imbued in contemporary America. That is, abortion sympathizers protect it under the venerable right to choose for oneself. In addition, to be *pro* is positive, which is attitudinally superior to being negative and restrictive. By discussing the pro-choice camp first, I am assigning to them the liberal, dynamic role, and relegating the opponents to a conservative, static role. Given the history of the subject, this seems logical enough.

But consider the pro-life camp. Their natural position is really antiabortion, and, further illustrating the preeminence of choice in our society, they are painted as antichoice by their opposition. But our collective consciousness prefers *pro* to *con*. Therefore, the logical thing to do is to find an ideal to support rather than one to reject. The ideal ideal for this purpose is, of course, life. It is because the promise of choice is so powerful a concept for the American public—it is this that has become our manifest destiny—that the countervailing slogan has come to fix upon life itself. Only life itself can outweigh freedom to choose, although Patrick Henry's "give me Liberty or give me Death" is a powerful rebuttal.

I suspect that the pro-lifers would reject my deconstruction of their term. They simply state that abortion is murder. And murder, the termination of life, is of course unacceptable. Therefore, if one is antimurder (and who isn't?), one must be antiabortion. As we said above, it's better to express things positively, as in this case, "pro-life." And life is the only player worthy to challenge the dynamic lure of choice.

The year 1973 was a pivotal year, and not solely on account of *Roe v. Wade*. The United States had just ended hostilities in Vietnam. The progressive 1960s—which were in reality the preceding ten or so turbulent years—were coming to an end. By this point in time the societal transformations that had begun a decade earlier were beginning to be consolidated. Ideas that had been radical just a few years earlier were becoming widely acceptable. Representative of this, the Supreme Court abortion ruling, which strengthened the rights of individuals, provided a fitting punctuation to the start of a new era. The 1960s were a cauldron of conflict, much of which revolved around the oppositional axes of the individual and group, and even more around the notion of opposition itself. It was a watershed era; things would never be quite the same again.

The stormy 1960s conjure up various feelings and images in our minds—strong ones for those who lived through the period. Experience, however, can give rise to selective memories. While I will not pretend to give a comprehensive summary, what I will do is present an overview with an eye on the themes of this book.

A number of issues are central to this historical period. They can be construed as oppositional, usually in some obvious sense; additionally, they form a number of interrelations that are integral to the emergence and influence of choice. In the intellectual and cultural domain, the 1960s are the period most contributory to the fall of modernism as the reigning model. One manifestation of this that we will discuss is the collapse and fragmentation of modern art.

Socially, the 1960s were a time of liberation; more precisely, an ushering in of greater independence and opportunity for many who had been relatively disadvantaged. The beneficiaries form two somewhat overlapping categories, each with different objectives. One category is that of minority groups, who sought to increase their opportunities through society's divestment of traditional but unequal treatment. The largest efforts with this objective were the civil rights movement and, as it was called, women's liberation. The other category focused more generally on the individual, although it had its greatest realization for youth. The objective was not equity but freedom. Freedom to choose one's lifestyle. The most tangible application of this sought-after principle was free love, but ironically (because it was organized by the government) the most metaphorical message of freedom was found in the space program.

Before delving into some of the events of the 1960s it is worthwhile to ask, why did it all come about? One catalyzing factor could have been alienation. The older generations in the West had experienced one or two destructive world wars and a crushing economic depression in between. Having grown up with difficult lives, they gratefully accepted their hard-earned prosperity that was realized in America in the 1950s and that would later reach Europe. But this prosperity was received very differently by their children, who grew up materially comfortable but with the dissonant and unprecedented specter of annihilation from a cold war that always threatened to go hot. When there is change, all generations have gaps, but this one seemed unusually large. Logically enough, when the younger generation was called to fight a dubious war in Vietnam, they balked.

Another catalyzing factor was the increased presence of choice. The 1950s had seen prosperity like never before. The older Depression generation perhaps had some lingering guilt regarding consumption. But, as writer David Halberstam points out, the 1950s was the era when (in the United States) "In God We Trust" started appearing on money. People had to be coaxed into feeling they deserved numerous goods, and thus spending and material aggrandizement was sanctified in a recapitulation of the Protestant ethic. For the younger generation, however, entitlement was the name of the game. And after college ranks had swelled post–World War II, and the increased capacity was maintained, this younger generation was the first where one could *expect* to grow up comfortably and then attend college in preparation for a *choice of career.*

The 1950s, as we realize now, was not a uniformly bland decade celebrating the newly arrived American dream. There was plenty of vocalized conflict and dissent, from the McCarthy accusations to the exhortations of the Beats. However, the voices of conflict did not penetrate through to the majority of the people. A decade later, they would.

The 1960s began in much the same way as the 1950s ended. There was no single galvanizing episode, although a chronological check of the records reveals an acceleration of events. The first "happenings," dynamic mixed-media artistic experiences, occurred in 1959. In 1960, federal courts ruled that *Lady Chatterley's Lover* was not obscene. The first birth control pill went on sale in 1961. Amnesty International was created in 1962. The civil rights movement gathered steam in 1963, as did anti-nuclear-weapons protests that increased in number and size (London, 70,000; Japan, 100,000). In the same year, Betty Friedan's *The Feminine Mystique* appeared. There were more voices, and they were louder and more widely understood.

Culturally, however, there were signs of devolution rather than evolution. As historian William O'Neill remarks, critic Dwight Macdonald was perhaps the first to perceive the fading of the avant-garde. "Midcult," the meeting point between high and mass culture, was eroding the avant-garde by sucking it into the mainstream. For example, forty years earlier Dada had sought to provoke, to satirize, and to shock. It was playful but it was serious. In 1960, the emerging Pop Art lacked Dada's conviction—but was much more accessible. Accessibility implied a lower common denominator, and through it the avant-garde was becoming disenfranchised.

Art's Peak—and Fall

Art critic Robert Hughes, in *Shock of the New* (1981) expanded on the theme that modern art was losing not only its power to shock but also its political role. For one thing, in bygone days, art did not compete with other media such as books, newspapers, magazines, and television. It was therefore more important and "contained possibilities of social threat and intellectual disturbance that it no longer possesses." Indeed, since Hughes's writing, the only shocking news we hear about art revolves around auction prices and obscenity (or is it that the auction prices are obscene?). Not that high prices and obscenity didn't exist before 1980. But for decades now art's shock has come from pieces that many find to be shock for shock's sake, like Andres Serrano's *Piss Christ* or Damien Hirst's sawn-in-half pigs in tanks.

Hughes notes how the market has destroyed the significance of artistic works. Moreover, the market, a bourgeois instrument, now serves to disarm—and quickly—any rebellious purpose that avant-garde art might have. The more revolutionary the work, the more rapidly it is converted into a mere purchase. Ironically, "The price spiral led to the discouraging paradox that works of art, once meant to stand apart from the realm of bourgeois luxury and display their flinty resistance to capitalist values, now became among the most eagerly sought and highly paid for."

The progression of insurgency and subsequent acceptance of avant-garde expression—modernism, in other words—had been the reigning orthodoxy for at least a hundred years. But by the 1960s this upward-spiraling dance of progress was becoming exhausted. One factor was the rise of cultural relativism. As Hughes notes, cultural pluralism had become so powerful a force that it overcame the sense of historical progress that reinforced the success of the avant-garde. For O'Neill, the disappearance of values in art foreshadowed the loss of values in society. Now virtually anything could be a work of art, and anyone could be an artist. Objective, or at least, established standards regarding truth or beauty were discarded, and this abandonment carried over to standards of conduct in other facets of life.

There were other factors present. According to Hughes, "American tax laws . . . in their benevolence towards the visual arts . . . destroyed the 'outsider' status of what used to be the vanguard. Modernism is now our official culture, and we have no other. The most vivid indication of this is the American museum." One function that a museum has, of course, is to preserve history. It is interesting to note, as Hughes does, how the founding of the (New York) Museum of Modern Art seventy-five years ago, along with the explosion of university courses in modern art post–World War II, played an instrumental role in turning the avant-garde into history, and simultaneously multiplying its monetary value.

Another effect that had snowballed was the elevation of art to almost transcendental status. Hughes writes, "Over the last half-century, the Museum has supplanted the Church as the main focus of civic pride in American cities. (At the same time, European churches were busy converting themselves, for survival, into museums.)" It is hard to disagree with this assessment; if you have any doubt, visit the Metropolitan Museum of Art or the Louvre again so you can be trampled by what seems like half of humanity. As for the analogy with the Church, Tom Wolfe had made the connection back in 1964: "The fact is, the Route through the art galleries bears approximately the same relation to Art as church-going, currently, bears to the Church." Despite its proliferation and mass accessibility, art has remained Art. It is holy and evokes a considerable amount of reverence. It is eternal (they say) and demands protection. And the museums and galleries aren't sufficient to satisfy our appetites through regular pilgrimages; we enshrine it in our homes as our pocketbooks will allow.

Another dynamic that became fossilized in the historical record by the 1970s was that of art movements. As Hughes puts it, "By 1975, all the isms were wasms, while the only people heard talking about 'movements,' and wistfully at that, were dealers, who missed a regular supply to punch the market along." By the 1970s there was no clearly identifiable mainstream to move against. Instead the art world saw the whirlwind of a tremendous multiplicity of styles, turned out by a glut of art grads, teachers, and unemployed artists all seeking to do anything provided it had not been done before.

So just what happened in 1960s art? Something important to observe is that art—and creative activity in general in the 1950s—was still a refuge for high culture. Hughes tells us that at that time, most serious artists, writers, and composers could not tolerate an association of images or values between high and low art. But the ever-more-present commercialization and media assaults on the senses would break down the barriers and force even artists to consider products and choices. Artists were sensitive to their surroundings, and this sensibility launched Pop Art in the late 1950s.

Richard Hamilton, the first user of the term "Pop," supplied a brilliant prototype with a 1956 collage entitled "Just What Is It That Makes Today's Homes So Different, So Appealing?" This work displays a buffed Adam-and-Eve couple at home, surrounded by a slew of products that more or less conform to Hamilton's characteristics of Pop Art, which include low-cost, expendable, mass-produced, yet—and notice the paradox—glamorous. (And indeed, by 1960, much of the developed world could obtain a household of affordable, glamorous items.)

Perhaps a remark of artist Robert Rauschenberg sums up the zeitgeist: "I was bombarded with TV sets and magazines, by the excess of the world. . . ." But imagery overload and glut are only the beginning. The ads that Rauschenberg and everyone else saw on television are there to give us choices and to sway our choice. Indeed, the ad was to become enmeshed with the world of high art shortly after Hamilton coined "Pop." At the same time that Roy Lichtenstein was elevating the comic strip and James Rosenquist, the billboard, to art forms, Jasper Johns and Andy Warhol finished what Hamilton began, with Johns's flags and ale cans and Warhol's Factory-produced tableaus of Campbell's soup cans, Coke bottles, celebrity images—and dollar bills.

Pop Art was by no means the only influential wave of the 1960s. As mentioned above, any number of artists and wannabe artists were attempting to push the frontiers of artistic expression. But the frontiers had virtually disappeared. Artists were starting to go around in circles. As writer Octavio Paz remarked, "the avant-garde of 1967 repeats the deeds and gestures of 1917. We are experiencing the end of the idea of modern art." And the oppositional art of the 1960s often merely revisited Dada's themes but it lacked a social or cultural message.

Dada had grown out of the despair of World War I. That war, as we had previously observed, went a long way toward shattering the optimism that the modernist program fed on, and Dada, epitomized by the Cabaret Voltaire in Zurich, 1916, equally shattered Art's complicity in the program. Ironically, although the Dadaists sought to save mankind (or at least themselves) from the ravages of warfare, their re-creation of art—utilizing "readymades" such as urinals, newspaper shreds, or even garbage—as well as their poems, which were composed of random words, served as the perfect *anti-art*. Never again could art be taken seriously. And what did Paz mean about 1967 recapitulating 1917? Two of the more celebrated works of the newer era were Piero Manzoni's series of his own canned shit (thirty grams each), and Yves Klein's empty exhibition (which recalled John Cage's earlier silent [musical] composition). Both Klein and Manzoni, incidentally or not, died before age thirty-five, as if to amplify the message that there is nothing else left to do. After fifty years, the completed cycle announced the same "art is dead" chorus that was, perhaps unwittingly, composed earlier. Pop Art and anti-art thus effectively completed the program that Dada (with more honorable intentions) had begun fifty years earlier: the equation of art and anti-art, aesthetic and antiaesthetic, profound and superficial, culture and commerce, handcrafted and machine made, single and multiple, object and subject. But after the half-century interlude, the world was aware of the score (blank or not) and the news was old. This time, when modernism clashed with its own extreme, it unraveled into postmodernism.

More Upheaval: Freedom and Rebellion

Art, of course, was not the only arena of opposition and confrontation. Popular music underwent an enormous upheaval, as rhythm and blues was transformed into rock and roll. The event (in the United States) that seemed to accelerate the acceptance of the new sound—and its associated lifestyle—was the televised appearance of the Beatles on the Ed Sullivan show in February 1964. But their image was, at least at first, clean and unthreatening. Just eight months later, the Rolling Stones made the same pilgrimage, but eschewed any conservative gestures in their appearance. Their press photo shows them in a variety of outfits, including sunglasses and striped pants, and a conspicuous absence of neckties. The establishment was quick to embrace the new genre; for example, Queen Elizabeth II bestowed the Order of the British Empire on the Beatles in 1965. However, rock and roll quickly drifted away from the love songs and catchy dance tunes of those early years and became a celebration of counterculture and a vehicle for social consciousness and rebellion, presumably not exactly what the Queen had in mind.

Rebellion—and the shedding of the past—was spreading everywhere. By the end of the 1960s most of Africa had gained independence from colonial rule.

The Vatican abolished Latin as the official language of Roman Catholic liturgy in 1964. And in that same year, the peacefulness of the growing civil rights movement gave way to riots, first in Paterson and Elizabeth, New Jersey. A year later more serious rioting would take place in the Watts area of Los Angeles.

The year 1965 was pivotal. People started burning draft cards, and then themselves, at antiwar demonstrations. Nothing was sacred and secure from scrutiny. Ralph Nader published *Unsafe at Any Speed,* a withering indictment of the Detroit auto industry. At universities across the United States, professors and other intellectuals joined students at antiwar "teach-ins." After 1965 the new movements were absorbed more quickly into the general culture. And even before youth culture was transformed into a more general counterculture, the cultural revolution itself, like avant-garde art, was being co-opted by the marketplace. The cycle time from shocking vanguard to common commodity was only a couple of years (now it is even quicker). O'Neill quotes theater critic Robert Brustein, who remarked in 1965, "'Now that the cultural revolution has become an arm of big business, the mass media, and the fashion magazine, values have all but disappeared from artistic creation, and a crowd of hipsters and their agents are cynically exploiting the fears and pretensions of a semi-educated public. Must we choose between a discredited Establishment and a careerist avant garde?'"

One of the hallmarks of the 1960s was the breakdown of the division between high and popular (or low) culture. We have already noted Macdonald's victimizing of "midcult." But the erosion was widespread, reaching far beyond a particular cultural intermediary. For example, the early 1960s saw rock-and-roll dancing (a low art form, to many) spread through the privileged classes like wildfire—witness the journalism of the day, stating "In recent weeks, throngs of Jet Set socialites have jammed the dance floors of such once-staid bastions of New York cafe society as the Stork Club and Peppermint Lounge, not only to twist but to jerk, poney, wiggle wobble and frug till the wee hours." O'Neill makes an interesting remark about the Twist: it "celebrated both individuality and communality . . . a hallmark of the counter-culture, the right of everyone to be different in much the same way." We note that, stylistically, it took two or so decades for people to manifestly express their "right to be different" in *different* ways. The 1980s and 1990s saw a multiplicity of styles, as well as a multiplicity of mixed styles, no doubt a symptom of postmodernism (which we will leave for later). But the individuality that the 1960s brought would remain.

The 1960s also saw a veritable explosion of fashion (as did, I must point out, the 1920s) in which stylistic diversity held sway. But—as with rock-and-roll dancing—like never before, this trend came from *below,* as O'Neill and others have noted. "Fashion had always been dictated from above, by Parisian couturiers and other authorities. But in the sixties it was the young . . . who set the pace. . . . By mid-decade even the great couturiers had accepted the new wave."

Mod, in all of its variations, was one major branch of 1960s fashion, and down-to-earth hippie handcraft was another. The latter garb was supposed to demonstrate one's connectedness to nature, as if the person wearing the clothes had fashioned them in harmony with Mother Earth. But the innocence, or at least well-intentionedness, of the hippie movement was quickly ruined. Dubious hangers-on were out simply for sex and drugs (and rock and roll). For many, drugs became the principal vehicle not only for expanding consciousness but also for widening individualism and choice of experience. But money did not disappear as a necessity—and neither did its attendant vices, crime and violence.

Another element of this new age of freedom and self-exploration was a surge in religious interest. But, as could be expected from such rebellious times, traditional practices were not the draw. Instead, young people turned to alternatives: Zen, sorcery, magic, and for those less adventurous, any number of spin-offs of the old Western standards. In the same vein, many turned to spiritual or self-help programs in the form of cults like Esalen and Synanon, or variants like T-groups and encounter groups. Some social critics see the age dominated by rationality, as represented by science and technology; others perceive a dominance of spirituality. Certainly the renewed interest in religion would indicate dissatisfaction with the purely rational. But politically, it pointed to a rejection of technology as embodied in the military-industrial complex wreaking death and destruction in Vietnam. There were thousands of mind-and-body groups that seemed to mediate between sensualism and sensibility, rationality and spirituality, technology and humanism, more or less offering a packaged version of getting in touch with one's senses—within reason—to the working middle class. All in all, these efforts seemed targeted to correct imbalances that were commonly perceived to be rampant. The important point, though, is that finally the mainstream was willing to listen to alternative messages and explore alternative philosophies. By now, enough constraints had been lifted. Freedom—freedom to choose—was becoming universal. It had reached critical mass.

To recap the points of this chapter, the liberal concepts of pluralism and freedom had finally broken through to the populace at large. These concepts spread along two axes. One was rights for subgroups (as defined by race, gender, sexual orientation, etc.) to obtain unbiased recognition and fair treatment within the larger community. The other was the right, for the new generation of privileged youth, to self-determination on an individual basis. But as with any social transformation, such a breakthrough does not come without a price. In the 1960s this price had various manifestations, for example riots and racial friction, or the considerable loss of young people (the "dropouts") from roles in "productive" society. Social rebellion—albeit costly—certainly evidenced the general notion of opposition that was central to civilizational progress.

In the cultural sphere, though, the motif of opposition, the very engine of modernism, seemed to peter out. In art, music, and fashion, the boundaries between high and mass culture dissipated. As subjectivity rose and objectivity fell, modernism—in its eventual absorption of the alternative—had become the establishment. Therefore what was acceptable or not became generally unclear, and creative expression began to either cycle around and borrow from previously visited ideas or to search for ways to generate shock for shock's sake.

After this trend continued into the 1970s, critics sensed that the new, eclectic sensibility was here to stay. The dominant cultural mode of modernism had no sooner become the accepted cultural ethos when it began to recede. What replaced it was, of course, postmodernism. Postmodernism, as we will see, was somehow simultaneously a hypermodernism still pushing the envelope, but also an antimodernism, bent on rejecting dogma, dissolving oppositions, and embracing diversity.

One aspect of the 1960s we have touched on is how the dissolution of the high–low cultural rift affected art, music, and other outlets. Let's turn now to some other consequences of this cultural fusion.

One of the important themes in the 1960s that we touched on in the previous chapter was the dissolution of the boundary between high and low (or mass) culture. As we have said, when high culture and low culture become one and the same, or to put it differently, when low culture is elevated through its adoption by the upper classes, and high culture—which now is no longer distinguishable as high culture—is co-opted by market forces and disseminated to the masses, there are repercussions. One is that the power, in both progress and message, of the avant-garde is blunted. Another is that standards—and underlying them, a sense of objectivity—will erode.

The Triumph of the Vulgar

Another way to express this concept is that through the intermingling of styles, a society's sense of *taste* is dulled. Suddenly it is difficult to tell the refined from the vulgar, the good from the bad. As critic James B. Twitchell writes, "We live in an age distinct from all other ages that have been called 'vulgar' because we are so vulgarized that we have even lost the word in common use, and, in a sense, the aesthetic category." When bad taste becomes inoffensive, we enter into what Twitchell calls *Carnival Culture*. And this quagmire has its roots in cultural relativism and the loss of the absolute.

Twitchell studies three media—books, movies, and television—and concludes that, because of the takeover of media management by business concerns, vulgar themes have driven out higher-class ones. In his version of Gresham's law, bad taste has driven out good. Various facts or events indicate that the barbarians have not only arrived at the gates, but have broken through. For one thing, the gatekeepers have by now generally either departed or have been replaced by impostors. But more on that later. Twitchell points out that by

1992 entertainment products had become America's number two export, behind military hardware. In 1988 and 1989, television network news programs spent an average of thirty-eight minutes a month on showbiz stories; in 1990 this average shot up to sixty-eight minutes. These programs are regular features now. Nintendo, a mere toy, in 1989 grossed more than a quarter of total U.S. book sales. And, apropos of our museum remarks, in 1990 the Museum of Modern Art staged an exhibition, "High and Low: Modern Art and Popular Culture." Finally the arbiters of taste had given in to validating low, popular expression, in which "the vulgar was at last accorded equal time and better space." Clearly for Twitchell, the trend that had begun around 1960 predominated within thirty years.

Admittedly, it's hard to say when high- and lowbrow cultures began to mix. For generations, and indeed, for thousands of years, new works or styles have appeared that were considered vulgar at the time but that eventually became acceptable, sometimes even esteemed classics. As Twitchell notes, in the 1890s Max Beerbohm reported that bicycle riding at Oxford "'was the earmark of vulgarity.'" Tourists today gape at the quaintness of the bikes, which seem to us clearly consistent with the slightly surreal and indeed nearly caricaturish high-culture environs. Perhaps more insightfully we can ask, when did high culture begin to get influenced by low culture (or the reverse), to borrow from it, to permit, even sanctify, a "trickle-up" cultural process (with no aquifers to reduce its toxicity)? And, as has surely been pointed out before, is this the same as asking, when did men stop wearing jackets and ties and hats, and women dresses, everywhere?

Back again to the 1950s. Jackets and ties were still the norm, but people were starting to get addicted to a new kind of commodity—and with it, new norms: television. Television may have been a barrel (well, at least a tube) of laughs for its growing audiences, but a few people—intellectuals namely (all of whom, through nature or nurture, represented high culture)—were pretty angry about it. Dwight Macdonald declared that "mass culture" (as exemplified by TV) was a "cancerous growth on high Culture." Art critic Clement Greenberg more innocuously called it the medium of kitsch. Of course, this dialogue has not disappeared today. Critics rail against television just as vehemently, and yet, not much changes. Everyone—especially the networks—knows that TV is mostly trash. (Recall an ABC ad campaign emphasizing that using 10 percent of our brain is far too much anyway.) Nevertheless, we continue to watch.

The Frankfurt School theorists cast the creators of television and other media as an evil and manipulative "culture industry" that, in its desire for maximum profit, sought to exploit the gullible, simpleminded masses. This view remains commonplace among the intelligentsia. Opponents would claim, however, that the creators and distributors of mass culture, rather than manipulating a befuddled public, are actually giving discriminating consumers *what they want*. And this latter camp has a powerful argument vis-à-vis today's (and less so, the 1950s) market: the consumers have the power to choose. In any event, Marshall McLuhan's famous "the medium is the message" taught us, among other things, that television, both in its content and more aptly, as a medium, provided *entertainment* like never before. And, whether a snobby intellectual or not, one seems compelled to admit, whether citing a least-common-denominator argument or Gresham's Law or through mere observation of what's on, the majority of what has been aired since TV's inception has been generally entertaining for the majority of the audience. (One also has to concede, incidentally, that with the advent of cable, there is quite a lot of worthwhile programming available. But we digress.)

That television transmits, on the whole, low culture, is not newsworthy. It is important to note, however, that early on, TV, like radio, offered its viewers a *choice*: to change the channel. Eventually, the advent of cable and the facility provided by the remote control gave rise to a new, virtually national, pastime: channel flipping. In fact, channel flipping, along with its direct descendant, Web surfing, enjoys a central role in today's postmodern life. It provides action within passivity. Pick news or movies, commercials or programs, sports or talk shows, dramas or sitcoms. Have a picture within a picture (for an extra $100). Concentrate on one program (these days, this is admittedly extreme) or endlessly cycle through the one hundred channels. Pay-per-view, or not. Above all, television actualizes what we want most: choice.

Of course, TV is not the only medium of low culture. The low culture revolution has penetrated everywhere; not least of all, it has percolated up to spark high culture and to pilfer a few things.

One thing that the sweaty masses are taking from the *haute bourgeoisie* is their travel destinations. Be it jet-set locations or local museums, the barbarians have long ago stormed through the gates. It is worthwhile to note that the jet age began just before 1960. In its infancy, only the privileged jet set could hop aboard. Ironically it was the jet airplane itself, in its capacity for passengers and its contraction of the globe, that eventually spelled the jet set's demise.

Maybe I harbor blurred memories of false realities, but it seems to me that certain locations used to be exclusive: say, Nassau, Acapulco, Saint-Tropez. Nowadays, Nassau is an inexpensive package trip for anyone wishing to hit the beach and throw a few bucks down the casino drain. A stone's throw away was Hog Island. Tom Wolfe tells us that this spit of sand was originally converted into "a resort for refined people" by upper-cruster Huntington Hartford for twenty-five million 1959 dollars. Now this resort is called Paradise Island and serves the same largely unrefined Nassau crowd. Formerly glamorous Acapulco has for years been locked in desperate competition with other "Mexican Riviera" towns and has had to rely on aggressive marketing to preserve whatever is left of its image. And Saint-Tropez has long since been buried by wannabes who are looking for Saint-Tropez. À la Heisenberg, when they turn up to look, *voilà*, it has changed.

Of course, the destinations themselves share complicity in their loss of exclusivity, and although we always vilify the developers, they simply act in their own perceived self-interest. This is even truer of museums, now forced under dwindling state funding to increase revenues. As the masses take over not just the sites but the entire *domain* of travel, the museums profit by being a must-see on every itinerary. (And witness the proliferation of those necessary guide-books.) No wonder the museums have become our churches.

As jumbo jets and hydrofoils continue to ferret out the upper classes and their exclusive enclaves, "getting away from it all" has itself become a valued commodity (as long as there is Internet access in the room). But the ants are ruining the picnics everywhere—and the upper classes, to protect what is left of their culture and sense of status, or at least, their lifestyle, have been forced to two refuges: walled villas and a disguised form of price discrimination that Robert Frank calls the "charm premium."

We can't climb over the walls of the villas. But we can all freely observe the charm premium. I first have to float an old and somewhat dubious assumption: that the upper class and the wealthy are synonymous, and that they are the purveyors, providers, and defenders of high culture. Although this assumption has perhaps been truer of the United States than Europe or elsewhere, I think it used to be a reasonable approximation, a decent working hypothesis. Now, things aren't so clear anymore (a sure sign of postmodernism).

The charm premium exists when a certain product costs more, usually much more, than a similar, functionally substitutable one. The more desirable product is differentiated by a small but distinct improvement in quality or features.

For this there is a surprising price gap. *Gulp*. To exaggerate, those who can afford the product do not need to ask its price, like the proverbial shoppers for a yacht.

The whole point of the charm premium is that the added value one obtains is largely the signal that one is able to afford the added value. Of course, the signal must be some (visible) characteristic, perhaps identified by the item's insignia. The additional versatility or greater quality—that is, the added value—is itself not worth the whopping premium. We don't get what we pay for. And this is not fair; those of us without beaucoup bucks are, indeed, discriminated against.

What we *do* get for the extra money is, of course, a status symbol. This psychology, as we discussed in chapter 5, operates in the domain of brand names and designer labels. (Note: to emphasize the physical manifestation, we say "brand" and the French say *marque*—the mark or brand that, as synecdoche, is what you are actually procuring, as image and label itself.) It is hard to say in general whether the labels are in fact higher quality goods. Probably some are, while some aren't. At the mundane, day-to-day level, most of us pay a small premium for certain things, like call drinks in bars or certain brands of beer. Equally, we avoid generic store-brand pharmaceutical products that are identical to the brand-name drugs. What all of this behavior adds up to, is an unfortunate and dangerous spiral in which the moneyed classes seek to distance themselves, and the lower classes tenaciously attempt to catch up. It used to be called "keeping up with the Joneses" but is more prevalent and insidious now than it was forty years ago.

It is safe to say, with Tom Wolfe, that back in the 1950s the upper classes wielded considerably more power and influence than they do now. And, although the inroads of the masses were worrisome, it was believed (at least by some critics) that Macdonald's triumvirate of highbrow, midcult, and masscult would endure. That is, that highbrow culture would be able to ward off poisonous influences and survive.

There Goes the Neighborhood

But Tom Wolfe has been taking society's pulse for a long time. And back even in 1963, he found, "Once it was power that created high style. But now high styles come from low places, from people who have no power." Wolfe found high society seeking refuge via "various esoteric understatements," symbols such as "Topsiders instead of tennis sneakers." Over the years, in a consumer world increasingly thick with products, it seems almost as if the upper classes and the producers of certain designer items have conspired to save their distinguishing symbols through the charm premium. (A Marxist or Frankfurt School devotee would surely blame this on a calculated move of the fashion industry to repress the proletariat.) The idea is that the stiff increase in cost for the premium goods would serve to exclude less wealthy wannabes. A game theorist would call such a pricing strategy a *separating equilibrium*. But is it possible to thus maintain the divisions in our society? Ordinary, but upwardly mobile middle classes have quickly learned to exude, even shout, wealth through a few choice purchases (a Mercedes or Lexus; a Frontgate grill; a Rolex).

This manner of consumption, especially typical since the 1980s, spelled, in part, "there goes the neighborhood." It was to get much worse. As the glut of products grew, so did a glut of counterfeits. People of *all* classes could equip themselves and acquire the requisite symbols for virtually nothing. But counterfeit goods aside, the problem of preserving high-class goods for high-class people became insoluble. No degree of charm premium could save the day. There were too many people laundering drug money by purchasing the most exalted status symbols at any price. Therefore the symbols lost their facticity of (representing) high class; that is, the equation of wealth and high class was invalidated. And, hip to react to this trend of vulgarism—contamination, more precisely—designers like Tommy Hilfiger and Nautica (not even a person) came along to sell the (white) suburban preppy looks of leisure (the outdoors, land and sea, health and joy) and winked as they inflated their prices and watched their merchandise get gobbled up in the inner cities too.

As could be expected, there was a backlash against this designer trend. Columnist Roy H. Campbell reported such a movement in the *Philadelphia Inquirer* in late 1997. He embedded the issue in the larger one of the struggle for civil rights, for equality and freedom. In this case the freedom is found in the purchase of clothing presumably requiring a great deal of disposable wealth. Campbell cited a small but growing backlash among blacks, who are exhorted by (presumably black) critics to reduce their materialism and increase their investment in their community. Rappers, for example, had recently begun to speak up: "Already, the Wu Tang Clan [a black rap group] . . . is rapping a diss on designer goods." Some time has now passed, and I don't believe the backlash has caught on.

To further complicate (and postmodernize) this topsy-turvy world of brand and designer semiotics, the upper classes, as Wolfe spotted so long ago, began to gravitate to and adopt the low, popular styles. At this point, when a Mercedes rolls by, much of what it used to stand for is lost. Consistent with postmodernism (as we will discuss), class-separating equilibria are largely disappearing. However, there are other signs, such as the runaway costs of higher education, that perhaps certain things will reemerge as they "should"; and these signs won't be arbitrary like Tom Wolfe's topsiders.

In so many places the high and low are forced to intermingle (if not always interbreed): supermarkets, airports, malls, drug stores, highway rest stops. What is flogged at these places is aimed at everyperson, since, naturally, the market adopts a lowest common denominator. In addition to this, and especially disturbing to the defenders of the highbrow, we are often indulged with product endorsements from on high. Andy Warhol noted long ago that Coke is drunk in the White House. In Britain, you can find Her Majesty's seal on a bewildering array of common foodstuffs. And back at the Oval Office, we used to see Bill Clinton's gluttonous testimonials for McDonald's. (Neither of the Bushes would step that deeply into American popular culture.)

At least foods themselves don't seem to have a legitimacy problem. Outside of the pizza battles in New York, there don't seem to be widespread problems of brand or restaurant misrepresentation. But with most other commodities nowadays, genuine or not, brand merchandise is well and truly *branded*. Isn't this lack of discretion a bit vulgar, a bit low-rent? Perhaps it used to be— when men still wore jackets and hats and ties. Now, it's capital letters, front, back, and sides. And more: certain goods come with a detachable proof-of-purchase, proof-of-authenticity tag or pendant: say, Coach bags (classy products marketed as exclusive); or, Nike shoes (omnipresent and clearly mass culture). On what fair basis can we distinguish motivationally between the wealthy, coiffured blonde and her Coach accessory, tag dangling from the strap, and a poor, inner-city teen with a filthy jacket but a Nike or Timberland tag dangling from his shoelaces? Vulgar? Good taste? Bad taste? Which one?

And speaking of taste, can bad taste become good? Culture critic Susan Sontag discussed this inversion in *Notes on "Camp"* in 1964. "Camp asserts that good taste is not simply good taste; that there exists, indeed, a good taste of bad taste." But camp is not simply bad art. It is a sensibility. It focuses on style, exaggeration, artifice, extravagance. Camp rejects traditional aesthetic categorizations. Just as dandyism was "the 19th century's surrogate for the aristocrat in matters of culture, so Camp is the modern dandyism." But unlike the dandy, "dedicated to 'good taste,'" camp "appreciates vulgarity. . . . [T]he connoisseur of Camp sniffs the stink and prides himself on his strong nerves." To Sontag, the critical distinction between high and low culture was found in the difference between unique objects and mass-produced ones. Camp does not differentiate among such categories, and thereby "transcends the nausea of the replica," finding "more ingenious pleasures . . . in the coarsest common pleasures, in the arts of the masses." High culture, for Sontag, is "basically moralistic." Avant-garde art and other extreme expressions act by creating a "tension between moral and aesthetic passion." But camp becomes entirely aesthetic by eliminating the moral issues. Sontag had conflicting feelings regarding her explication (and therefore "betrayal") of something that, at the time, was well-known but little analyzed, being "almost as strongly offended" by camp as she was drawn to it. In spite of this friction her essay resonates with positive sentiments. We are made to feel that the arrival of camp was necessary to counter the stuffy edifice of high culture, which had created and perpetuated the high–low bifurcation. This notion is consistent with the title essay of her larger volume *Against Interpretation*, which rebels against "the project of interpretation," the bulk of criticism as it has developed—a purely intellectual reaction to art. "What is important now is to recover our senses. We must learn to *see* more, to *hear* more, to *feel* more." Criticism has become a highbrow activity that ought to be cut down to size.

Not surprisingly, in mainstream media, criticism *has* been cut down to size, at least in one regard: the introduction of lowbrow criticism. We increasingly see more casual (mass-culture) reviews, ostensibly aimed at ordinary people. For example, from neighborhood newspapers to the *New York Times,* we see write-ups of budget-priced restaurants, written in plain style and with a lowbrow focus. Or we hear a New York City radio station with a mock critic doing movie reviews in which she breathlessly discusses the screening room's air-conditioning, how many snacks she had (and what they cost), how good-looking the actors were, and so on. Although this is definitely worth a laugh, don't forget that most of us are generally reduced in movie conversations to little more than comparing lists of recently seen films (the names of which are sometimes already forgotten) and exchanging penetrating comments like "it was good."

In this lead-up to a discussion of postmodernism I have aimed to show that the dissolution of the high-culture-versus-mass-culture distinction, which gathered momentum in the 1960s, has been a theme central to contemporary society. But we see that this theme is concerned with the question of the preservation of the *symbols* of high culture, class symbols in fact. And the current reality is that the purveyors of the products that have signaled class differences have succumbed to the forces of the mass market. The upper class has been hoisted with its own petard, as items like the Mercedes-Benz hood ornament signify almost anything—a purchase; a lease; clean money; dirty money—and therefore nothing. And tied to branding is the very notion of authenticity itself, and thus the issues of "the real thing" and more broadly, reality itself and its manifestations or characteristics—facticity—reappear.

Classics Are the Real Thing

One notion our society has tried to hold on to is that of the "classic." Alas, even this category, never exactly clear-cut to begin with, is becoming fuzzy. To turn back to movies, consider Akira Kurosawa's *Rashomon,* which, being an old film and a masterpiece, is presumably a classic. But how is this designation decided? One attempt to bestow the appellation "classic" on a film is to remake it. It used to be the case that remakes were done after twenty or thirty or forty years. But now, remakes confer historicity on the originals after only a small gap in time. Some remakes dispense with the historical dimension altogether. Such films basically provide a straight reproduction of the same product with a different cast (and, sometimes, a different language) only a short time after the original has been released. What's more, the film landscape is getting cluttered with any number of restored originals playing at first-run theaters, some of which boast a few "significant minutes" of previously edited footage. Additionally, Hollywood has started to cash in on prequels as well as sequels. Also flooding the market are behind-the-scenes, documentary-style pieces, which give each individual viewer the intimate special-guest-only, backstage feeling and therefore confer added value far beyond mere how-it's-done curiosity.

Other films that proliferate nowadays are just higher-budget, feature-length versions of television series, which in turn are (sometimes) partly based on an actual event (for example, *The Fugitive*). Still others are loosely based on books, often with an (actual) historical component. In true postmodern fashion, the totality of these efforts levels the playing field among history and fiction, old and new. And nostalgia?—we discover that merely revisiting the previous decade is enough to satisfy many pangs of sentimentality.

As we have mentioned before, the cycle time from introduction to mainstream has been decreasing. The fall of modernism and the rise of cultural relativism have ensured that the alternative is not at odds with established norms. The mainstream is now licensed, as it were, to gobble up whatever comes along. This happens pronto, thanks to the ever-more efficient distribution networks and the upward-spiraling demand, reflective of a society that is increasingly receptive to the pluralistic tradition. Increasing variety has expanded choice, and through this our collective appetite for choice has become self-generating. The rapid absorption of new expression serves to blur distinctions between new and old, contemporary and classical. When *Pulp Fiction* came out (just two years after the release of *Reservoir Dogs*) Quentin Tarantino was suddenly an established (and emulated) filmmaker with a style that seemed to have been around forever.

Such observations need not be confined to the domain of cinema. Now 1970s' and even 1980s' rock is virtually classical music. A computer game that's five years old can be dubbed a classic (for example, SimCity is marketed this way), and a computer game that's twenty years old is positively ancient. Another history blurrer is the fairly recent phenomenon of biographies of young people, usually athletes in their early twenties. These days, after one good season, sports figures garner multiyear, multimillion dollar contracts, often with the result that their subsequent performance flops, or they're gone forever with an injury. So just as quickly as these athletes come and go (not to mention how frequently they move from team to team or how often the teams move from location to location), their notoriety must magnify within a small ribbon of time. Hence, out come the biographies, one step ahead of their retirements.

Reprise: Reality, Objectivity, and Subjectivity

Now back to *Rashomon,* a 1950 film based on the story "In a Bush" by Ryunosuke Akutagawa. *Rashomon* tells the story of a renowned Kyoto bandit, Tajomaru, who waylays an elegant couple as they travel on a path through heavy woods, attacks them, and is subsequently captured. Just about the only clear facts are: the three relevant identities; that Tajomaru ties up the man and forces himself on the woman; and that the man dies. Three others who are waiting out a rainstorm skeptically recount different versions of the incident. Their scenes serve to punctuate and narrate the episode, which is otherwise cinematically depicted from four successive points of view.

The first version, Tajomaru's, shows the woman eventually giving herself, so to speak, to him in front of the bound husband. She then demands that one of the two men must die (and thereafter she will belong to the other one). Tajomaru releases the husband and after a valiant sword battle, prevails. The wife, in the meantime, has run off.

The wife's story is similar only in the general setting and scheme. The most glaring difference is that in her version, after she is attacked and Tajomaru has fled the scene, she approaches her husband with a dagger and then faints. She forgets what happens next but by her own admission she seems to have stabbed him to death.

The husband's story is relayed to us through a medium. As with the other accounts, the three storytellers are extremely cynical about each version. But what gives each story its facticity is the film segment that we view. Had *Rashomon* been a courtroom trial, any witness's oral testimony could be found to be persuasive or wanting. We would hear their words but we wouldn't *see* their story. But *Rashomon* presents to us the filmed sequences—which, to our eyes, carry more veracity precisely because they're filmed. We forget, for example, that the husband's version is told through a medium, because the only "medium" that counts is the filmed account.

The husband's story diverges from the others. In this report the woman goes off with the bandit, and then attempts to persuade him to kill her bound husband. Tajomaru, nonplussed, then releases the husband, who in turn commits suicide.

There is a fourth account, but whose? It turns out that one of the three storytellers happens to have observed everything. Finally it appears that Kurosawa's circle of subjectivity will be broken. The observer relates that after the rape, the bandit begs the woman to marry him. She refuses and is able to free her husband. The husband, who must now confront Tajomaru, refuses now to risk his life for his wife. But she exhorts them to fight it out, and they do, with Tajomaru killing the husband.

We have no time to relax in the satisfaction of having found out the truth. The observer's account is challenged. It seems now that *he* may have killed the husband and stolen a valuable inlaid dagger that may have played a role, and he therefore had incentive to falsify his story.

The entire presentation of *Rashomon* pits mendacity and skepticism against the filmic facticity of the four accounts. On the one hand we are constantly reminded that the protagonists have exaggerated, have lied. "Men are weak, they lie," we are told, and "women fool themselves." But on the other hand, for each version in succession, the very medium of presentation—a film within a film—provides incontrovertible evidence for that person's description being the correct one. These ostensibly objective segments give way to conflict and subjectivity. By pitting logic against photography, Kurosawa has brought the dance between subjectivity and objectivity, truth and fiction, to a higher level.

Inevitably, discussion of the objective–subjective rift will bring us back to the physical sciences. The paradox presented in *Rashomon* is powerful and compelling, but ultimately we reassure ourselves, as we do with small children, that it's just a story. We have already discussed paradoxes in physics but the next one, dating from 1965 (that year again), shakes our belief in objective reality to a greater degree than the others.

Thanks to widespread popularization, much of the educated public is familiar with the Heisenberg uncertainty principle and Schrödinger's Cat, two paradoxes of twentieth-century physics that we have already discussed. A third paradox that is lesser known, but additionally responsible for eroding our beliefs in objective reality, was introduced in a thought experiment by physicists Einstein, Podolsky, and Rosen (EPR) in 1935 and rebutted in a real experimental format by John Bell in 1965. Bell's work, like so much of modern physics, defies our intuition. In the end, objective reality is not further compromised but there is ample opportunity for third-hand (and third-rate) interpretations to arise that support various unscientific phenomena such as telepathy. Although unintended by the physicists, these interpretations tend to diffuse, enhancing our feelings of a loss of the absolute.

The EPR experiment in its more modern form (which Gell-Mann attributes to David Bohm) goes like this: a certain particle at rest and without "spin" decays into two photons. The laws of physics dictate that the photons have identical polarization. This polarization has two components, circular and plane polarization, and just as in the usual statement of the Heisenberg uncertainty principle, where both momentum and position cannot simultaneously be specified, circular and plane polarization cannot both be simultaneously given, either. But in this experiment, if you measure, say, the circular polarization of one photon, you know what the circular polarization of the other one must be. But then, by measuring the plane polarization of that photon, you would know *both* polarizations of the first photon, an apparent contradiction. Therefore EPR concludes that something is wrong with quantum mechanics; it cannot completely describe reality. Or, if quantum theory is correct, then *either* the photons do not exist in an objective state at a given point in time, which is bizarre, *or* the state of one photon instantly affected the state of the other one, far away! This instantaneous action at-a-distance is what inspires claims of telepathy and other phenomena such as communication faster than the speed of light.

Pagels carefully describes Bell's deeper investigation. The initial decaying item is an atom of positronium. The atom decays and the photons fly off with their polarizations perfectly correlated. A "polarizer" is set up for each photon. When set at a certain angle, the polarizer has a certain probability of blocking a photon. What Bell does is to vary the angles of the polarizers relative to one another. (You can get the feel of this by playing with two pairs of polarized sunglasses.) *If* the states of the photons are objective (that is, the states exist and are not a matter of opinion) and *if* what happens at one polarizer does not influence what happens at the other, *then* Bell shows a certain mathematical inequality must hold. But, in actual experiments, the mathematical condition is violated. This is confusing—now it sounds like the experiments confirm either action-at-a-distance or the nonobjectivity of the subatomic world.

To rephrase Bell's argument, the experimental violation of the mathematical inequality need not rule out subatomic objectivity. After all, various physicists had postulated the existence of hitherto undiscovered "hidden variables" that lurk underneath the indeterminacies of quantum theory and provide an objective model. But on account of the violation of Bell's inequality, belief in an objective quantum world would seem to necessitate the acceptance of surely absurd long-distance causality. Here Bell shows that there is an escape from the horns of the dilemma. The polarizations of the two photons are perfectly correlated. Because of the probabilistic nature of a photon's passage through a polarizer, its getting through is a *random* event. The same is true for the other photon. Now consider a sequence of photon pairs and recordings. What we have is simply this: two random streams of information. These sequences just happen to be correlated—but not due to any sort of long-distance causality.

Bell brings this completely down to earth by describing an eccentric he calls Bertlmann (as retold by Gell-Mann). Bertlmann always wears one green and one pink sock (sometimes on different feet). If you observe just his left or his right foot, you see a random sequence of green and pink socks, since Bertlmann randomly chooses a sock to put on, say, his right foot. But the sequences on his two feet are perfectly correlated—you need only to observe one foot to know what color sock is on the other foot.

One interesting thing to observe here is the slithery escape, in this interpretation, of the physicists by invoking noncausal correlation. Usually this defense is used by social scientists, who need to remind us that two things that *vary together* (which is what correlation is really pinpointing) need not causally affect one other.

You may have wondered if there is some explanation of this EPR–Bell conundrum in terms of the many-worlds theory. There is. Gell-Mann briefly brushes away the confusion by saying, look: the two measurements in the EPR scheme (that yield the impossibly precise circular and plane polarizations simultaneously) simply take place on two different, mutually exclusive branches of history. But EPR requires that the measurements be used together—which, in the many-worlds version of quantum theory, is not allowed. The paradox is thus dissolved. But as we've already seen, the many-worlds theory, however elegant, involves plenty of potential weirdness; to remind you, Gell-Mann says that we can not rule out the possibility of the existence of other equally real, but different, worlds that continue to diverge.

So, maybe we've come full circle. In all this uncertainty, what *is* clear is that our grip on physical reality, as best as the physicists can understand it, has become strange and fraught with contradictions and choices of measurements and interpretations. And this development is very well correlated with the increasing complexities, contradictions, and choices that most of us face in our personal lives.

Einstein himself, the towering giant of so much of modern physics, could never accept the paradoxes and uncertainties inherent in quantum theory. Even after his friend Kurt Gödel rocked mathematics in 1931 by showing, roughly speaking, that mathematical theory itself must be incomplete—that there exist truths that cannot be discovered—Einstein sought, in vain, a complete and unified theory for physics. Ironically, Einstein, through relativity theory, was perhaps the most influential of all in eliminating the primacy of a single, objective, point of view. But hopes for an ordered, sensible Einsteinian world are all but dashed, and with them, our sense of authority dwindles further. The absolute has been lost.

Over a century ago, we began to lose our faith in religion (or in God). We obtained little relief from science, which too often had frustrated us with its inconsistencies and eternal secrets. And, as we have seen, high culture eventually lost its veneration too. Over time we naturally increased our emphasis on the subjective—ultimately focusing on ourselves. And that focus, though it makes us vulnerable, though it precipitates existential crises (and made a couple of generations of analysts rich), and though it weakens our sense of community, liberates us.

Throughout this book I have been teasing with the notion of the postmodern. Postmodernism seems to be many things: it intersects with the postindustrial information age; it is at once both antimodernism and ultramodernism; it is the realm of blurredness, a jumble of styles. Or perhaps postmodernism is all of these and yet none or them—perhaps it is simply a catchy term for the contemporary era. In any event it warrants the attention that follows.

Attempting to define postmodernism is a difficult task. The term is overused. Often it's misused. Some casually call it "PoMo." Many seize on it as the all-defining feature of modern (or is it contemporary?) life, shaping the future as well as the present. Certain exponents—critics, artists, architects, and writers—who are exalted as exemplary practitioners of postmodernism declare that they have nothing to do with it. And there are those who claim it means nothing at all. Most of us outside the fray don't know postmodern from modern. We ask, didn't the ancients think they were modern? It seems likely they did, although Richard Appignanesi and Chris Garratt (et al.) claim that the first use of the term "modern" in the sense that we use it was by the Abbot Suger in the twelfth century. And, we naively query, if we're postmodern, what about future generations? (Neopostmodern?)

The typical scholarly approach is to note that "postmodern" seeks (if we use some editorial whimsy and allow the term some activity) to differentiate itself from "modern." So, one continues by trying to pin down "modern" and "modernism"—at least, retrospectively—and then distill from contemporary culture, just what it is we do and think that transcends the merely modern. In other words, to use a postmodern term, we will analyze a *paradigm shift* that has taken place.

Modernism and Progress

To reiterate what we've seen in previous chapters, modernism is basically the following. There is a certain, well-defined, recognized establishment, or mainstream. Challenges, in the form of competing, alternative styles or ideas, are mounted against this status quo. The bold creators form the avant-garde. Often the new material is largely ignored or rejected, and it disappears. But sometimes, the alternative, the avant-garde, catches on. There is a snowballing effect, a trend. And if the trend is pervasive and enduring, it can supplant the status quo. The new movement is the dominant one now—and is therefore the new establishment, the next mainstream. A paradigm shift has occurred. This is modernism. Viewed as a system, modernism continually undergoes evolution and growth through an unending sequence of revolts, each one of which temporarily establishes a new equilibrium. This evolutionary turnover process sounds natural and timeless. Why "modern?" How long has this been going on, what happened before, and why has it ended? It's difficult to imagine progress as occurring through any other construct.

All of us have been trained by our experiences to view progress as natural. Indeed, over the past century, it has always been present for us, and therefore it is something to expect. But progress didn't always exist. Looking back on the so-called Middle Ages, we all know how the Renaissance took us "forward." But remember that the typical Renaissance theme (the rebirth, right?) was to recapture the truth—and beauty—of the ancient Greco-Roman teachings and styles. This mindset was to reestablish absolutes—artistically, philosophically, and scientifically (science in the form of "natural philosophy," as it was called). Of course, this typical perspective I remind you of is oversimplified, and moreover, not really the case. The Renaissance that we mentally place in the fifteenth and sixteenth centuries in fact began much earlier—around 1300. It was a complex period of vast social and economic, as well as humanist and artistic, change. As an engine of transition, the Renaissance ultimately had less impact as a recovery operation in search of ancient perfection than it did as a vehicle of transformation and an agent of exploration and discovery.

Progress? When the dominant ethos is the recovery of lost ideals, progress reverses chronology. But consider the era of exploration (of sea, land, and eventually sky) that followed the Renaissance. It redrew the map, and taught Europeans to think beyond their boundaries. At the same time, the Reformation broke down the uniform hold that the Roman Catholic Church had on religious thought. New questions were being asked, and sometimes, the old answers were insufficient. The earth was not the center of the universe, and large rocks did not fall faster than small ones. The debunking of the classical truths, the fragmentation of Christianity, and the expanded world view begat the spirit of the Enlightenment: the search for knowledge and betterment. The ancient absolute was being overthrown, and replaced with the certitudes that science was uncovering. This was *progress*. This was the beginning of the revolution-and-overthrow pattern that characterizes modernism. Philosophically, this was the paradigm of Hegelian dialectic—progress via thesis, antithesis, and, ultimately, synthesis, reconciling the oppositions. The mainstream swallows (and digests) the alternative, only to find itself utterly changed. (You are what you eat.)

Progress involves the ever-ascending pattern of learning more about the world, and using that knowledge to improve our conditions. Most direct, and easiest to comprehend, are physical and material improvements. Not surprisingly, scientific and medical advances, and their concomitant technologies, are easier to come by than social change. Therefore, for three hundred years, advances in scientific thought, by which we mean the successive installation of theories, each one purportedly eclipsing its predecessor as a (more) faithful *model* of *reality*, have been the primary sources of progress for us.

Our successes in science, however, have led to the ever-building confidence in our ability to *control* our world. The often-ignored downside is that we take too much for granted and ignore our tenuous relationship with the natural world which, I remind you, is still out there (albeit shrinking). Every so often we receive a wake-up call—for example, the huge Lisbon earthquake of 1755, which obliterated a large port city at the height of the Enlightenment, or the catastrophic tsunami in late 2004, or the appearance and spread of HIV, first noticed in 1981 (and, as of this writing, still infecting millions and still incurable). The Lisbon earthquake shook the Europeans' confidence in a benevolent God (even if, for many philosophers, it was God as designer of, and not participant in, the universe). The HIV/AIDS crisis, still construed by some as a religious message, is shaking our confidence in our ability to control—author William Irwin Thompson would say, "replace"—nature.

Progress? What about socially, and morally? What about our spheres of expression—literature, music, art, architecture, and so forth? Obviously, the theme of modernism was not lost on these domains; if anything, they appropriated the progressive model that science had established, and indeed, when the term modernism is tossed around, it is with respect to these categories of expression and their successions of styles, not science. We refer to *modern science*, but not modernism in science. The striving for new knowledge, the spirit of exploration, and the successes that science gave us inspired similar challenges in arts and letters. Having said this, it is immoderate to make the claim that scientific progress led to modernism in the arts. To explore this question is to deal in the apples and oranges of the objective (what scientists believe science approximates) and the subjective (what is to most of us, the raison d'être of the arts). Einstein subsumes Newton; but does Stravinsky replace Bach, or Matisse, Rubens?

Although the modern project of scientific progress is 300-odd years old, Clement Greenberg saw modernism as a self-conscious, self-referential mode of thought begun by Kant just over two centuries ago. Greenberg identified modernism by its absorption with self-criticality, writing, "Because he was the first to criticize the means itself of criticism, I conceive of Kant as the first real Modernist."

In art, according to Robert Hughes, modernism also dates back to about 1800. The avant-garde required the formation of a European bourgeoisie steeped in the liberal thought of the Enlightenment, and therefore it could not have emerged until 1800. And moreover, Hughes writes that prior to 1800, because of the system of patronage, "'subversive' innovation as the basis of artistic development could not have occurred." The French Revolution of 1789 went a long way toward demolishing that system. In replacing the monarchy, the bourgeois audience "did create the permissions within which the artistic variety the salon had come to express by 1820 could ferment and nourish an avant-garde." Hughes also points out that the first use of the term "avant-garde" in the cultural (and not military) sense was by Henri de Saint-Simon in 1825; a protagonist of his invention exclaimed, "'The power of the arts is in fact most immediate and most rapid; when we wish to spread new ideas among men, we inscribe them on marble or on canvas.'" But for Hughes the first major avant-garde artist, fresh and provocative, was Gustave Courbet, an outspoken and influential preimpressionist.

Still others have marked the start of modernism in art at around 1860, when Édouard Manet established painting as a self-conscious and self-referential activity, with one eye on the historical life that works acquire through their presence in the museum, and another eye on the (bourgeois male) onlooker. This observer, merely by viewing, was implicated in dalliance with unclothed paramours in works like *Olympia* and *Le Déjeuner sur l'herbe*. At the same time, Charles Baudelaire (Octavio Paz and Jürgen Habermas tell us) developed an art criticism in which "color, lines, sounds, and movement ceased to serve primarily the cause of representation; the media of expression and the techniques of production themselves became the aesthetic object." Baudelaire also sought to add art to the existing vehicles of progress, the physical and social sciences.

Judging by the way modern art has been taken seriously, alongside enjoying a long-standing popularity boom and an astronomical rise in value, this Baudelairean ethos seems to have been generally accepted.

Society Undergoes Specialization

We have reviewed how the turbulent 1960s saw the beginning of the end of modernism as the dominating theme of Western culture. And we have described several aspects of postmodernism that took over fairly rapidly. Before exploring postmodernism in more detail, it will enhance our perspective to consider another dimension of modern life that we have only touched on—the compartmentalization of various societal functions, analogous to the division of labor that had helped forge the effectiveness of the Industrial Revolution.

One cultural division that much has been made of is the gulf that has developed between the sciences and the humanities, decried and belabored by writer C. P. Snow. But I am referring instead to social theorist Niklas Luhmann's thesis that modernism began with the breakdown, beginning in the seventeenth century, of the "natural unity of society." Luhmann's idea is that society instituted the substitution of ideals in place of natural norms. For example, philosophers and others conceived of *happiness* as something for everyone to aspire to. This substitutive pattern accelerated; at the height of the Enlightenment in the mid-eighteenth century, artificial ideals such as moral principles began to replace natural ones. One consequence was the focus on equal rights that was brought to political systems. We note that this shift parallels the artificial replacement of nature as carried out by the emergent Industrial Revolution. However, Luhmann asserts that the substitutions that took place were attempts to create or maintain a unity within society, to neutralize differences. Increased emphasis was put on developing a normative framework, for example, the interest in utopianism.

But by the late nineteenth century, Luhmann claims, there existed a significantly broadened division of labor among sectors of society. Consistent with this, the principle of division of labor, as noticed by Adam Smith early on in the Industrial Revolution, would reach its fullest impact in the mechanized assembly lines that sprang up after Henry Ford introduced the first one in 1913. Division of labor entails *specialization;* the more division of labor, the higher the specialization—and the higher the output in a productive system. Luhmann sees the sectors of society as not only increasingly specialized (legal, economic, scientific, etc.) over time but also as emergent *systems* acting on their own. The less concert that exists among them, the more the potential for one to cause problems in the others; for example, science and technology led to the development of nuclear weapons, which in turn has led to problems in the political sphere. Thus the modernist project of building unity in society started to crumble. The upshot of this fragmentation and discord is our post-modern society: the loss, through the division of labor and specialization of our functional systems, of modernism's strides to maintain unity of purpose.

Certainly, vastly increasing specialization has been carried out in the intellectual sphere. In universities, reorganization has repeatedly occurred as academic disciplines have been defined and developed and differentiated. Although at times like the present, there is some perception that the divisions have been carried too far, and various efforts to develop interdisciplinary programs crop up, specialization remains the dominant academic culture. For example, an academic will risk being ostracized by doing research in a field not in one's own well-defined realm—a realm defined in part by association with mentors or through mere presence in a particular institution. Whether the prevailing distrust of outsiders is justified, the aura of specialization that pervades academics is consistent with the division-of-labor paradigm that we have discussed. To be fair, by the twentieth century virtually no one could master multiple fields of study anyway, simply on account of the explosion of information and advances that had been amassed in countless areas. In the mid-nineteenth century you could have been, say, a "natural scientist" with a strong grasp of, and ability to contribute to, diverse areas. Not so a hundred years later. Moreover, generally speaking, the Renaissance man is gone. To be at the top of one's field, for most who conduct research, necessitates relative ignorance in most other (even closely related) pursuits. Only those who have an extraordinary capacity for information as well as a bottomless curiosity and boundless energy can manage expertise in different areas. Virtually no one can be at the cutting edge of discovery in two or more fields simultaneously.

Division of labor—at the societal and intellectual levels, not to mention in the factories—and the specialization that it generates are consistent with the development of choice as a societal focus. Specialization entails opposition; and we have observed the connection between opposition and choice. But Luhmann's interesting thesis seems a bit removed from the nuts-and-bolts of our actual cultural happenings since the 1960s. More important, it doesn't help us understand, specifically, what postmodernism is.

Features of Postmodernism

It is necessary to discuss postmodernism in some depth because many theorists feel that postmodernism is the most characterizing feature of our times. My goal is to convince you that the key attributes, if not the entirety, of postmodernism are tied to choice. By "tied to" I have to be slightly evasive; I mean in part derived from, in part fueled by, in part correlated with (again, in the sense of two elements correspondingly manifesting themselves, being associated though perhaps not by cause and effect). A convincing connection can be made when we realize how much of postmodernism's themes are oppositional.

In a broad sense, postmodernism can be viewed as inherently oppositional: as antimodernism. Theorist Fredric Jameson gives examples of such reactions across a range of creative media. These, which include "the pop buildings and decorated sheds celebrated by architect Robert Venturi in his manifesto, *Learning from Las Vegas;* Andy Warhol and Pop Art, but also the more recent Photorealism; in music . . . John Cage [and] Philip Glass . . . in film, everything that comes out of Godard . . . in contemporary novels . . . William Burroughs, Thomas Pynchon and Ishmael Reed on the one hand and the French new novel on the other," are some among the many instances and types of what we call "postmodern." As pure opposition, there is nothing new here—just challenges to an established order (the order being that of modernism itself). A reaction against modernism and its monuments (those singled out by Jameson include Abstract Expressionism and the works of Joyce, Stravinsky, and Mies van der Rohe) does not by itself change modernism's underlying operation. But something different has nevertheless been underway. Under modernism, each successful wave of style or fashion becomes canonized as a classic, theorist Jürgen Habermas tells us. But this seemingly limitless theme was beginning to get weary by the late 1960s, when, as we have seen, artists resorted to shock for shock's sake, and found value primarily in novelty. What other contemporary symptoms can we identify that differentiate the postmodern from the modern?

A telling feature of postmodernism, noticed by countless theorists, is its effacement of the ordinary linear march of history. This trend has been felt most in the United States, which, Baudrillard claims, "having known no primitive accumulation of time . . . lives in a perpetual present." In addition, Baudrillard notes, "Octavio Paz is right when he argues that America was created in the hope of escaping from history, of building a utopia sheltered from history, and that it has in part succeeded in that project, a project it is still pursuing today." The result of this project is, in part, an emerging erasure of historical perspective.

Jameson describes an aspect of historical inversion in, for example, the novels of E. L. Doctorow. Although, Jameson argues, all historical novels create an interaction "between what we already 'know' and [what is] seen to be concretely in the pages of the novel," to him "Doctorow's procedure seems much more extreme than this. . . . [T]he designation of both types of characters—historical names and capitalized family roles—operates powerfully and systematically to reify [the] characters. . . ."

A similar manipulation of "what we already 'know'" can be found in novelists Caleb Carr or in Anne Rice. To surprise and amuse the reader, Rice's vampires break some of the time-honored rules to which they are mythically bound. These updated vampires are, in her setting, the real thing precisely because the storyteller has gained authority through warning us about fictitious behaviors. The reader is on the one hand comforted to know that certain of his or her "factual" beliefs about vampires are "true," validated right there on the printed page, and on the other hand can see some of the regulations refreshingly lifted. This technique therefore strikes a balance between satisfying our need for security (the vampires are anchored in known territory) and our thirst for the new (provided by the fresh facts of vampire activity).

Going back to film remakes, we see that the same process is taking place. When the characters and setting are updated—revised for the contemporary audience—a new, more *alive* layer is constructed over the older foundations that in turn sink below the ground (but remain on top of all the previous versions). Only an excavation can reveal the layers of historicity.

The blurring of history has trickled down to everyday mass media. In the movie and television industries, there has been a proliferation of mock documentaries and television docudramas that have used a variety of techniques, including the mixing of fictional and historical characters, the interspersing of newsreel footage and video clips, and the commingling of color and black-and-white media. These tricks enhance the hyperreality of fictional material by incorporating segments with putative veracity, and they also confound the usually well-understood arrow of time. Another, less subtle technique is illustrated in a radio ad for a furniture store that ran a few years ago in the Philadelphia area. Tourists are on a tourbus, and the guide says something like, "on your left is the famous Mount Laurel [an actual suburb], where General Grant defeated Julius Caesar [mild ooh-ahh murmuring], and on your right is

Such'n'Such Furniture, they're having a sale"—and the tourists go wild, the bus screeches to a halt, the tourists scramble out, and so on. The history-blurring joke with Grant defeating Caesar (and moreover at Mount Laurel, New Jersey) is in fact ironic, since in all likelihood, only a small minority of Americans actually know anything about Grant or Caesar. History is losing its chronology. We have professional basketball players who are unaware that they play for Hall of Fame coaches. We watch televised bombings of places whose histories we are blissfully ignorant of. If something's old it's old; it doesn't matter whether it's ten years old or a hundred or a thousand. Present-day personalities are turned instantly into historical objects simply by their appearance in the media; conversely, historical characters, viewed in the same media, are made to look very much alive. Thus history is past and present and even future, whether it's Jesus Christ, Ben Affleck, Margaret Thatcher, or the Pope. If you have any doubts about this, round up some teenagers and test them on historical events, or, if you are unwilling to go to the trouble, just test yourself!

Another principal feature of postmodernism—contrary to the antimodernist theme—is that it constitutes a more complete modernism than modernism itself. Modernism as intellectual and artistic development was historically concurrent with the massive social transformations brought about by the Industrial Revolution. These social transformations naturally took time and gave rise to various juxtapositions of the old and the new. Thus Jameson in part typifies modernism as "what Ernst Bloch called the 'simultaneity of the nonsimultaneous,' the 'synchronicity of the nonsynchronous,'" for example, as illustrated by "peasant fields with the Krupp factories or the Ford plant in the distance." What they are saying is that the modernizing *process,* which effected tremendous industrialization, brought farm laborers to cities, and literally transformed our landscape, has been carried out to such a great degree that we are forgetting its novelty and contrasts and are losing our sense of the new. In fact this project is largely complete. On this point Jameson claims that modernism is identifiable by its "incomplete modernization." As the opposition between old and new vanishes, so does our sense of modernism. Summing this up, we can quote Jameson again (quotation being another prevalent manifestation of the postmodern): "postmodernism is more modern than modernism itself." Modernism's sense of the new was acute because of the contradictions between old and new. Now that those contrasts are waning, our sense of modernism is, too. What was novel and exciting—in *process* as well as in *content*—a generation or two ago is ho-hum, business-as-usual today.

Another angle on this aspect of postmodernism is that the theme of modernism, founded as it is on oppositions, has won the day. The rebels, as it were, have become the establishment. There is no one left on the battlefield. As we have pointed out previously, alternative expression is now absorbed almost immediately into a society that has been weaned on pluralism and diversity. The life cycle of consumption, discrediting, and exhaustion of styles and trends is Andy-Warhol short. Hence postmodernism's being hypermodern, that is, more modern than modern. It is a cultural mode founded on oppositional themes, but operating in a world where anything goes.

In this we see postmodernism working largely to dissolve, or at least soften, contradictions, oppositions, and conflict. One example of this that Jameson cites is the significant use of pastiche nowadays. For Jameson pastiche relies on the mimetic features of parody but it lacks parody's satirical dimension. "Pastiche is blank parody, parody that has lost its sense of humor;" it is "without that still latent feeling that there exists something *normal* compared to which what is being imitated is rather comic." As an example of creative work in this direction, Jameson offers what he calls "nostalgia film"—movies like *American Graffiti* (which recreates a 1950s atmosphere), or *Chinatown* (the 1930s), or, in a somewhat different sense, *Raiders of the Lost Ark* (let me add the more recent *Sky Captain and the World of Tomorrow*). These are not historical films. Films in this category—even a film like *Star Wars,* set in the future—evoke a certain sense of the past, and thereby "gratify a deeper and more properly nostalgic desire to return to that older period and to live its strange old aesthetic artifacts through once again."

Pastiche has the additional connotation of hodgepodge, of mix and match. Those who deride postmodernism often point out the loss of unity of expression, the clashing styles, and, ultimately, the loss of (absolute) standards. In such a world, anything goes. Very few things shock us anymore, and the zeitgeist is to accept anything new (as long as it is different) as "cool." You can listen to Gregorian chants *and* heavy metal, or surround yourself with El Greco *and* Mapplethorpe. There's no need to worry whether silk clashes with tweed, as bothered a gangster in Godard's *Breathless*. Associated with this anything-goes contemporary ethic is the notion that, freed from the constraints of *either* conformity *or* narrowly defined rebellion, people can *choose* themselves. They can choose motifs that they like without being tied to a certain established style or politicized antistyle. This freedom of choice is refreshing; it was seductive even to the modernist architect Philip Johnson, who famously joined the ranks of postmodern architects ("I try to pick up what I like throughout history") with his Chippendale pediment topping the AT&T building in New York.

At this point let us summarize the above differences between modernism and postmodernism. One view is that postmodernism is a more inclusive modernism. It is modernism without an opponent; it is modernism in which opposition to the alternative has been disbanded. In postmodernism the establishment's modus operandi is to immediately embrace the alternative. Challengers to the cultural scene are no longer confronted at the door.

A different, more confrontational, spin is that postmodernism is antimodernism. In this view, postmodernism rejects the works that have become accepted by the establishment as classics of modernism. In this view, postmodernism carries on, angry and antiestablishment, railing against the establishment of modernism itself, not just the latest cultural norm.

Regardless of which spin we put on it, postmodernism seems to employ techniques that don't fit modernist conventions. One is the use of historical inversion, the blurring of history. Another common device is pastiche, appearing both as neutral parody and as hodgepodge, mixing and matching as one pleases. This last feature in particular fits our world of choice—in postmodernism our creative urges need not be channeled through a single theme, style, or message.

Time and Space Get Squeezed

But there is another, more theoretical, angle on postmodernism that we should consider. Social theorist David Harvey, in his work *The Condition of Postmodernity* finds that the waves of modernism and postmodernism that we have seen over the past one hundred fifty or so years have been instigated by a series of crises, each "derived from a radical readjustment in the sense of time and space in economic, political, and cultural life." These periods were, first, 1847–1850 or so, when modernism began to accelerate; second, around 1910–1914, when modernism took off yet more rapidly, as witnessed by the incredible burgeoning of creative works of literature and art (witness the impact of relativity's shocking revelations about space and time that we have already discussed). Interestingly, this explosion of creative work was accompanied by the advent of scientific management in both theory

(Frederick Taylor) and practice (Henry Ford). The third crisis was the social upheaval of the 1960s and the emergence of the latest cultural wave (i.e., postmodernism).

The "space-time compression" that Harvey refers to has had different manifestations. In the older, industrial era, the advent of cable and telephone communications and the introduction of railways and automobiles shrank the globe and transformed our notions of time and distance. More recently, we have seen similar transformations in, among other things, the consumer landscape. Harvey notes that the rapid and flexible production techniques of the 1970s and 1980s led to "accelerations in exchange and consumption." And just as the fashion market was mobilized to quicken the "pace of consumption not only in clothing, ornament, and decoration but also across a wide swath of life-styles and recreational activities"—bringing out products with shorter and shorter lifetimes—the newly emerging service economy was similarly crafted to provide "very ephemeral services" as well.

The result of all of this has been a newfound emphasis on trend, change, and speed. We have become a "throwaway" society, to use Alvin Toffler's term, and what we dispose of are not just short-lived commodities but "values, lifestyles, stable relationships, and attachments to things, buildings, places, people, and received ways of doing and being." It is not hard to see that with this sort of ethos in place, many businesses have given up any serious hope of planning for the long term, and this attitude, generally speaking, has eroded loyalty on the parts of both management and labor.

Harvey's book was published in 1989 but it is not difficult to extend his argument to the Internet era. Note, for example, the crisis and dislocation in the Arab countries, which has been blamed on the too-rapid modernization they have undergone. The world has shrunk yet once more, and we possess a truly awesome ability to communicate and receive news in an instant.

The role of "space-time compression" in the genesis of modernism and postmodernism certainly is important, because at each new crisis our newfound abilities for transport and communication have reshaped how we think about the world. However, these crises have not been acute and discrete but rather they have unfolded gradually, and the argument that they have directly brought about various cultural transformations is quite tenuous. So although space-time compression is noteworthy, it still seems to me that the emergence of ice is a much more direct and tangible influence on our social and cultural lopment over the past century.

Individuals, the Public, and the Private

As I have already argued, the relatively newfound choice that permeated much of Western society by the 1970s was a phenomenon that impacted heavily on the notion of personal freedom. Freedom, of course, intersects with *individuality,* and this latter notion is one that Jameson and others have contended has been under siege. There are different aspects to this loss of individuality. One dimension is that the successive waves of modernisms possessed a clear identity, an unmistakable style. This unity of vision has been lost in postmodernism's creative expressions, which whimsically quote and freely mix and match motifs and referents. In this setting, Jameson writes, "nobody has [a] unique private world and style to express any longer." To distinguish yourself, you'd have to go to unnatural lengths—like wearing red all the time, or listening to nothing but Mozart.

Consistent with this free-for-all is a notion that we have already mentioned—the death of the author (Barthes). Here, as theorist Hal Foster remarks, modernist works are "unique, symbolic [and] visionary" whereas postmodern texts are "'already written,' allegorical, [and] contingent." These malleable expressions have lives of their own now, because choice has breathed multifaceted life into them. This gesture is simply the corollary of our newfound freedom to break from convention. We are free to interpret. Moreover, because these outputs have been divested of their creator's intentions, originality has, to a great extent, become passé, and hence pastiche fills the artistic void.

Another dimension to this loss of individuality is the erosion of the boundary between the public and the private. Baudrillard points out that we have reached the point where the most intimate aspects of private life are brought to us via television. On talk shows, it hardly matters whether the guests are actors paid to simulate real-life crises, or ordinary people truly revealing their extraordinary situations. What Baudrillard calls the "ecstasy of communication" penetrates all aspects of our lives. We have to dodge calls from telemarketers who range from the illiterate to the obnoxious, we receive e-mail messages about nasty new computer viruses, and we receive *urgent* junk mail envelopes clogging our mailboxes. As Baudrillard puts it, "all secrets, spaces, and scenes [are] abolished in a single dimension of information."

It's pathetic when ordinary folks appear on talk shows and air the melodramatic and the sensational in their desperate grasps for money and celebrity; it was already bad enough that every aspect of celebrities' lives became not just publicly available, but practically unavoidable. But we're all evolving public personae; give people wireless phones, and they're all too eager to show off and share their conversations with anyone within earshot (and, since everyone tends to speak loudly on cell phones, earshot is pretty far). Give people the Internet and they're thrilled to share intimate thoughts and photos with complete strangers. Not so long ago, Sundays were reserved for quiet, private times. Forget tranquil Sundays and evenings; time itself has been commodified, like everything else, by the postmodern market: everything nowadays is 24/7.

With information dispersing at (nearly) the speed of light and with communication becoming our primary preoccupation it seems that the public and private spheres have intersected permanently. As Baudrillard says, "The one is no longer a spectacle, the other no longer a secret. . . . [T]his opposition is effaced in a sort of *obscenity* where the most intimate processes of our life become the virtual feeding ground of the media. . . . Inversely, the entire universe comes to unfold arbitrarily on your domestic screen (all the useless information that comes to you from the entire world, like a microscopic pornography of the universe, useless, excessive, just like the sexual close-up in a porno film): all this explodes the scene formerly preserved by the minimal separation of public and private. . . ."

We do seem obsessed with the surreal, often hyperreal aspect of exploring, even absorbing, the lives of others through the larger-than-life saturating voyeurism that we are accustomed to. This is what has drawn viewers worldwide to "reality television," beginning with *Big Brother* and *Survivor*. Putting aside our skepticism about the "reality" of these shows, they do celebrate the transport and exaltation of exhibiting oneself, of sharing oneself with a potential infinity of strangers. Thus the erosion of the tacit public–private divide that once existed is woven into the blurring of reality, the blurring of oppositions that characterizes so much of postmodernism, the blurring driven by choice.

Another dimension of postmodern blurring is presented in the Peter Weir film *The Truman Show,* written by Andrew Niccol. The title character's very life calls into question the effacement of two boundaries: between public and private and between real and artificial. Unknown to Truman, his entire life— friends, job, wife, sleep, *everything*—takes place on an artificial set, a city-sized studio. Everyone who interacts with him uses a script; even nature is fabricated. Truman's activity is tracked by five thousand cameras, and the resulting 24/7 "show," funded by product placements, is seen live around the world, like a soap opera. When Truman eventually discovers the set-up he wants to know, "was any of it real?" He is told that *he* was.

To just set up a hidden camera is to merely invade privacy. The viewed product lacks intrigue because there's no interplay, no tension, between the public and private or between the real and artificial. At the other extreme, plenty of people have recently been installing cameras to broadcast their "private" activities on the Web. Consent is understood, and therefore the product loses its authenticity, as is the case with reality shows. What makes *The Truman Show* provocative is its half-and-half quality. Though the actors and the set are fake, Truman is genuine, and the resulting interaction is precisely what breaks down both the public–private and the real–artificial barriers.

Despite the rash of blurring of the real and fake, I believe that one enduring search for the real will be the popularity of "hardcore" genres—for example, in music. This term, generally speaking, connotes loud, gritty, no-holds-barred, furious primeval sound devoid of subtlety, finesse, tenderness, and so forth. In deconstructing the term, observe that it means stripping something to the kernel—by removing the pulpy exterior, the ultimate, indestructible essence is exposed. People sense this and therefore, I believe, some seek in "hardcore" a pure and therefore truer emotion, unadulterated by pretense. Hardcore will always contrast against the increasing blur of sensibilities found in popular expression.

More Oppositions, More Blurring

Another blurred opposition is found in the meshing of the local and the global. National and international products, stores, and media are effecting various degrees of universal standardization. Regional differences—which, like them or not, are interesting—seem to be disappearing. When people go to the mall they experience the same thing whether they live in Virginia, California, Texas, or Illinois. Maybe it's called Nordstrom's in one place, Bloomingdale's in another and Marshall Field's in another, but what's the difference? In Britain too all the "high streets" are virtually carbon copies (Boots, W. H. Smith, Marks & Spencer, Dixon's, H. Samuel, etc.). And the proliferation of national and international chains: Borders, Barnes and Noble, Bed Bath and Beyond . . . and some that don't begin with "B," like Gap and Ikea and Friday's and the ubiquitous Chinese restaurant (not a chain but just as familiar). On top of this there is the global reach of the Web. The unique stores must go mass-market if they are to survive. Overall, the effect is exactly what we have called the *inversion* of choice.

Again, modernism was an oppositional ethic, and so much of what we call postmodern seeks to move beyond the tension that opposition creates. Postmodernism, in its pastiche, can emphasize contradictions without taking them seriously. You can feel perfectly at ease with a fat-free health salad followed by a greasy meatball sub, or by washing down a gigantic ice cream sundae with a Diet Coke. But generally, the postmodern ethic is to soften conflict, to have your cake and eat it, too. Postmodernism enables choices and therefore promotes inclusion, but it also postpones decisions and the exclusion that the choices would involve. It is no coincidence that postmodernism resonates with pluralism. As choice has become for the many, so have the features of postmodernism—and thus we are brought full circle to the high culture–low culture divide that our society is erasing.

There are additional distinctions that are fading. One development has been the difficulty at times in telling the difference between postmodern theory and practice. In other words, do certain postmodern practices exist because someone theorized about them, or was the theory developed in order to codify the behaviors? Probably, the process is autocatalytic—much of the theory is advanced to explain various behaviors but some of the behaviors are inspired by the theory. Similarly, as the mass market turns everything into a commodity, we are starting to identify, metonymically, products with their images (as we have discussed vis-à-vis name brands). What exactly is it we purchase? Do we take our kids to the fast-food places for the food or the toys? And in some academic circles, the specialization that mushroomed for a century is partly being dissolved. Jameson has proclaimed the "end of philosophy," meaning that it is now impossible to differentiate its discourse from that of other disciplines like sociology or literary criticism. It's all "theory" now.

Postmodern Themes in Architecture

For many, the first, and ultimate, expression of postmodernism has been in architecture. When did postmodern architecture commandeer the reins from modern architecture? Critic Charles Jencks claims that the "death of modern architecture" took place on July 15, 1972, about 3:32 P.M., when the notorious Pruitt-Igoe high-rise public housing project in Saint Louis, Missouri was imploded. (Public housing is now [among other things] horizontal rather than vertical.) But there were signs of change well before 1972. Author Jane Jacobs advocated pluralism, which in this context is the mixing of functions, styles, and ages, as early as 1961. Pluralism implied complexity and diversity. Others too in the early 1960s expressed dissatisfaction (or boredom) with the "univalent" modernism that had dominated most of the twentieth century.

One of the factors that Jencks identifies as crucial to the development of postmodern architecture is society's increasing focus on commerce. He writes, "Architecture obviously reflects what a society holds important. . . . In the pre-industrial age the major areas for expression were the temple, the church, the palace, agora, meeting house, country house and city hall; while in the present, extra money is spent on hotels, restaurants, and . . . commercial building types. . . ." But, he continues, "Commercial tasks are more democratic than the previous aristocratic and religious ones." Substituting "mass culture" for "democratic," we see from these remarks that architecture was deeply influenced by the melding of high and mass culture that was becoming noticeable in the early 1960s.

But what *is* postmodern architecture? For too many critics, it's a jumble, it's pastiche. For Jencks, it is complex, pluralistic, contextual; it is multiple-coded, abstract, eclectic; it contains suitable content; it has relevant ornamentation. And it is bound up with choice. Jencks notes that "eclectic" means "I select." Part of what is being selected is the particular employment of a past form, whether for a serious purpose or just for amusement. Strictly speaking, resurrecting past forms is not new. Architects from the Renaissance to the twentieth century have been reusing classical forms all along. Postmodern architecture, though, goes much further, "quoting" from particular works as well as from various eras. This spirit Jencks calls "radically inclusivist." The quoting is not arbitrary, as the postmodern architect attempts to match the structure to the surroundings. If we conceptualize the neighboring forms linguistically, we see that postmodern architecture communicates through a vernacular, as opposed to the more rigid universalism that modernist architects would employ.

Another aspect we should explore in a bit more detail is the postmodern sense of self-consciousness, self-reference, and facticity. A superb illustration of these themes is found in one of the medical faculty buildings at the University of Louvain, Belgium (Lucien Kroll and Atelier). One wall shows us the literally upward evolution of the building's skin. At the base a brick and rock pile cascades away from the wall; by thus getting your attention, you are forced to contemplate the ascent from the ground up, of the refinement from rock to brick to tile. The observer is also confronted with a demonstration of the authenticity of the building process—the material is literally of the earth; also, the haphazardness of the rock and protobrick indicates "man-made" and not "machine aesthetic." Finally, we are able to receive the architect's self-conscious message, "I am relating a story, and you know it, and I know that you know it," and so on.

As an aside, such self-conscious self-reference pervades other forms of expression. For instance, over the last few years, in its marketing of several animated features the Disney Corporation has placed significant emphasis on self-consciousness as well as authenticity. Their ads and trailers show the animators' black-and-white sketches. As with old-fashioned flip pads, we see the pages riffled to provide motion and scene change. So, in a curious and effective inversion, the animated cartoons (often based on ancient mythical figures) gain a human grounding by showing us that they were created by artists' hands. (Again, *not* machine-, or rather, computer-aesthetic.) We are comforted to see the product deconstructed for us in charcoal-and-ink drawings whose creation we can understand. The underlying technology is veiled in order that we welcome the product as something humanistic. Finally, the whole presentation, with its blatant "let us show you how we did it" message, provides the same satisfaction in exactly the same fashion as the "making of" pieces that we have discussed previously.

This technique is neither monopolized by Disney nor terribly recent. Back in the late 1970s, while making *Apocalypse Now*, Francis Ford Coppola was involved in producing a "making of" short documentary. This may not have been the first such instance, but since then, a whole genre of behind-the-scenes production has spread. Now, these "making of" works are taken for granted (of course, DVDs are marketed and assessed partly on the strength of this supplementary material, and as for Coppola, his 2001 *Apocalypse Now Redux* tacked on forty-nine "never before seen" minutes to the original work). The cable station VH1 runs a "Behind the Music" series, and Universal Studios, as another example, has adopted the motif to the public setting of a theme park.

But back to architecture. In the work of Cesar Pelli, for example, Jencks finds an adaptability to the "visual grammar based on the local context." But Pelli also emphasizes authenticity; the visible layer is always treated "as a thin curtain wall that reveals—for those who care to look—the reality of the steel construction underneath." The same emphasis is found in the work of James

Stirling and Michael Wilford. In discussing their Cornell University Center for the Performing Arts, Jencks notes that "if you get very close and examine the cracks [between marble blocks] you find the, by now, standard Post-Modern non-joint joint, the sharp black void that tells you these are stones which do not 'stand' on each other, but 'hang' from a steel frame." The notion that the heavy blocks are load bearing is audaciously inverted, and by allowing us to discover this the architect is revealing the underlying truth about the construction.

In summary, postmodern architecture seems to incorporate all of the dialogue of opposition (and its softening) that we have discussed with other forms of expression. It is concerned with the progressing dissolution between high and low culture; it addresses the struggle between singular and plural codes; it brings attention to issues of real versus artificial; and it weighs the questions of large scale versus small and mass production versus personal aesthetic. In a word, postmodern architecture is *complex*. This sketch of postmodern architecture completes our survey of the transition from modernism to postmodernism. Let's continue to explore postmodern themes before we consider some criticism of the era.

In the previous chapter we reviewed the hatching of postmodernism, as it were, from modernism's egg. Having established the conceptual issues, I would like to briefly present some additional postmodernist themes and behaviors, and then explore various ramifications of one of these themes, self-reference.

Designers, Buildings, and Dressing for the Gym

We have already discussed, to some degree, both designer labels and postmodern architecture. Is there any connection—say, designer architecture? Certainly: back in 1994 the *New York Times* ran an article entitled "Label Living." Almost all one hundred twenty-four units of a new Miami Beach condominium were sold out before the ground was broken. Its attraction? Being named after a fashion designer best known for a line of perfume. On the surface, this is nothing more than a clever application of a designer label, but note that this trend is extending to branded fashion hotels, as witnessed by Palazzo Versace on Australia's Gold Coast, and the opening in 2005 of a chain of hotels by Giorgio Armani. Such "value-added" strokes of genius occur almost every day—although an edifice with a designer logo certainly seems to extend the frontier. Lurking beneath the surface, though, is an issue of legitimacy. The *Times* article assured us that, although the Miami Beach designer was not the architect of the eponymous building, he did contribute to its creation, make changes in the plans, and grant final design approval. But after all, the obvious reason the article was newsworthy is because, essentially, a designer's name was applied to a product that not only the designer didn't design, but couldn't have designed. And this is what is pushing back the frontier, not the mere fact that designer architecture is a new concept.

What's more, this designerless designer product is not a line of, say, household appliances with the logo of a couture creator. We're talking about an enormous, multistory, highly visible block of expensive apartments. This is as public as one can get. The rooftop "label" advertises the building's insincerity on a grand public scale. Indeed, in contemplating the small-fry nature of our own private, label-exhibiting shirts, toiletries, luggage, electronics, and, at the top of the heap, automobiles—we realize that the designer building, reminiscent of something like the Arc de Triomphe, is literally and truly monumental.

One thing this project has demonstrated is that a designer label can be sold to a collective of individuals. Although each condo buyer purchased an individual unit, presumably without consultation with other prospective residents, they were of course aware that each owner would be sharing a dubious virtual commodity. Although the residents get to live *inside* something "designer," and although for many this feature also may have had the attraction of joining a club with its implications of exclusivity, the developers had to contend with the following problem: designer labels are for personal effects, and for good reason—the item is supposed to be tailormade for *you*. How, then, could the developers be confident that a sizeable designer building would have appeal? Put differently, how could they expect to extract added value from a label that had to be publicly shared, thereby deindividualizing it and possibly stripping it of all cachet?

Whether its success was predictable or not, in likening the building to the Arc de Triomphe I mean that both are monuments to conquest—in the building's case, conquest of a new market. We can now expect a hoard of designer buildings, designer estates, and designer resorts to sprout up; I'm surprised that progress on this front has not been faster.

Directing the designer theme back to clothes, not everything sartorial in the postmodern world is designer. In the 1960s, as we have already mentioned, there was a movement underway toward what sociologist Angela McRobbie calls a "second-hand style." She claims that vintage clothes were catapulted into the fashion mainstream by the 1967 appearance of the Beatles' *Sergeant Pepper* album. The wearing of vintage clothing prompts various questions. "Stuart Hall saw in this 'hippie movement' an 'identification with the poor,' as well as a disavowal of conventional middle-class smartness." And despite the overt rejection of such middle-class values as material wealth, McRobbie also sees in this dressing down (as did Tom Wolfe and Angela Carter), an additional class motivation: rich kids mocking the poor. As Wolfe himself pointed out, the poor kids wouldn't want to wear the hippie clothes; "they'd vomit."

McRobbie also notes social-economic dimensions. Second-hand clothes are not just retro-cool but have a wider clientele—the unemployed, young single mothers, travelers. Plus the second-hand markets themselves are attractive in various ways. In some cases these markets have served to revitalize blighted areas and have paved the way for commercial development. Of course, they are not immune to prevailing capitalist forces; there is a savvy business side, an entrepreneurial element to them as well. Interestingly, this has led to an upscaling of the second-hand market: preowned designer gear.

Although our era has seen greatly relaxed standards for dress, the blurring of styles and of protocols can get a bit confusing at times. Clearly, dress-up standards have been lowered. But, in another inversion, sometimes we have to dress up when dressing down. Consider the fashion industry for women's athletic gear. Over the past generation there have been three major changes in this market. One is sheer volume. Another is the evolution from the simple, monochrome palette of T- and sweatshirts, gym shorts and sweatpants. But most interesting has been the impact of advanced technology and the resulting space-age fabrics that have been introduced. Concomitant with this has been a rise in prices and profit margins.

As has been pointed out before, Umberto Eco tells us that we purchase an attitude along with a garment. Naturally the garment industry has relied on this notion to great advantage. The image associated with the high-tech garment is one of a higher plane of fitness. Spandex, for example, unlike fleece-lined sweats, hugs the body. But if you are to capitalize on this feature of the fabric, you'd better have the shape. Fitter is sexier, and the outfit reinforces the point by providing a smooth, silky uniformity. And therefore we have a corollary: the ones in the sweats are probably hiding some unwanted flesh.

Perhaps the fashion industry has manipulated yet another consumer sector to amazing degrees (the more high-tech, the hotter). But consider the woman of modest means who begins a fitness regimen and decides to join a health club, partly armed with the hope that her monetary investment as well as the communal dedication will together bolster her resolve. Let us suppose that either in a preference for natural fibers, or a need for thrift—or else a conscious desire to hide those extra pounds—she purchases a couple of primitive (let me use this word) outfits of the T-shirt-sweatshirt-sweatpants variety. Such comfortable clothes have mass appeal, but obviously lack the technological superiority and performance of the new fabrics.

So off she goes to the club, and as if those digital, computerized machines weren't intimidating enough—the woman cannot help but notice the others in their nylon and lycra-spandex leotards and leggings, sexy outfits in coordinated, hot colors on firm (and even not-so-firm) aerobicized bodies. Fashion momentarily aside, the newcomer in the sweats will probably not be able to keep up with the more experienced people in the aerobics class, and if she tries the machines, after the trepidation and frustration involved in learning how to work them, she will surely be exhausted in just minutes—but those others seem to keep on going forever.

Despite the rationalization that it's only her first week, and so forth, the woman will have experienced the validation of the superiority of the other outfits. Even if she sits down and convinces herself in a cold and rational manner that leotards and bicycle shorts do not in fact contribute more to fitness than do sweatpants, there is no denying that those other women are *in shape;* the literalness of this last phrase settles the issue.

Reflecting on this, our fleece-donned newcomer to the scene will surely turn to the mirror. As we are so unfortunately socialized to do, she will see in her reflection the eyes of those others on herself. And in that inevitable competition that we engender, she will capitulate to the consideration of issues altogether outside the domain of her initial quest for fitness. The initial choice she made was, of course, to join a health club. Perhaps she shopped around for a suitable club; perhaps she weighed gray sweats against blue, but these factors pall in comparison to that primary decision (with "just do it" echoing in her ears). With the initial decision settled, the woman expected to be able to concentrate on the next step in the fitness program—working out in earnest—without any distraction. Meeting new people, although perhaps welcome, is a secondary sort of distraction. But for now, she is dismayed by those outfits.

Perhaps at first she prevents herself from concentrating on clothing. She becomes accustomed to the health club, develops a routine, masters the equipment. She stays with it. Her fitness improves, and perhaps she perceives changes in her body or on the scale. But regardless of her social interactions while working out, she will project that critical self-reflective gaze onto others. She will overhear conversations in the locker room and see how the other gear transforms the body. The signals will accumulate, and only a Martian could be oblivious to them. Of course, in any society the pressure to conform is difficult to withstand. So inevitably she will have to seriously consider the issue of the high-tech outfits. With any small amount of perspicacity she'll realize that she is forced to make a decision. Quite possibly she'll resent coming to this crossroads. Moreover, not only would the new purchases demonstrate submission to a shallow set of principles, but they would signify her allegiance to the converts already outfitted.

On the other hand, her rejection of the vogue would now be intentional, and as such, would certify her as chic-less and shapeless too. This signification would thus be felt from inside as well as from the (self-reflected) outside. Does she buck the trend, or give in and conform? Her dilemma, induced by the fashion industry's inversion of high style for exercise, is typical in our era of choice.

Postmodern Food

Another area in which the latest trends encroach on our lifestyles has been food. One development hard to miss over the past decade has been the proliferation of coffee bars. Several years ago, when the coffee craze was becoming established, the *New York Times* ran an article linking it inextricably with choice. One coffee-bar owner indicated that he had five different kinds of milk ready, which hints at how many varieties of coffee might be available. The key notion was that "Americans tend to see limitless choice as almost a constitutional right." Moreover, it was posited that with coffee, choice also operated as a capitalist mechanism to convert a 50-cent cup into a $3.50 latte. Now whether megaoptions or something else is what gets us to the coffee bars, the significance of the article is that it serves as a barometer of how people are starting to become aware of the wide-ranging role of choice in their daily lives.

Coffee bars are not the only new item on the gastronomic front. In fact, throughout the past couple of decades, there have been many choice-related developments in the culinary arena. For one thing, salad bars and tapas bars have caught on; their chief attraction is that they offer tremendous variety, the sampling of which is controlled by the individual. The diner need not commit to a single dish, but can mix and match.

This postmodern mix and-match theme extends beyond the restaurant medium; it's in the foods as well. Pizzas come with a bewildering variety of toppings. It wasn't always like this. Sodas too, come in a zillion flavors in addition to diet and caffeine-free options. In general, whether it's coffee, juice, ice cream, cereal, or almost anything else, there are more pure flavors *and* more

mixes readily available than ever before imaginable. Are the companies pushing these varieties on us or are they merely providing the products we demand?
It's a moot point; what matters is that the issue of choice has transformed the
food service industry. The underlying sentiment is that people are no longer
content with choosing between chocolate and vanilla. Sometimes they want
both, sometimes they desire other flavors, and sometimes they want even
more—for example, when Marlon Brando reputedly used to order the entire
dessert tray, unwilling or unable to choose.

Culinary variety involves not only mixing available items but also expanding the food base. Although, no doubt, cooks have been introducing foreign
ingredients into their dishes for centuries, Marian Burros tells us that only in
the 1990s had this practice become well-defined, under the name of "fusion
cooking." This trend of creating novel and exciting tastes has caught on as a
way of stimulating "the palates of jaded diners who have seen it all."

Indeed, at any trendy restaurant in any major city, the menus are dominated
by dishes of what seem to be a jumble of ingredients, many of which change
seasonally and most of which are calculatedly exotic. Sometimes one suspects
that this is merely the pastiche of postmodernism at work (or play) in the
kitchen, with competing chefs outdoing each other in variety and complexity.
Burros confirms our suspicions by quoting cooking expert Nina Simonds, who
claims that often, in America, fusion cooking is a "mishmash that doesn't add
up." Successes, we are told, take place when chefs learn their ingredients and
master the matching of complementary tastes and textures. Sadly, though,
when mix-and-match for its own sake predominates, many of us suffer. Indeed,
now some chefs, to buck the trend, are going back to simplification.

Trendiness and Shorter Life Cycles

Trend, of course, is hardly limited to athletic gear and cuisine. It is all around
us, to the extent where we wonder if trend itself has become a defining feature
of our culture. Edward Rothstein contends that we "have created a culture
founded almost entirely on trends." Happenings in pop culture and in intellectual circles are coming and going with gathering speed. And, confusingly,
not all trends are new—some are created out of recycled nostalgia. Increasingly, we—the consumers—are determined to keep up with what's in and out.
Consequently, trend spotting has itself emerged as a trend, and our growing
obsession to discern some sense of direction out of the chaotic assortment of

new styles that bombard us with increasing frequency is becoming a pseudo-scientific mission to unearth the true metatrend.

Rothstein goes on to state that the intensifying and arbitrary flux that we see in cultural spheres is not going to yield an underlying Holy Grail of direction, of progress. All it will do is undermine any sense of tradition and stability that culture has had, and replace it with pure trend and change for its own sake. However, he notes, until contemporary times (say, perhaps, until the 1960s), trend and change itself, and indeed the impetus for change, resided in the very existence of an established tradition. His argument is that postmodernism and its seemingly mix-and-match, cut-and-paste ethos has departed, irretrievably, from the orderly modernist progression wherein rebellions against the establishment at first shock the system but are eventually reconciled and absorbed.

The argument is that we are losing our long-running balance between trend and tradition. The very notion of tradition is itself being transformed into an unattractive, rigid burden. The consequences of adhering to the current zeitgeist and its diminishing of tradition are ominous, including the slow extinction of classical music as an evolving organism and the increasing shallowness of, and the vanishing of historical richness in, mass-media entertainment. Even intellectual life, it is claimed, is succumbing to emphases on trends and mass appeal. We have lost our sense of importance to such a degree that the study of shopping malls equals that of Western iconography. To summarize, our zeitgeist has lost T. S. Eliot's "presence of the past." For Rothstein, the intervals of *zeit* become ever briefer and the *geist* hardly exists anymore. Thus, our shared experiences have become tenuous and ever more meaningless.

It is difficult to argue with the main points of this thesis. That our society has become more and more commercial, and less and less community minded, humane, and compassionate, that we are displacing human values with commodity bundles, just as we are replacing human voices with voice mail, is such a central cliché for us that we cannot even determine its verity. The loss of tradition as a polestar—even one we disregard—seems to be an obvious consequence of our societal hollowness.

But, we may ask, don't trends reverse themselves? Don't things work in cycles? Can't we expect, or even foresee, a reinstatement of tradition, a healthy balance between the classic and the avant-garde? Will the modernist processes that have fueled civilization's engine from the Enlightenment to the 1960s return to supplant the helter-skelter PoMo that rules today? And is this, in fact, to ask: will there be another Renaissance that future theorists will wistfully rhapsodize about?

To try to answer these questions, let's look at the essential dualisms present: tradition with its familiar, static, and well-worn comforts, versus trend with its novel, dynamic, and untested excitement. Accepting that both of these complementary notions are fundamental to the way we view our world, then it follows that tradition is not going to vanish, any more than religion did under the Soviet regime.

But what if you reject the idea that tradition is an essential component of our character? After all, judging from popular culture, we're not exactly desperate to keep it. Here are some perhaps more convincing arguments. For one thing, I believe that people need, and indeed cultivate, areas of common ground. Although, admittedly, this common ground has greatly shrunk—that Shakespeare quote everyone used to know might now get no reaction—people will always need to be understood, to connect. And to do that we require a common language. That language, in part, derives from our need to express shared thoughts. Example: when we sit around and discuss films (or places we've been), we have an unfortunate tendency, as I've already mentioned, to trade lines like, "Did you see x? It was really good." Because x is no longer the only film in town for weeks, we have evolved to the point where only a minority of films (and other experiences) are shared. But, you have to admit, it is those *intersections* that provide spark. It's one thing to hear that Jamie saw x, and maybe you'll make a mental bookmark to see it; it's another, and much warmer, event, to hear that you and Jamie have shared x. We treasure the connection, even if we have become so inarticulate as to simply reply, "yeah, it was really good."

Moreover, cultural relativism aside, we establish certain preferences. We are always, sooner or later, going to think, I'd like to see (hear, taste, feel) that again. Not surprisingly, others will share our taste; when these preferences are strong and pervasive, a classic is in the making. Some things we want to keep around. As an example, classic rock albums are big sellers, and not just to the 35- to 60-year-olds who grew up with that music. For years now, musicians on the top of the charts a quarter of a century ago have dusted themselves off and have been touring successfully. Some of their most avid fans weren't even born when the old bands first broke through. And another point, short and sweet: if tradition didn't exist, someone would reinvent it. Traditions and classics will not go entirely by the wayside. However, we do seem to be preoccupied with trends and with trend itself. What else typifies our postmodern world?

One trend that we have noted is that of shorter life cycles. These fleeting spans seem to have infiltrated many aspects of our lives, from the trivial fashions that briefly possess us to transient spells with cars, houses, careers, and spouses. We want to choose, to taste as much as we can, and consequently, hardly anything permanent seems worthwhile anymore. Economists speak of "durable goods" (for example, appliances), but the fact is that such goods are now purchased and replaced with alarming frequency. Think of how many people seem to be constantly upgrading their kitchens, suddenly a normal activity in an era when home makeovers are broadcast on television and have quickly become part of our culture. Everything is now disposable. This ethos has taken hold in our public culture, our private lives, and in our capitalism as well.

When we think of capitalism, we conjure up one of two competing paradigms: the older industrial capitalism, concerned with the manufacture of physical commodities, and the newer postindustrial variety, focused on information, communication, and the exchange of financial instruments. The older model resides in massive factories, in sweat and smokestacks; the newer version is sleek and digital, with panoramic views from gleaming offices. Older capitalism was there for the long run. It built empires, which required far-sighted commitment to the accumulation of capital as well as its restrained reinvestment. This long-term attitude bears the stamp of delayed gratification.

But now, upstart telecommunication companies tell us that "no empire lasts forever." We see ads about the Internet in which a young guitar peddler tells us of his hopes to sell enough guitars to retire. The spirit of capitalism is being rewritten, largely under the weight of new information-age entrepreneurs, typified by dot-com start-up companies. But unlike Microsoft, an information-technology firm built to last (some believe rule) in the older behemoth style, most of the upstarts aim to cash out and retire. Indeed, "cash out" has nearly become a motto for our times. Far from establishing empires, the start-uppers hope that IBM (which has spent the last decade reinventing itself as a service, and not a manufacturing, empire) will buy them out, if they haven't gone IPO first. They do not want to take the heat in the kitchen too long—the ranch in Nevada or the farm in Oregon beckons. They do not envision their children and their children's children on the throne; they're too myopic. And who could blame them? Supernovas burn out. The world is changing too quickly and it's too hard to keep up.

As for the sought piles of money, the Russian chess master Aron Nimzovich's maxim, "the threat is stronger than the execution," is apt. Money's characteristic as a convertible medium of exchange has become intensified in our era of choice. Money has become a prize far more valuable as potential energy than the physical commodities it can provide. Ironically, in our present times of market volatility and paper wealth, cyber-worth is often as virtual as the companies that generate it.

Will the new entrepreneurs leave a legacy? Most of them won't. They grew up with the Andy Warhol fifteen-minutes-of-fame mentality. The old-style industrial robber barons were not always the least ruthless of individuals, but they *did* set aside some of their money to build monuments—concert halls, museums, colleges, and so on. Most of the current small fry seem reluctant even to fund a chair in those colleges—they know that no one cares who Smith Jones of the Smith Jones Chair in the Informative Sciences is or was anyway. The corollary to the fifteen-minutes-of-fame-outlook is that our memories become exactly that short.

But perhaps the most significant point is this: in our world of multimillion dollar contracts, get-rich-quick schemes are becoming normal, if not yet the norm. There is a great deal of wealth being spread around, and the culture of instant gratification has embedded itself. Take the money and run—the possibilities are endless. (And then open a restaurant, or start a mutual fund, or. . . .)

Another symptom of the shorter life cycles in our society is the growing tendency that we have to refuse to wait for one task to be finished before we begin the next one. Increasingly, we are turning to multitasking—perhaps a good metaphor for our times. By multitasking I don't really mean the ability on your computer to quickly switch back and forth between applications that are running. I do mean behavior like talking on the phone while driving (which probably increases one's accident risk), or talking on the phone while ringing up customers at the cash register (which sometimes results in the wrong change given out). Call waiting is another good example. But there's more to multitasking than our active attempts to simultaneously take care of multiple things at a time. Gradually and perhaps insidiously, multitasking is creeping into passive domains as well. Our waiting time, for example while "on hold," is now being appropriated by advertising pitches. And even the interval in between television shows is being utilized in a leaner, more efficient, multitask manner:

up until the 1996 season, TV shows would end, credits would roll, and then the ads would run for a couple of minutes until the next program. Now, the credits roll as a sidebar, and the network promotes the rest of its evening lineup on two-thirds of the screen. Since the promos are aural as well as visual, it seems that the intention of the networks is to use the marginalized credits as mere reminders of the preceding program, as well as to appear to do justice (however minimally) to those involved in its production. A similar example is the "crawl" that is now commonplace across the bottom of so many news channels. Such multitasking—another dimension of our attempt to fit more into our lives—is potentially dangerous, not just because we might lose control of our vehicles while on the phone, but because it can increase our tendency to marginalize *everything*.

One more example of shorter life cycles is the shorter movie runs nowadays. First-run films used to stick around for eight weeks, more or less, and now even the high-grossing films are gone sooner, sometimes after only a month. The reason for this is surely economic, but the result is that movies are spending less time in the national consciousness and thereby becoming more of a quick entertainment snack, here today and gone, almost literally, tomorrow.

Museums Are Not Always What They Seem

If so many aspects of our society, of our very culture, are becoming ephemeral, what exactly do we hold sacred? For modernism, as we have noted, museums became the houses of worship. What is happening to museums today? One development is the revival of the "sideshow-and-wonder-cabinet" exhibits of two centuries ago. For example, there is the American Dime Museum in Baltimore, where authentic fakes—museumlike pieces—take their places among genuine curiosities. Some insight into this trend is provided by Lawrence Weschler, who has written about David Wilson's Museum of Jurassic Technology (MJT) in Los Angeles.

This museum too is a throwback to the wonder cabinets that were among the first modern museums. The small-scale MJT exhibits a collection of curiosities of natural and technological phenomena. But the curiosities themselves, in the manner they're exhibited and documented, induce a strange incredulity in the viewer. This is not the ordinary astonished reaction, simply registering our surprise that something amazing is actually real; it's astonishment with a healthy dose of speculation. Well, it's more than that: you can't believe it because in fact, museum or not, you suspect it's phony. And if you probe deeper, there's something that's not quite right. It's not like a *real* museum. The captions on the displays, for example, are dubious. Monographs for sale are published by "the Society for the Diffusion of Useful Information," listed in California but with a British postal code (which, after investigation, turns out to be the same as the Ashmolean Museum's in Oxford, England). The Society's branches are located in, among other places (I can't resist this), Billings, Bhopal, Bowling Green, Dar es Salaam, Dayton, Düsseldorf, Mar en Beg, Mar en Mor, Pretoria, Teheran, Socorro, Terra Haute, and Ulster. Everything seems to be, in Weschler's words, at times "stupefyingly specific, at other times maddeningly vague." Wilson, the director, maintains an ironic persona, answering, but not answering, the visitor's questions. As Marcia Tucker, a director of a different museum, relates, "the literal-minded way in which [Wilson] earnestly and seemingly openly answers all your questions, his never cracking or letting you know that, or even whether, he's in on the joke," adds to the fog. In true postmodern spirit, the museum blurs the real and the fictive. Weschler brings great skepticism to his detective work as he seeks to uncover the *truth* behind the exhibits. But each display and caption is an onion's layer, and as he peels the layers away he succeeds in uncovering any number of curious connections. Surprisingly, most of his findings—not all—in fact corroborate what is shown and described, and Weschler, in "go figure" disbelief, more astonished than merely astonished, is almost back at square one, when he first asked, "Um, what kind of place *is* this exactly?"

We can't pretend that the majority of the museums of the world are given over to stimulating the visitor's tension in discerning among the real, the unreal, and the hyperreal. But the MJT takes a step beyond the ordinary in raising our consciousness concerning the veracity of its contents. And it is this quality that is consistent with contemporary society's burgeoning explorations of ways to both create and disarm oppositions. In this case we again see the blurring of truth and fiction. However, the way it is brought to our attention is unexpected, and is the product of a dissonance between detail and vagueness, authenticity and deception, that calls into question the very nature of the institution. The dialogue that develops is essentially one of the museum's pressing us to question its purpose; this dialogue, then, has an element of *self-reference,* in which the museum initiates its own doubts. In the postmodern spirit, pervasive self-reference and self-consciousness are two more hallmarks of our age.

Tattoos, Cloning, and Self-Reference

The recent explosion in the tattoo business invites thought as to whether, for many of us, it is time that the body itself became a museum of sorts, part wonder cabinet and part canvas. And speaking of trends, tattooing has lasted longer than I would have predicted. As for any trend, though, there are always those who seek unexplored territory. Maybe I was slow to pick up on it but only in mid-1997 did I notice the emergence of a new frontier of body decoration: scarring. Tattoos had become passé, having trickled up and down, and indeed in every direction, through society. For some—like those who window-shop tattoo joints in my Philadelphia neighborhood—it seems to have become second nature. Tattoos and piercings have been adopted as a norm of dress and personal ornamentation.

Now scarring, it would seem, has two characteristics that extend the boundaries. One, scars are ugly and antiornamental, in opposition to decorative tattoos. Two, scars are a lot more difficult to remove than tattoos; as such their relative irreversibility sends a tougher, more hardcore message.

Reflecting on this, I saw—and still see—the next wave as being amputation. Scars, although ugly, are not, in the literal sense, dysfunctional. And, although scars may not be easy to address surgically, they are, at least in theory, reversible. Amputation, though, pushes the envelope by diminishing one's functional ability (yet preserving the rebellious attributes of antiornamentation and increasing the authenticity of and commitment to this rebellion). Of course, I am not being original here. Worse, I had in mind the relatively tame lopping off of the tip of a pinky finger or middle toe; but my friend Martin Czigler tells me that a film exists of a man having his penis amputated.

Perhaps piercing, scarring, and amputation is not your idea of self-reference, or of the body as museum. And it's pretty low-tech, especially for the turn of the century. What about creating a clone—the ultimate technological self-reference? We were all caught by surprise in early 1997 when researchers in Edinburgh, Scotland announced that they had successfully cloned a sheep. Within the same week, more cloning was reported in Oregon, and the race was on. The events were high profile; the public was momentarily spellbound.

But strangely, every scientist covered by the media came out against the cloning of human beings. The British government stopped funding the sheep replicators. The Clinton administration pushed for the same censorship in the United States. You could not get enough of scientists, bioethicists (that's a profession?) and politicians on the air, embracing high morality. Cloning was suddenly morally reprehensible. But these were *scientists,* for Christ's sake. Hadn't even *one* of them wanted to be Dr. Frankenstein? Didn't they ever see *Blade Runner,* or read *Brave New World,* or the tons of science fiction about cloning itself? Most likely, these scientists were just being circumspect. Much easier to keep in line with public sentiment, proclaim that cloning is reprehensible, and then retreat into the lab to work more of it out.

Notably, just months later, the *New York Times* wrote, "'Never' Turns Swiftly Into 'Why Not.'" Suddenly, after initial reactions of disgust and outrage on cloning humans, the scientific community was saying, "it's just a matter of time" and "the risks aren't that great," and asking why is cloning less acceptable than creating an embryo from a donated egg and sperm, and so on. In late 2001 a Massachusetts company announced the cloning of human embryos, in an attempt to form stem cells. Although lawmakers reacted negatively, with some expressing a desire to ban such research entirely, it seems that human cloning has edged closer to inevitability. Every few months now we hear about another new advance—most notably, the cloning of human embryos in South Korea in 2004.

Obviously, cloning allows us to progress toward the realization of genetic engineering. And on this subject, scientists are quick to seize on the possibility of eliminating predispositions to Alzheimer's disease or cancer. However, we all know that once such basic necessities are dispensed with, what we are really going to become obsessed with are things like intelligence, height, and eye color. Sooner or later (I believe sooner) we will have to face this issue, rather than deny it and promise never to clone. The issue is vast, covering a multitude of scientific and philosophical questions. Bioethics? The metaphysical issues of existence and identity are broached by cloning, as well as by its distant relative, artificial intelligence. When—and, at this early time, I must write "if"—the human brain can be "backed up" (in the cybernetic sense), we will enter the fourth phase of civilization, *immortality.*

Before closing this chapter on postmodern manifestations, let's explore the concept of self-reference in more depth. To backtrack, we have earlier in the book considered at length the loss of the absolute, realized in the emergence of the individual over the past century and our unprecedented emphasis on, and acceptance of, the subjective. But there's more: "individual" is too clinical and also too general. We want to express our individuality but this in fact means the exposure of the core within—the *self.* Self-knowledge, which starts with self-awareness, is not exactly new, as Plato's "know thyself" indicates. However, as we have seen all along, one powerful indication that an idea has had impact is to witness its application in cultural and scientific expression. And there has been a bountiful harvest over the past century of scientific ideas that center on self-reference. Just as postmodern theory has roots in art and criticism that predate it by half a century, scientific notions employing self-reference go back many years also.

Self-Reference and Mathematics

I have mentioned Kurt Gödel's incompleteness theorem of 1931 as an event that shook mathematics to its core. This result showed that any self-consistent, useful number system contains *undecidable* statements—statements that are true but are *unprovable* within the system. This should seem outlandish to most of us. We think that math is math, and that its truths—theorems—are out there, waiting, and able, to be discovered. And Gödel's theorem informs us that all the geniuses and speedy computers in the world will never be able to unearth everything we would like to.

Just a few years later, in 1936, mathematician Alan Turing obtained a related result. Of David Hilbert's challenges for mathematics presented in 1900, there were three main issues concerning the foundations of mathematical theory. One was whether mathematics was *complete,* that is, whether all of its statements could be proved true or false; the second was whether mathematics was *consistent,* that is, not self-contradictory; the third was whether mathematics was *decidable,* that is, whether there existed a general procedure that could be applied to mathematical statements to correctly decide whether they were true. In 1900, Hilbert claimed, "Every definite mathematical problem must necessarily be susceptible of an exact settlement." Twenty-five years later he reiterated, "in mathematics, there is no *ignorabimus* [we will not know]." This sounds almost self-evident. But Gödel, relying, as we shall see, on self-reference, showed two things: that mathematics could not be shown to be consistent, and the more famous result stating that even *if* mathematics were consistent, it was *incomplete,* since it contained unprovable statements. But the third question—could a well-defined step-by-step procedure be developed to determine the truth of a particular statement in a finite amount of time—was still unanswered.

From our point of view, this last question is, "can't they just program a computer to crank out mathematical theorems?" Such theorem-proving programs do exist, and play a significant role in artificial intelligence, but they don't generally turn up too much that is new *and* of interest. What Turing did was to devise a hypothetical computational device now called a (universal) *Turing machine* that can carry out any calculation that *any* mechanical device could perform. This was a novel and important conception; as it turned out, twelve years later Turing led the first successful British effort to construct a modern computer. But what Turing showed was that there existed *unsolvable* problems. Consider an "infinite loop," a headache for a programmer in which, due to an oversight, a sequence of instructions will cycle around forever (and eventually crash the system). An example of the type of unsolvable problem Turing had in mind is the following: create a computer program that can check whether any program contains an infinite loop.

As for self-reference, Gödel's proof relied on a mathematical coding of the ancient Epimenides paradox. Epimenedes, from Crete, stated, "All Cretans are liars," which, written in a more mathematically formal way, could be, "This sentence is false." Of course, the statement is not mere self-reference. If false, the statement must be true; but, if true, then it's false, and so on, an example of what author Douglas Hofstadter calls a "Strange Loop." Referring to Russell and Whitehead's *Principia Mathematica*, Hofstadter paraphrased Gödel's (numerically coded) statement as "This statement of number theory does not have any proof in the system of *Principia Mathematica.*" Gödel's effort ensures that this is a true statement, and therefore unprovably so!

Turing, for his part, devised a formal proof to demonstrate that no method existed that, within a finite time, could decide whether a given mathematical statement was true. His proof was based on Cantor's method of showing that there are more irrational numbers than counting numbers. But Turing devised another argument to prove undecidability that relied on self-reference. Consider the issue of an infinite loop in a computer program. If a program could be written to detect infinite loops in *any* programs, then it could detect an infinite loop in its *own code*. But this would be an impossible task; in detecting such a loop, it would have to try it out and therefore loop around forever. Therefore such a program cannot exist.

From Self-Reference to Self-Reproduction

The idea of self-reference makes plenty of other appearances in mathematics and science. One place it pops up is in *recursion,* which has to do with nesting (a dream within a dream, or, to use Hofstadter's examples, a film within a film [or a parenthetical remark within a parenthetical remark]). A simple arithmetic notion that illustrates this is something you should have learned in school, called "factorial," written as a number followed by an exclamation point. As you (may) remember, $n!$ is equal to n times $(n-1)$ times $(n-2)$ and so on, all the way down to 2 times 1. A recursive way to define this is to set $n!$ equal to n times $(n-1)!$; but when we set things up in this fashion, we need a place to stop. Here we stop at $0! = 1$. The stopping point is what prevents us from going on forever; for a mathematician, it also describes an elementary instance of the expression. Those of you who have programmed computers quickly learned about subroutines and loops. You "called" subroutines, sometimes over and over, to obtain some useful output for the input you sent it. Loops, once entered, would perform some repetitive sequence of identical operations; if you weren't careful, you would stumble into an infinite loop as described above.

More sophisticated programming uses *stacks,* which are meant to simulate those cafeteria stacks of plates that push down onto, or pop up from, a spring. Thinking about the parenthesis-within-a-parenthesis motif, we realize that when we encounter a (left) parenthesis, we temporarily put things aside and then delve into the new encapsulated material. If, before we hit a right parenthesis and "pop" back out to the main text, we run into *another* left parenthesis, we go to *another* level of operations, as if we've put another clean plate on the stack, temporarily hiding those below. This nesting quality is very useful.

As a final example of recursion, consider the task of manually sorting a pile of numbered items. Suppose you don't know how high the numbers go. The following "divide and conquer" method is quite efficient: divide the items into two (roughly) equal piles, and sort the two halves separately. This, in turn, requires you to divide those two piles into two more piles each, and so on. Finally, you have a bunch of two- or three-item sets, that can be easily sorted and recombined.

Although computer programming has been done since about 1950, and logicians, as we have seen, were thinking about machine instructions since the 1930s, it wasn't until quite a bit later that there was widespread exposure to programming in university courses and through wide-scale industrial application. The year 1970 can serve as a turning point. (As a digression, the first IBM "third generation" computer, the S/360, came out in 1965; the S/370, an updated version, was announced in 1970. Integrated circuits, which enabled the miniaturization we take for granted today, came out in the late 1960s, and the first commercially available microprocessor, the four-bit Intel 4004, appeared in 1971.)

In 1970 the mathematician John Horton Conway created a computer game called "Life." This game is not the kind we're currently used to—it does not develop kids' aggressions by bashing enemies. Imagine pixels on a computer screen—in which each pixel is either on, that is, alive (and lit up), or off, that is, dead, at a given point in time. With every clock unit of time, the screen undergoes a transition, according to a simple, strict set of rules. Each cell's next state depends on its present state and its eight neighbors' states.

This game doesn't sound very exciting. It's not interactive; the player's only role is to set up an initial configuration (and this privilege can be relinquished). Moreover, given an initial setup, the rest of the transitions are strictly determined. All you do is simply watch the images on the screen change.

But how they change! First of all, despite the deterministic behavior, the transitions are surprising and (visually speaking) unpredictable. Some robust-looking patterns die out, some fragile ones strengthen, and certain figures actually pulse or drift across the screen. Life enthusiasts have come up with quaint names for a host of these special patterns. The most important feature, justifying the very name of the game, is that new Life forms can be created from certain interactions. What's more, Conway was able to show, at least in theory, that Life patterns exist that are *self-reproducing*. This is stunning news—that a large checkerboard of initially random chosen squares can give rise to shapes that grow and shrink, move and interact, create new shapes, and even reproduce themselves.

Obviously, dots on a computer screen—*codes*, if you like—are no substitute for *real* life. But there is a connection to the great breakthrough of biologists James Watson and Francis Crick in discovering the double-helix structure of DNA, and the still-ongoing human genome project. I should point out that long before Conway, and also before the Watson-Crick discovery, John von Neumann was able to demonstrate in the abstract the existence of a self-reproducing automaton. (Von Neumann's sketchy proof was later filled in by Arthur W. Burks.) As William Poundstone points out, von Neumann's work is of interest not because anyone would want to build a robot based on his schema, but because he showed that reproduction need not require divine intervention, and in addition he hit on the idea that a self-reproducing entity needs to have a description of itself stored somewhere, and needs to be able to pass this encryption down to its progeny. This is essentially the mechanism of DNA. It performs double duty both as an instructional code (i.e., program) to create offspring and as a descriptional code that can be passed along.

Very roughly speaking, the DNA helix is a two-stranded zipper that temporarily is undone to allow transcription in which our genetic "self-description" is matched and efficiently copied by strands of messenger RNA. These mRNA strands leave the cell nucleus (where the DNA encryption is permanently stored) and are worked on, in a process called translation, by ribosomes that inhabit the cell's cytoplasm. The ribosomes, by reading the mRNA code, produce proteins (i.e., life) by sequentially cranking out amino acids.

Uncertainty, Chaos, and Adaptation

If we pause here and consider where these deliberations on self-reference have led, we see that *information coding,* whether genetic or digital, seems to be the key feature. But isn't there a difference between the mechanically based, strictly deterministic modus operandi of the game of Life, and real life, which surely must have a random element?

Of course, one of the basic truths of science that we have come to know over the last century is that the world is *not* governed solely by deterministic laws. Everyone seems to know that reality—whatever it is—is not Newtonian. Overall, the way our *modeling* of reality has improved that is pertinent here is the introduction of a stochastic, that is, random, element in our scientific analyses. Different sciences have resorted to different techniques to account for uncertainties, but one general approach—probably overrated—has captured a great deal of public attention over the past fifteen years: chaos theory. Evidently, people like the oxymoronic notion that disarray can be formalized. The element of the uncontrollable within a rigorous system seems to resonate romantically in many of us.

Science writer Ivars Peterson and physicist Murray Gell-Mann cite the mathematician Henri Poincaré, in 1903, as already having summed up the fundamental implication of chaos: even *if* the laws of nature were completely deterministic and known to us, predictions cannot be reliable, because we cannot ever know conditions *precisely,* and because "small differences in the initial conditions produce very great ones in the final phenomena." As Gell-Mann points out, chaos theory is a mathematical theory of nonlinear dynamical systems (processes that change nonuniformly over time), but unfortunately, that catchy name is often applied to any phenomena that exhibit volatility or uncertainty.

What are some other ways scientists have modeled the vagaries of nature? Very often, they'll start with a deterministic model and tack on a stochastic feature. For example, the behavior of stock prices—the market is, after all, *some* sort of organism—could be represented by a number of terms that depend deterministically on other quantities, *plus* a random term. Depending on who's doing the talking, this random term is called noise, or drift. Often, the mathematical construct for this term is called Brownian motion, after the nineteenth-century biologist who studied the haphazard movement of such things as dust particles floating across your living room. Ultimately, however, the random term is just an addendum, a "fudge factor" that is computer generated from some probability distribution and added on to the other, deterministic, terms in the model.

A more recent—and more promising—approach that has appeared over the last decade is the interdisciplinary study of *complex adaptive systems*. Adaptation, of course, implies change to suit an environment. And a complex system is a collection of agents or components that interact in a multitude of ways.

The interest in this field of study is that it may allow us to explore and understand phenomena that seem either mysterious and outside the purview of traditional science, like social upheavals, or else have eluded science, like the functioning of the brain. The more researchers look, the more they find *self-organizing* properties of systems: spontaneous and unplanned events such as cellular morphogenesis, or the appearance of a market economy. These self-organizing systems do not merely appear. They are dynamic—they adapt and evolve. Furthermore, such systems seem to operate on a knife-edge in between a state of order and one of chaos. They are orderly enough to provide some stability, but volatile enough to allow for change and adaptation. The study of complex adaptive systems, apart from its promise, adds the interesting prospect of uniting researchers in diverse fields—physics, biology, economics, computer science, mathematics, cognitive science, and others.

What do these researchers do? How are the complex adaptive models set up? Clearly, there is more to them than some equations with randomness thrown in, and they are more than ordinary computer simulations. But simulation starts us on the right path. Think of the SimCity game, an interactive game in which the player guides the development of an urban environment. Continually, the player makes decisions on resource allocation and activity selection and the environment evolves. The structure that emerges depends, of course, on the player's input as well as on the game's own interaction rules (with a few natural disasters thrown in).

The complex adaptive systems seek to model an environment but without the human intervention of a game program. One model that has been successfully applied to a variety of areas is the genetic algorithm technique due to computer scientist John Holland. As could be expected, this method incorporates mechanisms that biologists have documented in the real world. The basic idea is that behavioral schema for adaptive agents in a complex system are encoded as strings of binary digits. Chunks of these digits have a certain meaning or serve as a particular instruction. These procedure codes operate, and also compete, within a changing environment; their ultimate performance (assuming this can be measured) indicates their "fitness." Some of these schema may turn out, over time, to be fitter than others. Holland employs natural selection to eliminate the weak schema. But what about adaptation? What about random events? The solution again is to imitate nature. One natural element of randomness is mutation. This is incorporated in the genetic algorithm by occasionally changing a randomly picked digit, say, from one to zero. As in real life, this will probably have an adverse effect on fitness, but could occasionally improve it as well. Another way to generate new and possibly more adaptive schema is sexual reproduction. At various junctures, the genetic algorithm will select two of the fitter schema and combine them via genetic crossover. That is, at a certain crossover point, the codes are each chopped apart and the resulting segments are mixed and recombined. The new schema that result— offspring, as it were—are added to the group of agents, while the least adaptive members are dropped from the mix (i.e., they become extinct).

Genetic algorithms are appealing in providing us with a way to incorporate reproduction, mutation, and above all, natural selection, in modeling a competitive environment. They are by no means the only tool that has been developed in the arena of complex adaptive systems. Another approach has been to introduce so-called neural networks, which obviously are modeled, at least loosely, on the connectionist structure of the human brain. So finally, at the beginning of the millennium, we have methods to model natural and even artificial phenomena that are *dynamic,* that *evolve,* that *self-organize.* As these mathematical structures develop over time, they surprise even their creators. They seem to live their own lives unpredictably.

But something else is present. Logic, algorithms, computer science, biology, adaptation, evolution, in fact *problem solving:* all of these are, in part, building blocks of the ambitious program of artificial intelligence (AI). The ultimate goal of AI is to create an artificial entity—call it a robot or a computer or a machine or whatever combination of hardware and software you like—that can imitate or even improve on human thought. Most researchers trace AI back to a paper written by Turing in 1950. The article begins, "I propose to consider the question, 'can machines think?'" Turing went on to suggest a simple way to determine whether a particular artificial entity has achieved AI's goal. His method more or less remains the acid test fifty years later.

Artificial Intelligence and Free Will

Imagine you are having a real-time, interactive conversation via e-mail, except that you can't tell whether your correspondent is a bona fide human being or a computer program. A program good enough for people to be fooled about half of the time has passed the "Turing test."

Acid test or not, you can be sure that some day, when (and if) there is an artificial entity that can pass muster—pass itself off as a person, at least via electronic discourse—there will be many who insist that the computer is still not really able to emulate the mind. The critics will invoke concepts like emotion and creativity; they may mention *free will*.

More than a decade ago, Roger Penrose argued that there are aspects of the human mind that machines will never be able to mimic. Basically, his claim is that "there is an essential *non-algorithmic* aspect to the role of conscious action." This is tantamount to saying that certain components of our thought are noncomputable, literally not able to be arrived at through the machinations of *any* kind of computing machinery.

Penrose points out that quantum theory has a random element, and that "various people leapt at the possibility that here might be a role for free will." But, as he continues, if this randomness is "*really* random," then is our free will merely the product of random events? Is it an illusion?

But what about the random element? The usual popular descriptions of chaos theory instruct that the fluttering of a butterfly's wings on one side of the globe could be responsible for a catastrophic event on the other. Similarly, we wonder whether a quantum event—say, the spontaneous decay of a subatomic particle—could be responsible for (OK, I'll say it: *cause*) a particular thought to occur, and further, a physical act to result. The jury is still out on this. But suppose it were possible; suppose that it happens all the time. Then we can safely claim that our thought processes and our resultant actions are not deterministic. Does this ruling save the day for whimsy, for caprice, for creativity and spontaneity? Have we answered that old philosophical chestnut: free will or determinism?

Not so fast: first of all, reconsider Spinoza's classic case for determinism, that we have no more freedom of choice, that is, free will, than does a projectile in motion. A conscious projectile could believe itself free to turn, but nevertheless it selects the straight path that it will indeed follow. We believe that we freely choose, but are simply ignorant of the causes of our thoughts and actions. If quantum theory is correct, or at least correct in its nondeterminism, we have to either reject Spinoza's argument or else update it by appending random causal events to his determinism. (The deterministic viewpoint was recently restated by Daniel Wegner, whose book title, "The Illusion of Conscious Will," gets right to the point.)

But can we accept a free will that is based on random, uncontrollable causes? The causal factor is the crux of the issue now, not determinism. And if you insist that we are truly free to choose, and that our actions are not completely determined by exogenous forces, random or otherwise, can you propose a physical theory to support your claims? Here, possibly Hofstadter has the right idea when he speculates that consciousness and free will "are based on a kind of Strange Loop, an interaction between levels in which the top level reaches back down towards the bottom level and influences it, while at the same time being itself determined by the bottom level."

And back to AI: clearly it is easy to introduce a random (or, for purists, a pseudorandom) element into an artificially intelligent (or quasi-intelligent) system. Randomness and unpredictability are not the issue. Free will is, and there are many who claim first, that we have it, and second, that computers don't and never will. Surely—and in the not-too-distant future—we will one day build quasi-intelligent systems. One such system will probably be confined to our computers. It will browse the Internet for us, take dictation, write letters, inform us of quirky happenings, read our mail, shop for us, and so on. A personal secretary, if you like. However, it will be more difficult to create an intelligent robot that will cook and clean for us, pick up all of the stuff lying around, and maybe go out and get a quart of milk. Nevertheless, imagine one of these quasi-intelligent systems, either the software or hardware type, with which you could share a joke. You both emit peals of laughter. Who are you to decide that the software-driven guffaws aren't real? What if the program tells you that it's sad—its favorite entertainer has just died, or its favorite football team has just lost? Will you respond that it doesn't know, can't comprehend, doesn't *feel, real* sadness? What if you step on the robot's foot, producing a gasp? Tell it it's not actual pain? And who is to say that your actual pain isn't any less electro-chemical-mechanical? Think it over!

Well, you've thought it over (a bit) and you still insist that there is a difference. Perhaps there is, and this is why I'm covering myself with the term "quasi-intelligent." But what *is* the difference? A soul? Or free will once again? If programmers put a randomizing feature into your personal software secretary, it could easily become more whimsical than anybody you've ever met. "I decided to write you a sonnet today, in Italian," or "I thought you'd like to check out some pictures from this biker site," or "No, I just don't feel like downloading the *Times* for you today, but I *did* order some outerwear for you from Land's End. I figured you might learn to like fuchsia. Oh—and I got you an extra-large; you've been gaining weight lately, and I bet you'll need the next size by the fall." Maybe this is a little too much free will, or just not the right kind.

If you capitulate on free will, or at least the capacity to simulate it, you may not give up on the *soul* as a uniquely human feature. What is the nature of this soul? For perhaps the same reasons that so many people cannot give up faith in God, many people (the same ones?) hold on to the prospect that they have this mysterious essence—their soul, spirit, psychic force, or whatever. Three-and-a-half centuries ago Descartes not only founded our very existence on the (apparent) fact that we think, but also formulated the classic dualism between the thinking (but not material) mind, and the material (but not thinking) body. Clearly, for Descartes and for so many of us, the mind is the "I." For Descartes, "I am not only lodged in my body as a pilot in a ship but . . . I am . . . so intermingled with it that I seem to compose with it one whole." Anticipating the question of how a nonmaterial entity could interact with, and indeed seem to causally affect, the body, Descartes housed the contact point in the newly discovered pineal gland. (He also gave an explanation of the causal apparatus that would make any New Age author proud.)

Long ago, most philosophers, like Gilbert Ryle, had rejected the Cartesian "ghost in the machine" and other such dualisms, but then, it's not clear whether philosophical arguments ever get anywhere, or whether the realm of philosophy is merely language. We naturally seek harder proof in science. It's no secret that over the past decade, scientists have been finding more and more behaviors that are physiologically, and ultimately chemically, caused, and further, that the causes of (or at least predispositions to) these behaviors are genetically based. An unusual but notable such result was accidentally stumbled on by UCLA researchers working with an epileptic teen a few years ago. The scientists were electrically stimulating various lobes of the girl's brain. At one point, laughter was produced. Perhaps you dismiss this as a "reflex," a tickling of the brain. (I wrote "laughter was produced" in the passive voice to encourage your skepticism.) But get this: the sixteen-year-old, fully conscious during the entire procedure, reported actual amusement, self-cognizant humor in, for example, the way the researchers were all standing around her. The electrical stimulation was perhaps not so different from the giggly effects of marijuana (known long before Descartes, let alone modern science).

To sum up the possibilities for AI to someday succeed: the materialist philosopher La Mettrie wrote *L'homme machine* back in 1747, in an era when today's progress would have been virtually inconceivable. If he were alive now, there is no chance that he would reverse his belief that "Nature constructed, within the machine of man, another machine which proved suitable for retaining ideas and producing new ones" (from *Système d'epicure*). It is possible that AI will never succeed in duplicating human thought processes. But it will probably get pretty damn close.

There is a certain hollowness in realizing that our mysterious and unique core is neither; that all of our secrets will be revealed and replicated by scientists, or—sadder to say—computer programmers. Even if this does come to pass, we will always have that special feeling of being unique and transcendent. We will retain the perception of free will—that we are unpredictable and in this we have something that no one can ever discover. This polarity of mind and body, spirit and matter, indeed mysticism and science, will continue to torment us. To some extent it always has, but only since Kierkegaard and Nietzsche have we become liberated enough—increasingly so in the era of choice—to make the self and its cogitation the primary focus of philosophical investigation.

Through the vanishing of absolute standards and the plentiful self-absorption that followed, through the proliferation of goods and the plentiful choice that resulted, people in the twentieth century gained a widespread and unprecedented sense of conflict and opposition that has manifested itself in numerous cultural and personal spheres. Friction appears even when we are spoiled for choice, as is so often the case today. But as our wealth grows, so does our ability to overcome the disjunctions that choices present—more and more, we *can* have our cake and eat it, too. A generation ago this theme began to supplant the oppositional, modernist mindset. What has resulted is a culture still beguiled by exclusionary choices but also aware that some choices can be tamed. They can be blurred. They can be inclusionary. More significantly, the very way we think about choices has been changing at an accelerating rate. Choice itself has gone from being a means to achieve happiness to an end in itself. And our realization that choice is not merely a vehicle but an objective has fueled so much of what has been termed postmodernism. Furthermore, our increasing awareness of our individuality has been matched by an increasing sense of self-awareness and the growing practice of self-reference in a variety of directions, the ultimate one, perhaps, being the program of artificial intelligence.

I don't want to give the impression that *every* dualism in our society is being blurred and broken down, or that once an opposition has softened and gone fuzzy, that any underlying problem it might represent is on its way toward being solved. One conflict that has become increasingly threatening to our society is the aforementioned clash of the individual and the group, and I will return to its discussion shortly. Prior to that, though, let's review what some critics and social theorists have had to say about various directions in which we have been recently heading.

William Irwin Thompson: We Are Replacing the Natural with the Artificial

One postmodern blurring that we have examined involves the intermingling of the true and the false, the real, the fictive, and the hyperreal. In some settings, the ability to cloud the distinctions among these categories requires a considerable technological ability to create the artificial. Armed with this power, the next and tempting step for us, which we call progress, is to apply it. We replace the natural with the man-made. America, William Irwin Thompson argues, has made the replacement of nature a way of life, a theme, a principle on the global rise and poised to redirect everyone's future.

And what is wrong with that? Thompson asserts that a mighty struggle has been underway. Nature's violent actions such as hurricanes, floods, and droughts lash out against humanity's technological insurrection. As for global warming, ozone depletion, runaway pollution, epidemic disease, out-of-control bacteria and mutant insects—we ignore them, except for the occasional sensational headlines. Technology plows full steam ahead.

Thompson states, "It's the technological process and not the natural product that is important." Furthermore, "history is replaced with movies, education is replaced with entertainment, and nature is replaced with technology," in a "peculiar wedding of low kitsch and high tech." To wit, Thompson selects some of our accomplishments: Cheez Whiz, Cool Whip, tasteless fruit, Sylvester Stallone movies, AstroTurf, and Disney World. The last item is actually, he claims, a meticulously planned, controlled, and manipulative attempt to replace culture itself (culture, at least, as it used to be known). The primary strategy Thompson implicates is Disney's installation of its own products as historico-cultural icons in its visitors' minds. In a clean, cheery, crime-free environment, you wait in a well-managed queue and listen to Disney songs, "old favorites" that get your nostalgic juices flowing. (Meanwhile, you have paid so much money that you are determined not to be disappointed.) You visit the various Worlds at the EPCOT center, literally larger than life, and in doing so, freed from your automobile and thereby rediscovering bipedal locomotion, you are at once reconnected to our Planet Earth (while being swept off your feet).

So swept away are many visitors, that they have converted (without quite knowing it) to what Thompson calls "the world's cleverest and most successful new religion," one that is transforming a world of education and reflection into an entertainment-immersed "postliterary culture." Disney, of course, has other methods of drawing your attention to their realm. One, for example, is self-referential: Disney owns ABC, and the two promote each other—on New Year's Eve on ABC you will see events at Disney World as well as at traditional sites. More generally, Disney is successful at developing an omnipresence similar to that of Christmas. What I mean is that Disney's interwoven umbrella of entertainment products creates a sentimental core of fantasy and nostalgia that even intelligent and thoughtful people wallow in—just like Christmas. The process is begun in childhood and is therefore very powerful, because by appealing to that pure, innocent, almost atavistic id, it is able to stave off the critical, cynical superego. Christmas is a fantasy period, whereas Disney is a network of fantasy products. Christmas is able to occupy our thoughts for a couple of months and invade them occasionally the remainder of the year. And Disney has developed similar power. Its wide and complex web of products and advertising is usually able to tempt us with that unrestrained joy of childhood, triggering a desire to plug into it once more.

In a wider sense Thompson is right—that attractions like "Disneyism," loud music, electronic culture, chemical addiction, and more generally, the expanding and polluting habits of consumption, are replacing the good old values of preservation, the exchange of ideas, and education—that is, *culture*. But like so many others steeped in the good old days, he forgets that most people, now *and* then, virtually devoid of his intellectual and critical faculties, are (and would have been) thrilled to reach the Age of Entertainment.

What else has America replaced? As art became the religion of modernism and museums its cathedrals, entertainment has become the religion of post-modernism and color monitors its shrines. And, as much as we find it natural that time marches from past to present to future, Thompson claims that we are watching this flow erode through that evil scapegoat, television. For him, CNN in particular is the prime suspect, presenting us with varied, simultaneous transmissions that compress not only twenty-four-hour time periods but also larger, historical ones—"tribal, preindustrial, industrial, or postindustrial"—in its "electronic collage." CNN's coverage of the 1991 Gulf War (as well as more recent conflicts, like Iraq in 2003) blurred the distinctions among news, live footage, docudrama, entertainment, and history, and it also served as its own best commercial for future viewing. (Interestingly, regarding live war coverage, the Gulf War signaled a sea change to both Thompson and Baudrillard; consistent with this, the writer Paul Theroux noted in 1982 how *little* live coverage of the Falklands conflict was actually aired in the U.K.)

But as the 1990s rolled on, and the market shares of the traditional networks plunged, they too had to resort to increasing globalization and the warping of time and space. By 1997, the tragic end to Princess Diana's life would galvanize all of the media into a self-conscious, open competition in which their coverage of "The Death of Princess Diana" was an event beyond the actual event itself. Reporters were dispatched to London, Paris, and everywhere else; the time zone differentials were erased at the expense of a few bleary-eyed and well-paid stars, and before you could say, "where's the royalty," a host of books had appeared on the Duke of Windsor's abdication sixty years earlier. The overall argument—that television (now augmented by the Web) is destroying the arrow of time—is not particularly convincing; yet Thompson is correct in noting that Americans' sense of history, always poor, has reached new depths. As he points out, when today's kids see Humphrey Bogart or Charlton Heston on the tube, they're just old guys lumped together with the Beatles, Louis Armstrong, Babe Ruth, or even George Washington. It's all history. And, after writer Nathanael West, he remarks that "history [in Los Angeles] becomes a movie set that spatializes time: on one studio lot you have Caesar and Cleopatra, while next to it the Sioux are defeating Custer. For the young raised on electronic media, there is no historical past, there is only an eternal present in which all time is going on now."

This eternal present manifests itself in our surroundings and our gear. "Furniture for the young is . . . a poster of a celebrity, a Coca-Cola wastepaper basket, a Mobil gas pump light, and a war-surplus inflatable life raft. These signs, whether they are worn around as furniture or on as clothes, have a recognizable nostalgic feeling to them, but no real history." And when history becomes smeared, we tend to become less responsible for our actions. Thompson thus explains the defacement of a synagogue by thirteen-year-olds: "if the adults in Hollywood have made so much money with the Nazis, why should we be surprised when kids in the hormonic rush of puberty turn history into a Halloween costume parade for skinheads and heavy metal freaks. Jew and Nazi, cowboy and Indian, CNN's American and Iraqi, or Disney's Pirates of the Caribbean—what's the difference?"

In today's world, where innovations and new editions leapfrog one another in ever-faster cycles, where obsolescence is not only planned but quickening, where ballplayers (and their teams) seldom last more than a few years in one place, our sense of era, generation, and time itself has been hopelessly deformed. Computing is perhaps an extreme example, but those of us who used punched cards in the 1970s now see them symbolizing distant Dark Ages. The 286 machines of the 1980s are almost literally ancient history. When the laptop I bought in 1994 crashed five years later, it was so old by then that the manufacturer told me that model was not serviced anymore. In an age where computers have penetrated every aspect of intercourse (almost), when it's routine for the pizza place to know your address simply from caller ID, B.C.E. might as well mean "before computers existed." For kids today, 1950, as well as 1850 and 1450, are B.C.E.; it's all old.

Thompson tackles our American penchant for devouring chemically enhanced, if not completely artificial food, and the (un)natural extension to this—a general reliance on man-made chemicals to which, through habit or otherwise, we become addicted as well as dependent. Novelist William Gibson saw where this would lead. In the futuristic *Neuromancer*, real food is almost nonexistent, and a character comments on the great expense of raising a "whole animal for years" just to produce steak.

It seems that our technological obsession is widening the bifurcation between engineer and poet, and that the engineers are winning. However, Thompson tells us, it's not so simple. Technology has its spiritual underside; art and poetry can catalyze cultish fascism, for example, so who's to say what the possibilities are or how the battle will continue. Every once in a while there is a catastrophe in which spiritualism has intersected badly with technology, like the mass suicidal demise of Marshall Applewhite's Heaven's Gate cult—the sort of calamity Thompson seemed to be alluding to (before its time).

Perhaps you're an enthusiastic, committed technologist, or, more likely, a passive technologist, happy to have word processing and DVD and e-mail and voice mail (when it's all made accessible). Either way, I suspect Thompson's invectives will sound rather Luddite-ish, and in any event, they're largely ineffective (Thompson admits much the same himself). Nevertheless his points deserve scrutiny. One of Thompson's main targets is the chemical and biomedical megaindustry, whose goal seems to be the attainment of immortality (and the cashing in on the attempt). Reflecting on Thompson's list of chemical nasties that this industry has spawned (including DDT, thalidomide, dioxin, and to which I'll add breast implants, diet pills, and vioxx), I find the fortunes of Prozac most interesting. The *New York Times* reported that in Germany, by mid-1997 the nonprescription preparation Saint John's Wort *(Johanniskraut)* was far and away the most popular antidepressant, outselling Prozac by four to one. Even doctors in the United States were starting to prescribe it—by 1998 it was well established. (Here is a victory, albeit minor, for naturists.) I began to wonder what the Prozac sales directors would do—make physicians offers they couldn't refuse, or maybe try some of that *Johanniskraut* themselves. Imagine the ignominy of your product losing market share and getting humiliated by a two-thousand-year-old herbal preparation!

Neil Postman: Technology Is Taking Over

William Irwin Thompson is not the only one to lament our growing love affair with and dependence on technology. Neil Postman adds another voice of concern. He pinpoints the sources of our technological obsession in some unlikely places. One is Cambridge, England, 1792, where a tutor named William Farish first assigned grades to students' papers. Another is René Laënnec's invention of the stethoscope in 1816. He picks out some more usual suspects too, like James Watt's steam engine (1765), Samuel Morse's telegraph (1836), and Frederick Taylor's book, *The Principles of Scientific Management* (1911). Postman adds Auguste Comte, Adam Smith, and Henry Ford, for good measure. To Taylor, Farish, and Comte, we owe the notion that natural behavior can be analyzed through breaking it down and quantifying it. To the inventors, we are indebted for obtaining ways of making life easier, which is especially gratifying in an era of losing faith in our religious systems, if not exactly in God. To Adam Smith in theory and Henry Ford in practice, we owe the ideas that division of labor and greed both work for the greatest collective good.

Postman defines a *technopoly* as a system in which all aspects of cultural life are dominated by technology. In such a system, he warns us, we substitute technology or a technologically generated item for the real thing. For all its merit, technology crushes our moral structures and deprives us of some of our most human values. The United States, of course, is the leader in this dubious race. Much of the explanation goes back to at least to the 1800s, when de Tocqueville observed that the United States was a nation on the move and in search of improvement—which was found in newness. Abetting this search are factors like our immigrant makeup (people choosing to start over again), our frontier mentality, and our abundant resources.

The accelerating introduction of new technologies seems to quench our thirst, at least temporarily, for the new and improved. But our obsession with technology and our elevation of the science that drives it has proved, in part, harmful. On this Postman presents three points: that we suppose techniques of the natural sciences can be used in the social sciences; that social science generates organizing principles for human behavior and society; and that "faith in science can serve as a comprehensive belief system." This belief system causes us to push quantification and science into places they don't belong. Science becomes the only path to truth, and as a result, we often develop pseudoscience when we don't know the answers or when we need a persuasive mechanism. When we equate science and truth but mistake pseudoscience for science, we deceive ourselves—almost anything can be sanctified if it is termed "science" and involves "experts." In general, our "the computer says so" mentality testifies to the widespread acceptance of technology and quantification. What's more, the equation of science and pseudoscience leads to the strange inversion that people believe what they want to believe anyway. As an example, a long time ago a friend of mine became convinced, after observing a casino gambler, that you can win at roulette simply by simultaneously placing different bets. I spent a long time explaining that the different bets do not improve your chances, and that even though the gambler might have won at least one bet on almost every play, he was losing most or all of the other bets. My friendship and the trust that it would presumably generate, combined with my advanced degrees in applied mathematics, could not shake the belief that multiple bets will beat the house.

science has spawned an era in which we don't
is or who does it, since everybody is now a scien-
lette player who covers the table with chips. (Tan-
onic that despite this reverence for the scientific,
ers *studying* science. About half of the scientific
d in the U.S. go to nonnatives.) This trend toward
rvades even the least plausible areas, for example
ite of contests is broken down into tenths of a
t more precision and therefore greater worth and

ue of the scientific–humanistic division is traced
w (whom Postman, not without cause, lambastes
d the division as well as the general ignorance of
s. Others, like Postman and Thompson, believe
There's another camp: Susan Sontag holds that
act an "illusion," and what has transpired is the
" grounded in the novel dynamism of contem-

Postman and Thompson are correct, can the hu-
I believe so, for two reasons. One is that, as the
op up after their victory (and, in a narrow sense
dgets in any decent university), all of their tools,
cs, will have saturated our collective conscious-
e them all for granted. This is already happening
drugs are advertised with various effects com-
(placebo is too hard a word); the stock market's
to the hundredth of a point; sports analysis is
e trivia, and on and on. For the moment we are
statistics, by so-called fact; but soon this vogue
eby cheapened. Like any other (economic) com-
e, quantification and the science and technology
value (and certainly its novelty value). Conse-
o things —that we currently deride as "touchy-
the derision, or perhaps contempt, that some
their human resource class or engineering stu-
s)—is being plowed under, it will become un-
d stock, it will eventually be rediscovered.

My second reason for not counting out humanism is that human beings have not changed much emotionally over the last couple of thousand years, and I don't expect them to in the next few hundred. As in all oppositions, some amount of balance must be struck; if it weren't we would seek it out. As long as our hearts beat fast and our pupils dilate and we shed tears, our feelings will not be subordinated to some numerical scale. We will retain our humanist sides and our humanist experts who chronicle those feelings and help us get in touch with them and live more fully. In other words, if you're exhilarated, you're exhilarated, and knowing that this rush is an 8.7 out of 10 is not going to be the main thing. (Although, on the other hand, the 8.7 will mean *something*.) Thus science versus nature is and will remain a fundamental dualism. Some will continue to believe that science and its deputy, technology, are appropriating all of the turf, and others will see nothing but New Age crystals and channeling and lack of rigor in the schools and conclude exactly the opposite.

Confounding the issue of nature's struggle against the artificial that Thompson documents, or the allied battle between humanism and technopoly that Postman presents, is the blurring of the entities of reality, fiction, and hyperreality that we have already discussed. Suppose you pick up a package of chocolate-covered raisins. Careful—that chocolate may not be *real*. What hath science wrought? The "chocolate" has been processed with a "great tasting" fat substitute, so it's "healthy" (especially with those raisins). We face this sort of quandary daily. It's not real chocolate but it tastes all right—perhaps better than certain real chocolates. But what's this fat substitute? Is it natural (well, you know what I mean—even natural foods have chemicals)? Is it organic? In the context of replacing the real with the fake, the truth with fiction, where are the lines drawn? It's like watching a film: "This is a true story." Down to what level, what details? Which features of the actual story are conveniently omitted? There's no more "true story" than there is a single true newspaper account of a complex event. And, increasingly, in this media-saturated world, it's difficult to tell the science from the pseudoscience, and the chocolate from the imitation.

Gene Rochlin: The Consequences of Computerization

Gene Rochlin is another critic of contemporary trends whose focus has been the consequences of computerization. His primary argument is that wholesale computerization of all of our organizational spheres, from financial trading to the armed forces to air traffic, nuclear power, and other operational controls, will reduce the autonomous human elements to dangerously low levels. A central premise of Rochlin's argument is that computers will never be able to duplicate the ability that humans have in certain sensory-cognitive dimensions. Computers will never develop the intuition and "tacit knowledge" that people build up over years of experience. For example, they will never know that an engine sounds a bit wrong, and stop to check it out. On one level, Rochlin contends that as human command and control is replaced by automation, inevitable and unforeseen catastrophic situations will develop—situations that humans might avert but which are not preventable by computer systems.

Rochlin also fears, on a higher level, that we will lose "the capacity to nurture, enhance, and expand" human skills that are ordinarily honed through trial-and-error and trial-and-success. In addition, we will lose " 'slack,' the human and material buffering capacity that allows organizations and social systems to absorb unpredicted, and often unpredictable, shocks." Moreover, we will perhaps lose even the hypothetical ability for humans to intervene in the control of complex systems.

But perhaps the most intriguing of Rochlin's fears concerns the computer at the heart of the issue of human autonomy. Some years ago, the proliferation of desktop microcomputers proved to be significantly liberating for those who used them. Lack of standardization and networking technology made information exchange difficult, and therefore elevated the importance of the autonomous desktop user. Organizationally, one saw a certain decline in centralization correlated with an increase in individual autonomy.

However, the autonomy of individual users was short-lived. As information systems and network technology developed, centralized operational control became more extensive than ever. And, as organizationally integrative software becomes prevalent, not only do blue-collar workers become mere adjuncts to automated physical processes (as has already happened), but white-collar workers become equally subordinate to automated management processes. As Rochlin points out, this struggle for individual autonomy within an organization revisits Frederick Taylor's introduction of scientific management to factories a century ago. Back then, skilled workers were transformed through division of labor into cogs of meticulously planned, repetitive, mass-production processes. Similarly, today's managers are finding their organizational functions replaced by software, leaving them to fit in as subordinates whose locus of freedom is shrinking.

In a larger sense, some of the fears that Rochlin articulates come under the umbrella of choice. The conflict that is being played out by countless organizations between the forces of company centralization and individual autonomy may be tipping in favor of centralization. And the corollary to this is that, in the workplace, the decreased autonomy that we persistently mention roughly translates to a loss of empowerment through the loss of the ability to make one's own decisions. It is a restriction of choice in an era where choice is becoming paramount. On the other hand, though, it is entirely possible that workers will gain heightened powers and status due to the expanded set of functions that computerization entails. Or it is possible that the traditional, vertically integrated organizations that form the bulk of discussion here will migrate toward newer, more horizontal structures. Perhaps the visions of *1984* and *Brave New World* will not be upon us so very soon.

Obviously critics play a vital role. After all, they are supposed to criticize and act as our conscience. However, unremitting criticism becomes onerous. One begins to wonder if things are really that bad, or if perhaps the critics are simply reminding us that every significant advance carries a downside too.

There's Good News Too, Reports Gregg Easterbrook

In light of this, journalist and author Gregg Easterbrook gives us some much needed perspective when he details just how much things have improved, in *The Progress Paradox: How Life Gets Better While People Feel Worse*. As you can tell from his title, we might not believe that conditions in the world have been improving, but they have—markedly. Easterbrook carefully documents the advances we have made over the past century in facets of our lives as diverse as life expectancy, recreation, education levels, income and living standards, and more. Crime is on the decrease (for now, at least). There's more equality for women and minorities than ever before (although obviously, things are not perfect yet). Our environment is getting cleaner, despite some perception to the contrary. And, globally, poverty and starvation are on the decline (but we still have a long way to go).

It's encouraging to see that things are not really as bad as we think, but why are we feeling worse? More specifically, why are so many of us depressed? Clinically speaking, there *has* been a distinct rise in depression, and Easterbrook turns to psychologist Martin Seligman for the identification of a few root causes. One is the rise in individualism. There is now less religious affiliation and less community involvement. Families are smaller and more spread out. So naturally we tend to focus on the "I" more, and when things are going badly, there are fewer ways for us to reach out and seek support. This focus on individualism, in turn, seems rooted in the loss of the absolute that we have already discussed.

Another cause of our current wave of depression, according to Seligman, is the "'teaching of victimology and helplessness.'" This is one aspect of responsibility avoidance. As victims we curiously testify to being unable to control our fate—an inversion of choice!—and we get caught up in looking to blame others for any misfortune.

A third cause of contemporary depression is "runaway consumerism." We use consumption as a "shortcut to well-being." As Barry Schwartz has also noted, such consumerism seems to have no limits. As we require ever more things to satisfy our urges, we become literally insatiable.

Clinical depression aside, Easterbrook notes that the choices available to us create a burden like never before. He cites Robert E. Lane, who claims that one reason citizens of market democracies are becoming unhappy is, "There are too many life choices . . . and demands to discover or create an identity." And as Easterbrook puts it, "Today freedom and choice in all things create a pressure that previously did not exist, and can make whatever does not work out in your life seem a reflection on you. This problem might be called 'the choice penalty.' The choice penalty may be especially high for women . . . now women have so many options that choice itself has become a source of anguish."

Easterbrook provides a number of antidotes to living in our current high-stress world, his prescriptions ranging from changes to our personal mind-sets to recommendations for public policy. If only we could act on his advice, our glass would be more than half-full.

Lawrence Levine: More Good News

An even more refreshingly positive critic is Lawrence Levine, whose book, *Opening of the American Mind,* has three major themes. First, Levine debunks the myth that American (and Western) civilization has had a little-changing canon of classics over the past few hundred years. In fact, Levine tells us, this revered humanities canon was itself always in flux, and had become a canon for only about a fifty-year span during the twentieth century. Second, Levine reminds us that multicultural studies have an intrinsic worth; from a historian's point of view, elitist history is simply not complete and is therefore inaccurate. Third, opening (and not closing) our studies is not only healthy, but we have always had such a tradition. Pluralism is not just the product of recent radicalism.

Levine substantiates his points in various ways. For example, he demonstrates that the long-standing "classical" curriculum in the West was actually more concerned with the fine points of Greek grammar than with the content of the works. Even as late as the 1860s, an author like Shakespeare was not elevated to the status of the Greeks. And science held a lower status than Shakespeare did. Surprisingly, that era had very similar battles over modernization of the humanities curriculum to ours today—which contradicts the notion that our current dialogue on the same issues is raw and unprecedented.

The origin of the "canon" sentiment, according to Levine, developed during World War I. Many could not see a clear role for the United States in that conflict (echoing our involvement in remote regional conflicts today), and therefore America's eventual entry into the war needed considerable justification. Justification required education (and propaganda), which in turn developed into the standard Western Civilization courses that traced European thought and progress from the ancients through to the 1900s. The content and relevance of these courses was challenged in the social and intellectual foment of the 1960s, when they became, in part, modified or dismantled.

As for pluralism, Levine shows that the fears we harbor today about immigration, derived from racial, ethnic, and linguistic differences, are exactly the same fears that our forefathers harbored one hundred, two hundred, and even three hundred years ago. For example, there are those who pessimistically speculate about the future of English in the state of California, given the growth of its Mexican-American population. Levine finds analogous fears about Irish immigration in Massachusetts and German immigration in Pennsylvania going back to the 1700s. He documents fears of a swelling wave of crime in mid-nineteenth century New York that was blamed on its Celtic population, and reports numerous past exhortations to limit the influx of various ethnic groups. A hundred years ago the "natives" said identical things about Italians, Poles, and Jews that are often said about Asian-, African-, and Hispanic-Americans today. Perhaps some things will never change—but Levine's point is that our fears are unfounded and always have been. Americans might resent foreign immigration, but the fact is we have ceaselessly thrived on it. The mixing of cultures, whether called melting pot or tossed salad, has, despite its tensions, been the force behind America's vitality and the uniqueness of its culture.

One difference between the eighteenth-century fears of being overwhelmed by immigrants and those of the turn of this century is that the contemporary fears are driven by sophisticated-sounding demographic forecasts. The assumption in these forecasts appears to be that certain groups will continue to have many kids per family, whereas the natives average less than two. Then by the year 2030 or whatever, the majority of Americans (Californians, etc.) will be different (speak Spanish or whatever else is the source of concern). Since the fears seem to be grounded largely in the difference in fertility between immigrant or ethnic groups and other Americans, it would be well to speculate about the underlying concerns.

An obvious source of concern for those threatened by an influx of other peoples is their mistrust and fear of difference. Mitigating this apprehension is something I will address in chapter 19. But the fertility issue is a related one and is, I believe, highly influenced by choice. One important and detrimental dimension of fertility is the high number of children born to teenagers; a recent UNICEF report, for example, indicates that children born to teenagers are more likely than other children to grow up in poverty, do poorly in school, abuse drugs and alcohol, and to become teenage parents themselves.

The UNICEF study (of twenty-eight of the world's richest countries) finds that the United States has by far the highest rate of teenage motherhood. The U.K.'s rate is second highest. Countries like Japan and the Netherlands, however, have very low such birthrates. Therefore wealth, as measured in the aggregate among nations, is not a determining factor for births to teenagers. However, family poverty and low educational background are highly correlated with such births. What does choice reveal here?

There is a large gap between rich and poor in the United States (and a considerable, but smaller gap, in the U.K.), and not only is the gap widening, but increasingly the mores of this nation rest on the accumulation of material goods. Although this amassing is achievable for the great majority, it is not achievable for all. As we have discussed, the United States (and to a lesser degree, other developed countries) have developed a "now" culture that is shortening the cycle time between desire and possession. The culture of delayed gratification that Freud considered so important for the maturation of an advanced civilization is starting to unravel. This shows in our trade deficit, in our personal debt, in our advertising, and most of all, in our lifestyles of ever-increasing conspicuous consumption. Envy, as the economists are keenly aware, is a powerful motivator. And driven by envy, as Frank warns us, the accelerating patterns of conspicuous consumption by the wealthy have rapidly trickled down to the middle classes and below. Unfortunately, though, in a culture that screams consumption in its every nook and cranny, those who are excluded from that consumption will seek a compensatory mechanism. In the case of our lower-class teens—especially those who do poorly in school and who sense very few opportunities down the road—having a child can be a way out, at least in the short term.

Obviously, there are stages to bearing a child. The first, of course, is that of having sex itself, which in this context can be interpreted as the exercise of choice by those who do not, and believe they never will, have the opportunities that abound in the larger society. The fact that pregnancies result from the lack of birth control reveals at least two facts: one is that birth control is expensive; another is that a conscious gamble is indeed underway. The next stage, the possibility of abortion, also is multifaceted. For some, abortion is simply too expensive, or is outside moral boundaries. But for others, the pull toward having the child outweighs that of termination. Contrast this urge to have a child with the sentiments of many at the other end of the socioeconomic spectrum: birth rates have been declining among the middle classes in the developed world. Dare I suggest that the endless individual potential that has emerged in the era of choice—potential not just to consume but to shape one's life—has been influential in decreasing women's drive to have children?

Getting back to choice and delayed gratification, one notion that heavily impacts our decision making is long-term planning, which depends on what Robert Axelrod calls "the shadow of the future." For those disenfranchised by the society at large, the future does not cast as long a shadow. The effect of this discounting is to emphasize outcomes that provide short-term joy. Having a baby is one of the few such "low cost" activities. It is self-generated (important in a society that excludes those who can't afford to play consumer) and yet serves as a priceless commodity. Unfortunately, such children are too often treated as commodities and status symbols as well.

We can easily forget how not everybody is overwhelmed by choice (go to the supermarket; go to the mall; go to the sixteen-plex movie complex; go to the Home Depot; or just stay at home and surf the Net or watch TV). But all of us are immersed in our environment, and thus we are trained to live with choice. It is so central to our lives that if we are deprived we almost literally don't know what to do with ourselves. Most of us find, or at least look for, some meaning in material accumulation. But when our poor are forced to wade through our omnipresent consumer cornucopia, adrift in a land where normal people have mountains, or at least, housefuls of possessions, and they can't live like they are *supposed* to, then obviously there will be consequences.

Given that we seem to define so much of ourselves by our possessions, there is no more profound evidence of poverty than one's inability to say *yes* to very much. Henry David Thoreau may have claimed that a person's richness came from being able to say *no* to things, but the obverse of this coin is that you start with what you possess, and go up from there. Why else would designer labels have become so sought after by the underprivileged, if not to announce, I have money, I can consume with the best of them—with the article of clothing itself being the facticity of wealth. The same may be said for gold adornments. Beyond gold, many poor people blow considerable amounts of money on what others in society would view as dubious purchases. This behavior, as with gambling, is surely motivated by the desire to prove that one is more powerful than the money, that one can withstand its loss. One way or another, though, everyone gambles or gets some designer gear (or gold) but everyone sees through it also, and no one is any happier. Thus consumption becomes to some extent necessary but not sufficient, in our quest to appease our envy. Something else is required to address envy and emptiness, and a baby, a free and yet priceless miracle, often fits the bill.

A couple of generations ago (and we have to note that for some, the generations are getting shorter, while for others, longer) social pressure was sufficient to prevent most teen pregnancies, partly since few incentives, psychological and economic, existed to encourage them. But times have changed, and individuals, even underage ones, have clout enough to challenge the greater society. Thus we have another example of the important struggle between the individual and the group, a conflict that is far from equilibrium and is threatening to dislocate much more than our moral systems. Let's revisit this struggle again.

A bit of a recap: I have claimed that, over the course of human history, only as the twentieth century advanced did most persons in the developed world achieve a standard of living that generated plentiful amounts of discretionary wealth as well as time in which to enjoy it. What we have obtained with these surpluses is a heightening sense of the centrality in our lives of having to make choices. This omnipresence of choice in our lives is correlated with the growing prevalence of choice as a major theme in much of our cultural expression. Choice has manifested itself either directly or indirectly; the indirect effects include the many oppositional motifs that we have discussed. Opposition itself constitutes an important dimension of modernism, which in turn had been the chief vehicle of progress in our cultural sphere for over a century.

In the 1960s modernism seemed to come to the end of its dialectical line of avant-garde innovation and subsequent absorption into the mainstream. There was little to rebel against; modernism itself had become the establishment. The division between high and mass culture was deteriorating. Partly spurred by this, the loss of the absolute had advanced sufficiently for pluralism—in general, the notion of accepting the alternative—to begin to be accepted. In turn, creative expression would generate less and less shock value and begin to re-trace its half-century-old steps. Finally, the synthesis of these factors led to a strengthening desire for freedom—freedom to determine one's way in the world, freedom to choose. This last struggle was played out on several over-lapping battlefields, including the civil rights movement, the conflict over the war in Vietnam, the hippie movement, women's liberation, and gay rights.

By the mid-1970s many commentators sensed that the old oppositions had softened and that the dominant mode of modernism was beginning to be eclipsed by something new, something more eclectic and inclusive. This new cultural mode was dubbed postmodernism. In some ways postmodernism was more modern than modernism, and similarly thrived on the knife-edge of opposition. But in other respects postmodernism in its inclusiveness looked to soften oppositions, to overcome contradictions, to have its cake and eat it too. As we have pointed out, these objectives seem to characterize so much of our personal lives as well as our cultural expressions.

Not all oppositions in our society are disappearing. Furthermore, the erosion of an opposition is not necessarily a beneficial occurrence. Oppositions may be tense, but often their balance helps maintain equilibrium in society. For example, the United States in the 1950s had at least the appearance of stability, and was in no apparent turmoil over the separation of high and mass culture, or the relative lack of heterogeneity that generally prevailed in the media. But the dissolving of such a system can lead to disequilibrium. And, as economist Lester Thurow points out, disequilibrium "means great threats as well as great opportunities." An important disequilibrium today, as mentioned at the end of the last chapter, has arisen from friction between the individual and the group. Why is this friction such a central issue in our society?

As stated in chapter 11, Adam Smith's invisible hand has been the chief axiom of free-marketers, some of whom advocate an extreme hands-off approach to the economy. In its favor, there is a certain elegance to the invisible hand. Moreover, in many circumstances Adam Smith has been correct in his related observation that private individuals are more capable than governments of investing their money to profitable ends. However, although free markets certainly have widespread utility, not every good in society should be treated as a privately tradable one. In chapter 11 I appealed in part to a natural division of goods into public and private ones—those that are either shared or are not—which is a consequence of recognizing our structural predilection for viewing the world as a system of differences and categories. Knowing that some readers will still disagree with this point of view, I now want to strengthen my position.

Conspicuous Consumption, the (Not So) Silent Killer

We have already discussed Robert Frank's remarks concerning the runaway "luxury fever" that is consuming us. As already mentioned, this is one aspect of the vicious spiral of choice. In addition, we have already discussed how keeping up with the conspicuous consumption of others will lead to a situation in which no one's relative standing has been improved, but everyone is worse off. It is as if everyone defected in repeated plays of a many-person prisoner's dilemma. In addition, such behavior has led to the low savings and massive personal debt and bankruptcy rates that we have today. And, as we will see, these conditions are by no means the most serious consequences. Although it is true that much of our consumerism has been good for our economy in the short run, it is also true that we are in for serious long-term effects if our spending patterns continue.

As we know, social traps form counterexamples to the invisible hand theory. But although many have believed that social traps like overfishing or overpolluting can year after year be ignored with impunity, Frank shows us that conspicuous consumption is increasingly becoming a serious threat to our well-being. It's a silent killer, like hypertension.

Frank first argues that—as we've discussed—conspicuous consumption leaves everyone worse off. But is this really true? What American family feels worse off when they have a big house, three cars, three TVs, a couple of computers, numerous phones, and a cornucopia of other commodities, and the only downside is that they work long hours or perhaps carry several thousand dollars of debt? The key to this argument is, as we have discussed before, many studies have shown that we adapt rapidly to pleasures and improvements in the domain of conspicuous consumption (larger homes, luxury cars, fancy watches, etc.). But once we adapt, we are no happier than before. Therefore, not only is our direct pleasure from conspicuous consumption evanescent, but because everyone else follows suit, our relative standing does not improve either.

Next, Frank points out that there *is* a category of spending in which we would all be better off; this is the less flashy domain of *in*conspicuous consumption, in which the United States has been declining over recent years. There are numerous examples where increases here have been shown to have long-lasting, positive payoffs. Where can we obtain some real improvement in our standard of living? In buying a new SUV, or in spending more time with friends? In having a roomier house, or in additional vacation time? Through buying luxury wines, or by exercising regularly?

Perhaps these examples do not convince you. But studies show that possessing goods like new SUVs or larger houses or top-rated wines make us no happier in the long run. However, spending time with friends, vacation time, and exercise all have been demonstrated to have long-term positive effects on our health or well-being. But you want harder evidence.

Inconspicuous consumption can be public as well as private. Over the years, as our national wealth has been growing, we have suffered inadequate levels of public spending in a variety of important sectors. Could an increase in public spending result in everyone's benefit? Absolutely. Frank notes how our aging municipal water systems could use attention, which would decrease the levels of toxic metals in our drinking water. Our air quality could similarly be improved. We have shortages of food inspectors. Our bridges and highways are deteriorating. And we are equally penny-wise and pound-foolish when it comes to drug treatment and drug prevention programs. In each category, a small fraction of what we collectively spend on luxury goods could go a long way toward improving the quality of life for *everyone* in our society.

Perhaps it's not enough to know that various public goods like water quality and road conditions can be improved. Perhaps most of us are happy with the current state of affairs in that sector. After all, it is our choice as individuals to decide where our money should go, and our overwhelming desire seems to be for better cars and bigger homes, and not safer roads and cleaner air. Unfortunately, though, we are slowly but surely paying a price for our acquisitions. While we spend little on public transportation, for example, all those cars we purchase are clogging the roads and increasing the amounts of time we spend stuck in traffic. Personal bankruptcies are at an all-time high—according to Frank, in one out of every seventy households. The longer hours we are working, combined with increasing job insecurity, are causing measurable increases in our stress levels. This additional stress precipitates physical and emotional disorders.

On top of this, the quality of our public amenities has, generally speaking, been declining over the years, and sooner or later this degradation will reach dangerous levels. Frank provides numerous details regarding the declines in expenditures for successful drug prevention programs, road and bridge maintenance, public school teachers' salaries, and FDA food inspections. Some of these categories are time bombs waiting to explode. Others are already troublesome. In the last chapter I mentioned the issue of children being born to mothers, often young and single, who do not have adequate resources to care for them. Although this problem is becoming pervasive, it is still predominant in the inner cities. Many of these children are born to drug-abusing parents, require extensive, expensive hospital treatment as infants, and suffer long-lasting behavioral and learning disabilities. Addressing this issue by spending some money on social programs and drug treatment and prevention would generate a handsome payback for all members of our society.

I hope by now it is clear that, on the whole, our capital is not being spent optimally. The problem is that each of us realizes that doing the right thing individually will not benefit us or anyone else very much and we therefore spend our money in ways that make us happy. As Frank points out, there is a correspondence to Darwinian theory. Just as "Male elks would do better if all had narrower racks of antlers, and peacocks would do better if all had shorter tailfeathers . . . many spending decisions that are adaptive for the individual are maladaptive for society as a whole." We know that an SUV, for example, uses more fuel and pollutes more than a small car, but the additional pollution we create is, in the scheme of things, negligible. We also know that the proliferation of heavy, high-riding SUVs makes life in a small car a bit more dangerous. So, like the elks who evolve large antlers, we splurge for 4×4s. Similarly, many of us who live in cities may believe in public schools. But we are faced with public schools that have deteriorated over the past thirty years. Many private schools—if we can afford them—will provide a better education for our children, and therefore many urbanites feel that they have no choice but to go private, even though they are aware that this decision leaves the public schools worse off for others.

Sometimes we don't even realize that we are compromising others' situations. In the suburbs, we shop around for houses with the school district reputation as a high priority. But those homes go for a steep premium, for which we have to work harder and earn more. As Frank notes, "The person who stays at the office two hours longer each day to be able to afford a house in a better school district probably has no conscious intention to make it more difficult for others to achieve the same goal. Yet that is an inescapable consequence of his action."

Invisible Hands and Visible Greed

Even when we are not measurably compromising others, the invisible hand attitude manifests itself in a variety of dangerous ways. One is the Panglossian "best-of-all-possible-worlds" philosophy where we believe that human ingenuity will always rise to the occasion and save us from doom. In 1798 the "dismal scientist" Thomas Malthus warned of the dire consequences in store for us on account of population increases outstripping the growth in food supply. Two hundred years later, we stand at six billion people worldwide and yet, although our distribution systems are inadequate, we still have the *resources* to feed everyone. In other, similar predictions, the Malthusians, although seemingly in possession of an incontrovertible theory, have been proven equally wrong. No wonder we have evolved the belief that things will always work out for the best. But even then, we too heavily rely on the *market* to solve our problems. As an example, because fossil fuels have been so cheap over the past two decades, we have neglected the development of renewable energy. Too many of us see nothing wrong with the market solution, which is to use fossil fuels until their scarcity will drive prices up. Only through that eventual economic pinch will we hasten to develop large-scale alternative energy sources. The problem is, over the intervening years fossil fuel use will continue to wreak havoc on our environment. Why prolong this nasty situation?

Another, not unrelated, example is that of a suburban family of four or more persons who have to share only two or three cars. Given the monetary resources, they might spring for an additional vehicle so they don't have to go ferrying each other around. If you were to point out to them that this sort of behavior is bringing on traffic congestion, the answer is invariably that if the congestion gets bad enough, then public transportation will reemerge. The idea, of course, is that only when the congestion is sufficiently annoying will the inconvenience of public transit compare favorably, for enough people, to the hassle of traffic jams. And the market will naturally respond to this, increasing public transit when there is demand and eliminating it when there isn't. Unfortunately, the configuration of American suburbs is already not very amenable to public transportation, and so the market solution for this worsening problem is therefore unworkable.

At this point, we are left to reject Adam Smith's invisible hand, or at least reject its wholesale application to all economic affairs. The crux of the issue is that, as Frank states, since "each individual's well-being depends on the actions taken by others," then "the individual pursuit of self-interest will not result in the greatest good for all." Our shift in spending from public to private and from inconspicuous to conspicuous is only exacerbating our growing problems. Adam Smith himself had the foresight to recognize this trap. He realized that people, driven by a strong desire for material possessions, are led to perform a tightrope walk just to manage their consumption. In the end (i.e., old age), we realize that the value of these possessions is illusory, that we'd been taken for a cruel ride. I believe we can safely conclude that advocating the invisible hand has profound negative implications for a society where progressively, the individual is gaining greater independence and autonomy. Whatever balance we may have had between the individual and the group is being upended.

There is more to be said about the rise of the individual to preeminence in our society. Generally speaking, casual observation can be quite convincing that people are caring more and more about themselves and less and less about others. We're more self-centered than we used to be. One small but telling symptom I find is that people are talking more than they used to in movie theaters. Moreover, when asked to be quiet, they often do not seem to understand why. Maybe too many of us are used to watching movies at home, and are thereby conditioned to ignore the presence of others.

Movie theater conversation is surely not the coming of the apocalypse, but there are too many other symptoms of growing egoistic behavior. Too many drivers, impatient with the red light and seeing no traffic coming, will drive off before the light turns green. Others barely slow down, let alone stop, for stop signs. Many do not yield the right of way to pedestrians in the crosswalk. And the pedestrians just saunter across, red or green. There used to be a joke about a foreigner pushing ahead of the queue to board an English bus. One of the people patiently waiting would remark that the hasty person must have thought he would arrive first if he got on first. The reality now is that plenty of people push ahead. Perhaps something I witnessed on a route in north London sums it up: at a bus stop a crowd of schoolchildren pushed ahead of an elderly man to board. Indignant, the man cried out, to no one in particular, "the only thing anyone cares about any more is money."

In Philadelphia, we have any number of people who register their cars out of state in order to avoid high auto insurance rates. Ironically, the rates are high in part because the dearth of properly registered and insured vehicles leaves a high proportion of vehicles with no insurance at all. In Florida a disproportionate number of drivers obtain handicapped status in order to be able to park their cars in better spots. On our urban subway trains many youths, deprived of the opportunities of others, stretch out an arm or leg to claim the only choice they're going to get—the temporary possession of the empty seat next to them. And all over, college students are seeking special status under a spreading umbrella of disabilities, their primary objective being to have more time to finish exams.

The overall impression here is that too often, we are trying to get ahead, usually at the expense of others. And I don't think that it's going out on a limb to correlate these behaviors with ones typical of what I have called the "now" generation, for which there is a serious departure from the old-fashioned delayed gratification ethic. Nor are these observations inconsistent with those from critics who remark that we are losing our sense of *civitas*, or theorists who bemoan our conspicuous consumption. In general, this is also congruent with a pattern of diminished public expenditure. And in the latter arena, there are even those who wish to redefine public goods for personal gain. Among them number, not surprisingly, Donald Trump. Some Atlantic City landowners refused to budge from land that Trump wanted for a casino. He brought a court case against them, citing eminent domain, through which the local government could take over and then demolish the structures. Trump lost the ruling; the judge noted that eminent domain applied only to schemes for the good of the people (i.e., public goods like a library, etc.). So, at least as of July 1998, casinos were not (yet) considered to be public goods.

From what we have noted regarding the loss of the absolute, it is not surprising that as individuals we may be focusing more on ourselves and less on others. What could surprise some is that economists have had such a strong tradition of egoism, beginning with Adam Smith.

In One Corner, Sympathy and Commitment; in the Other, Egoism

The economist Amartya Sen provides a different approach to rejecting the egoistic precept. Sen traces the modern economic model of competitive analysis back to Francis Y. Edgeworth in 1881. Edgeworth claimed that "'the first principle of Economics is that every agent is actuated only by self-interest.'" This self-interest has become, in the modern jargon, "rationality." Sen observes that Edgeworth was well aware that this notion was not realistically applicable to our decision processes. But, he adds, Edgeworth felt that moral, utilitarian considerations were not relevant in war and commerce, and could not outweigh our uncontrolled selfishness or our impulsive self-interest.

Nearly a century later, not too much had changed. In 1971 theoreticians Kenneth Arrow and Frank Hahn remarked that "economists from Adam Smith to the present . . . have sought to show that a decentralized economy motivated by self-interest and guided by price signals would be compatible with a coherent disposition of economic resources that could be regarded, in a well-defined sense, as superior to a large class of possible alternative dispositions." Although Arrow and Hahn's language is somewhat guarded, no one would argue that they have described the canonical theory as it stood. As for the intervening years, a good deal of work, particularly in relating economic theory to biological behavior, would bolster the thesis that self-interest is not only how we operate, but that it generally works out satisfactorily. Of course, we have already discussed some of the opposing evidence, for example, Axelrod's evolution of cooperation.

Sen notes that in both Edgeworth's and in more contemporary analyses, egoistic principles result in markets with two basic characteristics. The first is that the market self-regulates into a *competitive equilibrium* where all agents buy and sell commodities at specific market-clearing prices and, given what everyone else is doing, no agent is unilaterally better off by not adhering to the equilibrium program. The second—from a different angle—is that the market is efficient, that is, no agent's outcome can be improved without making someone else worse off (which is called Pareto optimal); in addition, all agents are at least as well off by participating in the market as they would be left alone (called *individual rationality*), and, no group of agents could defect from the market and obtain a superior outcome (group rationality). These conditions of efficiency, individual rationality, and group rationality correspond to what is called the *core* of an economy. (Remarkably, it can be shown roughly that if the number of agents is large enough, the set of core, i.e., "undominated," outcomes will coincide with that given by the competitive equilibrium.)

These results form a good part of the cornerstone of modern economic theory. But Sen points out that even Edgeworth realized the market structure and its equilibrium outcomes may leave those who start ill endowed no better off, and that "utilitarian good society" would require that competition be "'supplemented by arbitration.'" Despite this, Edgeworth, and especially those who champion free markets as the paradigm to treat all economic activity, consider the egoist-competitive market approach to be both a realistic model as well as one leading to the achievement of the general good.

Sen's primary attack on the egoistic foundations of economic theory involves two distinct concepts that he calls sympathy and commitment, each of which is essentially excluded from the neoclassical models. Sympathy is where "concern for others directly affects one's welfare," and commitment involves taking action on account of this concern, although the concern as such does not decrease one's welfare. He observes that although behavior based on sympathy is essentially egoistic—since one's own satisfaction (utility) has been affected—most of modern theory treats it as an "externality" and through this mechanism, avoids dealing with it.

But commitment, according to Sen, which is intimately related to our moral structure, "drives a bridge between personal choice and personal welfare, and much of traditional economic theory relies on the identity of the two." That is, incorporating commitment into a wider behavioral theory would nullify the traditional market-based theory as applied to individual and social welfare.

Sen admits that the traditional, noncommitment-oriented theory does apply well to a large sector of economic activity, for example, to private consumer activity, or more generally, to consumption of private goods. (Adam Smith and free markets are fine for private goods.) Once again, the freedom for individuals to compete is indispensable in fostering innovation and sustaining a vigorous economy. But private goods are not the whole story. Commitment pervades the domain of public goods economics, which is concerned with provision, as we have said, of resources like roads, parks, defense, and perhaps health insurance or even communication and information systems. These goods are *shared*. One way to see this is to consider the well-known free rider problem, in which each individual attempts to shirk fiscal responsibility for supplying a public good. This results in the good's failure to be funded, despite the positive net benefits it would have bestowed on the community. If all public goods were treated as private ones (or if government vanished), self-interest would clearly lead to inefficiency.

Commitment, Sen points out additionally, profoundly affects the area of production via the problem of motivating personnel. People are not the utility-maximizing *Homo economicus* creatures they are often declared to be. "'Where is the railway station?'" Sen amusingly asks, "'There,' I say, pointing at the post office, 'and would you please post this letter for me on the way?' 'Yes,' he says, determined to open the envelope and check whether it contains something valuable."

Sen even critiques the usual analyses of subjects who experimentally play the prisoner's dilemma. Often, social scientists and game theorists ascribe players' refusal to follow the (optimal) selfish strategy to a lack of intelligence or strategic sophistication. Sen wonders whether asking if the players are "*more* sophisticated than the theory allows" would be more appropriate. In this remark, Sen is referring either to strategic sophistication or to the realization that the indicated payoffs in the experiments do not represent all that is meaningful to the players, or both.

To recap Sen's argument, modern economic theory, although good for understanding markets, is often neither realistically descriptive of human economic behavior nor optimal with respect to social welfare. The primary factor that is unaccounted for he terms "commitment," which is an internalized morality (or, perhaps, although he doesn't mention this, an instinct) that causes our behavior to deviate from predictions of market theory. Additionally, Sen finds two important lacunae in market theory, or, rather, areas to which it does not seem applicable: public economics and production. Sen opposes the egoism that is preeminent in both economic theory and socioeconomic behavior with a utilitarianism in which we ought to focus on total social welfare rather than on individual wealth maximization. That is, our individual objectives should be subordinate to the objective of producing the greatest good for the community, as represented by the sum of wealth. What might be the retort of the free market advocates?

With respect to Sen's commitment, the laissez-faire supporters could respond that, at the present time, competitive theory works well in the absence of this supposedly moral substrate. But suppose this commitment does exist in certain situations. Everything has a price, and therefore in theory, the price put on commitment would serve merely to adjust the market-clearing prices that neoclassical theory so admirably supplies. At most, this might require something of a paradigm shift—like going from Newtonian to Einsteinian physics—but it is theoretically manageable. As for public and production economics, perhaps the competitive market theorists could wriggle out of the difficulties Sen and others pose by claiming that their theory can be made to work with sufficient modifications (that simply haven't been developed yet). Or, perhaps there is a powerful argument that all so-called public goods can be provided as private goods.

It is natural to conclude that in the domain of private goods, that is, those that are used by individual units of an economy (a person, a family, a business) but not shared among them, the traditional, competitive market approach is reasonable, provided that it does not lead to outcomes that are demonstrably group suboptimal, like Frank's class of smart-for-one-dumb-for-all behaviors. Proposals like the consumption tax he suggests may be the right way to curb such social traps.

In the domain of public goods, which are shared among individual units of the economy, the competitive models, based on the rationality of self-interest, must give way to methods that are social, that is, community based. But the sticking point, as we have discussed earlier, is, just which goods in our rapidly changing world are public, and which are private? What is important to realize is that semantics is not the issue; what we hold as inalienable rights, *is*. Although vastly beyond the standard of living of the seventeenth century, our world is still one of constrained optimization. To what extent can we transcend Locke's "life, liberty, and property" (and what sort of property did he have in mind)? Putting Locke aside, what Americans have to come to grips with (more than Europeans and Asians do) is how willing we are to engage in *subsidization* as an integral part of our social contract. It is most unlikely that we will be able to construct and maintain mechanisms through which citizens of a community or state pay for, and only for, the public goods that they use, without succumbing either to the related problems of adverse selection and moral hazard, or else to a general impoverishment of available goods and services. It is inconceivable, for example, that we would eliminate AIDS research just because its sufferers couldn't raise enough money. Subsidization involves Sen's notion of commitment, nowadays called "doing the right thing." And this is at the core of the fundamental opposition of selfishness versus altruism, that is, the individual versus the group. Free markets do not help us share.

With respect to the issue of individual wealth versus communal wealth, moral philosopher John Rawls goes further than Sen, rejecting even community-valued utilitarianism. Rawls champions a "justice as fairness" criterion built on the social contract of Locke, Rousseau, and Kant. He rejects utilitarianism on the grounds that it is individually irrational. Why should an individual "accept a basic structure merely because it maximized the algebraic sum of advantages irrespective of its permanent effects on his own basic rights and interests"? Better, for Rawls, is to focus on the least advantaged persons in society and ensure that their welfare is improved when there are gains to be shared. That is, "social and economic inequalities are to be arranged so that they are . . . to the greatest benefit of the least advantaged. . . ." This "maximin" criterion, under which one attempts to maximize the welfare of the minimum-level members of society, can certainly conflict with the utilitarian total-welfare-maximization allocation of goods as well as with that stipulated by the egoistic, market-driven solution. It is notable that Rawl's desire for justice in the form of fairness for each individual in society leads him to promote social welfare allocations that, at least in the aggregate, are community suboptimal.

Obviously there are social welfare solutions that consider more than the mere distribution of wealth. Perhaps a satisfactory equilibrium could be reached where all capable persons in society would devote a few hours a month, say, to some sort of community service. Or maybe—as proposed by Bill Clinton, in a scaled-down version—each of us, on graduation from high school or college, would put in a year of service and would then be free to pursue what he or she wanted in a career. Possibly the kind of consumption tax that Robert Frank and others have advocated would generate enough revenue that, redirected toward productive projects, would solve many of our societal problems for us.

Global Tensions and the Clash of Civilizations

The tension between individual desires and group norms can ripple through a society and precipitate instability. At the same time, though, on the global stage, we also experience the pressures brought about by the growing self-determination of various factions. Historian Samuel Huntington has pointed out that ethnic and civilizational wars have repeatedly developed in the power vacuums formed by the departures of ruling (often colonial) powers. The efforts of the remaining factions to create lasting destinies are remarkably akin to the self-actualization processes that individuals experience. And, as in the criticisms of individual self-actualization, we find on the societal level that attempts by one group to win freedom are inextricably tied to the subjugation, or even elimination, of another. (Of course, as with any social situations, these circumstances are not ever very clear-cut. Other factors related to local warfare have been documented: Huntington lists historical inability to coexist without enmity, demographic shifts, and even curiosities like the percentages of 15- to 24-year-olds of a group exceeding 20 percent of its total population.)

Huntington rejects both Francis Fukuyama's "end of history" hypothesis as well as its antithesis, essayed by Zbigniew Brzezinski and Daniel Patrick Moynihan and dubbed "sheer chaos," as comprehensive models of our geopolitical situation. Since we live in a complex world, it is unlikely that on the one hand, a universal Western civilization is sweeping the globe, or that on the other one, international relations are devolving into pandemonium. As with so many of the oppositions we have considered, the agents of change—which are ethnic groups as well as nations—synthesize both opposing elements.

The world is indeed modernizing, but Huntington argues that it is not Westernizing as much as we (Westerners) presume it is. He believes, for example, that the United States' predominance in the sphere of entertainment media will not create a universal popular culture. Nor will English, despite its modest role as a lingua franca, generate a long-term cultural effect. After all, Russian as a second language waned in popularity as Russian power declined. And it seems inevitable that U.S. influence will decline too.

Huntington's main thesis is that the future of international relations will be determined by the clash of major civilizations. Many factors are and will remain important in how these civilizations are differentiated. However, Huntington finds religion—not language, race, or ethnicity—to be the primary cultural factor in defining civilizations. The continuing Balkan conflicts provide a good example of how peoples with a common language and ethnic traits can be torn apart by religion. But haven't we established the general decline of religion over several generations? Perhaps not. The loss of the absolute extends beyond religion. It refers to a general plurality of beliefs that have evolved over the past century-and-a-quarter. Science, technology, and liberalism eroded our trust in the absolute authority of the Church. As we obtained discretionary time and wealth, we gained empowerment over our own decisions, so any role of an Almighty would necessarily diminish. But liberalism and science had their limits too, and did not eliminate people's beliefs in *something*. More to the point, as long as alienation is present, religion will provide a mitigating influence.

Just as modernization is not likely to homogenize the world's cultures, it will probably not dispense with religion. Huntington details how religion has enjoyed a worldwide revival—*"la revanche de Dieu,"* as Gilles Kepel has called it—over the past two decades. Since the spectacular revolution in Iran in 1979, violent fundamentalists have wreaked havoc in Egypt, Algeria, and Israel's occupied territories, and religious war and its associated terrorism are at the forefront of everyone's mind after September 11. In quieter ways we have seen fundamentalist inroads in the United States in the conflicts over school prayer and the teaching of creation "science." But *la revanche de Dieu* is not merely the rise of fundamentalism. It pervades our everyday lives and even sways government policy. Interestingly, Huntington finds that this resurgence of religion, often strongest among the middle classes, in fact is *caused* by the modernizing processes of "urbanization, social mobilization, higher levels of literacy and education, intensified communication and media consumption, and expanded interaction with Western and other cultures." It is plausible that the dislocation and alienation that accompanies this modernization, carried out in Asia and other areas much more rapidly than it had occurred in the West, induces the need for "new sources of identity, new forms of stable community, and new sets of moral precepts." Religion seems to satisfy this need.

But religion, however important a determinant of civilizational difference, is only one dimension of it. Another axis that Huntington emphasizes is the individual–group one. He finds that our Western tradition of individualism is "unique among civilized societies." One interesting observation is that emphasis on the community can confer a competitive advantage. For example, Asia's rapid modernization, as Huntington quotes Lee Kuan Yew (the former prime minister of Singapore), was supported by the "'values that [their culture] upholds, such as the primacy of group interests over individual interests.'" But Huntington also contends that China's Confucianism, with its emphasis on "authority, order, hierarchy, and the supremacy of the collectivity over the individual," presents problems for democratization.

The religious orientation of a society can influence its political orientation, and this in turn will certainly impact on its economic behavior. Huntington quotes a Singaporean white paper that lists that republic's "shared values" of "Nation before community and society above self," "Family as the basic unit of society," "Regard and community support for the individual," "Consensus instead of contention," and "Racial and religious harmony." Singapore's commitment to democracy, Huntington observes, is absent from the list. And interestingly, he contends that the statement on support for the individual (which in part contradicts the first principle) was added to the other four to explicitly counter the Confucian emphasis on hierarchy and family. We can attribute this, perhaps, to a market-driven need for Singapore to differentiate itself from China as well as from the West.

East–West; Group–Individual; Yin–Yang

As we have remarked about religion, the desires for freedom, democracy, and individualism cannot be suppressed. They will always surface, especially as a global culture of choice continues to gain momentum. But perhaps we in the West have placed too much emphasis on the individual. In light of the various problems we increasingly have to confront, we might explore alternatives. As is constantly being pointed out, the experiment with communism failed. What can we learn from Eastern philosophies like Confucianism and Taoism?

The Tao is, roughly, "the right way." "Confucianism," writes physicist and author Fritjof Capra, is "the philosophy of social organization, of common sense and practical knowledge" with the objective of following the Tao, and Taoism is "concerned primarily with the observation of nature and the discovery of its Way. . . ." One principle that Confucianism adheres to is *propriety*, that is, good taste, manners, ceremony, ritual, tradition, and carrying out one's role in various relationships. Another is the development of our humanity, which includes the practices of respect, loyalty, honesty, and diligence. Following these principles will lead to the establishment of the harmonious social relations that characterize a good society.

Confucianism and Taoism form a complementary pair of approaches. Taoism is mystical whereas Confucianism is practical. But, according to Capra, the "principal characteristic of the Tao is the cyclic nature of its ceaseless motion and change" as seen in the adage, "going far means returning." Capra's point that "Modern industrial society which is continuously trying to increase the 'standard of living' . . . thereby decreases the quality of life for all its members" is a good illustration of this principle.

The duality between yin and yang provides a model to illustrate the motion of the Tao; their dynamic interplay indeed represents our natural duality even more comprehensively than the binary oppositions of French structuralism. Originally depicting the dark and light sides of a mountain (which can switch places), yang came to symbolize light, male, creative, and strong, while yin was dark, female, receptive, and yielding. There's more: yang is dynamic, yin static; yang is motion, yin rest; yang is rational, yin intuitive; yang is summer, yin winter.

Capra notes the similarity of the Taoist concepts of flows and dualities with the remarks of the philosopher Heraclitus ("everything flows; you can't step in the same river twice"). For Heraclitus, "cold things warm themselves, warm cools, moist dries, parched is made wet." For the Taoists, change, which is continual, occurs through the interplay of dual opposites. And each pole has, at its core, a kernel of its own opposite.

The Confucian-Taoist thought outlined here is important for us because it illustrates the centrality of the balance between oppositions. We are losing the balance between the individual and the group in contemporary Western society, especially in the United States. With respect to the similarities and differences between the way Western and Eastern cultures view oppositions, the key difference seems to be that in the East, oppositions are seen to be linked organically ("going far means returning"). There is a literal, systemic belief in this, as well as in that each extreme harbors the nucleus of what it is diametrically opposed to, and further, that cyclical movement between the poles is a fact of life. In the West, we reject this. Progress need not involve regression and the road to wealth will not lead to destitution. Excess is, therefore, not to be avoided. If anything, we believe in the slogan, "too much ain't enough."

To be sure, we do acknowledge a necessary entanglement of opposites here in the West, both in formal and folk expression. At the formal extreme, Sartre's very notion of being necessarily involves its negation, nothingness. In ordinary speech, we frequently offer the clichés, "what goes up must come down," and "the bigger they come, the harder they fall." I can vividly remember from my childhood how when I was sick, my father would say, "it'll get worse before it gets better" (although he didn't mean it in the Taoist sense—not that kind of guy). I would hope that he was wrong, but more significantly, I'd reflect on the necessity implicit in the adage. "*Why* does it have to get worse?" I would wonder.

Of course, just as we in the West sometimes push for an Easternizing influence, many in the East praise the ways of the West. On the eve of President Clinton's trip to China in 1998, the *New York Times* ran a front-page article on the recent flowering of personal freedoms in China, complete with a large and provocative photo of lovers openly smooching at Beijing University. The article was concerned with the "growing realm of personal freedom in China that allows ordinary people to make choices about travel, work, study, and love" and noted the recentness of the trend. "The issues that most people care about most—choosing a job, a place to live, a mate—have gained a degree of flexibility that few could have imagined 10 years ago." Despite some crackdowns that Beijing has recently imposed on Hong Kong, there is no doubt that personal freedoms in China continue to accelerate.

Reports like this one (though obviously written by a Western reporter for a Western medium) persuade us that the questions of choice are indeed universal. Though choice can be politically or economically suppressed, the desire for it is culture free. And although, as Huntington claims, the core civilizations outside the West such as Islam or the Sinic civilization may resist Westernization, they are not resisting modernization. And modernization brings choice.

No society is perfect, and I am not packing my bags for East Asia. However, I believe that East and West still have much to learn from one another. Our unmitigated quest for personal aggrandizement has led, through both inequitable initial distributions and unequal abilities within our populace, to a society in which the gap between the successful and unsuccessful is alarmingly wide. Accelerating conspicuous consumption is sucking valuable resources away from worthy public projects. We are starting to work harder than we used to and have fewer enduring benefits. As we travel up this vicious spiral, we will be faced with increasing complexity and less time to manage it. At the other end of the spectrum, our underprivileged class continues to grow. We have not done enough to help them help themselves. Instead we have created a situation in which both choice and consumption seem to be everyone's inalienable rights, and when this promise of entitlement is not delivered, the consequences are too often violent. On the individual level, crime is a frequent recourse. And on the group level, widespread rioting and looting, even on celebratory occasions (for example, when a sports team wins a championship), has become commonplace. Our response is to continue to build jails and lock people away at ever-increasing rates. Few who serve time get rehabilitated, and we can expect that as our prison exit populations match the record entry populations, those who are released, full of rage and lacking normalization, will not mesh well with the society that they rejoin. Our quality of life is beginning to erode.

A very natural response to the preceding concerns is to point out that we are more prosperous, healthier, and living longer than ever before. In one century we have transformed most lives in the developed world from ones of drudgery and toil to ones positively affected by the availability of choice. True, our conditions are not utopian, but given past progress, we have every reason to believe in a sumptuous future.

Thus the Panglossians address the Malthusians.

In this chapter I want to ask if, in the course of human history, we have ever before been in similar, or at least, analogous circumstances. If the answer is yes, then we need to examine the parallels among the common eras and attempt to learn from our forebears. If the answer is no, I certainly do not suggest dispensing with history as a prescriptive force. But it will be significant to know how and why our society is, in many important respects, in uncharted waters.

The Seventeenth Century: The Dutch Golden Age

One reasonable place to search for parallels to our time is seventeenth-century Holland. For one thing, this golden age seems to provide the first example in history in which wealth and prosperity seem to have been fairly pervasive throughout a nation's population. Historian Simon Schama notes that his study of Dutch wealth and culture in this era does not include the very poor, but neither does he catalogue solely the elite; he is confident that his lens captures a wide view of the population. Another similarity to our times is found in seventeenth-century Holland's blurred cultural stratification. Schama claims that there existed a mix in attitudes and culture among the elite, bourgeois, and masses. For example, a common text of the day might appear in both a fine and a plain version. Although the volumes were segregated by the quality of the binding, the reading material was nevertheless understood to be universal.

Before documenting in great detail the abundance of commodities that Dutch households of even modest means accumulated, Schama emphasizes the pervasiveness of the moralizing theme that excessive consumption will reap its just and disastrous recompense. This message cut across class: "For most of the seventeenth century . . . preachers and moralizing writers made no social distinctions in their attacks on corrupt manners. Their assumption was that abundance was a common, if unevenly distributed patrimony, and that the middling and common people quite as much as the elite needed warning of the dangers of drink and gluttony before they incurred the inevitable wages of sin."

Schama demonstrates the overabundance of goods in Dutch society with a corresponding profusion of evidence. He relies on historian Jan de Vries's data, which confirm various anecdotal accounts of the relative wealth of the Dutch. The anecdotal evidence itself is prodigious. Travelers like William Aglionby often commented on, for example, the remarkable variety in the diet of laborers, and expressed their awe of Dutch towns by observing that there were "'more palaces than country people's houses. Tis here where we must admire the magnificence of the citizens. . . .'" Aglionby also noted, according to Schama, that "signs of prosperity and ease extended right through the population."

Beyond food and housing, there are all indications that Dutch conspicuous consumption had a long and varied reach. Amsterdam, for example, boasted districts devoted to particular goods, including books, stationery, nautical supplies, hardware, dyes and fabrics, furniture, printing, haberdashery, medicines, shoes, and so on. Schama goes to great pains to catalogue the broad extent to which "middling" families possessed varied and bountiful food stocks as well as household furnishings. The reader is peppered with observations such as "relatively modest households could be well stocked with furnishings," or "The most common 'luxury' items in middling households were the mirrors that the clergy denounced as the tempters of devilish vanity," or that "pictures . . . hung in such profusion in middle-class households," or "It was perhaps in their kitchens and parlors that the Dutch middling sort were most lavishly equipped."

Much of Schama's interest lies in the contradiction of the Dutch appearing, at times, as "free-spending prodigals" while supposedly being "Europe's most tight-fisted burghers." The solution of this conundrum would shed light on

Max Weber's thesis that Dutch Calvinism tended to accumulate capital through restrained consumption. But in cataloging various conspicuous displays of Dutch wealth—the extravagant furnishings of private mansions, the magnificent streets, private buildings and gardens in numerous Dutch cities, and lists of prizes offered regularly in minor lottery drawings, Schama concludes that Weber's belief that the Protestant work ethic would serve to restrain consumption "does not seem to hold true for the Netherlands, the most formidable capitalism the world had yet seen."

It would appear, then, that the advanced capitalism developed in seventeenth-century Holland might well have been a sufficient condition for a culture of choice similar to ours to have emerged. But given that this does not seem to be the case, we have to ask why. I believe the primary answer lies in the presence of an absolute that we began to shed only in the late 1800s. Schama demonstrates just how ubiquitous the messages of "ministers and moralists" were, warning that "spending sprees, and the addiction to opulence . . . could only have one end: a material and moral enfeeblement that would inevitably culminate in collapse." Initially, the extremely influential clergy perpetrated these admonitions of impending doom and destruction. But these pervasive moralizing cautions were promulgated not only by the Church, but often by others, including artists and humanist critics, and appeared in the form of commercial regulation carried out by municipal authorities. The huge output of moralistic canvases during this era is testimony to the depth to which the cautionary messages had penetrated society.

As with our own apocalyptic predictions—some related to millennium fever—the Dutch in the mid-seventeenth century entertained plenty of anxiety in the form of doomsday forecasts. These utilized, as Schama notes, themes like "the ephemerality of the bubble, the robbery of the vain and foolish, the folly of Dame World and the despotism of Queen Money." There was, of course, one spectacular such fall from grace, the tulip speculation and frenzy that precipitated a crash in 1637. A general anxiety, though, fueled by the intermittent wars with Spain, England, and France as well as the occasional natural disaster, would continue deep into the eighteenth century. I believe that the self-consciousness and worry that stuck with the Dutch throughout the golden age was an important factor in inhibiting their freedom—the moral liberty and independence from an absolute that is the other necessary catalyst of choice.

I also believe there were additional factors that retarded any large-scale movement in seventeenth-century Holland toward our present-day concept of choice. Certainly the Dutch of the time enjoyed more buying power than their neighbors, but it cannot be said that their lives were as easy as those of their descendants three hundred years later. Although Schama goes to great lengths to illustrate how prices of various goods compared to wages, it is not clear how much discretionary money or time was available to the average person (although there seems to have been at least a modicum of resources left over for gorging, sozzling, and whoring). Certainly Dutch life, although more pleasant than elsewhere in Europe at the time, still had to be difficult. In particular, the standard of living must have been significantly inferior than that, say, in 1850 or 1900 (and recall that the latter were in turn far from today's measures).

Interestingly, a drive toward eclecticism featured in the demise of the golden era. According to Schama, "The most well-to-do . . . aspired to a more international style of dress, speech, diet, and architecture. . . ." Of course, there were other, and probably more important, factors. Dutch competitive advantages in areas like shipbuilding had eroded, eventually undermining conditions available for workers, many of whom then emigrated. Fiscal troubles and excessive tax burdens also figured in the reduction of Holland as a major power. And although the Dutch Republic didn't by any means collapse, its standard of living simply fell more into line with that of the rest of Europe. It is instructive to examine the material wealth as well as the self-consciousness of a thriving nation like seventeenth-century Holland. But it seems clear that the differences between the Dutch of that era and the developed world of today largely outweigh the similarities.

An Earlier Golden Age: Greece

Thomas McEvilley proposes that we have an entirely different type of predecessor—a cultural predecessor—in the ancient Greeks. Let's consider his thesis more closely, starting with the statement, "It is important that we realize that our Modernism is not unique." In the restricted universe of art, McEvilley first discusses quotation, which clearly is a historically oriented device. There is one type of historical quotation that he dismisses as mere learning about alien cultures and the resulting diffusion of various characteristic icons. In this sense the "Egyptians quoted the Sumerians; the Greeks the Egyptians; the Romans the Greeks; the Renaissance Italians, the Romans," and so on. This sort of quotation is merely the processing and subsequent posting of received material. The artistic quotation we have developed in the twentieth century differs due to its radical purpose and its sophistication. Dada advanced quotation "as a critical instrument," to question our traditional artistic products as well as the very nature of art. Fifty years later Pop Art, as we have already discussed, in large part recapitulated Dada; but McEvilley points out, although "Dada vulgarized the iconic," Pop "iconized the vulgar." Rather than merely introducing an unfamiliar form, Dada and Pop Art used already familiar images to make a point about society or challenge our suppositions about art. But quotation in this sense did not end with Pop—Pop was where quotation took off. In what we call postmodernism, artists have employed the quotation in numerous ways, for example, in copying an entire work, by incorporating, in an original way, various allusions to past styles, or by transforming the context of a familiar icon. For McEvilley, the accumulation of postmodern artistic quotations provides an "inventory" of both classical forms and contemporary insights into the older works.

The modernism McEvilley discusses is "the conviction that with reason, pragmatism, and good will, human communities can identify and solve their problems, ever more perfectly implementing the ideal of the greatest good for the greatest number," a sensibility he derives from pragmatist John Dewey. This is a reasonable mix of Victorian liberalism combined with the optimistic ethic of progress, although it dispenses with the social and cultural mechanisms of avant-garde rebellions against a potentially absorbent mainstream. McEvilley contends that today's postmodernism, which has surpassed Dewey's modernism, in essence had visited Western civilization before, in Alexandrian times.

To justify his thesis, McEvilley first identifies various practices that emerged in Athens after about 530 B.C.E. One is that potters and vase painters began to sign their work, contrary to the anonymity customary among the earlier Greeks and the Egyptians. This practice, for McEvilley, demonstrates the concept that art is not something to be merely copied from ancient forms, but is instead personal expression. He claims that what brought this modernism on is the emergence of democracy and market forces, where the new middle class championed meritocracy as opposed to the privileges of birth.

In this observation we see in ancient Greece an elevation of the individual analogous to what we have seen over the last century. This emphasis on the individual, especially in one's transcendence, McEvilley claims, is a common theme in Western consciousness. For example, in our myths and literature we repeatedly have posed the ominous challenge to our uniqueness through the introduction of an artificial (human) being. Examples that McEvilley cites are Ankebuta, an ancient Babylonian who wrote about creating an artificial human (as passed down in Hebrew cabalistic texts), the "golem, a being created by a rabbinical successor of Ankebuta," and Frankenstein's monster. All of these attempts turned out horribly because, McEvilley writes, "the attempt to create a person is always perceived as impious in cultures [including ours] that have a myth of the soul." This observation is consistent with the current aversion to human cloning, at least in the West. It is interesting to note McEvilley's point that Japan, which has accepted robots relatively easily, has no such tradition of soul mythology, as its culture is largely based on "the Buddhist idea of not-self, or soullessness." The above remarks, by the way, contrast somewhat with those of Daniel Boorstin, who points out that we in the West affirm the Judeo-Christian narrative that God created us in his image, and therefore we have inherited the mimetic urge to create. No such immanent desire wells up in non-Western peoples, since their gods were not creator gods, even in the case of Islam. In any event many of us in the West are afraid of robots, cloning, and artificial intelligence, just as we were afraid of Darwinism, all of which threaten the immutable soul—the self—and its underlying free will. These fears, as McEvilley continues, are traceable all the way back to the conflict between our Greco-Roman and Judeo-Christian roots. The Judeo-Christian tradition, as we have discussed, is founded upon faith, whereas the Greek tradition is based on doubt, criticism, and reason.

There are other parallels between the golden age of Greece and our modernism. One that McEvilley cites is how Aristophanes breached the proscenium arch. By having actors throw water on the audience, Aristophanes punctured the membrane that separated the artificial universe of the stage from the actual world of the spectators. And just as the twentieth century has seen an explosion of interest in art and pilgrimages to museums and art galleries, during the golden age, McEvilley tells us, "galleries began to appear, for the first time on record . . . for no purpose other than aesthetic delectation." In addition, he writes, during the golden age books on art history by Xenocrates and Antigonus appeared, which examined the development of art, particularly with respect to creativity. Artworks themselves became commodified and began to have tremendous barter value in the expanding economy, much as they have had in recent times.

We begin to understand that quite a few modern innovations are not so modern after all. Just as Aristophanes anticipated 1960s' performance art, we find that the Greeks developed various techniques that later generations only rediscovered. Another example is the origin of linear perspectival drawing. We attribute this "vanishing point" technique to early fifteenth century artists like Alberti and Brunelleschi. But, as McEvilley finds, even this Renaissance technique dates back to the ancient Greeks. Vitruvius indicates that the use of a vanishing point was originated by the stage designer Agatharchus in the fifth century B.C.E. The perspectival method was preserved in Arabic texts like Alhazen's *Perspectiva,* and McEvilley finds compelling evidence linking this text and other studies to the Florentine masters. In sculpture and poetry, as well as in the fine arts and theater, the golden age was a dynamic period of innovation. It seems as though the Hegelian concept that historical progress was a law of nature, with a direction and a goal, was already well in operation. Therefore McEvilley's claim that "the tradition of the new was fully in effect" indeed may sum up the situation.

The golden era of Greek modernism eventually petered out after 350 B.C.E. as first Greek hegemony and then even self-rule collapsed. The era that immediately followed, the Alexandrian age, saw, according to McEvilley, a reversal of the tradition of the new, where the "inner imperative of Greek art and culture turned toward its past." This culture revolved around a "nostalgic longing" for works of a much earlier era. Here is the parallel to our contemporary postmodernism. In what ways can this correspondence be made more precise?

We have seen how the turbulent 1960s ushered in our postmodern era; similarly for the ancient Greeks, political strife brought on the Alexandrian age. The protracted war between Athens and Sparta ended with Athenian surrender in 404 B.C.E. and with this came a decline in Athenian prosperity. Eventually the Greek city-states all fell under Macedonian control in 338 B.C.E., and in particular, under Alexander the Great himself in 336. These events, it can be argued, precipitated a rejection of the dynamic, but failed, culture. The demise of democracy plunged Greek modernism into a nostalgic postmodernism. The forward-looking ethos of innovation and progress gave way to a historicist culture that attempted to revive the ancient traditions that the modernist waves had swept away. McEvilley describes several examples in art and literature in which there were widespread efforts to revive or imitate more classical Greek works, such as epics styled on Homer or poetry crafted after Sappho. More interestingly, McEvilley contrasts Alexander the Great's colonialism with that of the Enlightenment and post-Enlightenment era. Alexander seemed to hope that his Hellenistic culture would meld together with those of the various peoples he overran. He took on Persian customs. He and his officers married foreign women. One wonders, though, whether Alexander really believed in his visions of brotherhood, longing for the "one world" that so many of our songs dream of, or if he simply was attempting to unify his far-reaching territories and pre-empt rebellion. Regardless of his motivation, his pluralistic endeavors are strikingly postmodern, and diverge from the inflexible methods of modern-era European colonialism, which attempted to impose its value system universally.

A higher-level way to consider what happened in both ancient Greece and the latter half of the twentieth century is to frame, as McEvilley has, the fall of modernisms and the subsequent rise of postmodernisms as "an oscillation that has returned many times." This oscillation is rooted, for McEvilley, in the opposition between reason and faith, where his claim is that historically, moments when the two poles "seem to mix more or less equally tend to end in confrontation." Artistically speaking, we can align the transcendental and romantic elements in art with faith, and the self-conscious, critical elements, with doubt.

This faith versus doubt opposition is expressed in the struggle in art between form and content. The Platonist and romantic traditions would have seen content inhering in form, as Clement Greenberg did, in which works of art need not signify external items or relate to anything outside themselves. McEvilley quotes Greenberg as saying, "'The avant-garde poet or artist tries in effect to imitate God by creating something valid solely on its own terms. . . .'" Despite resistance from the structuralists, who, like Lévi-Strauss, hold that "'Form and content are of the same nature, susceptible to the same analysis,'" the mainstream of art criticism continued into the 1960s to emphasize form at the expense of content. For McEvilley, this sentiment reached its apogee in remarks such as Susan Sontag's "'Interpretation is the revenge of the intellect upon art,'" and poet Marv Friedenn's "'in order to feed a thought you must starve a sensation.'" (How zero-sum, constant-energy, Freudian, and restrictive this last declaration is.)

We have already discussed the literary parallels to the overemphasis on form, where context, referents, associations, and intentions are stripped away to leave the text itself. In this vein, the form-bent, modernist, "new critics" still held on to a Platonist, objectively grasped aesthetic, in which a work is self-contained but still analyzable by objective, competently trained critics. However, the deconstructionists that followed them rejected that objectivism in favor of multiple interpretations.

Parallel to the trend away from objectively grasped form in art, Frankfurt-School-influenced critics also challenged the form-dominated mainstream, but from a different perspective. Their Marxist grounding led them, McEvilley claims, to emphasize the socioeconomic forces influencing creative expression as well as the aesthetics of the work itself. For this brand of criticism, "any act (including any art act) is saturated with political meaning." Against the background of conflicting theoretical bases, many artists, McEvilley observes, rebelled and attempted to evade categorization and thus to "bypass the process of commodification." They rejected any objective standards that might have survived at that point, and gave themselves over to works of expression and performance that were, to exaggerate, all content and no form. This explanation of the 1960s transformation, anchored in critical theory, provides a different slant on the emergence of postmodernism.

It seems reasonable to address the form-versus-content issue as we would any opposition. Art that is all form and no content is sensory but bypasses the intellect. Friedenn notwithstanding, we are thinking and not merely sentient beings and deserve more than content-free art. Of course, on the other hand, art that is all content and no form is not art. And if the two stray far out of balance, it is reasonable to assume, à la Voltaire, that a movement will surface that brings art back to where neither form nor content vanishes. Another way to consider this issue is McEvilley's invoking the Saussurean principle that form and content represent the two dimensions of a sign (the signifier and signified, respectively), and therefore are not separate entities. They are intertwined. Either way, it would seem that only a balance between the two can be sensible.

Chronologically, the overall picture is that modern art, steeped in expression, initially inhabited the transcendental sphere—form over content—but then, beginning with the 1960s, began to swing toward the critical pole. Such oscillations have recurred, McEvilley believes, in various societies over time from Rome (as essayed by Seneca) to Asia. These cycles or recurrences, then, presumably of different intensities, render the progress of Hegel or Dewey a mere myth. As McEvilley sums up, postmodernism is about shedding the myth of modernism. "History no longer seems . . . to be going any place in particular." It "has dissolved into mere time, into Averroes's endless succession of moments. . . ."

Will Modernism Cycle Forever?

McEvilley takes his place firmly among those who see history as endlessly cycling. His primary thesis is that the postmodernism that we have evolved over the past two generations is in fact one postmodernism among many. While I believe McEvilley has succeeded in what seems to be a secondary objective, which is to bring out the philosophical, artistic, and historical underpinnings of the transformation from modernism to postmodernism, as opposed to the usual emphasis on literary criticism, linguistics, sociology, and psychoanalysis, I will nevertheless argue against his principal theme. To begin with, McEvilley is largely concerned with art, whereas my scope of exploration, including science, technology, and lifestyle considerations, is broader and more comprehensive. But fundamentally, many of his points can be directly assailed.

McEvilley's chief objective is to demonstrate that the transition in ancient Greece from the golden age to the Alexandrian age significantly mirrors ours from modernism to postmodernism. In part, his evidence is compelling; convinced or not, the reader must concede that perhaps we are not as (post)modern as we believe, or maybe that the ancients weren't so ancient. If we accept McEvilley's somewhat narrow categorizations of modernism and postmodernism, his argument has some force. It focuses on an Athenian "tradition of the new," flourishing under a democracy that enjoyed a regional predominance for over a century. But was this golden age tradition rooted in the same broad sense of progress that we have had for over two hundred years? I believe the answer is in the negative. Although McEvilley cites a number of new works in literature, fine arts, music, and theater, I am not convinced that the Greeks worshipped the tradition of the new with the same fervor that we have worshipped progress and trend. I am not convinced that the Greeks carried out our paradigm shifts in which the avant-garde is absorbed into, and changes, the mainstream, in a pattern of punctuated equilibria. It is arguable that Dewey's modernism—where through the pragmatic use of reason, we can improve the lot of humanity—was a guiding light for the Greeks as well. And against the assertions that the Greeks developed socialism in this period, even with the burgeoning of the new mercantile class, we have the flip side—that roughly one-half of the Athenian population were slaves or metics, and only about 15 percent were adult male citizens.

Many of us, when given the stimulus "progress," respond with thoughts of science or technology. In this regard it is problematic to compare the golden age with the industrial age in the West from the late 1700s onward. The tremendous role that scientific and technological progress has had for us over the past two centuries in transforming our individual conditions as well as our social institutions, is unparalleled in ancient Athens.

No doubt, there were modernist themes in Athenian culture. The Western notion of the self seems to have originated there—though not the twentieth-century self that would seek to dominate nature. One example is the self-attribution practiced by potters and painters that contrasted with prior anonymity. But was this the emergence of the self, or was there a large economic impetus as well—to distinguish among artists, as collectors and critics combed the newly created galleries?

The transformation to the more historicist Alexandrian culture was initiated by the loss of regional hegemony and, following this, the disappearance of self-rule. In this period McEvilley reports a wave of nostalgia, reversing the tradition of the new. There was widespread quoting in sculpture and literature, including the revival of out-of-fashion works. We can augment McEvilley's thesis by remembering the establishment of great libraries—repositories of the past—at Alexandria and Pergamum. And we can note that Hellenistic civilization, widespread but politically fragmented, adopted various unifying policies, often centered on classical works. For example, gymnasia were now city-state run, with curricula that included the poetry of Homer. Disparate dialects were merged into a common Greek language, and new urban centers sprang up that were modeled on existing Greek cities. Even Euclid was primarily organizing already-known results.

However, rather than simply rehashing classical genres, the Alexandrian age saw a great deal of innovation too. In drama, comedy sought to dispense with politics and reject classical themes. In philosophy, new schools of thought, Epicureanism (after Epicurus) and Stoicism (after Zeno)—in a general sense complementary to one another—to some degree supplanted the more traditional schools of thought of Plato and Aristotle. But the main thrust of progress was technical. For whatever reasons, the Greeks did not extensively parlay science into applications (i.e., technology). Perhaps, like Plato, they were content with ideal forms. But the Hellenistic era from Alexander down to the Roman conquest fostered more scientific and technical progress than had the golden age. Perhaps Archimedes found engineering "ignoble," as Plutarch claimed, but he nevertheless devoted a great deal of effort toward practical applications of mathematics. In medicine, the practices of dissection and vivisection expanded the frontiers of knowledge. In geography and astronomy, bold new theories were advanced, including a heliocentric system with an earth that not only revolved around the sun but also rotated on its own axis. In this vein of newfound progress, the Hellenistic era resembles our industrial era more than our postmodern, postindustrial age. And, unlike *la Revanche de Dieu* that we have seen over the past twenty-five years, the Hellenistic, and not the golden, age saw a general diminishment of traditional Greek religion.

As we have discussed, most expositors of postmodernism mention several characteristics, most of which are outside the scope of ancient Greece. One aspect of our postmodernism is the erosion of the high–low culture gap. Another is the blurring of the public–private boundary; another is the tension, in criticism, between the synchronic and the diachronic. None of these dimensions appear to be relevant in the Alexandrian period. Another theme we have discussed is the blurring of reality. With respect to this, McEvilley points out the breaching of the proscenium arch. Admittedly this was clever and prescient, but it does not compare to our complex contemporary mix of reality, artificiality, and hyperreality.

Ultimately, McEvilley's thesis, if it still stands, is greatly reduced. But the real lesson here does not reside in a debate about modernisms and their sequels. Nor does it involve the obvious fact that some cultural trends and artifacts cycle around. The 1990s ushered in a great deal of adornment—tattoos, piercings, body sculpting, and so on—but who knows, perhaps soon we will worship the pure unblemished body. And although nobody dresses up for the theater anymore (clearly symptomatic of the breakdown of the high–low divide), note that even cruise operators, themselves the quintessential purveyors of jet-set leisure for the masses, request that their customers don formal gear for a couple of nights on the ship. (These trends are trivial but they provide plenty of material for social historians of the future.) In the appropriate contexts, cyclical theories can still be useful for historians, but in general, the idea that abandoned intellectual or artistic movements will someday return to the limelight is almost tautological and therefore ineffective.

The fuss about whether our postmodernism is unique is only a sideshow. The principal forces that impact our era emanate from the almost universal availability of choice in the twentieth century and beyond, not the collapse of modernism in the 1960s and its segue into postmodernism. This pervasive choice, in turn, arose from a technologically advanced production and distribution system as well as on a profound loss of the absolute—conditions that are unprecedented in human history.

I have two goals for this closing chapter. One is to consolidate and summarize the diverse material we have discussed. The other is to deliver on a promise I made at the outset, which is to provide some prescriptive analysis. It's all very well to identify choice and its concomitant oppositions and dilemmas as an integral issue in our lives and our cultural expression, but omitting a sense of how to use this realization beneficially would be unsatisfying, if not downright negligent. The following observations and their important policy implications, though not always original, derive directly from our preceding themes.

Choice, being pervasive in our society, engenders continual oppositions and conflicts, big and small, for almost all of us. Although in this book we have largely concentrated on how choice increasingly affects us on the individual level, it is clear that similar problems exist (and always have) at the group level, whether between factions or among states—problems of how to balance one's actions against those of others. These problems, far from disappearing, seem if anything to be proliferating too. How can we learn to resolve conflict and opposition both at the micro, or personal, level, and the macro, or intergroup, level?

Balance the Familiar and the New

The generic suggestions that I will advance have been outlined earlier. First we must accept the structuralist notion that human beings will always form oppositions. It is our character to classify, to seek out similarities, and—perhaps more so—to discover differences. Whether these differences are physical or linguistic or ideological, they will always be present among people and peoples. From this simple observation, we can draw various conclusions. One is that we can never hope to all be the same. It is naive to wish for a homogeneous world where differences and the conflicts these differences naturally engender have been eradicated. In this context we can apply Voltaire's remark, "If God did not exist, it would be necessary to invent him," in numerous circumstances. Difference is something we have to live with.

On the other hand, it is tempting to focus on difference and lose sight of our complementary need for commonality. There are various manifestations of this need, both societally and culturally. For example, as we discussed in chapter 15, it can often seem, in our world of pastiche, trend, and change, that we are losing the balance between trend and tradition, the new and the familiar. Perhaps this is indeed happening in the short term. But, once again, if tradition didn't exist, someone would reinvent it. We *need* common beliefs and common experiences; they provide essential connections. Very few of us can stand constant change where we are always on the edge, where we reject the comfort of the old and familiar. Therefore a balance must, for most of us, be sought.

This principle applies to a variety of situations. Consider travel. Virtually all Mediterranean beach resorts are, in summer, swarming with western Europeans. In one sense, the vacationers are simply seeking sunny destinations, and therefore Britons, Germans, and Scandinavians journey to Greece or Spain as naturally as Americans gravitate to Florida. In another sense, though, the beachgoers are well aware that they are heading abroad, and this means dealing with the unfamiliar. Novelty, of course, is stimulating, but too much unfamilarity breeds discomfort, so the host sites attempt to find the right balance by accommodating, for example, their visitors' culinary and linguistic limitations. This way, the masses that want the excitement of a plane trip and a week in an exotic, dazzlingly sunny locale without having to speak another language or eat dubious food are catered for, provided they are willing at times to speak English loudly and slowly. The trick for the resorts is to maintain an effective equilibrium between preserving local charm (in architecture, natural features, shops, and restaurants) and adapting to the visitors' cultural expectations (food, language, convenience). Too much local charm and not enough familiarity, and the resort won't draw on a wide customer base; but eliminate the charm, and the resort will descend in attractiveness, value, and, subsequently, quality of life.

Travel is a good medium to appreciate the opposition between the risk of the new and the security of the tried-and-true. As mentioned in chapter 10, when planning a trip you have to weigh the advantages and pleasures of returning to a familiar spot versus the adventure and novelty of trying somewhere new. Some people, of course, prefer to minimize their risk and they always bask in the comfort of the expected and familiar. Others live at the opposite extreme, preferring the continual freshness of the new. Most of us live in the middle ground, occasionally trying somewhere different, sometimes returning to a comfortable haunt. (Interestingly, scientists in Israel and the United States have identified a gene, the presence of which seems to increase our predilection for novelty and adventure.)

The same theme reappears in so many aspects of our lives. When we return to that favorite location, we desire continuity and immediately seek out salient, characteristic landmarks and images. If too much has changed, we feel dislocated. But if we satisfactorily recapture the essence of our memories, we say, "it's as if we never left." This is partly how we behave when we meet old friends after lengthy passages of time. We say, "you look exactly the same," somewhat sincerely, partly not, and largely just conscious that we have identified those essential qualities that have endured. In this context, we don't tolerate extremes on the familiar-versus-new axis. Going further than skin deep, if we find that someone has changed excessively, we probably decide at the end of the evening that there's not much held in common anymore, but if they're the same old person, we see stagnation and lack of growth, and we feel disdainful.

This theme, indeed, crops up in all sorts of arenas, for example, in food, fashion, and radio station programming. Some of us enjoy particular dishes at certain restaurants. We may even visit an eatery on account of a particular dish and would be quite disappointed to find that this item is no longer on the menu. Therefore restaurants—which in our trendy times are under pressure to stay dynamic and explore new plates—run the danger, when changing their menus, of alienating their customers. The thematic advice here would be to retain certain classics, but forge ahead experimentally with other offerings, that is, specials.

This direction has not been followed sufficiently in the athletic shoe industry. In recent years the market leaders have frenetically turned out new style after new style, each one more garish than the last. Although a few classic styles are occasionally available, there is generally little hope of finding a sneaker style that will be around tomorrow. Not surprisingly, what has happened is that hiking and work shoes of more conservative and stable designs have made enormous inroads into the casual shoe market. These shoes give us the stability—literally and stylistically—that we sometimes crave.

The sneaker manufacturers provide just one example of being sucked into a dependence on trend. In our culture, the term "new" has become almost synonymous with "superior." Unfortunately, this is often misinterpreted with the result that new styles appear just for the sake of being new. The designers forget that some old styles (maybe from last year) might be worth keeping. Again, the thematic advice is to retain both a classic line and a trendy line of items.

Some industries have learned this lesson very well, recognizing the importance of maintaining a balance between the familiar and the new. Beverage companies like Coca-Cola, for example, have learned how to diversify their products instead of tampering with a successful one. (Coke learned the hard way—changing the cola formula some years ago was a disaster and they now market their original formula as "classic.") Clothing stores may emphasize that they carry more classics as well as more of the avant-garde. Radio stations boast of airing more oldies and more new music.

Obviously, one can't solve all the dilemmas. On the consumer side, when you are buying that next pair of athletic shoes, perhaps you can't decide between a plain, inoffensive style and an outrageous new one. Or maybe it's Friday night, you're tired, and you're planning to stay in and see a movie (without all the guests). There are so many films you'd love to see again, but there are plenty that you've never seen and have always wanted to. Or it's time to plan your vacation, and you can't decide whether to return to the Cape or to visit a Caribbean island where you've never been. You'll never quite be able to resolve even these happy problems satisfactorily.

Emphasize Unity within Diversity

A related dualism to the familiar-versus-new is that of heterogeneity versus homogeneity, brought about by the introduction of diversity into a homogeneous culture. Many in our present society feel threatened by plurality and multiculturalism because of its unfamiliarity. But like trend versus tradition, the opposition between a single- and a multiculture will not disappear. The consistent advice in this sphere is to emphasize *both* the unifying, common aspects of our different elements of society *and* the features in which we differ. The logic is clear. We will never reach some point in time where we are all alike—either physically, culturally, or ideologically. Differences will always be noticed, and will always be potential sources of suspicion and alienation. Therefore the only sensible way to bridge these gaps is to celebrate these differences, but at the same time, celebrate the far more important qualities that we all share. We need to more clearly demonstrate our many universal and profound qualities; we too easily forget that we're all human, and have so much in common. At the same time, by celebrate our differences, I mean to conceive of them positively, as features to find interest in, to enjoy, learn from, and respect. Note that this dual emphasis is not intended to suggest a compromise, or a mix, or a melting-pot blend, or a commingling of watered-down cultures. Dual emphasis means to maintain diversity *within* unity. By strengthening both poles, our walls of distrust, ignorance, and contempt will crumble.

The basic idea of emphasizing both diversity and unity has been expressed before. For example, Murray Gell-Mann has written, "The tension continues today between our need for the universality envisioned by the Enlightenment and our need for the preservation of cultural diversity." Although "particularism in all its many forms" threatens the future of humanity on the planet, "cultural diversity is itself a valuable heritage that should be preserved. . . . One of the principal challenges to the human race is to reconcile universalizing factors . . . with particularizing factors. . . ." Samuel Huntington notes that our "Founding Fathers saw diversity as a reality and as a problem: hence the national motto, *e pluribus unum*. . . ." Huntington proposes a "rule for peace," namely, "the *commonalities rule*: peoples in all civilizations should search for and attempt to expand the values, institutions, and practices they have in common with peoples of other civilizations."

Do we have any viable alternatives to the dual emphasis I outline? One alternative is to aim for a day when all of humanity is homogeneous. Aside from this being genetically unfavorable as well as impossible (at least for now), think of how boring it would be. At the other extreme, we can carve up the planet as has happened in Yugoslavia. This is often convenient and in the short term may be politically expedient, but it is likely in the long run to exacerbate the problems that ignited friction between the factions in the first place. It's more sensible to educate ourselves about how we differ and what we share—and to enjoy these qualities—than to either pretend they do not exist, attempt to erase them, or create antagonistic, xenophobic pockets. Thus we have no choice but to cheerfully attempt to manage our diversity. To this end, a framework that provides an understanding of how choice impacts on the way we live and conceptualize our world will be central to an age in which managing diversity will grow in importance.

I am not endorsing a complete relativism, in which objectivity has all but vanished in favor of subjectivity. In a great many aspects of human life there is a need for standards; it behooves us to compare, along whatever criteria are relevant, different alternatives and rank them accordingly. It is fine to appreciate and treasure different contributions in a variety of areas, for example, literature or art, without imposing a value *system*. But doing this need not preclude attempts to compare them either. And clearly, there exist more concrete situations for which a value system is quite necessary, for example, in evaluating the efficacy of disparate medical approaches. Sometimes there is better and worse, right and wrong.

Regarding the diversity–homogeneity divide, one of the important discoveries of the twentieth century is that diversity is, in general, a good thing. Not only is diversity beneficial in a scientific sense—for example in evolutionary biology, where diversity in the gene pool is crucial in preserving adaptation to a dynamic environment—it has become valued in our social fabric as well. And even in the cold world of market economics, various types of organizations have recognized that diversity in their staffing or in their products can boost their market competitiveness.

There are many applications of this theme. For example, much has been made of how book superstores are starting to overwhelmingly dominate their market, not only wiping out the small independent stores that provided variety, but even influencing the publishing process. The superstores do in fact pay lip service to variety by stocking impressive numbers of titles. However, we note that to compensate, they keep shelf lives short and push only a small, high-volume subset of titles, so as to maximize volume sold. Now Internet sales are changing the entire bookselling landscape. Perhaps the only way the brick-and-mortar locations will survive is through their accentuating the non-virtual—by enhancing customers' personal interactions with books and with other people, and in offering complementary products. Hence, the book superstores provide seating, readings, and coffee/juice bars. What about the small independent stores? Can they develop a niche?

It may be too soon to count these small operations out. Consider the resurgence of low-budget, independent films. Just as the Hollywood studios were consolidating the industry in the early 1990s by relying more on standard, formulaic scripts as well as on remakes, a few hugely successful (especially by revenue–cost ratios), fresh, and innovative movies demonstrated that the public wanted more than just Hollywood's predictable offerings. Diversity prevailed.

The same thing, at about the same time, happened in the U.S. beer market. A handful of indistinguishable (and undistinguished) lagers had the market virtually covered except for a few snobs on the East and West coasts. Suddenly, small, diverse, independent microbrews appeared that appealed even to middle America. This gambit was mimicked by the major breweries—the mainstream gobbling up the alternative—but diversity has its foot solidly in the door.

Essentially, when the major breweries produce microbrew-style beer, they are adopting a boutiquing strategy reminiscent of how department stores lay out floors of designer zones. These strategies, of course, are intimately tied to the diversity–homogeneity issue as well as the inclusive–exclusive opposition we have discussed. Recently there have been all sorts of applications of this idea. A colossal Las Vegas hotel, the Mandalay Bay, offers a Four Seasons hotel tucked away within it. This alliance extends the Hilton "Towers" concept, in which the top floors of their hotels offered slightly more upscale accommodation. Universities have been capitalizing on the same principle in various ways. One has been the development of honors programs within the larger university structure. This elitism is meant to provide a more exclusive product within the larger, inclusive institution, while hopefully not signaling an implicit inferiority of the other degree programs. Another scheme has been the emergence of "name brand" colleges in which a division or professional school within the university takes on the name of a (usually) generous benefactor. In the latter cases, the fact that a professional school has a name seems to elevate it to a higher status. This is verified when most students and alumni use the narrower designation instead of the larger institution's name.

Increase Your Flexibility

Boutiquing capitalizes on exclusivity within inclusion, but in the wider picture it is a device to provide more choice (as long as the less exclusive options do not vanish). There are other ways to increase consumers' choices. One theme that we have discussed is the softening of choice by eliminating the irreversibility of the alternative actions. All sorts of retailers continue to enhance their applications of this notion, by offering consumers easier and easier ways to try their products—whether vacuum cleaners, computers, or lipstick—at no cost. Just return the item (almost) painlessly for a full refund. In the university setting, there is a proliferation of travel-study alternatives for students. One type of offering is the online and videoconferencing courses that have sprung up, so students can gain credits at remote locations. Another option is presented via course selections at partner institutions. In addition to the older "junior year abroad" programs, students now can more flexibly travel to various world-wide sites to take classes. I suspect that this trend will mushroom, so that the typical undergraduate will no longer attend college at one location for four (or five) years. The norm will surely become more flexible: a semester at home on-line, a summer here, a summer there, perhaps a co-op job in between. Consistent with this, a lot of companies are seeking alliances with complementary firms. For example, you can tally frequent-flier miles by chatting on the telephone. And you can use those miles on different airlines. I expect to see a burgeoning of this type of alliance and versatility, as it enhances consumer choice.

As we come to expect more flexibility from life's situations, we will probably make career changes the norm. You study to become an engineer; ten years later you retool to become a chef; eight years of that, and you become a social worker. As a society, we will have to accept this lifestyle and try to lower the cost of career changes. Incidentally, there is an analogue to this retooling in just-in-time manufacturing, when lowering the changeover costs (setting up production from one product to another) allows producers to support a larger product line. Such improvements are paving the way for the new industrial world of mass customization.

The flip side to our expecting more flexibility is that more flexibility will be expected of us in return. As authors Stan Davis and Christopher Meyer and others have pointed out, traditional economic roles are changing. Knowledge is becoming predominant in our information-driven society, and with that we are seeing value shift away from organizations and toward individuals. Also, things are changing so fast that very few endeavors can be expected to endure, whether they are sneaker styles or start-up companies. Because of this, the notion of a long-term career, in many instances, may become outdated. The only way to stay marketable will be to constantly acquire new skills.

The shortened life cycles in our careers have been preceded in our personal lives by shorter spans with partners. Social critic Barbara Dafoe Whitehead has attributed our rising divorce rates to our "sense of well-being" becoming "more dependent on the richness of [our] emotional lives . . . and the variety of opportunities for self-expression," predicated on the spreading affluence post-1960 and the rise in the demand for instant gratification. Regardless of whether these reasons constitute the whole story, the facts seem to indicate that the pressures against divorce have lightened, rendering it more of a viable choice than it was in the past. Interestingly, Daniel Bell has pointed out that more than half of American women who have been divorced have remarried within five years, which leads us to conclude that we are not rejecting the married lifestyle, but rather the premise that partnership is forever.

Divorce is simply becoming part of the expanded palette of lifestyle choices that are now available, as are open marriages, the once-controversial "living together," and the ubiquitous single parenthood. Clearly, our very conditioning and our expectations for choice have broadened our approach to lifestyles, forcing age-old stigmas to rapidly recede. As more categories of lifestyle, as it were, become acceptable, more of us actualize our dispositions. And despite some painful break-ups, the process seems, for most, to be liberating.

It is evident that the issue of choice will continue to penetrate every aspect of our public and private lives. Choice has permeated so many areas of our existence that it seems like a natural goal—indeed, a requisite—in nearly all circumstances.

In recent years the topic of school choice has become hotly debated. I find it somewhat amazing that so many people seem to think that the ability to choose a school will be a panacea for our ailing educational system. Perhaps it will. Or, on the other hand, perhaps choice is an empty promise of power. But before resolutely setting out to provide school choice, we should think long and hard about the following three points. First, let's assume that not *so* long ago—say, around 1960—our educational system was in better shape than it is now. Suppose we have a decent grasp of the factors that have contributed to the decline of our schools. Given the sustained presence of these factors, will the availability of school choice really serve to improve the education of our children?

Second, in light of the many unfavorable comparisons we make of our schools and our students' academic performance with those of other developed countries, what are we doing differently, and probably poorly, at home and in the classroom? School choice may not address these practices. Indeed, school choice is not the normal model in any other nation.

Third, I believe that part of the motivation for school choice derives from our society's increased mobility in recent years. This physical feature is a manifestation of the shorter cycle times in our careers and our personal lives that we have discussed above. Movement, after all, is dynamic and seductive. Its prevalence could well lead us to believe that shifting our kids from school to school in the same fashion that we transfer from job to job, house to house, and partner to partner will improve our schools and be educationally beneficial. This philosophy of movement has taken root in various school administrations. For example, the Philadelphia school district has been moving principals around like a shell game. If a principal doesn't improve a school (as indicated by test scores, often measured for just one grade), he or she is simply transferred to another school (while a different, perhaps worse, principal takes over). The real problems are untreated. Will the availability of school choice improve education? Perhaps an experiment would be worthwhile, but I suspect we are barking up the wrong tree.

Another example in which the ability to choose has taken on disproportionate importance is the field of medical care. As we face out-of-control costs, we have mounting pressure to reduce bills without compromising our medical services. One way to tackle inefficiencies in our health care system is to nationalize it to some degree. Doing this, though, is seen as a measure that would reduce our choice among physicians, and is therefore dead in the water as a candidate for legislative consideration. Indeed, the ability to retain choice among doctors and institutions has become nonnegotiable, outweighing far more important considerations like scope of treatments and quality of standards.

We have seen that the ability to choose, both directly and indirectly, is a major force in determining public policy. As a direct factor, choice is becoming a sine qua non in policy areas like education and health care. Indirectly, the by-products of choice—the oppositions and dilemmas that choice creates—will continue to loom, as evidenced in our wrestling with societal issues like diversity. The policy recommendation congruent with the emergence of choice is to emphasize both oppositional poles. As previously stated, we should underscore neither pure diversity nor pure homogeneity, but attempt to highlight diversity within our commonality.

Complicating this landscape is the phenomenon of shorter cycle times in both the public sector and in our private lives. This is coupled with heightened expectations, even from the poorest sector of our society, of what constitutes "inalienable rights." But as we more frequently change our domiciles, careers, and partners, as well as increase our consumption (expecting growing satisfaction all the while), we simultaneously shorten our delayed gratification fuses. We are becoming more of a "now" society and individuals are developing briefer time horizons over which they are willing to work toward a goal. As we saw in chapter 16, this foreshortened "shadow of the future" has policy consequences too. Incentive programs, particularly those to elevate the underclass, must be designed in such a way that tangible rewards are neither too distant (when they lose meaning) nor too hurried (when they are taken for granted).

Easing Your Personal Choices

The previous discussion has dealt with general principles that can be applied to a wide variety of policy applications. But it is a good idea to also mention some tangible ways to deal with choices on an individual level. Barry Schwartz has given a number of insightful, concrete suggestions for improving personal decision making, some of which I relate here.

First of all, recall that Schwartz has shown that the multitude of choices and experiences that we encounter, although often wonderful, can be debilitating for us. We adapt to experiences and develop higher expectations, which are often not met. We regret the paths we did not take. We perceive inadequacies when we compare ourselves to others. More choices can produce greater anxiety. Things that used to be good enough no longer are. These issues are more than just bothersome. What can we do to improve our well-being?

Perhaps the most central of Schwartz's suggestions is to "satisfice more and maximize less," that is, "settle for something that is good enough and not worry about the possibility that there might be something better." Most of us are often focused on making the *best* choice. If we could relax this obsession by satisficing—picking something good enough—we would reduce some of our unease.

Of course, this is easier said than done, and part of developing a satisficing strategy would involve another of Schwartz's rules, "choose when to choose." Don't fight every battle. And, hand in hand with letting some decisions slide, we need to train ourselves, says Schwartz, to "regret less."

Some of Schwartz's decision-making rules require that we gain a better understanding of how our minds work. If we understand how we have adapted to new phenomena in the past, for example, Schwartz notes that we might be able to "anticipate adaptation" in the future and temper our choices accordingly. Similarly, if we comprehend the way in which our experiences have altered our expectations, we might be able to harness this knowledge from now on.

Two other of Schwartz's rules strike at the very core of choice by asking us to impose constraints on our behavior. Frequently I have mentioned how the softening of oppositions and the dissolution of conflict have become central to our thinking. In this regard, we seek to escape commitment, to make our decisions reversible. Schwartz sees this behavior as problematic, and he suggests that we make our decisions "nonreversible." To see the merits of his point, consider our attitudes toward marriage. If a particular marriage ends in divorce, we naturally conclude that the couple is fortunate that divorce was an option. But Schwartz argues instead that the flexibility of divorce "might have played a causal role in the marriage's failure." Perhaps, as he puts it, "when we can change our minds . . . we do less psychological work to justify the decision we've made." If the deposit, so to speak, is refundable, maybe we don't size up the situation as well as we would if there were no turning back.

Related to this is Schwartz's last rule, "learn to love constraints." This is another counterintuitive but compelling notion. Over the last couple of generations we have learned to prize freedom, but we have also learned, albeit slowly, that there is a price to pay. Sometimes, establishing some rules for ourselves can preclude a dose of angst (*I will never have more than three drinks,* or *I will never cheat on my spouse,* etc.). Yes, of course, rules are tough to follow, but adherence to some good ones can be rewarding.

Closure

It is time to bring this book to a close. As I write this, I recall one way I had considered starting off the book. It was to describe a feeling that I had some years ago. I was sitting at an outdoor café on the Boulevard Saint Germain in Paris on a warm and sunny July afternoon, nursing another *bière* and realizing that I was precisely and unequivocally *where I wanted to be.* I felt no distress, no conflict. No decisions to be made. Perhaps the alcohol had gone to my head, but reflecting on my strange sense of inner contentment and satisfaction, I felt, somewhat dangerously, that I *had no desires,* that *there was nothing at all remaining for me to do.* Despite the impression that has remained with me, the feeling is a clichéd one. Certain food or sex, people say, is "to die for." Unfortunately, though, the occasions we truly experience in this zone are few and far between, and the remainder of the time we are stressed by managing the sundry choices that confront us almost constantly.

We face a multitude of grave dangers to our planetary civilization—nuclear holocaust, destruction of our ecosystem, and others. But aside from averting them, our greatest challenge is and will be to manage the abundant choices that we will have to make in our lives. As we raise our standard of living, our society will move toward an era of *almost* unconstrained optimization in which mortality will be practically the only check on our activities. In such a world our goal will always be, at least metaphorically, Paris on that sunny day. And more than ever we will be preoccupied with managing the continual choices en route.

This book has been about the large-scale emergence of choice in our lives. By the late nineteenth century, two fundamental changes were underway in the developed world. One was the result of a hundred years of the Industrial Revolution: a growing proliferation of goods available to the ordinary person. The other was the loss of the absolute: a multifaceted decline in the feeling that either God or mankind was in control. This decline in objectivity led to a rising emphasis on the individual and the subjective.

The expanding role of the individual was complementary to the abundance of consumer goods in creating an atmosphere in which choice would emerge as a major—in fact, a predominant—influence in our lives. Freedom without choice does not breed a preoccupation with decision. But neither does a plenitude of alternatives when one has no sense of personal power, control, or destiny.

The evidence for stating that choice has become a predominant factor in our lives rests on its various direct and indirect manifestations. As a direct influence, in our personal lives we see the existence of choice as an issue in its own right in such important spheres as education and health care. More generally, I have tried to show how what I call the "vicious spiral of choice" is occupying more and more of our attention and our resources. At the same time, the desire to soften choice and diminish irreversibility, to have one's cake and eat it too, has led to a "now" generation in which many of us are deserting the guiding principle of delayed gratification. Consequently, we are moving toward a world of shorter cycle times as exemplified by our briefer sojourns with careers, spouses, and other formerly enduring aspects of our lives.

Choice has also had many direct manifestations in our intellectual domain. We have discussed the twentieth century's development of decision science and related techniques such as risk analysis, prospect theory, linear programming, and game theory. All of these endeavors are driven by the desire to quantify and thereby improve individual decision making. Existentialism, a branch of philosophy with strong literary roots as well as implications for psychotherapy, is entirely focused on the process and implications of a human being having to act, having to make a decision. And choice has played a major role in various other intellectual developments of the last century. In physics we have discussed the central role of choice in the many-worlds approach to quantum theory, in Bohr's Copenhagen interpretation of the nature of light, and in Schrödinger's Cat. In computational science we have seen the analysis of branching choices expressed as nondeterminism, which has a parallel in the branching paths that our lives describe.

The indirect role of choice is derived from oppositions that, as we have seen, have grown to dominate so much of our lives. Having to make a choice results in a fundamental opposition of inclusion (of the chosen alternative) versus exclusion (of the rejected options). But the issue of choice generates a multiplicity of other oppositions too, as the ability to choose opens up the consideration of competing factors that would not otherwise come to the fore. Indeed, structuralism would claim that classification, especially that based on binary oppositions, is a natural feature of our thought processes. The first thinker to systematically analyze such oppositional categories and their implications for our thought was Saussure in the early twentieth century. His insights into diachronic and synchronic, signifier and signified, and language as a system of differences not only initiated semiology but also led to profound work in anthropology and literary criticism. And accepting that so much of our thought is based on an oppositional structure helped lead to the acceptance of the very notion of opposition itself. As we have seen, the notion of cultural relativity, ironically associated with Einstein's relativity theory and fueled by the growing loss of the absolute, merged with this concept of the acceptance of opposition to build the emphasis on multiculturalism and subjectivity that we have today.

At the same time, the acceptance of opposition itself precipitated the fall of modernism in the 1960s and the subsequent rise of postmodernism. The modernist process wherein rebellious avant-garde concepts clashed with an initially hostile but potentially absorbent establishment ceased to be effective by the 1960s, since the very notion of the acceptance of the alternative had come to dominate the mainstream. The tradition of the new—and of progress—was blunted, and a postmodernism that sought to incorporate a variety of historical icons as well as avant-garde expression began to dominate creative domains.

Several other dualisms in which our newfound choice has played a contributory role have proven influential in twentieth-century life and thought. The breakdown between high and mass culture has, starting in the 1960s, tremendously influenced our expression and has significantly restructured society and its symbols. We have seen a similar breakdown in the divide between what used to be considered public and private. This dissolution of another traditional boundary has been manifested not only in our personal lives but also in issues of national policy. Related to this, the increasing emphasis on the individual in our society has been extremely liberating at the personal level but has reduced a great deal of community influence. The repercussions of this shift have been disturbing increases in conspicuous consumption combined with decreases in inconspicuous consumption (including public spending). Another blurred dualism central to our recent era has been that of the distinction among the real, the artificial, and the hyperreal. Never before have we had to worry so much, in so many avenues, about the nature of the true and the false. This blurring has had profound effects in our conception of mathematics, science, information, and interpersonal interaction. It will be increasingly felt through our advancing emphasis on the virtual.

A cautionary note is worth repeating. While I hope to have demonstrated the overwhelming role choice has played—and will continue to play—in so many aspects of contemporary life, I believe it would be futile to attempt to prove that our ability to choose, having reached a critical mass in the twentieth century, has been a direct *causal influence* on these phenomena. What I have illustrated instead is the *correlation* of the emergence of widespread choice over the past century with its manifestation in the many phenomena that we have discussed. I believe the relationship between the introduction of extensive choice into our lives and the marked change in our lifestyles as well as our intellectual and creative movements is clearly drawn.

With the ability to choose comes a responsibility for one's actions. This is an area of human behavior in which we have much to learn. One great challenge we face is that of generating guidelines for individual and group behavior that will, over time, reduce the amount of friction and conflict among people and peoples. Part of such a program will necessarily involve the integration of incentives, public choice procedures, legal proceedings, and moral codes that are consistent and suitable for all sectors of our society to flourish. We are not moving in the right directions yet. For example, our recent trend of attempting to dissolve social dilemmas by shifting the responsibility onto legal arenas fails to address the underlying issues. The current mushrooming of lawsuits in which individuals and municipalities are suing tobacco and gun producers will not elicit a dialogue that really speaks to what, if any, public consensus can be reached on constraining smoking and firearms.

Finally, I have developed a framework, a set of guidelines, on oppositions and equilibria that I believe can be applied with some success to public policy issues such as the handling of diversity, or those of school choice and health care. If the reader has detected a political bias or agenda, it is because I fervently believe that not all of our socioeconomic problems can be solved by resorting to an implementation of free markets and privatization for goods that are naturally shared. I think it is clear by now that continuing on our present path will exacerbate the great dangers that the future already holds for us. If we can fend off these perils, life's prospects in the era of choice might become very bright indeed.

Bibliography

Abrams, Robert. *Foundations of Political Analysis: An Introduction to the Theory of Collective Choice*. Columbia University Press: New York, 1980.

Andrews, Edmund L. "In Germany, Humble Herb Is a Rival to Prozac." *New York Times*, September 9, 1997.

Appignanesi, Richard, and Chris Garratt. *Postmodernism for Beginners*. Icon Books: Cambridge, 1995.

Arrow, Kenneth J. *Social Choice and Individual Values* (2nd ed.). Yale University Press: New Haven, 1963.

Arrow, Kenneth J., and Frank H. Hahn. *General Competitive Analysis*. Holden-Day: New York, 1971.

Arthur, W. Brian. *Increasing Returns and Path-Dependence in the Economy*. University of Michigan Press: Ann Arbor, 1994.

Atre, Jatin, and Elihu Katz. "What's Killing Television News." Working paper, The Annenberg School for Communication, University of Pennsylvania, 2004.

Axelrod, Robert. *The Evolution of Cooperation*. Basic Books: New York, 1984.

Ayer, A. J. *Philosophy in the Twentieth Century*. Vintage Books: New York, 1984.

Barthes, Roland. *Camera Lucida: Reflections on Photography*. Farrar, Straus, and Giroux: New York, 1981.

Baudrillard, Jean. *America*. Verso: London, 1988.

Baudrilard, Jean. *Cool Memories*. Verso: London, 1990.

Baudrillard, Jean. "The Ecstasy of Communication." In *Postmodern Culture* (Hal Foster, ed.), Pluto Press: London, 1985.

Bell, Daniel. *The Cultural Contradictions of Capitalism*. Basic Books: New York, 1976.

Bell, Daniel. *The Coming of Post-Industrial Society: A Venture in Social Forecasting.* Basic Books: New York, 1973.

Bernstein, Peter L. *Against the Gods: The Remarkable Story of Risk.* John Wiley and Sons: New York, 1996.

Binmore, Ken. *Fun and Games: A Text on Game Theory.* D. C. Heath: Lexington, Mass., 1992.

Boorstin, Daniel J. *The Creators: A History of Heroes of the Imagination.* Random House: New York, 1992.

Bottomore, Tom. *The Frankfurt School.* Ellis Horwood/Tavistock Publications: Chichester and London, 1984.

Brams, Steven J., and Peter C. Fishburn, "Approval Voting." *American Political Science Review* 72 (1978): 831–847.

Brandenburger, Adam M., and Barry Nalebuff. *Co-opetition.* Currency/Doubleday: New York, 1996.

Broda, Christian, and David Weinstein. "Globalization and the Gains from Variety." Federal Reserve Bank of New York Staff Report no. 180, March 2004.

Brooks, David. *Bobos In Paradise: The New Upper Class and How They Got There.* Simon and Schuster: New York, 2000.

Browne, Malcolm W. "Who Needs Jokes? Brain Has a Ticklish Spot." *New York Times,* March 10, 1998.

Burros, Marian. "Invigorating Western Palates with Eastern Influences." *New York Times,* April 23, 1997.

Campbell, Roy H. "Status Debate." *Philadelphia Inquirer,* November 30, 1997.

Camus, Albert. *The Myth of Sisyphus.* Alfred A. Knopf: New York, 1955.

Camus, Albert. *The Stranger.* Alfred A. Knopf: New York, 1946.

Capra, Fritjof. *The Tao of Physics: An Exploration of the Parallels Between Modern Physics and Eastern Mysticism.* Bantam Books: New York, 1977.

Chadwick, Owen. *The Secularization of the European Mind in the Nineteenth Century.* Cambridge University Press: Cambridge, 1975.

Chatwin, Bruce. *What Am I Doing Here?* Penguin Books: New York, 1990.

Chronicle of the Twentieth Century. (Clifton Daniel, ed.). Chronicle Publications: Mount Kisko, N.Y., 1987.

Cooper, Douglas. *The Cubist Epoch.* Phaidon Press: London, 1971.

Cox, W. Michael. "The Consumer Will Prevail." *New York Times,* October 2, 1998.

Davis, Stan, and Christopher Meyer. *Blur: The Speed of Change in the Connected Economy.* Addison-Wesley: New York, 1998.

Faison, Seth. "China Lets 100 Flowers Bloom, in Private Life." *New York Times,* June 23, 1998.

Dostoevsky, Fyodor. *The Brothers Karamazov.* Penguin Books: Harmondsworth, U.K., 1987.

Easterbrook, Gregg. *The Progress Paradox: How Life Gets Better While People Feel Worse.* Random House: New York, 2003.

Eco, Umberto. *Travels in Hyperreality.* Harcourt Brace Jovanovich: San Diego, 1986.

Everett, Hugh. "'Relative State' Formulation of Quantum Mechanics." *Review of Modern Physics* 29 (1957): 454–462.

Feynman, Richard, Leighton, Robert B., and Matthew L. Sands. *The Feynman Lectures on Physics,* volume 1. Addison-Wesley: Reading, Mass., 1963.

Feynman, Richard. *Surely You're Joking, Mr. Feynman: Adventures of a Curious Character.* Bantam Books: New York, 1985.

Foster, Hal (ed.). *Postmodern Culture.* Pluto Press: London, 1985.

Frank, Robert H. *Luxury Fever: Why Money Fails to Satisfy in an Era of Excess.* The Free Press: New York, 1999,

Fromm, Erich. *Escape from Freedom.* Holt, Rinehart, and Winston: New York, 1941.

Frost, Robert. "The Road Not Taken." In *The Complete Poems of Robert Frost.* Holt, Rinehart, and Winston: New York, 1967.

Garey, Michael R., and David S. Johnson. *Computers and Intractability: A Guide to the Theory of NP-Completeness.* W. H. Freeman: San Francisco, 1979.

Gell-Mann, Murray. *The Quark and the Jaguar.* W. H. Freeman: New York, 1994.

Gibbard, Alan. "Manipulation of Voting Schemes: A General Result." *Econometrica* 45 (1973): 665–682.

Gibson, William. *Neuromancer.* The Berkley Publishing Group: New York, 1984.

Graunt, John. "Foundations of Vital Statistics" (1662). In James R. Newman, *The World of Mathematics,* volume 3. Simon and Schuster: New York, 1956.

Greenberg, Clement. *Art and Culture: Critical Essays.* The Beacon Press: Boston, 1961.

Habermas, Jürgen. "Modernity—An Incomplete Project." In *Postmodern Culture* (Hal Foster, ed.), Pluto Press: London, 1985.

David Halberstam. *The Fifties.* Ballantine Books: New York, 1994.

Halley, Edmund. "First Life Insurance Tables" (1693). In James R. Newman, *The World of Mathematics*, volume 3. Simon and Schuster: New York, 1956.

Hampson, Norman. *The Enlightenment*. Penguin Books: New York, 1968.

Hardin, Garrett. "The Tragedy of the Commons." *Science* 162 (1968): 1243–1248.

Harvey, David. *The Condition of Postmodernity: An Enquiry into the Origins of Cultural Change*. Basil Blackwell: Oxford, 1989.

Heidegger, Martin. "The Way Back into the Ground of Metaphysics" (Trans. Walter Kaufmann). In Walter Kaufmann, *Existentialism from Dostoevsky to Sartre*. Meridian Books: Cleveland, Ohio, 1956.

Herszenhorn, David M. "Widowed Homeowner Foils Trump in Atlantic City." *New York Times,* July 21, 1998.

Hofstadter, Douglas. *Gödel, Escher, Bach: An Eternal Golden Braid*. Basic Books: New York, 1979.

Holland, John H. *Adaptation in Natural and Artificial Systems: An Introductory Analysis with Applications to Biology, Control, and Artificial Intelligence*. The MIT Press: Cambridge, Mass., 1992.

Hughes, Robert. *The Shock of the New*. Alfred A. Knopf: New York, 1980.

Huntington, Samuel P. *The Clash of Civilizations: Remaking of World Order*. Touchstone: New York, 1997.

Impressionism, by the editors of *Réalités*. Chartwell Books: Secaucus, N.J., 1973.

Iyengar, Sheena, and Mark Lepper. "When Choice Is Demotivating: Can One Desire Too Much of a Good Thing?" *Journal of Personality and Social Psychology* 79 (2000): 995–1006.

Jakobson, Roman. *Child Language, Aphasia, and Phonological Universals*. Mouton: The Hague and Paris, 1968.

Jameson, Frederic. "Postmodernism and Consumer Society." In *Postmodern Culture* (Hal Foster, ed.). Pluto Press: London, 1985.

Jameson, Frederic. *Postmodernism, or, The Cultural Logic of Late Capitalism*. Duke University Press: Durham, N.C., 1992.

Jehl, Douglas. "'No Disrespect' Meant to Islam, President Says." *New York Times,* November 30, 1993.

Jencks, Charles. *The Language of Post-Modern Architecture* (6th ed.). Rizzoli: New York, 1991.

Jones, W. T. *A History of Western Philosophy: Hobbes to Hume* (2nd ed.). Harcourt Brace Jovanovich: New York, 1969.

Kahneman, Daniel, and Amos Tversky. "Prospect Theory." *Econometrica* 47 (1979): 263–291.

Kalakota, Ravi, and Marcia Robinson. *e-business: Roadmap for Success.* Addison-Wesley: Reading, Mass., 1999.

Kaufmann, Walter. *Existentialism from Dostoevsky to Sartre.* Meridian Books: Cleveland, Ohio, 1956.

Kennedy, Paul. *The Rise and Fall of the Great Powers: Economic Change and Military Conflict From 1500 to 2000.* Random House: New York, 1987.

Kierkegaard, Søren. *Fear and Trembling.* Princeton University Press: Princeton, 1941.

Kierkegaard, Søren. *The Sickness unto Death.* Princeton University Press: Princeton, 1941.

Kline, Morris. *Mathematics: The Loss of Certainty.* Oxford University Press: New York, 1980.

Kolata, Gina. "On Cloning Humans, 'Never' Turns Swiftly Into 'Why Not.'" *New York Times,* December 2, 1997.

Lane, Robert E. *The Loss of Happiness in Market Democracies.* Yale University Press: New Haven, 2000.

Lebergott, Stanley. *Pursuing Happiness: American Consumers in the Twentieth Century.* Princeton University Press: Princeton, 1993.

Levenson, Edgar, quoted in *New York* magazine, October 20, 1997.

Levine, Lawrence W. *The Opening of the American Mind: Canons, Culture, and History.* The Beacon Press: Boston, 1996.

Lévi-Strauss, Claude. *Totemism.* The Beacon Press: Boston, 1963.

Levy, Suzanne. "But Is It Really Italian?" *New York Times,* December 22, 1993.

Luhmann, Niklas. *The Differentiation of Society.* Columbia University Press: New York, 1982.

Marcuse, Herbert. *Eros and Civilization: A Philosophical Inquiry into Freud.* The Beacon Press: Boston, 1955.

Marcuse, Herbert. *One-Dimensional Man: Studies in the Ideology of Advanced Industrial Society.* The Beacon Press: Boston, 1964.

McEvilley, Thomas. *Art and Discontent: Theory at the Millennium.* McPherson and Company: Kingston, N.Y., 1991.

McLuhan, Marshall. *Understanding Media: The Extensions of Man.* McGraw-Hill: New York, 1964.

McRobbie, Angela. *Postmodernism and Popular Culture*. Routledge: London, 1994.

Muller, Jerry Z. *Adam Smith in His Time and Ours*. Princeton University Press: Princeton, 1993.

Newman, James R. *The World of Mathematics*, volume 3. Simon and Schuster: New York, 1956.

Nietzsche, Friedrich. *On the Genealogy of Morals*. Vintage Books: New York, 1969.

Nietzsche, Friedrich. *Thus Spoke Zarathustra*. Penguin Books: New York, 1978.

Nietzsche, Friedrich. *The Birth of Tragedy*. Oxford University Press: Oxford, 2000.

O'Neill. William L. *Coming Apart: An Informal History of America in the 1960s*. Times Books: New York, 1971.

Owen, Guillermo. *Game Theory* (2nd ed.). Academic Press: New York, 1982.

Pagels, Heinz. *The Cosmic Code: Quantum Physics as the Language of Nature*. Bantam Books: New York, 1983.

Patterson, Orlando. *Freedom. Volume 1: Freedom in the Making of Western Culture*. Basic Books: New York, 1991.

Penrose, Roger. *The Emperor's New Mind: Concerning Computers, Minds, and the Laws of Physics*. Oxford University Press: Oxford and New York, 1989.

Pirsig, Robert M. *Zen and the Art of Motorcycle Maintenance: An Inquiry into Values*. Bantam Books: New York, 1974.

Pirsig, Robert M. *Lila: An Enquiry into Morals*. Bantam Books: New York, 1991.

Polman, Dick. "Prosperity." *Philadelphia Inquirer Magazine*, September 20, 1998.

Postman, Neil. *Technopoly: The Surrender of Culture to Technology*. Alfred A. Knopf: New York, 1992.

Poundstone, William. *Prisoner's Dilemma: John von Neumann, Game Theory, and the Puzzle of the Bomb*. Doubleday: New York, 1992.

Poundstone, William. *The Recursive Universe: Cosmic Complexity and the Limits of Scientific Knowledge*. William Morrow and Company: New York, 1985.

Rapoport, Anatol. "Experiments with N-Person Social Traps I." *Journal of Conflict Resolution*, 32 (1988): 457–472.

Rawls, John. *A Theory of Justice*. Belknap Press/Harvard University Press: Cambridge, Mass., 1971.

Rochlin, Gene I. *Trapped in the Net: The Unanticipated Consequences of Computerization*. Princeton University Press: Princeton, 1997.

Rothstein, Edward. "Trend-Spotting: It's All the Rage." *New York Times,* December 29, 1996.

Sade, Marquis de. *Justine.* Grove Press: New York, 1990.

Sartre, Jean-Paul. *Being and Nothingness.* Philosophical Library: New York, 1956.

Sartre, Jean-Paul. *No Exit and Three Other Plays.* Vintage Books: New York, 1959.

Satterthwaite, Mark. "Strategy-Proofness and Arrow's Conditions: Existence and Correspondence Theorems for Voting Procedures and Social Choice Functions." *Journal of Economic Theory* 10 (1975): 187–217.

Saussure, Ferdinand de. *Course in General Linguistics.* Open Court: La Salle, Ill., 1986.

Schama, Simon. *The Embarrassment of Riches: An Interpretation of Dutch Culture in the Golden Age.* Alfred A. Knopf: New York, 1987.

Schwartz, Barry. *The Paradox of Choice: Why More Is Less.* Ecco Press/HarperCollins: New York, 2004.

Sen, Amartya K. *Choice, Welfare, and Measurement.* Basil Blackwell: Oxford, 1982.

Silver, Vernon. "Label Living." *New York Times,* February 20, 1994.

Smith, John Maynard. *Evolution and the Theory of Games.* Cambridge University Press: Cambridge, 1982.

Snow, C. P. *The Two Cultures.* Cambridge University Press: Cambridge, 1959.

Sontag, Susan. *Against Interpretation.* Farrar, Strauss, and Giroux: New York, 1966.

Sperber, Dan. "Claude Lévi-Strauss." In *Structuralism and Since: From Lévi-Strauss to Derrida* (John Sturrock, ed.). Oxford University Press: Oxford, 1979.

Sturrock, John. "Roland Barthes." In *Structuralism and Since: From Lévi-Strauss to Derrida* (John Sturrock, ed.). Oxford University Press: Oxford, 1979.

Sturrock, John (ed.). *Structuralism and Since: From Lévi-Strauss to Derrida.* Oxford University Press: Oxford, 1979.

Spielvogel, Jackson J. *Western Civilization,* volumes 1 and 2 (2nd ed.). West Publishing: Minneapolis/St. Paul, Minn., 1994.

Tagliabue, John. "In Italy's Piracy Culture, Black Market Is Thriving." *New York Times,* July 3, 1997.

Theroux, Paul. *The Kingdom by the Sea: A Journey around the Coast of Great Britain.* Penguin Books: New York, 1995.

Thompson, William Irwin. *The American Replacement of Nature: The Everyday Acts and Outrageous Evolution of Economic Life.* Currency/Doubleday: New York, 1991.

Twitchell, James B. *Carnival Culture: The Trashing of Taste in America*. Columbia University Press: New York, 1992.

Unamuno, Miguel de. *Tragic Sense of Life*. Dover: New York, 1954.

UNICEF. "A League Table of Teenage Births in Rich Nations." *Innocenti Report Card* no. 3. UNICEF Innocenti Research Center: Florence, Italy, July, 2001.

Vander Zanden, James W. *Human Development*. Knopf: New York, 1978.

von Neumann, John, and Oskar Morgenstern. *Theory of Games and Economic Behavior*. Princeton University Press: Princeton, 1944.

Waldrop, M. Mitchell. *Complexity: The Emerging Science at the Edge of Order and Chaos*. Simon and Schuster: New York, 1992.

Weber, Robert J. "Comparison of Voting Systems." Cowles Foundation Discussion Paper no. 498, Yale University, 1977.

Wegner, Daniel. *The Illusion of Conscious Will*. The MIT Press: Cambridge, Mass., 2002.

Weschler, Lawrence. *Mr. Wilson's Cabinet of Wonder*. Vintage Books: New York, 1995.

Whitehead, Barbara Dafoe. *The Divorce Culture*. Knopf: New York, 1997.

Whitfield, Sarah. *Fauvism*. Thames and Hudson: London, 1991.

Wolfe, Tom. *Bonfire of the Vanities*. Farrar, Straus, and Giroux: New York, 1987.

Wolfe, Tom. *The Kandy-Kolored Tangerine-Flake Streamline Baby*. Farrar, Straus, and Giroux: New York, 1964.

Yalom, Irvin D. *Existential Psychotherapy*. Basic Books: New York, 1980.

Index